THE
WORLD VIEW
of
REMBRANDT

by Jane Roberts

THE EARLY SESSIONS

The Early Sessions consist of the first 510 sessions dictated by Seth through Jane Roberts. There are 9 books in *The Early Sessions* series.

THE PERSONAL SESSIONS

The Personal Sessions, often referred to as "the deleted sessions," are Seth sessions that Jane Roberts and Rob Butts considered to be of a highly personal nature and were therefore kept in separate notebooks from the main body of the Seth material. *The Personal Sessions* are published in 7 volumes.

"The great value I see now in the many deleted or private sessions is that they have the potential to help others, just as they helped Jane and me over the years. I feel that it's very important to have these sessions added to Jane's fine creative body of work for all to see." –Rob Butts

THE SETH AUDIO COLLECTION

Rare recordings of Seth speaking through Jane Roberts are available on audiocassette and CD. For a complete description of The Seth Audio Collection, request our free catalogue. (Further information is supplied at the back of this book.)

For information on expected publication dates and how to order, write to New Awareness Network at the following address and request the latest catalogue. Also, please visit us on the Internet at *www.sethcenter.com.*

NEW AWARENESS NETWORK INC.
P.O. BOX 192
MANHASSET, N.Y. 11030

www.sethcenter.com

THE
WORLD VIEW
of
REMBRANDT

by Jane Roberts

Published by New Awareness Network Inc.

New Awareness Network Inc.
P.O. Box 192
Manhasset, New York 11030

Cover Design: Michael Goode
Photography: Cover photos by Rich Conz and Robert F. Butts, Sr.
Editorial: Rick Stack
Typography: Raymond Todd, Michael Goode

ISBN 0-9768978-2-2
Printed in U.S.A.

I dedicate
The World View of Rembrandt
to my wife, Jane Roberts,
who lived her 55 years
with the greatest creativity
and the most valiant courage.

Robert F. Butts, Jr.

SESSION 946 (DELETED)
JUNE 9, 1983 4:30 PM THURSDAY

(This little "session" actually consists of world view material, but I'm calling it a session simply for ease of filing and retrieval. Jane gave her last very brief session in St. Joseph's hospital on January 9—just five months ago. She held this one in the same hospital, after going back in on April 20.

(This afternoon's work might mark the beginning of a very significant development—Jane's urge to do creative work again. We'll see what develops. The material below, fragmentary as it is, began to come through late in my daily visit to her, in room 331 as I showed her a copy of ReVision *biannual journal of consciousness and change. Evidently someone has subscribed to it in our name, anonymously; we received our first issue last fall.*

(I was explaining to Jane the contents of a series of articles on art in this Spring 1983 issue, when I talked about a section on European art and the self. A self-portrait of Rembrandt is included, a very famous one. As I tried to explain to Jane how great art defied being dissected, she began to come through with impressions concerning Rembrandt. Later as she spoke I learned that this was world-view material. It certainly wasn't Seth speaking. Her voice was quite "normal."

(I didn't realize exactly what was transpiring at first, as Jane began speaking, so missed a few lines. That is, I had to ask her to repeat them as I got out a pad and pen.)

Sobriety deals with dark colors, but his original colors had glimpses of gold, and weren't as dark as they are now.... The twirling motions of damsels caught in skirts.... In still-lifes he liked to capture life's full scrumptiousness *("That's the word I keep getting"),* so that one object, if well done, was apt to suggest others of its kind—richness and opulence.

He was very fond of a copper color. A green he used in his portraits in flesh.... *(Repeated several times.)* You might say he had a gluttonous attitude toward life.

(4:50 PM.) From nature's sway no man escapes *(pause, one of many),* but even dissoluteness speaks of a world beyond nature's sway. Even meat that grows rotten serves a purpose that serves the painter's art *(pause),* and nourishes the needy portion of his brain. If woman's beauty must decay, still maggots have a life in miniature that still speaks of the beauty of their source.

Manure reels the senses with piled richness. *(Pause).* Tints of green and gold, implying loves that rot and yet live beyond decay. *(Then something in Latin I couldn't get.)* The scrotum swells like a sweet balloon, and the flowers burst their semen. Sweet balloons of nonsense that escape, and yet never escape this earthly sphere. There is more than painting, but painting is caught in life, and life itself is a tangle of colors so that even one suggests them all.

Fat ladies' smiles are orange *(pause, laugh)*, and no wicks burn down without ashes, which are the orange glints of the fat ladies' smiles.

("Can you die from gout?" Jane asked, as I talked about how little is really known of Rembrandt's personal life and correspondence—his writing—if he had much of any. I said that as far as is known he kept working until his death, or short-ly before, though the cause of his death is unknown historically.

(Jane smoked a cigarette at 5:05, while I got my stuff together preparatory to leaving. But she had more.) He had gout. He had swollen ankles at times, and gout, because he liked to eat. I also think there're some juicy comments about the clergy in there. I think it's a mixture of what I know about Latin and what he's trying to say. I think it's "gross domino"....

(Jane spelled it out, then at my request tried again:)

Gross Dominus. Like a takeoff on a litany *(and she tried to sing or chant what she was after)*. A contrast between Christ's poverty and the church's rich-ness....

(5:20.) I keep getting a stylus script. Lost in bills—he left some scribbled notes. He guarded the notes as jealously as any burgher hid his cash.... Hidden in a scarlet sack, at the first old address, the house where the children had typhoid. Hidden where no man would touch them, afraid of the plague's curse, or worse.... Something about 16 and 20 bushels gives a clue as to where they lay. Disguised in children's wear. He means hidden in baby clothes or something like that.

That's it....

(Jane didn't know if she was saying Rembrandt's notes still existed, were still hidden in that "first house."

(I'd told her along the way that at least some of what she came through with correlated with things I'd read about Rembrandt. That is, as an artist myself I under-stood them in ways that might not mean that much to her [although she paints also, of course].

(I particularly thought the material revolving around what she called Rembrandt's gluttonous view of life was very apt. I could see how this attitude could be interwound with his painting, its richness, its contrasting lights and darks, and particularly with his use of thick unfinished pigments and surfaces in his later works. And always the mystery of Rembrandt's work, its still-universal appeal, must be based upon deep and psychic intuitive understandings made physical in paintings that in my opinion have yet to be equaled, let alone surpassed. Jane's interpretation of his all-encompassing approach to life and art as being gluttonous would fit in very well here.

(I'm taking the session to read to her in 331 this afternoon. Perhaps she'll be inspired to do more on Rembrandt. At any rate, the issue of ReVision *and our conversation about art—and earlier about the current state of physics—had triggered her creative state.)*

SESSION 947 (DELETED)
JUNE 10, 1983 2:27 PM FRIDAY

(I read yesterday's session to Jane after getting to her hospital room at 1:30, and explained a few more things about Rembrandt's life as I remembered them from the books I have. The main thing here is that she's doing something, and as I told her during the course of the afternoon, it doesn't matter whether she produces a book, notes, essay(s), or if she does nothing at all with the material. In the meantime her material on Rembrandt's world view is very interesting. Already, it seems to have added impact or dimension, a force, to his life that's lacking in the books about him. That force is present in his art, so, I told Jane, her material could be furnishing an account of that emphasis verbally as he did it visually.

(Jane had a late lunch—she didn't get back from hydrotherapy until 12:30— and after she'd eaten I read yesterday's material to her while she had a cigarette. We talked about the notes Rembrandt had supposedly hidden away. Jane began to come through with more world view material:)

I think he meant stuffed inside a child's doll.... sewed right inside it. Somehow—you know, right inside it instead of stuffing.

And so it wouldn't be a soggy mess; the whole thing was enclosed behind snug bricks. He planned to save them for a nephew, but he never actually gave them away; and they were but dilly-dallyings, notes written now and then, thoughts that came to him in the night—and some ideas about the mixtures of colors, and the ways mild radiance could be suggested even though it didn't actually appear in the painting, and yet seemed to be there. Colors that made other colors brilliant simply by their presence and contrast. Purple remained in the background of royal enhancement, yet never appeared by itself alone.

Nobility and gout were faithful brothers, so even I had my touch of nobility in ways I had not planned. My feet sweated, my toes like sausages, fat and sometimes gooey. But such things are contained, and fall in the background as a man's life's art contains them all. They are elements of life's overflowing, the packaging in which life itself shows its splendid and sometimes nefarious ways.

(After a short break, resume at 2:36. Note above that at times Jane delivers the material as she would do herself through ordinary comment, while at other times she

appears to be quoting Rembrandt—or at least assigning a personal "I" to the material she draws from his world view.)

There were four bills enclosed with my notes meant for my nephew, yet never delivered. My families came and went like luscious apples, coming into their time, rounded and firm-fleshed, only to fall into the worm's realm. Worms also need their nourishment, so who should deny any of God's creatures their livelihood? So even in death there is life. Looking at one, you look at the other, and in one way or another each painting must reflect both life and death, for one without the other is meaningless.

Life is like a purse made of sow's skin, to be filled and emptied while the purse remains itself regardless of its contents. I care not what fills it, or whether it is empty, but it is always itself, waiting.

About the country, there is much I would know, for I know little of it, while people and places of urban design capture my imagination, and serve as nets for my hopes. The countryside seems too vast, too much like a supper, too large ever to be eaten, while people and urban places are there for the taking — amazing, amusing, but in doses that are manageable; portions to be captured, examined, and used by the painter's art. Or so I thought, and still think.

Silver and china dishes can suggest a full or empty harvest, and always there is man's sly knowledge of hunger and abundance.

(2:44 "Let me take a break and have something to drink before they come in to turn me," Jane said. She lay on her back. "A cigarette. Maybe I'll get more.... Then you can read me back a little of it. Okay?"

("Yes...." Jane asked me what I thought of the material, and I said things relative to the notes at the beginning of today's session. I added that I wished I had written down what I said. However, I was still intrigued by her original appellation of the word "gluttonous" to Rembrandt's life and work, I told her, and by the many connotations implied by its use.

("I got that he did scurry around a lot," Jane said as we talked, "hiding from bill collectors."

(2:55.) And good riddance to fools too dumb to take a small sketch for their <u>wares</u>. They buzzed—the bill collectors—like flies, noisy and quarrelsome, and I banged shut the doors, pulled the shades, and once or twice hid myself behind the draperies, there to contemplate my condition, for I did overspend— yet knew my paintings had their value, worth more than any tons of trinkets that I might, for my pleasure, collect.

There were Greek merchants I met in the marketplace, their pouches full of spices, they having traveled by their vessels, collecting spices and coins to their hearts' content. There were music boxes of exquisite delicacy, some made of shells, inlaid with pearl, and other music boxes of shells from the seashore, wrought with clever mechanisms *(delivery emphasized)* so that they made music and, so it was said, could tell the time. So I amused myself with such childish tokens. They cluttered my belongings, yet they added to my appetite for life, and in that way they nourished my paintings, which were never thin and wavering, but full of implications foreign to nature, yet like nature at once.

I tried to add more to nature than nature had, while being a part of nature itself I glanced slyly out of it, and if I fell I always picked myself up again, like a child learning to walk, with no nonsense about it.

I had a temper if harassed, even as sometimes the clear air bellows and sounds like a rusty horn. My raspy bellow could be like that—a horn played badly—but if left alone I was tranquil until the need for excitement once again drove me to our lusty hearth.

We boiled and brewed some colors until they were strong and rich. Anyone could tell ours was a painter's house, for its smell and odors were nefarious.

(3:38 PM. "At least I feel I'm doing something I'm made for," Jane said during a break. She said this several times during the afternoon, in between periods of dictation, nurses' visits with medication and inquiries, breathing exercises, and so forth.

(She also picked up something about a school for boys. "He either went there or it was nearby," she said during break. Then:)

They took mathematics, theology, geography. The curriculum was heavily loaded on the side of arithmetic—the sister to industry *(louder)*.

They handled slide rule[r]s (?), compasses, and learned to tell the time even in distant places. They learned the names of all of the saints, those dead but living dynamic souls counted among the church's own. Arithmetic was necessary to business, and the boys emerged clever-headed moppets, able to fend for themselves.

(3:41. "At least I feel like I'm doing something I'm meant to do," Jane said again. "Maybe it'll cut across all of this other stuff."

("I sure hope so," I said. I read to her what she'd produced so far. I took a break to look at some correspondence—which has been piling up lately, since I haven't felt like working on the mail—and read a few passages in ReVision magazine—the issue that may have triggered Jane's Rembrandt material. A couple of nurses turned Jane so that she lay on her left side, facing toward me as I sat beside her. I thought she was through dictating, but....

(4:23.) He never painted at the waterfront. It was too dangerous, because you could end up kidnapped and put on boats to work, and the same thing I

was getting was that they had pirate merchants. They'd lure you with the promise of selling you something real cheap that was of real value—they'd hit you over the head and you'd wake up on board ship the next morning, especially if you looked strong and healthy. They didn't want you if you looked sick and scrawny. Your best protection was to look thin and sickly—and he didn't look that way....

(That was it for the day. I said that as far as I knew Rembrandt wasn't a marine painter. I remembered—I thought—sketches he'd done in the countryside; cottages, canals maybe with small boats, etc. He was a studio painter interested in people more than anything else, I thought. But he had produced a few imaginary landscapes.

(Jane's material just above reminded me of reading about the old and notorious "press gangs," who would roam the waterfronts of Europe looking for people they could kidnap to man the sailing ships of the times—but I don't know what historical periods the press gangs operated in. Should be easy to determine. The term "impressing" was also used here, I believe—which I associated with the impressionist painters of several centuries later.)

SESSION 948 (DELETED)
JUNE 11, 1983   2:45 PM SATURDAY

(We continue the saga of the Rembrandt material, as soon as I arrived at room 331 this afternoon. Jane said she'd picked up some on Rembrandt this morning—that there were similarities between him and her father, and that these might be one of the reasons the material was available to her. [There are other reasons, too, which will become clear later in this session]. But as soon as she said this, and without even knowing what details she might be referring to, I felt I knew what she meant. And again, it was one of those things that seem quite obvious once known. The connections had already been made plain in the two previous Rembrandt sessions—if only one could see them.

(I might add a connection I made on my own—and that is simply that some of Jane's own characteristics fit in with both her father and Rembrandt's characteristics as she's been giving them so far. These revolve around her own approach to life—a strong, and yes, gluttonous one, as Seth himself remarked some years ago. For Jane is a person who plunges in, goes all the way when she's interested in something. She works in great bursts of inspiration, as witness these sessions themselves. Once she fastens upon something, that's it. She doesn't want to stop; she wants to forge ahead. This is all quite simplified, of course, but I see numerous similarities in her own makeup

and that of the 17th century artistic genius she's dealing with in these sessions. Most interesting.

(I suppose Seth would say that these psychic connections are vital to her ability to even tune into the Rembrandt world view to begin with—a common ground of being, out of which grew many similar interests. This isn't to note that there aren't many differences between Jane and Rembrandt, say, but evidently those dissimilarities do not interfere with her ability to come through with the Rembrandt material. Rembrandt's fixation on money [if that's the correct appellation] is quite opposed to Jane's more open acceptance of the belief that her talents will provide for her; she doesn't feel as though she needs the miserly approach—but then, some of those differences might be rooted simply in the different social contexts of the two personalities, and it could be legitimately said that both Rembrandt and Jane are interested in being paid for their abilities. And this kindred interest has obvious connections with her father Delmer Roberts' own secretive attitudes involving money.

(After the usual nursing services performed, including feeding lunch, as described in my notes for each day of Jane's hospital tenure, she began to come through with more Rembrandt material. Once again, she did this both as though she was simply relaying the information herself, and at other times as though Rembrandt was speaking through her. Meaning that, more accurately, she was drawing upon his world view and casting it in terms of the personal pronoun "I.")

I felt that Rembrandt had some of those same damn tricks my father had, of squirreling money away. And they had weights in the bottom hems of their drapes, and instead of weights in a lot of places he used to put coins. He'd sew them in, or have his wives do it, or in the folds of the drapes. And he had a money belt, but he didn't keep much money in it, because if they got too close the bill collectors would go right through your house and search it, or take a piece of goods to pay for the debt—so instead he squirreled away coins.

He loved clothes and had a lot of pantaloons, and when he went out he never carried much money so he couldn't get robbed. He tried lining his pantaloons with coins but they were too heavy. If you went out at night you could get robbed, so he wore old clothes to look poor. But as he said before, he was a man of property, and he didn't intend to lose it.

He had some crimson velvet-covered furniture of which he was exceedingly fond—two chairs and a sofa—

(2:53. A nurse came into 331 to ask Jane if she wanted to be turned on a side. Jane said no. She had to go over tomorrow's menu with the nurse, choosing each item she wanted for each of the three meals. I read the last few lines back to Jane. Resume at 3:00.)

A matched set. When he could he also sewed coins into the stuffing of the furniture, if he could, working from beneath.

(Pause. "It upset my concentration, working on that menu," Jane said.)

He loved the mirrors, in which he studied faces—

(3:02. Another interruption. A different nurse brought in a small cup of liquid vitamins for Jane to take.

(I felt that this interruption got Jane off the track, in that she might have come through with some material on Rembrandt's working methods. Even though the nurse left after a few moments, Jane resumed on a facet of her earlier material.)

He didn't believe in giving too much of an allowance to his children, either, to teach them the value of money. And he didn't believe in telling everybody his business, either. He was very careful about what he said about politics. He never gave away the meanings of his heart, but said what was expected, thinking that was the wise and prudent thing to do.

He was devout, but with a good eye to the church's chicanery, about which he said nothing but held his peace. He believed that children had their place, and met he sometimes acted the buffoon, playing with them on the floor, following their childish pranks and fantasies, telling them stories on the afternoons when the lighting was poor and the candles only served to make the rooms seem darker by contrast.

He hired many carriages—

(3:08. Once again the interruption precluded Jane following through on a train of thought. This time two nurses came in to clean up Jane, who for some time had been in the process of having a BM in bed, as she lay on her back on the disposable plastic underpad covering the sheet. Such activities of nature are a fact of life when one is confined to bed. In recent days Jane's slowly rotating bodily rhythms have led her to having a movement each day at about this time, whereas previously these had been taking place before noon. She's been going at about this time each day since giving the Rembrandt material [as well as for a few days before].

(After their ablutions were finished I read to Jane what she'd produced so far today. Now she lay on her left side, facing toward me. She repeated that today's material grew out of her father's habits with money.

("It sounds pretty hilarious," I said. "Almost like a compulsion or obsession."

(Whereupon Jane quickly said to me: "In answer to that—what you just said—?" And the following came through in the first person, as though my material had struck through to the Rembrandt personality itself:

(3:30.) I was not obsessed but prudent, and there were many men with habits as bizarre as mine, who guarded their habits as jealously, for I was surrounded always by a busy household—at its liveliest a man's delight—but there

were also issues that should be kept secret, held from women and children, who for all their beauty are not equipped to handle them. Thus in my way I did my families a service, until of course a wife was awakened by bill collectors at the door, yelling out in alarm. I admit I was tempted to hide beneath a bed or coverlet.

(3:35. A nurse came in to give Jane her scheduled eye drops.)

There were prayers and litanies to be said –

(3:40. Another nurse came in to take Jane's rectal temperature. I moved from that hard, unforgiving wooden chair back to the softer plastic-covered chair in the corner and tried to concentrate upon the mail. Lately it's seemed that most letters I've answered are from those who either want to come for a visit, or those who are having, or have had, mental problems. I haven't felt much like doing mail lately.

(After the nurses had gone I read to Jane her material from 3:30. Now she went back to her delivery in the third person.

(3:52.) He left the litanies and prayers to his wives and children—who prayed enough, it seemed to him, to serve an entire parish, for he believed that God knew a man's heart directly, and what his needs were, and thus to pray overmuch was almost a rebuke to God, as if one did not have faith in him—that God would not act without constant pushing and probing, supplication or adoration.

He often thought that man made God in his own image, instead of the other way around, since surely God himself would act on man's behalf without such constant reminders of man's need. So God had given him the need to paint, and so secure his livelihood—so in painting he thus served God's will as well as his own, a kind of blessed economy.

(Pause.) Thus prayers as such seemed needless, for in being himself he served his own ends and God's as well.

That of course would seem heresy, and so he kept his thoughts to himself, thinking, however, that if he thoroughly understood his art an understanding of God would come as well, so that both in a way were one, and God's power was in the colors he used, and in the brushstrokes themselves, and everywhere.

(4:00.) So let the people troop to their churches. He supposed God was there as well.

As to confession, he felt no man should bare his soul except to God, and no man could really act in God's behalf more than any other, or take on airs apart from those common to all men, but still I kept my counsel. Sometimes, in truth, I envied the church's wealth, the display of gold and silver that shone upon the altars and decorated the statues, yet toward all I maintained a certain tolerance, tried to be levelheaded and prudent—and prudent most of all.

(Note how in this delivery Jane switched in mid-sentence from her personal viewpoint to speaking for Rembrandt himself. I wonder what the word "prudent" sounds like—and how it looks—in Dutch.

(4:06. Jane asked me to light a cigarette for her. "This is your birthday present," she said, "because I know you're interested in art and in him. There isn't much else I could do—"

("Who needs anything else?" I asked. What a unique and loving present—and one so typical of her way of doing things. "You snot," I said. "I might have known you'd go about doing this this way...." And in return she smiled a certain kind of knowing smile, one that had a long history between us. She revealed a certain kind of satisfaction, a knowing that her creative actions were true—and obviously the best she's done in a long time. Was there still hope?

(4:10.) An artist in my time *(1606–1669)* hardly had the luxury of solitude. No man could mix his own colors or prepare his canvases alone, but assistants were always required if any painting were to be done at all. So I always had assorted assistants, mostly boys who harbored within their hearts to be artists too—some quite talented, and some as innocent of talent as an angel is innocent of evil.

Solitude, it seemed, was more precious than gold, yet on the other hand I did not know how to act on those few occasions when I was truly alone, facing only myself, and it happened so rarely that sometimes it seemed I beheld a stranger whose ways were hardly known to me, and whose thoughts belonged to another.

(4:14. I put out Jane's cigarette for her.)

It was then I scribbled down those strange thoughts that came to me: mine yet seemingly not mine, as if they were thought by another, so that I stared at them and then had to turn to recourse with others until the feelings of strangeness went away.

We had many sicknesses. That sometimes seemed to thrive upon the air itself, as multitudinous as flies in summertime; rashes and i-n-g-u-e-s-a-g-u-e-s *(spelled after several attempts at pronunciation: "I don't know what the hell that word is.")*, that came and went. Fevers and lassitudes, some blamed these on God or demons, but if one were patient they finally went away.... *(Pause.)* I paid them little mind, impatient to get to work again, though I swore at them as if they were sly tiny scoundrels that I could not see, but that were determined to thwart my best attempts at peace or peace of mind.

There was intrigue everywhere, and I kept my ears open, taking it all in and saying nothing. Or I seemed to agree with whomever it was I spoke, whether or not I did. Again, I found this most prudent.

I delighted as much as any man in gossip. Though I pretended, as most men do, that gossip was a woman's weakness and not a man's. I took no heed of rumors, though I listened to them all, pretending ignorance when I was asked. Thus did I preserve some stability, and kept my households intact.

(4:23. Jane took a brief rest.

(4:25.) There were always rumors concerning the downfall of the church, and dissenters' voices could be heard if one listened well. I could not see any organization, for all its faults, that could keep men contained, besides the church and state we had.

My painting always kept me busy—far different than a poet's estate, who required a mere script to express his art. There was always clamor and tumult *(pause)*, and in my heart I felt they were a part of man's plight, meant to push him onward. So I never, or hardly ever, wallowed in self-pity—except perhaps when my debtors became too fierce. And I could indeed, I'm afraid, momentarily take on the coward's ways.

(4:30.) I was no miser. I spent my money well. I shared what I had with family and friends *(pause)*, but I always kept extra coins hidden away to be on the safe side, and so I told no one where they were contained.

(A series of interruptions now began—nurses taking blood pressure, and so forth—the "vitals," as they called them. Their activities were part of the daily schedule for Jane at this time. My wife's signs always proved to be quite normal.

(4:41. "Do you want to rest for a while?" I asked Jane when we were alone again.

("I don't know...."

(Work for the day was over, however. Now I want to note some thoughts that came to me in connection with the Rembrandt material. Here are the notes I wrote at 10:10 AM on June 12, as I began typing this session:

("Could Rembrandt have used or driven his body to achieve his goals in the same way that Jane has done? I don't mean that he was arthritic or bedridden—no one knows how or why he died—but that he used his body as a machine or vehicle with a similar disregard or ruthlessness, something like Jane did. Another reason why Jane is able to tune into his world view?"

("Could be an important point here. Add to the notes at the end of the session [along with Jane picking up that "....he spent a lot of money in pharmacies.... but that the potions did little good."]

(Jane came through with that last tidbit just as I was getting ready to leave 331 at about 5PM today. I wrote it down when I got home. I should add that I think my notes above are a little strong—but also that I think they contain some sort of truth, some sort of intuitive connection that I made on my own. I'd say that mak-

ing such connections is very likely under the circumstances: one's imagination and intuition are bound to be stimulated—alerted—toward them as the material unfolds. The restless creative mind will always seek to put it all together in new syntheses made up of old parts.)

SESSION 949 (DELETED)
JUNE 12, 1983 4:45 PM SUNDAY

(A few notes: Depending on how far we carry the Rembrandt material, several facets of the history of his times in Holland—the 17th century—should be checked to see how Jane's material compares. For example, what religion(s) was paramount in his country? Jane used the word "parish" in the last session. Would this be correct? We could also use information on what houses Rembrandt lived in, if this is known, and his family history.... Jane referred to a nephew, for example. I've read of a brother; was he married, etc? I suppose I could also ask Jane to comment on some of these questions, if the material continues to develop—or they may be answered automatically. A list to refer to would be handy.

(Here are quotations from a note I wrote this morning while typing the 948th session.... "Jane is producing the Rembrandt material in the same manner that I think the artist probably used to produce his paintings—working all over the canvas at once. So as Rembrandt painted that way, she touches upon his personal life, his religion, his art, in a series of comments that all together add up to a fuller 'picture' of the man and his times, rather than laboring over details as she goes along. Rembrandt obviously had an orderly/intuitive way of working; without it he couldn't have possibly produced all of the work he did, with such great results. Jane likewise has her own orderly/intuitive way of working."

(The above isn't put very well, but can be developed if necessary. Rembrandt obviously began with a colored ground and a sketchy outline, and built up his paintings layer by layer upon a solid foundation so that results were almost guaranteed, if perhaps not always inspired. But at least he knew intimately how to perform the physical processes of producing a painting, step by step. Tie this in with the analogy of Jane producing her verbal canvas step by step.

(Upon reading over the two paragraphs above, the next day, I see that both of them are okay—so they could be combined eventually if necessary.

(At about 3:15 today [June 12] Jane underwent a hectic bout of movement, being lifted and turned several times while two and sometimes three nurses changed her sheets after one of them had accidentally let urine wet Jane's bottom sheet while substituting a fresh tube for the Foley catheter. Jane ended up on her left side, facing

me as I sat beside her in 331.

(Before all this happened I'd just finished reading yesterday's Rembrandt material to her, and she'd said she felt more there on Rembrandt's views on the saints.

I held the saints in awe and wonder—members of that scrumptious family *(pause)* of men and women dead and yet forever alive.

They each had their holiday, and for each day the church honored one saint or another with prayers and litanies. I thought that sometimes they existed more like allegories, yet that is not my meaning either—

(Jane was rather uncomfortable, lying on her left side, as the nurses had left her. She's been having spasms of the bladder recently, also; indeed, these have resulted in a slight leakage of urine on her underpads. The spasms aren't uncommon, according to her doctor, although she's been seldom bothered that way before. The spasms interrupt her concentration, though. She's been trying to deal with them through relaxation, and this approach has helped.)

—for their reality is far more valid, but the dimension of their existence is what mystified and eluded me as I sensed some rarefied atmosphere in which they had their lives, still alive and expressive, but alive in a different way than we know life. The same with angels.

In what estate did their existence actually happen? Were they somehow here and yet not here, and what did halos represent, besides being simply a mark of holiness? For I imagined in my mind that such rarefied atmosphere was everywhere, and that in painting it could be caught—but only when you were not trying to capture it, so that somehow its radiance simply appeared so that the artist himself knew that it was independent of the colors he used, but simply illuminated the painting with a light coming from everywhere. I was mystified in that angels were supposed to be men and yet not men, a blessed breed apart, not human yet fully divine, and I could sometimes sympathize even with Lucifer, in that he fell so low only because he tried to attain so much. Somehow he burst himself and fell apart in the fragments of tiny demons that then in the same way tormented men.

Long ago, when I was a child, I often envisioned angels riding in great radiance across the sky, or suddenly appearing at some poor bewildered man's bedside. Most likely the poor soul would be too shocked to speak, and die of a heart attack before the good angel could deliver the blessings he had planned.

So are angels to be given volume in paintings, or remain outlines? Do they have size as we have—weight and height—and what are they filled with if not blood? In that regard mystery has ever surrounded me, for in my heart I couldn't be sure if what I painted was real or not real, or if I painted truly. Yet these were mysteries each man had to fathom for himself, that pervaded his dreams sometimes, and hinted again of a strange life in between lives, and whose existence exists in a dimension that is ours and not ours,

Should angels be painted in perspective?—

(4:00. Just as I lost my place because of Jane's rapid dictation, a nurse came in to take my wife's rectal temperature, blood pressure, pulse, and so forth—"the works." Jane was still leaking a bit of urine because of spasms. She hoped they would go away if she relaxed, and the nurse agreed.

("Gee, Bob, I don't even know if they had perspective in those days," Jane said amid the ministrations. "Oh yes," I said, "it was common. Especially among the literal-minded Dutch."

(I'd left Jane's side to sit in the big plastic-covered easy chair in the corner of the room, where I usually worked on mail. etc. The nurses, by the way, were taking our new activities of dictation and notes in stride, though I doubted if any of them really understood what we were doing. "Writing a letter?" We agreed with any innocent comments like that, and kept working.

(Most of them know that Jane is a writer, though; I say little about my own activities. Strange—but some of them talk openly of their intuitional adventures. Other psychic abilities come up occasionally, as well as questions of life and death— the latter being hardly surprising, considering the hospital environment. Every so often Jane and I hear of a patient dying, even on the third floor where Jane is located. Walking down the polished halls to her room each day, I can't but help notice that most of the patients I glimpse are not young; they may range from the middle-aged to the very old indeed. [This ratio would obviously be much different in certain other sections, like pediatrics, for example.]

(I don't want to overdo a search for connections involving Jane's production of the Rembrandt material, but there could even be some as for questions about angels, life and death, the subject matter of some of Rembrandt's works—and Jane's hospital environment these days....

("Come on over [beside me] while I have a cigarette and give you some more material," Jane said at 4:13.

(4:14. Barely had she started smoking when a nurse came in to administer eye drops.

(4:16.) Should heaven—or the heaven—be painted in perspective? Were there places in heaven built according to an architect's design, or were there stranger perspectives than those we recognize — corners and crevices that existed only in the mind, or that the soul beheld?

The whole idea of strange perspectives in the heavens intrigued me, for if there were indeed other worlds than ours, it seemed to me that they must have perspectives of their own, and it seemed that one could glimpse such cosmic angles or distances that were distant yet not distant, as if the soul could perceive nuances that were always present yet usually not seen.

So I tried to hint in my paintings—later at least—of these bizarre if blessed strange perspectives of these other worlds, appearing out of some nowhere.

In what strange mood of mine could such perspectives be made to show themselves, and how could they be suggested in a painting? How could a man paint, in other words, what was not present to the immediate senses, when his very art seemed dependent upon normal vision?

If a man closes his eyes there is darkness — yet sometimes within that darkness light appears. Where does it come from? And how can an artist portray that which is not actually seen? I thought sometimes that an artist should have an inner vision quite as workable as physical vision is, and that such wonders might thus appear in their own realm, where they would seem quite reasonable and logical, with laws of perspective characteristic to themselves alone.

(4:27.) Many men—painters—took sport with perspectives, forcing an observer's eye to go in one direction or another, making distances appear on the flat surface. It seemed that a man's inner vision should somehow portray perspectives that had their own rules, so sometimes in my paintings I tried—inadequately—to portray such other <u>avenues</u> of perception.

The church itself had rules, saying that the church and angels and such must be painted in certain ways with certain characteristic colors. Should one paint Christ as a divine figure or as a human being? Should a painting suggest that Christ truly sweated? Should Christ look like a man or look like a god? But it seemed to me that the Son of God dwelled in those odd perspectives that disappeared when you tried to see them with ordinary eyes.

Again, sometimes a radiance appeared in my paintings that I could not explain, so that the effect produced was more than my colors could produce. I studied mirrors and reflections, reasoning that such odd perspectives might show themselves if one looked at the world backwards, so to speak, so that one tricked the mind into seeing perspectives that the physical eyes could not normally see.

Of such things I did not argue with my friends or assistants.

(4:35: Jane paused in her delivery, but this proved to be the end of dictation for the day. All was quiet and peaceful in the hospital. I thought that in an odd way it didn't matter what room we were in at such times, as long as we were together and doing something we enjoyed. Heretical thought, to have such feelings in a hospital! But the hospital environment—that very room, 331—is one that for many reasons we've chosen at this time. Right now it's a large part of our joint reality, no matter

what may happen tomorrow, say. I told Jane that if she wanted me to I'd bring in a book on Rembrandt tomorrow, so she could see some of his artistic solutions to the questions she'd posed on his behalf today. She didn't know whether to look at the paintings or not.)

SESSION 950 (DELETED)
JUNE 13, 1983   3:30 PM MONDAY

(Today I brought with me to room 331 the Harry Abrams volume on Rembrandt's paintings in Soviet museums. As soon as she knew I'd done so, she wanted to look at it. I held the book up and turned the pages from painting to painting. The book itself is gorgeous, and many of the paintings are world-famous and superb. We exclaimed over many of them. It was easy to point out examples that contained the lighting effects Rembrandt—or Jane—had referred to in the last session. I also showed her especially two paintings in which he'd painted angels as solid, three-dimensional individuals.

(While nurses tended Jane I scanned the long introduction to the book, looking for points about Rembrandt's life that might correlate with some of Jane's material. I believe I noted a few, but haven't given them any study. It may not be necessary anyhow.

(Jane was still being bothered by the spasms connected with her bladder and the catheter tube. She said she'd learned how to minimize them often through suggestion, however. She lay on her back, and had a cigarette after finishing a late lunch. Eventually she began to dictate.)

He used linseed oils. For some reason it was plural—I don't understand this. The tankers came in with supplies. And sometimes the oils he needed were spoiled—rancid—is that the word? *(I nodded.)*

He particularly had trouble like that in summertime. When everything like that was sticky. Tiny insects would even get on the paintings. And get caught.

It took a long time for the paintings to dry because of the sea air, so you had to be careful. One of the reasons he painted in the studio so much instead of going outside was because of the sea air. On some days it would leave tiny specks like salt grit on the paint, and even affect the brushes.

They had social hours occasionally when he and his cronies got together, for ale and good cheer, but even then he didn't discuss his techniques with other artists, but held them secret. He tried to keep his colors pure as possible. Even letting a good deal of time pass before laying one color on another. Only then

could his glazes work properly. Every now and then something in the weather
thinned his paint. He had no idea what it was to give such an effect. Then,
miraculously it seemed, they thickened up again. He had his assistants prepare
most canvases—time-consuming work with which the artist need not concern
himself. Brawn was required more than brains. Or art. While to bring the canvas —

*(Long pause at 3:38. Jane broke off her delivery to lay quietly while she con-
tended with more spasms. "I've learned a certain way to stop those spasms," she said,
explaining that suggestion was helping a great deal.*

(3:40.) Actually, he presumed that mountain air would be far better for a
painting. Keeping the consistency of paint more faithfully, for even his brushes
could become salty and stiff if they were not washed carefully. So in some
respects he and the salty air were enemies. And his clothes even became salt-stiff-
ened on some days.

He could not imagine how some painters could drive themselves to do
seascapes on location. Where the salt air was free to do its work—and so the
same could be said about dust, which drove him mad. There was always dust
everywhere—dust from the streets, from the draperies themselves, and these
could add a cloud upon the brightest colors if one was not as cautious as a cat.
Sometimes he forbade the women to work with their brooms, so as not to pro-
voke the nasty clouds of dust that then rose everywhere. His house was as tidy
as anyone's, and the women were always scrubbing. Yet dust it seemed was
everywhere.

(Pause at 3:45.) He had little use for soothsayers, yet certainly it seemed
that certain days were more propitious to paint than others, or charmed in a certain fashion, while other days were unhealthy, and the oils didn't work, as they
should. It was impossible to leave the mixing of paints to others, though some
artists might. He deemed the mixing of colors too intimate to trust to assistants,
however faithful their ways.

He didn't like to show paintings until they were finished, particularly portraits, for sometimes portraits showed qualities of the man's or woman's character that they were not willing to admit. One had to please the patrons!

*(3:52. "I'll have a cigarette," Jane said. "They'll be in to turn me any minute
now...")*

I also got that he studied dead men's faces, to see what had vanished from
what was once called life, to watch the strange changing of the colors in a dead
man's face. But he was very careful doing that so as not to be observed.

Sometimes he thought he noticed a halo effect in truth that glimmered
about the dead woman's or man's face, as if the unseen became visible and the

imagination impressed the physical mind with the sudden transformation. In a fashion he thought it was impossible to paint life without painting death as well, because the two were so intertwined. It was often quite difficult to receive payment from the family of a dead man, and he had to wait while the estates were settled. He did not wait like a vulture, but patiently—but still, on the business side of life such issues had to be considered, and who knew when today's living model might be dead tomorrow? There was so much involved on the business side, and he was no bookkeeper.

(Pause at 3:57.) He did not have the best reputation with bill collectors, but he did not believe in paying for work that was not well done, and so sometimes he held up payment for that reason.

(3:59. I took the ashtray away. "That [left] foot wants to go down," Jane said. I'd been helping her inch her feet down a bit at a time, and now with a little pressure I brought her foot down at least an inch—her best effort yet. There was an easily observable difference in the ways her legs were straightening. But she was still getting the bladder spasms.

(4:03.) It was very difficult to store supplies because the air was so damp.

(Long pause.) He was also not too agile about climbing ladders to reach the higher portions of larger paintings. And in later years it seemed he was always complaining of one indisposition or another, though these came and vanished.

(Later I explained to Jane that Rembrandt, 1606–1669, had lived for 63 years—no small achievement in itself in the 17th century!)

His ankles swelled, and on occasion even his fingers. Sometimes he fasted, and if not overdone fasting seemed to clear his general disposition and clean his system. He wondered sometimes at the color of a man's urine *(with a laugh)*, containing as it were the residue left from a man's food when he was done with it—or a color turned clear or cloudy, and held other tinges of color as well. *(Long pause.)* So he wondered how a man could manufacture such strange mixtures to be used for a painter's art.

He wondered sometimes, saying nothing, about using urine to thin his colors, or mix them *(long pause)*, but the smell was alarming and drew flies and other varmints, so his experiments along those lines were short lasting.

Temperas were difficult because eggs rotted, and the medium could not be controlled. It also was affected by the salty air, growing sticky.

(4:14. A nurse came into 331 to give Jane eye drops. She asked Jane if she wanted to be turned, and my wife said no.)

It was pretty unusual for his country, but there was a part of it where the earth was red, and it could be ground for colors—like in the south here—and the color was very stable. The dirt had to be very dry in order to collect the red grains, that red strain of earth. If the weather wasn't good, otherwise the color would just be muddy.

He often tried certain <u>grains</u> of color over flame, keeping them carefully in a dish that would not burn. Running the dish back and forth in the air over the flame. Sometimes he burnt his hands, so you had to work very quickly. He could also burn the pigments themselves in such a way. That particular work was hard on his temper, and when he got angry you could hear his bellow all over the house.

Some colors were so permanent that it seemed they would never fade or change, while others were quite untrustworthy, and would hardly last a day. He thought of his colors as he would of people: some were trustworthy and some were not. He could generally trust the earth colors. They seemed as enduring as the earth itself.

(4:27.) The reds had to be treated carefully. Some reds were scoundrels, and <u>appeared</u> permanent, only to vanish or turn into another color instead. This was particularly true of some yellows. (Long pause.) They could turn orangish at a moment's notice. He was amazed at the effects weather had on paints, and thought that for any preparation for life as a painter one would almost have to thoroughly study the elements as well. He did indeed follow the words of some soothsayers, who predicted when the winds would change and the rains would fall — but sometimes these predictions proved true but more often false. He thought that anatomy should be studied first of all by any artist, so the proper understanding of the body's parts could serve a man's art.

You could watch a dog or cat with immunity, or study a chicken's bones once it was dead, but the study of a man's body—or particularly of a woman's —was something else entirely. He never saw his wives truly naked, but only partially. He often questioned doctors about the body's anatomy. Some he knew studied corpses, but the church frowned upon such activities, and sometimes his own curiosity drove him almost into a frenzy.

(4:35.) He studied all the books on anatomy, and there was great controversy over where the soul existed—whether it be inside the body or without. Most considered it a thing apart, that hovered about the body but was not in it. But when they said, "The soul is gone," what did they mean? What then had vanished?

I decided that there must be different kinds of volume, different kinds of <u>thicknesses</u> than those we know. Sometimes I tried to paint cherubs more real than real, to suggest a stronger vitality and strength than that known by man. In my mind all things were basically united. A man's shit was full of the most amazing colors if one but looked—and again, I was often possessed by the idea of using some of man's own leftovers, or excrements, as a medium for painting itself. Of course it was impossible. The odors were horrendous, and urine faded, leaving only a stain.

There was nothing I did not at one time or another consider as a proper implement to support my art. Painting is so full of nature, so connected to the seasons, that it seems that a knowledge of the wind and air should be a prerequisite for any artist.

(Pause at 4:43.) So I sometimes despaired. Also, I felt my power as an artist and a man supersede all difficulties in some way that I did not understand, in that it endured as strong as ever.

(4:45. "Well, I guess that's it," Jane said. "I'll have a cigarette and relax before you leave. I'll relax if I can. I missed several times...." She referred to her spasms; they'd bothered her periodically, and had been accompanied by a slight leakage of urine onto the underpad. The nurses would be changing that item before long.

(A note: I couldn't help noticing that as she drew from Rembrandt's world view his comments on urine, she was having her own challenges involving that bodily product. Coincidence? Maybe. But I can safely say that if so, it's the first time that particular convergence of events has cropped up during our 29 years of marriage.)

SESSION 951 (DELETED)
JUNE 14, 1983 3:45 PM TUESDAY

(Jane hadn't had lunch yet when I got to her room at about 1:30. One of the nurses came in to feed her while I sorted through letters, manuscripts, notes, and so forth. [I carry a large brown paper bag full of supplies to 331 each day—and sometimes even that isn't big enough.]

(At 2:50 she began to read Session 949, which I'd finally finished typing. She lay on her back with her legs drawn up, and I propped the session against her thighs after clipping it to a piece of cardboard. She's read each session on the Rembrandt material this way and her ability to do so is a distinct improvement.

(The day was very hot; the temperature has been in the 90's the last few days. Her room is quite comfortable, though, with the fan on that's built into the register. She lies naked on the bed. The window is open but an inch or so. Jane asked me "if they had dry ice" in Rembrandt's time.

(This was a surprising question. She'd picked up this bit of information after I'd left yesterday afternoon. She asked me what dry ice consisted of, and I said that as far as I knew it was carbon dioxide, and that it was used in fire extinguishers and for refrigeration. I thought of it as strictly a modern-day product of technology. Jane

said she got that "they preserved stuff—food—with it, and that it originally came from China." She asked me to look it up in the dictionary and our encyclopedia.

(I said that I thought the very fact that she'd tuned into the subject was of interest. Even if it wasn't in use in Rembrandt's time, what associations on her part—and from his world view, say—had led her to come to such a question?)

I picked up something to the effect that he himself was portly a good portion of his life—but that was also deceptive, because the layers of a man's clothing made him look more portly than he was. He sometimes tired of frilled collars—both wearing them and painting them.

And some said he was rather gluttonous. They ate duck fairly frequently, which was sweet and greasy. And in one way or another he tried to suggest that sensual richness in his paintings, so that even the shadows came alive and were not dead. Shadows always added to a painting's mystery, and made light painting even brighter, and the colors more alive. Yet it never should be painted heavy-handed, but with an eye for delicacy, as if the shadows had the shapes sensed if not clearly seen. Shadows should not just be dull surfaces, therefore, and the palette knife could suggest an aliveness and elaborate designs that almost seemed to be there, yet were not.

(Long pause at 3:50.) Everything man knows is in one way or another human-oriented, so even the mysterious should have a human touch and appeal to a man's emotions, and not seem to be too distant or so lofty that a man cannot hope to understand. In one way or another the parables stand for men's universal situations, for experiences that in one way or another each man has had. So in painting parables, we paint more than the mere stories themselves, but give them new flesh *(long pause)*, by using today's men and women as models for the parables' stories.

We bring the parables to life by adding our own liveliness to tales that would otherwise appear too distant from our own concerns.

(Pause at 3:57.) You mentioned the Jews that I painted. Many cleverly went about in poorer clothes than they could afford, to arouse sympathy and to avoid others who might ask them to borrow. Instead they seemed almost like beggars themselves, but a few were truly penniless—

(4:00. There were interruptions: Two nurses came in to turn Jane. She screamed in pain as they rotated her to her left side, facing me: "Please be careful. Oh, please be careful." I thought they were rough in a way they usually weren't. One of them was called to the telephone by a third nurse midway through the operation, which didn't help matters any.

(Jane had a cigarette, and we talked for a while. She said she'd let me know if she got any more material. I moved to the other chair to work on mail—which I've

been letting pile up lately, by the way—but I barely got started.

(*4:09.*) He was fascinated about what the colors inside the body were—if they were closed and dark inside, or colorful, except for blood, which he knew was red. And the heart was red and the spleen was green. So was bile, or else it was yellow. He was interested in all the body <u>secretions</u>, thinking they were bound to carry information about the body itself—but who would ever think of painting a body inside out, so to speak? Such an endeavor would seem most offensive, not only to the church and state, but to people in general. Yet at times he thought of doing so.

He also wondered why he was given to such imaginings, when nothing could come of them, so prudently he tried not to wonder too deeply.

Surgeons and such did dissect animals. To be truthful, he didn't have the stomach for such proceedings, while still his curiosity was unbounded. Besides, cats and dogs were one thing and man another; since man had a soul he must be quite different from the animals, who did not.

(*Long pause.*) He tried to be industrious, to make his thoughts, even, count, so such imaginings bewildered even him, and he tried to lead his thoughts to more prudent ways. (*Pause.*) It seemed to him, though, that if even lice had life they must have something like a soul—some vitality given to them by God that was not their own.

Even the dullest rocks had a certain brilliance, and no gray was truly flat and black. And black in particular could seem to have tiny points and sparks of light.

(*4:18.*) Black indeed had a certain brilliance, though he never used it by itself alone. The mysteries of shadows demanded the cleverest blend of colors so they appeared, perhaps, black, but were not, and they carried the other glints of light that were carefully layered one by one.

Man was always caught in business, and so even those in repose in paintings should somehow seem to suggest motion, either coming or going, as if you caught a man in between motions, always about to move.

Certain vermilions could seem to jump back and forth, suggesting motion, but these were difficult to use, untrustworthy, and had to be backed up by other colors that kept them contained.

(*Long pause at 4:25.*) Each color had its own life, vitality, and characteristics. Like people, they were individuals. Some would run away and others seem immovable. The whites he tried in particular never to use alone, but backed up by actual color. Or often he used opposites to suggest a brilliance instead of white at all.

(*4:20. "I got that he used snuff,"* Jane said. *"It cleared your head out. Is that right?" I replied that I'd heard that was the case.*

(A note: Much hospital data, re times, medications, and so forth, in conjunction with these sessions can be found in my own separate notes that I make daily while at 331.)

SESSION 952 (DELETED)
JUNE 15, 1983 3:06 PM WEDNESDAY

(Add a mention of our prayer routine.

("A stray thought I just had," Jane said, "is that they had dry ice in China— that it came from there. It originated there, but I don't know...." I wrote down the question about dry ice, because I'd forgotten to look it up last night or this morning at the house. I'd been very busy, taking the car to the garage for replacement of the exhaust system, paying NY State and Federal income taxes, trying to catch up on these sessions, writing Eleanor Friede about Emir, and so forth. I told Jane that by "originating" in China she must mean the use of dry ice, since as a chemical compound it must be universal.

("Add that he—Rembrandt—collected snuff boxes," she said. At the end of yesterday's session she'd said the artist used snuff himself.

(A couple of nurses came in to turn Jane onto her left side, facing me, before today's material came through. "I'm just waiting to see if I get anything," she said, as though I might be expecting her to.

("It doesn't matter," I said, and meant it. She's been showing improvement recently, especially in the movements of her arms and legs, and that was of paramount importance. I'd told her I thought our prayer sessions, the Rembrandt work, the hospital stay, and our generally better attitudes were all contributing to that improvement, and that I hoped it continued. These sessions couldn't have come through not so long ago.

(On the way to the hospital this afternoon I'd stopped at the store whose personnel have ordered a small voice-activated tape recorder for us. Jane has been eagerly waiting for it to arrive for two weeks now. The manager called his distributor in Albany while I waited. Result: another two-week wait, as the just-marketed item makes its way from the manufacturer down to local outlets. At least, I said, we're doing things on our own in the meantime.)

He knew the Spanish used a lot of reds and blacks in painting, but he didn't go for that—it was too glaring—he thought it should be more subtle and mysterious. With a palette knife for the background of interiors you could suggest the finest detail without actually putting any detail in. Shadows should seem to engulf detail. Yet even then if the eye looked the observer should be positive he saw the details. The clever artist could suggest all kinds of flourishes and garnishes without actually producing them on the canvas at all. Nothing should be lost in the background—there should always be rooms that didn't show in the interior. This could be done by clever handling of lighting and assemblage of color.

Certainly the background should not appear flat. There were various planes *(spelled)* or levels within a painting *(pause)* that could each themselves serve as a shelf, so to speak, for any group of objects, but such planes should be complete in themselves—that is, done as carefully as the other portions or other layers, so that they were like paintings in themselves.

All objects should be painted with some glimpses of light, for in truth the light does reach everywhere, and nothing is completely engulfed in darkness. The various articles *(pause)* used along with the man or woman's portrait should somehow manage to express the person's character, and therefore be carefully chosen. For the articles used by people serve as exterior extensions of their minds and personalities.

(Long pause at 3:15.) Attention should be paid to the slopes of a man or woman's brow or cheek, so that these actually appear sculpted—a cheek sloping upward as surely as any hill does, or furrows sunken in as much as any valley.

The eye itself, of course, tells most of a person's soul, so the gentle slope of an eyelid should be painted carefully, for it has its own gentle fullness, while the rising eyebrows follow faithfully, it seems, a person's most secret moods, sculpted by emotion as certainly as leaves are by the wind—that is, it should he apparent that eyebrows move and possess their own agility. They may be as a squirrel's bushy tail, or thin and drawn, but they will always possess expression and motion.

The downcast eye is perhaps the most expressive of all, so that the eye is not seen head on, so to speak, but possesses a certain mystery, a mystery that can be suggested by the clever use of opaques, and then transparent light.

It should be remembered also that heads themselves have much weight *(spelled.*

(Pause at 3:22.) The eye seen looking directly outward is too bold *(pause),* so even in laughing paces the eye should not seem to stare right out in a frontward fashion, but have the head tossed slightly upward or downward so that the eye follows the curve of cheek or lips. The eye should also suggest its liquidy characteristics, for it moves more swiftly than any other portion of the body. The eye's motion is very still *(?).*

Some faces have smooth pores, and some have large ones, and according to the size of the portrait such characteristics should be apparent and not ignored, for no person's skin is smooth as parchment. Pores are not merely small dots, then, but through them some sweat secretions come, so they themselves have a certain kind of aliveness. A fat person's face, or an old face, for example, often possess larger pores, though this is not always the case.

In an adult the legs and arms stop growing, but remember that the hair still grows on and on and on unless you cut it constantly, or unless a man is bald, therefore never should hair appear as mere design, but as a freshly growing part of the head, like wheat to be harvested, alive with its own motion.

(3:30. Jane wanted a cigarette and some water, and asked me to flip her over onto her back. She felt that a bowel movement was coming, and wanted to be in position on the underpad. I began work on the mail while this was going on. A nurse came in later to check up, and give Jane eye drops. Jane asked her to return in a little while to clean her up. Now she wanted to do some more dictation.

(4:08.) The artist should also remember that the mouth is full of teeth and tongue, so that the lips are not painted in a surface fashion, but with the fullness of the interior always suggested. Painting the lips <u>parted</u> slightly is perhaps more propitious. To some extent the artist must understand the man's or woman's vanity, however, despite his own desire for truthfulness, for sometimes the person will want teeth painted in <u>where there are none</u>, while another will not care a whit. This is a most sensitive proposition, however, for many adults have trouble with their teeth, and women are more sensitive in that regard. Use some shadows in that area also. Remember, a mouth can open wide enough to eat an apple, so it has its own capacity for motion, and a certain elastic quality that should always be kept in mind.

Peoples' ears are not the same either. Some are bigger or smaller, some are pointed. Each person's ear is like no other, and in fact a person may have ears that do not match. All such actions should be taken to mind. Ears are not just stuck on, but are the body's appendages. They grow out of the head, with their own delicacy and fullness. If you look, some ears can be seen to have hairs that appear just beyond the curvatures.

And in the same way peoples' nostrils flare just like a horse's. The nostrils are not just holes painted on, but are openings into mysterious passageways, so this mystery should be suggested by the clever use of shadow.

(4:17. The nurse returned to start cleaning up Jane. "That's it for the moment," my wife said. Another nurse appeared. They also took Jane's "vitals," as they usually do at this time. When they were all through Jane lay on her right side, facing away from my chair and toward the south window.

(Jane had more material to give, so I moved around her bed and wrote stand-

ing up, using her bed table as a support for the pad. There isn't much room on the window side of her bed.

(4:45.) As anyone knows, there is a vast difference in the proportions of a young person's head and an older person's head, in relation to their bodies. The child's head is larger. Time has not yet done its work, and so the child's face is more flushed, firmer, and in a way immature. In some children, however, their character is already apparent, while in others their personality does not seem as well impressed upon the features.

I do not mean to suggest a vacancy, but an <u>expectation</u> of character to be filled. In the grownup's face the person's character is marked in every portion of the body. Even the body's wrinkles follow their own patterns, as if time itself had written scrolls upon the face. The wrinkles are time's hieroglyphics.

The child's head has a certain buoyancy that the adult's does not possess, as if the head were not yet full of thoughts. There are indeed differences between the faces of thoughtful men and less thoughtful ones. People who work with their muscles alone have a certain earthy substance. I do not mean to suggest that all peasants are happy people—but their faces indeed seem to have a greater gaiety than those of city folk, and their limbs seem more free for motion.

In this they bear a resemblance to children. That is, they possess a recklessness that is apparent in their figures that more cautious persons do not have. The background, imaginary or real, should carry out the body's characteristics, for in a way each body itself has its own theme. One person appears most often moody, or sad or sorrowful, while another seems at least to be crafty or vain, or even loathsome in his own fashion. So the backgrounds, imaginary or real, should carry through the themes that the model's character seems to suggest.

Often, however, a present-day person is painted in the guise of a well-known saint, or hero or legendary character. In that case the legendary character's characteristics overshadow the person's own, so that he or she is <u>elevated</u>, as it were, to a higher station.

Okay.

(5:00. "That was very good," I said.

("Yeah. I thought I was in it pretty good," Jane said. Her delivery had been fast and rather forceful. In it I'd detected something of the old days of the sessions. Today she'd done the best she had for a long while, as I told her.)

SESSION 953 (DELETED)
JUNE 16, 1983 3:45 PM THURSDAY

(Jean Sweeney-Dunn visited us in 331 at about 3:30 today, just as we were to start dictation. I'd fed Jane lunch because the nurses were short-handed and very busy, propped up yesterday's session for her to read, helped her have a cigarette, and so forth.

(Jean stayed for only 15 minutes. Jane was in the process of having a BM, but we went ahead anyhow. It was getting late. See my own notes for any necessary details re the day's events.)

It was very lively where he lived. The ships brought in all kinds of gossip and rumors, and so forth, and stories of people who lived in far places.

There's something about porcelain—I'm not sure what—I think something about <u>dolls</u> with porcelain heads and necks and maybe hands, and cloth bodies, because sometimes kids clutched them for portraits or held them or something.

(Jane paused. She was worried about having a bladder spasm. Her catheter had been replaced [see my own notes] recently, and she felt much better. At the same time she would feel twinges as though a spasm might occur. She's been instructed by her doctor—and the nurses—to drink as much liquid as she can.)

Kids also used little play wagons, and if he had children he tried to include some of their toys in the paintings. They even had some kind of dolls of black children—natives of some strange islands, they were supposed to be, and some French dolls.

(Long pause.) Oftentimes he had his models holding books or manuscripts, so that they appeared to be doing something, rather than just sitting for a portrait. This also added design and interest to a painting.

(Long pause at 3:52.) Religious themes often held his attention and interest, and since they had the power to stir imagination so strongly, and seemed to possess a life of their own, stories or parables seemed timeless in the same way that a painting did. That is, whether a painting was of the past or present in terms of subject matter, it still existed in its own time, contained by the frame, so that there seemed to be always a motion about to happen, and if you looked away a hand would toss a ball, or a person seemingly asleep in the painting would waken. So he did indeed try to somehow mix the contemporary and the eternal. A difficult task.

In other words, he liked to mix the practical, everyday lives of men and women with those eternal qualities that gave a man or woman vitality and motion.

Though theirs was a small-enough country, the commercial seaways opened it, so that even though it seemed remote from the world, it kept in touch with many lands and peoples because of the commercial seagoing vessels. The boats also brought dyes *(spelled)*, bolts of cloth, of course, different kinds of foodstuffs, and on occasion ammunition. There were always stories of smuggled arms, hidden arsenals and intrigues of one kind or another.

He supposed that if he traveled widely an artist might find a many fascinating subjects for his art, but he himself enjoyed his own homey location, mixing the elements of the marketplace with its failings and virtues with the aire *(spelled)* with which he felt the whole world itself was somehow held.

(4:00.) An artist with a clever imagination could imagine many foreign scenes and places, and use them to his heart's content. He didn't feel he had to go to a jungle to paint one putting up with testy mosquitoes, snakes, and the like, when in the studio the mind could suggest elements of jungle or mountaintop as the artist required.

(4:02 PM. Jane took a break for a smoke, but this was the end of Rembrandt for today. She wanted to be cleaned up. It's been trying to rain for some little while. Thunderstorms are predicted, Jean had said. I finally had to ring for a nurse at 4:15.

(Margaret Bumbalo has invited me for supper tonight. I suspect that she plans an early birthday celebration for me. I'm not actually due until the 20th.)

SESSION 954 (DELETED)
JUNE 17, 1983 3:42 PM FRIDAY

(After we'd finished yesterday's short session Jane had told me that she was picking up more on Rembrandt—about his death, and a "fantastic" apple tree that held apples of red and of gold. She gave me a little more, but things were rather busy in 331, and I didn't attempt to write down the material, or add it to the end of yesterday afternoon's session. I did hope she'd elaborate upon that material this afternoon, though.

(Lately the staff at the hospital has been so busy that I've taken on feeding lunch to Jane. Such was the case today. She'd returned from hydro, as we call it, not long before I arrived at 1:25, so with eating, cleaning her up after a BM, and the usual nursing ministrations on schedule, we couldn't get down to dictation until the time noted above. But when we did Jane started right in on the subject of Rembrandt's death.)

He didn't know what killed him. He just felt a dreadful twinge and couldn't get his breath, and then seemingly his breath just stopped. That is, he didn't remember anything for a long time, and then he came to.

He found himself on a delightful knoll, and in front of him was a fantastic tree, more real than real, yet utterly unreal—a tree whose branches were filled with fresh red apples—<u>and apples of gold</u>.

He knew the apples were of gold, and thus should be heavier than the natural ones, yet for some reason the golden apples didn't weigh down the branches any more than the natural ones, and all in all the tree was brilliant. The trunk itself glittered with dazzling earth colors. He heard a voice from nowhere say, "You may have an apple. Choose a red one or a gold one." Without knowing where the voice came from, he studied the apples carefully, and realized he was indeed hungry. He chose a red apple, though it was difficult indeed to pass the golden apples by. It was then he wondered who was speaking to him. He turned around. All ready to say, "Who is there?" when to his amazement he saw an angel, or what certainly seemed to be one.

(3:48.) This being (spelled) almost stunned his senses, for the angel managed to be somehow golden and natural at once, looking perhaps like a golden man with wings. While the gold itself had nature's great mobility and wasn't <u>immobile</u>, as gold is on earth, or heavy, or weighted down.

A statue of gold on earth would be heavy, but this gold was alive and fluid and moving. So I (note the switch to the first person) just stood there, gaping, mouth open. "This is the kingdom of the valley of colors," the angel said, and again I just stood there, aghast and incredulous. Before me spread out valley after valley filled with cottages and shops and people—but they were all composed of such changing glorious colors that I could only stare. It is impossible to describe, but while staying in their places, houses and rooftops, for example, their glorious colors gave the impression of constant motion, as if they flowed, and kept flowing while ever maintaining the stability of their shapes.

There were palaces and cottages, but one was not more glowing and mysterious than the other, and the cottages with their jeweled lighting glistened as if made of precious stones turned into a flowing liquid pattern. I should say patterns, but I could not take everything in at once — only that the cottages were as amazing as the palaces. And all the colors were so glorious that my heart ached.

It ached with yearning and with joy and with greatest delight —

(3:58. A nurse came in to take Jane's rectal temperature, pulse, blood pressure, and so forth. Jane was doing well dictating. "I was quite carried away," she said regretfully, later, at the interruption. I fed her a little ice cream and chocolate cake—the cake being part of the portion Margaret Bumbalo had given me last night after supper: The Bumbalos and son John had planned a tiny birthday surprise for me.

(Jane still lay on her back; I'd flipped her there from her left side so she could eat lunch. She had a cigarette. "I sure hope I can get back into it," she said.

(4:17. And she resumed dictation as though there hadn't been any interrup-

tion at all:)

—and with the greatest misgiving, because no artist could possibly learn to make such stunning hues. My heart almost ached with the deepest sense of loss that such beauty would forever escape my reach, but would go unexpressed, for no canvas could possibly contain such startling perspectives.

It was only then that I understood that I was dealing with entirely different perspectives than any I had ever known, in which both colors *(pause)* and objects existed in a way impossible to describe. Colors in themselves possessed their own startling perspectives—

(4:22. Jan, a nurse, came into 331. "It's time for me to turn Jane...." Once again Jane had been deeply immersed in her dictation. It took a while to get her turned and comfortable. Now she lay on her right side, facing the south window. The day was cloudy and windy now, threatening rain. There isn't much room between the bed and the window, so I stood up there, writing on the narrow bed table.

(I should note that Jane/Rembrandt uses the word "perspectives" in a somewhat different context than usual, I believe, assigning a sense of quality and feeling to the word as well as its usual meaning of depth, and so forth.

(And once again Jane resumed dictation right on target at 4:34:)

—that had nothing to do with one color being lighter or darker than another, but the colors in themselves interacted in a kind of communication, so that again I was filled with the deepest yearning when it came to my attention that the entire scene had a kind of *(long pause)* <u>musical</u> connection, as if the colors were also composed of majestic musical notes, and I realized that for some time I'd been straining to hear some strange, sensed but still inaudible music. The colors had some kind of musical reality just beyond my range, and I kept straining to hear it, and for just a moment or instant I almost did.

(Pause at 4:38.) That is, I caught sense of the sweetest, and yet most eerie music, as if perhaps all the birds on earth were singing their songs at once—each one, however, so melodious that the entire musical sequence shimmered— shimmered in musical colors, and I gaped once again like a child crying after a lost balloon rising steadily out of his sight into the skies. For surely that sublime beauty was beyond both the artist's and the musician's art as well.

I could hardly contain myself, and I know I made the weirdest sounds—

(4:41. A nurse gave Jane her eye drops. This wasn't too easy to do with my wife lying on her side. I read the material to her from 4:38. Then resume at 4:45:)

—bellows of agony and delight together *(pause)*, when mercifully a sudden cool and calm peacefulness settled gently about me, cradling me as it were, and I felt as if I were being gently comforted like a child after an overly busy day, and then I rested *(pause)*, and in some way I do not understand <u>time</u> came to comfort me—that is, I felt as if I rested comfortably with a full feeling of peace-fulness through endless nights and dawns, and that I was couched safely.

I also felt as if I was a changeling, and I began then to prickle with antic-ipation, as if undergoing some waited—for transformation.

Okay....

(4:41. "You don't have to worry about the time, Hon," I said when Jane paused. I'd seen her glance up at the clock taped to the top of the TV set. I'd pushed the set, which on its boom hovered over her bed, off to the side, and turned off the sound before she began dictating. I usually leave around 5:00. She was doing so well I didn't want to interrupt, though: the very fact that she was able to produce the ses-sion, as well as its intrinsic excellence, was of the utmost therapeutic value.)

Nothing bothered me, yet I felt somewhat like a child, half asleep, listen-ing to the voices of its family, murmuring, pleasant, and melodious.

I felt people around me, though I saw no one. I opened my eyes, or what certainly seemed to be my eyes, and space itself seemed to come alive and form itself into people or beings or inhabitants of this other perspective of which I have spoken.

It was then somehow that I understood that people themselves existed, or exist, in all of these perspectives and dimensions at once. It's a strange reality. In which the nearest is the furthest away at the same time, and that which seems far distant is closer than one's breath. All art exists in all of its forms at once. A painting is a musical composition also, and any art that exists in one form exists in all other forms at once. So a man's soul functioned in the same fashions, ever renewing itself. Each composition and each line is always transforming itself and being transformed, forming some truly celestial design that is more alive than life, and the more expressive than anything any artist could ever describe. Then once again I held my peace, or I was somehow lulled into a feeling of serenity, yet even then I felt that stirring of anticipation, as if I were some kind of changeling, already transforming myself into some other species indeed.

Once or twice I had the oddest experience while all this was occurring: I suddenly snapped to—back to the self I had been. I was in my studio, gulping and yawning the deepest yawns, cursing at the flies or whatever.

(5:00. There was thunder, wind, and some rain.)

Momentarily I felt the deepest love for that self I had been, and then it came to me that in one way or another I was that self still, and that miraculously all this was happening at the same time as I yawned deeply in my studio, or belched or coughed or whatever. Then once again I was somehow moved to a feeling of tranquility. I felt that days and nights and even centuries were passing somewhere, where the earth I'd known still continued its own ways, and I felt like I was a child in a hammock, resting.

(5:04. "I really felt parts of that," Jane said. She'd spoken along at a steady pace in her own voice, and her delivery had reminded me of those times in her regular sessions when she'd attained that same certainty and inevitability of expression—when I'd known for sure that she was clearly attuned to, and was a part of her source of inspiration. "That was good, Hon," I said. "It is good. I could tell you felt that way."

("I was really in it," Jane said. "I could see parts of it. You know—see it and not see it...." She could especially remember seeing Rembrandt in his studio, belching and scratching, she said. She felt as though she was "on the edge" of something more, so I waited. "I think of you and me having things like that," she said, probably meaning experiences.

(The rain was still slight, but now the thunder was heavier and rolling across the valley. The room was cool with the air conditioner going. No one was bothering us, and in the gathering gloom 331 had a comfortable, almost private atmosphere. For the moment, at least, it didn't matter where we were doing our thing. Jane said the supper tray wouldn't be showing up until after 6:30.

(5:15.) In the same fashion in some other portion of my mind, I met and spoke to all of those persons I had ever loved.

They spoke to me as clearly as they had ever spoken on earth. They carried on a dialogue, which gave the oddest impression, as if the conversations had been going on for centuries and yet were all happening at once. As if I was dividing them up so that I could understand them better.

Again, I realized that the dead and the living were all alive, and that death itself was part of a larger kind of life than ordinary life itself ever knew.

Sometimes I cried out with a certain kind of anguish; "Why didn't I know all of this before? And yet I realized—"Of course, of course"—that some part of me had known all of this all of the time. I realized also that I had my own part to play in the creation of the world itself, as I had known it, that I even played a part in the creation of its past—and in a way, if you knew how to read my paintings without trying to read them, you would see that all this was somehow implied, that one part of a painting implied the whole. Any painting shows far more than a man realizes, or than even the artist knows. It implies the kind of creature he is, the kind of species to which he belongs, and it even implies what I am now.

That's why some art endures—because the artist himself expresses *(long pause)* worlds that are beyond his present grasp, yet they come alive in his paintings. They illuminate all the colors.

(Pause at 5:25. A gentle rain had begun.) They express a reality into which the artist himself is growing, and the mark of the changeling is upon them. And

all who view such paintings know this without knowing that they know.

(5:26. "Well, give me a cigarette," Jane said. "Boy, was I really caught up in that," she said several times. It had been easy to tell. "I felt I was really with it—I think some of it is as good as any I've ever really gotten—certain passages of it, anyway." I said there was no doubt of it.

(I was still writing standing up beside her bed, using the bed table as a support next to the window. Resume at 5:42.)

The musician, I am sure, must see images as he composes his work, and those images must in one way or another serve to lead him onward, so that his musical composition begins to come alive in terms of color, line, and perspective, forming its own kind of multidimensional structure that grows into or from other mediums as well. That is, music must build up images that must exist as surely as the music, even when the musicians do not understand this. You should be able to <u>hear</u> a painting. For in one way or another it exists as a symphony also. And so the musicians' notes must build up their own form, their own painting, so to speak, establishing themselves in wondrous ways.

In the same manner the poet's inspired words surely also build form upon form, turning into images that establish themselves in this eternal yet ever-changing reality in which I am still only a babe, a babe who senses adults nearby—friendly relatives, comrades, colleagues. I realized also that I heard voices speaking directly to me. Yet I could not catch their meaning or resonance. I was only aware of their presence. And I certainly knew they were aware of mine.

(Pause at 5:50.) I found no words, even in my mind, to express their reality. On the other hand it seemed to me that we were all in one room, conversing about some learned subject, and that I was being asked questions. I did not know what the questions were. Even while one part of me understood that I was answering them.

My answers seemed to turn into a kind of purple sound, and I knew that colors spoke—literally, not just figuratively, and once more I was amazed and at a loss. Yet my voice did indeed turn into streams of colored sound. I had never heard of such a thing, colored sound, and then I realized that in some unaccountable manner I myself existed as some sort of living color, ever changing, that I turned into sound and back again into form. Indeed, I felt enchanted and bewildered all at once, and I realized that when I was alive, as people on earth term it, I was also expressing myself in colors that translated into sound and back again too swiftly for this physical being to understand in usual terms. And it was the same for all creatures, I saw, not one being left out, whether large or small.

And in the same manner, now and then I would return "briefly" to my studio to find myself coughing or wheezing or whatever, trying to remember something that I had forgotten. And what I had forgotten, of course, were those experiences that I'm only having now. For all of these strange experiences in some manner or another occur in their own spaces and times. They're only like musical sequences in which all other times fit so that the colors speak, and the times flow into the colors.

(*5:58. The rain was pouring down—quite heavily—with some thunder and a little lightning. The storm had been building all afternoon. I was getting tired, and a bit chilly, standing next to the air conditioner. "Boy, I was really out of it," Jane said again. "It's a great release."*

("It's also great to know it applies to everybody and everything," I said, as we talked about what had come through. Jane had a cigarette. The heavy rain was slowly moderating, but it looked like it would continue; I had to get out to the car.

(*But none of that mattered, I thought later, as I drove home in a downpour that had renewed itself so that the rain was heavier than ever. The material she'd delivered today made life worth it—it gave a view, a new perspective on daily life. If it was even half true, I thought, it was transforming knowledge, and it showed how little we really know in our physical lives, how limited our accepted "rational" really is, how far we have to go.... What a fitting demonstration, I thought, of Seth's often-repeated material about "consciousness getting to know itself."*

(*My clothes were wet from running out to the car in the parking lot behind the emergency room. The rain became so wild and heavy as I drove up Church Street that I nearly had to pull over to the curb and wait for it to subside a bit; the car's wipers could barely handle the load....*)

SESSION 955 (DELETED)
JUNE 18, 1983 3:27 PM SATURDAY

(*See my own daily notes for any additional info needed re these notes. So now we have to worry about the possibility of a strike by the nurses—only I refuse to worry. It's the hospital's responsibility to provide care for Jane.*

(*By 3:15 I'd trimmed her toenails, she'd read a very interesting letter from a fan, and the first seven pages of yesterday's session. We were alone in 331, although there was enough noise out in the hall. I have to water the Bumbalos' fuchsia on their front porch. They've gone to their cottage on one of the lakes for the weekend.*

(*Jane said she'd been picking up on her Rembrandt material this morning. I've noticed that in that material she seldom refers to Rembrandt by name, for some reason. Once again she talked about the inspired quality of her material yesterday, and how much she'd enjoyed delivering it.*

(*It's come to me also that if we ever do anything about publishing Rembrandt, she'll have to do an intro.*)

Right now I'm getting that at certain times he kept returning to the self in the studio, again, to find himself young or whatever, or staring at a painting, wondering what was wrong—when he realized that all the experiences he was presently having were still somehow in the back of his mind latent as he worked on his paintings, because he was painting in response to those inner visions that he seemed to be having now and only now.

So in—

(*3:28. Jean, the nurse, came in to ask Jane a question about food.*

(*3:30.*) It seemed impossible—but I was somehow reacting to my "future" experiences back in that "past," and I was painting in response to the experiences that I only now seemed to perceive.

(*Long pause.*) It was as if I was coming and going at the same time, and as if my past action were happening because of these future events. In the ordinary time sequence that I knew in life certainly my present action would be in the future. Yet I am now positive, or nearly so, that the original impetus for my paintings came from these events that now seem so new to me. It was like mixing past, present, and future together, as if they were indeed colors, or as if you found yourself peeking out at yourself in various designs and patterns.

(*Pause at 3:36.*) In ordinary earthly experience there must be time between actions, and one brushstroke must follow another. Now I feel that all actions happen at once; and that each seemingly separate time period is a part of every other.

I almost feel as if I were going back into the past in order to change any given painting, so that it is more in keeping with what I know now. But in the weirdest fashion, I began the painting because of this present knowledge.

(*Long pause.*) Once I heard Christmas carols, and found myself in my old studio, peering through the drapes to see a group of visiting Russians, dancing in the street outside, and singing carols.

(*A note for possible elaboration: The book on Rembrandt's paintings that I'd showed Jane on June 13—four days ago—consisted of collections of his works in Russian museums. A long intro, which I've hardly read, and Jane hasn't seen at all, details how the paintings were acquired; some, I believe by Russian scouts and agents traveling in Europe. I do not recall whether any of these representatives were active while Rembrandt lived, but their activities reach way back, I think, at least into the later years of the 17th century. Rembrandt died in the year 1669.*)

(*Long pause.*) The carols were musical colors, so that dazzling light emerged from the words they sang.

(3:43. "Humph," Jane said, pleased. "Oh, I guess I'll have a cigarette. What time is it?" A nurse came in, but couldn't get Jane's temperature rectally while my wife was on her back. She took blood pressure, pulse, and gave Jane eye drops.

(I explained as much of the Russian connection—if there was any—as I could. Jane wanted to know the dates for the Reformation. She mentioned Luther, and that she thought the low countries of Europe were largely Protestant by Rembrandt's time. I said a lot of our questions could be automatically answered as the material unfolds.

(Note, added later: According to our dictionary, the Reformation was the 16th century religious movement [in the 1500's] that aimed at reforming the Roman Catholic Church, and resulted in establishing the Protestant churches.

(3:56.) There were quite a few Russians that visited, and sometimes held Russian dances, where they did their folk dances and things like that. I'm getting that he felt more akin to the Russians than he did to the Spaniards, who seemed too <u>Mediterranean </u>for him—too sultry.

Rembrandt had to admit that the Spaniard's dances were emphatic enough, that their passion seemed to have a secret quality that might emerge explosively at any time, while the Russians almost always seemed hearty and somehow more open.

What he knew of the French he knew mainly about the French court—intrigues concerning the French royalty—and the French to him seemed more mercenary, even, than the Jews, for example, perhaps because he expected it of the Jews but not of the French. He expected the French to be extravagant, yet he did a few paintings for a Frenchman, and found them miserly in their pay, so it was hard for him to collect his dues.

There was also, he felt, a strange feminine nature to the Frenchman, and it confused him, as if the men were mimicking feminine habits. They were sometimes so slavishly polite in their ways that they struck him as being a trifle weak.

The Danes were much like the Swedes, rather clannish, yet good-enough businessmen and fairly trustworthy.

The guilds were strong, so it was best to go along with them. If one wanted to hire a carpenter or painter or whatever, then a man's guild had to be taken into consideration. A man from one guild dared not do the work of one from another guild.

In the French, he felt, the bloodlines were often highly questionable, where the Dutch lines were often simpler and cleaner cut, and there was less illegitimacy and fewer bastards.

(Pause at 4:05.) While he himself muttered about the prevalence of dust

or lice, still the Dutch were far cleaner than the French, he felt, and it was rumored that the Russians bathed themselves in snow even in the dead of winter.

He felt that the French paintings were more cluttered than he liked, and he felt also their colors were muddy in many instances. *(Long pause.)*

There was a mild—uh—but pleasant excitement one winter when nutmeg was introduced into Holland, and people used it—some in their brews. It was rumored to have strange powers.

(Long pause.) Many wealthy people traveled to the Mediterranean. And others took to the baths in those sunny climes. But he himself felt little need for such diversions. And often he had too many commissions ahead to allow himself a vacation of that sort.

He knew little of the Italians as a people, and he sometimes equated them in his mind with the Russians. They seemed plump, given to merrymaking, yet exhibiting the sudden dark moods that also seemed to possess the Russians. He tried to avoid such heaviness of heart, himself, and his paintings usually portray a variety of good, identifiable objects that were of a practical nature beauty implements, for example, or dishes or utensils, so that the viewer of a painting felt secure in his own world, practical and clean-cut, and was then the better able to contemplate those higher mysteries that were part of the painting as well.

(Pause at 4:15. Jane still lay on her back.)

He probably enjoyed the Jews as much as any other nationality *(? I mentioned this to Jane later)* beside his own—for they were mystical and practical at once; shrewd *(pause)*, and yet they lived their lives according to their sacred books and kept their own counsel.

Many people were jealous because the Jews did so well financially, and there were droves of tiny Jewish shops, while some of the banking concerns were also in Jewish instead of Dutch hands. But, he felt, enterprise will have its way. They charged good tough interest to anyone who would borrow from them, but he found them honest in their business ways, and no greedier than most.

(Long pause.) He enjoyed <u>glass cutting</u>, so this was very meticulous work. He knew of two glasscutters in particular whose colors were so bright and magnetic that he envied them. Light can shine through glass, of course, but it could not shine through a canvas but only fall upon it. He tried with glazes to suggest the colors, say, in a stained glass window, and was fairly satisfied with the results.

(4:22. "Oh, I'll have some chocolate Ensure," Jane said. "I was in that pretty good, too, and it was an entirely different kind of material [than yesterday's].... Oh shit. I didn't know it was that late...." I lit a cigarette for her. She asked for the liquid because everyone taking care of her wants her to drink as much as possible, to

help clear up the bladder condition.

(4:29.) There were certainly many difficulties connected with getting paid for your work. A mother might want to have her daughter's portrait painted, for example, in which case it was the mother one had to please. You had to keep an eye out so that you were certain as to who exactly was responsible for payment, particularly with group portraits, so that you did not have to waste time trying to collect from several persons at once. It was best to try to assign one man as representative for payment for the group.

There were—I'm not sure how to say this—a few dentists who required portraits that served as advertisements, and if the work was actually commissioned by the dentist, then the model had to be shown with even teeth— although sometimes it was permissible to show a glimpse of gold for a filling. And there were various businessmen who commissioned works to serve as advertisements for their trades—yet somehow it was still possible to follow one's own sway on such occasions, and to wind a patron's needs together with your own. At least he always tried to do so.

(Pause at 4:35.) One man might be ashamed of his pimples, for example, and beg an artist to ignore such imperfections, while the artist felt that the pimples were somehow the mark of a man's character. So in such a case the artist had to use good common sense, and a bit of flattery to convince the patron that his pimples were indeed a mark of character, and no disadvantage, so that then he could leave the pimples intact.

(Long pause.) Followers of high fashion wanted each frill to be exact, each elaborate hair dressing or hat to be faithfully displayed, so that when the painting was finished a friend might say, "From whom did you buy your delightful bonnet?" And sometimes the makers of high fashion would offer to dress the man or woman for a portrait in order to advertise their own trades.

(Long pause.) Sometimes a dressmaker, for example, might offer to pay the artist a trifle extra if the artist would show some characteristic of gown or waistcoat, hoping that the painting would send others to inquire as to who did such fine work, and then hasten off to buy a gown or cloak or whatever, at the tradesman's shop. Sometimes such bargains were struck right in the artist's studio. Such telltale design, he reasoned—

(4:45 PM. I heard two nurses talking in the hall outside 331: "We'll turn her on her side now, then put her back on her back for supper." And in they trooped. The interruption marked the end of the session. I told Jane before I left that she'd done well.

(These notes are added at 3:40 PM Sunday—the next day—after I'd read the session to Jane from page 3 on, since I hadn't typed all of it yet. But as far as I know,

there's no record that Rembrandt himself painted for tradesmen—signs, and so forth. At the same time it could be that he did so; that kind of work may not have had much survival value, especially if it had been mounted outside, for example.

(Another possibility is that his pupils could have undertaken such commissions as part of their training, under the master's tutelage, say, while learning their profession. In those days there must have been a steady demand for such signs for tradesmen's shops—perhaps the equivalent of the sign painter's art of today [and which I've practiced myself at various times]. I find the whole ambience here quite interesting, for certainly such work involved the artist of that time wholeheartedly in the business of daily life, art, and business. He must have felt needed, in demand in a way lacking, or at least quite different, today. After all, there was no one else to turn to for graphic expression—no magazines in color, no photography, no printed posters, no facile reproductions by the millions if needed. There were printed books, of course, though these must have been quite valuable, and etchings, dry point, and a few other small-scale versions of modern-day printing, but as far as I know that was it.

(I suppose there could have been limited editions of poster-like art, printed in color by wood block, or some other simple, similar process. If so, I know nothing about this.

(I mentioned to Jane also that on page 37 of the session she referred to the Jews as a "nationality." when they are members of a religion only. That is, there could have been Dutch Jews, French Jews, etc.

(Jane, however, is more worried that the Rembrandt material refers to the Roman Catholic Church—the statues, the wealth, the gold and silver, and so forth—whereas she thinks that after the Reformation Holland was supposedly largely Protestant. Their churches, she said, were plain and simple, with bare walls and wooden benches. There were no statues or colorful decorations. The Protestants didn't believe in those things.

(Such information can be checked—just as that on the dry ice question.)

SESSION 956 (DELETED)
JUNE 19, 1983   4:48 PM SUNDAY

("Give me a cigarette," Jane said, "and I'll see what I can do. I've got to do something today...."

(Her day had been an upsetting one. The details are in my own notes—but her situation seemed to be much better by now. She'd had much trouble with her catheter, and Jean, the nurse, had ended up changing it in order to bring about a normal flow of urine. Eating a late lunch, and efforts to get the old catheter

unplugged, taking medication and performing the "vitals," plus inserting the new
catheter, had eaten up most of the afternoon since I'd arrived at 1:20.

(Jane hadn't even had a chance to read the 955th session I'd brought in. I'd
had to sit in the hall while they changed the catheter. The hospital floor was very
noisy and busy; with nurses passing by, trooping visitors looking for certain room
numbers, and some patients crying out in what seemed to be endless rhythms. [I'm
writing a few separate notes about the general hospital atmosphere on the third floor,
and my view of it.]

(Jane lay on her back handling her cigarette with some difficulty in her left
hand as she began to dictate. She was quite naked.)

I was getting that when you came right down to it he didn't really trust
church or state. Yet he thought that man had to have some kind of organization
in order to live any kind of tidy life at all, or else man would just run rampant.
And he wasn't really in favor of that.

He didn't care either what religion a man had, but he did believe most
thoroughly in Christ. He had no idea of whether or not Christ was divine, the
Son of God or not, but he certainly believed that Christ had the greatest nobility of mind and spirit, and certainly it seemed to him that Christ was far more
than simply a legend. He did feel that Christ was somehow gigantic in his
<u>human</u> dimensions.

In all matters of church he held his peace. That is, he seldom argued,
either over religion or politics. In order to sell his paintings he had to have the
good will of other men, and so he felt it was only good sense to flatter them
occasionally, without overdoing it.

There was no doubt that the Vatican had inspired many artists, where the
works of art displayed there were truly spectacular. He said earlier that he didn't
believe any one man could pretend to <u>stand in</u> for God more than any other, in
the way he understood Catholic priests did, say, in the ritual of confession.

(Long pause at 4:55.) It was inconceivable to him that any person ever
believed any religion completely—but each person had his own version of any
given philosophy, and if you put all these differences together you'd probably
end up with another entirely new religion, and still another. *(Pause.)* Such issues
lay outside of his concern as far as painting was concerned, although he realized
that his own beliefs were bound to speak in his work. He never trusted people
who tried to appear too pious. Controversy took time, and he had enough to do
without indulging in it.

(Long pause at 5:00.) In a way he understood that the Dutch were somewhat more lenient indeed than some other nationalities—the Germans, for
example—in the matters of religion. He often thought that if the world looked

tidy enough from the outside, the Dutch were content. The Protestants believed in the Bible, and declared that each person should be free to interpret it for himself, but this was only as long as the new beliefs did not go too far. They didn't trust personal revelation, while on the other hand they seemed to applaud it. If God spoke directly to each person, it's too bad his messages didn't fit together any better.

(5:05.) There was a tendency in Protestantism to squash all gaiety, and of this he did not particularly approve. Some were for the banishing of dancing, or even of children's play, and the strictest followed a regimen of dreary praying and abstinence. This was particularly hard on the artists who were intrigued by color, yet he noticed also that many people found excuses to give them freedom from this process or another, and as long as the proper excuses were given all was well.

There was always talk about the ending of the world. There were always rumors that man's sinfulness had gone too far, and that God was ready to descend in all his awful majesty, one way or another, to inflict divine punishment. This he doubted simply because the world seemed unfinished to him in many ways, somehow lacking the fullness it would one day develop.

(5:10.) He tried to give such matters as little thought as possible, wanting merely to go his own way, enjoy his hearth, and paint, for the love of painting itself, and also for profit.

(Jane took a long pause, lying quietly with her eyes closed while waiting to see if she was going to have a bladder spasm.)

He certainly did not believe that the Pope (name?) was God's stand-in, nor did he think that anyone should hold as much power as the Vatican did. This hardly moved him to anger, however. He didn't believe in raging about affairs he could not prevent.

(Long pause at 5:14.) He didn't believe in squandering his thoughts or his money, nor did he believe in tithing. As far as beliefs were concerned, at the deepest levels he believed only in his painting, and if he clearly understood how he painted (long pause), he felt he would understand more about the nature of God as well. In the business of everyday living, however, such concerns bothered him little. He paid all taxes and dues and went his way. (Remember the earlier sessions about Rembrandt's troubles with bill-collectors.) He felt that he was well-enough liked, while not besieged by friends or social events, and he was not overly drawn to either sobriety or drunkenness. He cut as good a figure as any man, at least for a number of years, growing perhaps a bit stouter as time progressed, and he certainly felt religious yearnings at time, that seemed entirely and utterly private, having little to do with any churches that he knew.

He was fascinated sometimes by the changes in a person's face, and the colors, after death, though he did not feel that his preoccupation was strong enough to be dangerous.

(5:23.) Whenever he heard of a suicide he was appalled, and unless a person were extremely sick he could not imagine a man taking his own life. There was no escaping his own times, of course, yet certainly in his paintings he tried to suggest some freer yet eternal dimension, in which life itself possessed some wider scope.

The world at times did seem to him unfinished, as if God had done so much and left man to do the rest, but man's part was hardly done. Maybe God did nudge man along a bit by various illnesses or wars or such, that were the result of man's lack of action in the proper directions. He was sure that some philosophers could come up with a better explanation for man's ills, but that was his own explanation, and it served him as well as any.

There were people abroad, or about,that objected to any display of finery at all, and some of these felt that portraits themselves were forbidden ground, but since none of those people came to have their portraits done he did not pay them too much mind *(with humor.*

(Long pause at 5:30.) He did keep some extra clothes and supplies hidden away in case he were <u>forced to leave his country</u>, And he counseled his family to do the same. It was only wise to take such precautions, for church or state could suddenly turn ugly in unexpected ways. He had heard of some men being forced to leave their homes in the dead of night, to save their lives, and so he felt it was only prudent to take such precautions as those just mentioned.

Outside of his own family he had several aunts he fancied, a nephew and a brother-in-law, but all in all he loved his own wives and children, and he did not spread his emotions out <u>too thinly</u>.

(5:37 PM. "Well, give me another cigarette, and I'll see if I can get anything else," Jane said. If not you can go.")

SESSION 957 (DELETED)
JUNE 20, 1983 3:30 PM MONDAY

(When I got to 331 at about 1:30 I found that Jane had just come back from hydro, as we call it. Her lunch tray was in the hall. The new catheter was working well. At the same time, Fred K. is having a 24-hour sample of urine collected for two different tests, to check on how the bladder is functioning. The doctor is cutting his visits to Jane to twice a week, unless she wants to see him more often.

(Today is my birthday. I'm 64 years old. I hadn't been in Jane's room long

before the nurse, Jan, brought in a small birthday cake for me. They keep them on hand in food processing, and thaw them out on demand. I was really surprised; it turned out Jane had been telling people my birthday was coming up. We've made friends with many of the people who take care of my wife, of course. The cake was loaded with white and green icing, all decorated in swirls and shells, and incredibly rich in sugar. Jane and I each ate a quarter of it; Jan finished the rest.

(Last night Jane had dictated a little poem to one of the staff:

Dear Rob:
 May your days be sunny
 without much rain.
 Happy birthday from
 your loving wife Jane.

(And she'd dictated another one to Jan this morning, while waiting to go to hydro:

 Once upon a time
 my heart was dead
 but now, alive,
 it thrives on love.

(Jan is very pleased with Jane's liquid intake—it's up from 150cc daily to 250–300. Jane is eating well, too. I helped Jan feed her lunch. The staff is very busy. The strike possibility looms. Jane could eat more late at night, she said, after 11:00, say, but there's no one to feed her. Jan voted against a strike. She thinks the hospital will let the 200 RN's strike, then call in retired nurses, use supervisors, hire other people, etc. They even wanted me to feed Jane supper last night, but I had left.

(I read Jane the last few pages of yesterday's session, so she'd know where she was in the material. She lay on her left side, facing me. "They'll be in to check my blood pressure and stuff soon," she said.

("Don't worry about it," I said, pulling up a chair beside her bed.

("Okay. I'm not getting much.")

He usually had his apprentices prepare his canvases, which were made of the finest linen, and he was very meticulous in checking their work, making sure the canvas was stretched tightly enough yet not too tight, taking precautions so that it would not turn yellow.

The canvases came in bolts of linen. He was lucky because the seaport meant supplies came frequently. He understood that if you lived inland in some other countries, it took forever for some supplies to reach the inner hamlets from the coast.

(Long pause.) There were women who served as models, some used by several artists at once. They were great carriers of gossip if given the chance, which was another reason why he kept his counsel. He did the artwork for some calendars, using religious subjects for each month, depicting scenes from the Bible.

(A one-minute pause at 3:32.) He did more painting itself in the summer than in the winter, when the nights were so cold and dark. He tried to mix his colors in the winter, though—or at least he tried to do so—so he'd be ready for the summer days and longer light. He kept his colors in small jars, lidded. His palettes varied. Sometimes he used a kind of smooth pine, polished so it did not splinter, and on occasion he simply used white plates without designs or flowering.

His brushes were a kind of bristle, and kind of expensive so that he swore sometimes he'd cut off some of his cat's hairs use those instead—in which case someone always hurried to hide the cat in case he was serious.

(Long pause.) He usually worked by candlelight, which he could control, instead of natural light, which went its own way despite his wishes. This was not a definite rule, but was his usual custom.

(It was also one I've speculated about often—that Rembrandt may have worked by candlelight, the primitive forerunner of the electric light we take so for granted. I don't recall whether I'd mentioned such musings to Jane in years past. I had such ideas because of the overall richness and warm saturated, even hot, look of Rembrandt's work. I don't know what his contemporaries may have done about artificial light, but it seemed natural to me that he probably worked by candlelight. Naturally, of course, doing this created its own set of problems, for the warm illumination could lead the artist to make his reds and yellows and oranges too hot, to make them look right to the eye; whereas when the colors are viewed in natural daylight, they would then appear to be much too red, hot, etc. Perhaps practice enabled one to compensate in the doing. It might also be instructive to try painting a portrait by candlelight. What a joke, if one found that this simple method worked well....

(After the session I explained some of this to Jane.)

He wanted the important areas of his paintings to come forward to the eye as if they were sculpted. Particularly, he made sure that the folds of a shirt, for example, followed the body's motion, so that you knew there was a solid form beneath the britches of the folds of a skirt. He also tried to avoid flat areas, into which the paint seemed to sink, but instead used a variety of colors to suggest the shadows of a hand or arm, or to suggest a sofa's depth, the inner further objects of a room. The eye should seem to discover such details in a painting's background. As if it were in a real room, trying to peer through the darkness, and then make out the deeper depths, which should always contain some small glimpses of light.

(*Long pause at 3:50. The afternoon was darkening considerably, suggesting rain.*

(*I meant to add to my paragraph of commentary on page 44 that the age of Rembrandt's work also must play at least some part in their overall warm, mellow, yellow or hot look. After all, the paintings are 300 years old, more and less. Linseed oil is notorious for its yellowing properties, particularly when mixed with white. It seems logical that some of the look of Rembrandt's paintings is because of the yellowing of the oils and varnishes he used, in spite of the best efforts of museum restorers, etc. I think this is especially apparent in the overall yellow cast of flesh tones in many instances. I haven't seen any of his originals since my days in my early 20's in NY City. I was overwhelmed. The old combination of linseed oil and lead white—the only white he had to work with, as far as I know of those days—was a potent combination as far as discoloring went. I don't use lead white. Yet I think that he deliberately sought out a very warm ambience for his paintings, downplaying the cool colors considerably, and that this original warm feeling has become exaggerated over the centuries by whatever yellowing properties his materials possessed in themselves.*

(*Lead white is still considered to be the best white there is for the artist, but it possesses that vexing yellowing characteristic....*

(*For my own musings: Is this true of lead white when it's mixed with egg for use as tempera? I could make an experimental panel. Any oil-based varnish would also possess its own intrinsic yellowing qualities. [Damar wouldn't. I'm not sure about mastic.]*)

He enjoyed doing paintings of people at a table—their hands perhaps set off by the whitish tablecloth. The flesh seeming to rise out of the tablecloth itself as a hand lay carelessly upon it. In such cases he used profiles mostly, always feeling that profiles had great mystery. As he also believed that the lowered eye was most expressive.

In women, that look could appear to be both teasing or rebuking, according to the colors the artist used and the angles he chose to make more prominent.

Most often he liked to use friends as models, as sometimes he was haunted by a particular face or another, or a particular figure belonging to some stranger he saw on the street. In which case he would inquire after their surnames, and entice them to model for him, if they would.

(*Pause.*) It was almost impossible for him to look at a young boy and realize that such a tyke would grow up to be a man—so much larger, brawnier, so much heavier and taller. He felt that a boy must feel strange yearnings toward his growing manhood, trying to become a man too soon, so he tried to capture that feeling in his paintings of incompleteness yet of promise.

(Long pause at 3:58. "I've got to stop for a minute," Jane said. "I can't tell if I'm going to have a BM or not. Maybe it's gas...."

(She lay on her left side. I turned her on her back without much trouble, cut a chuck in half and made sure it was in position beneath her. A nurse came in to take her blood pressure; it was normal.

("I could ask any number of questions about any line of that material," I said, "but I haven't wanted to interrupt. It may not be that kind of work, or book, to begin with."

("What kind of questions?"

("Mostly about his work."

(Another nurse came in to take Jane's rectal temperature, so I moved back to the other chair in the corner to work on these notes. Jane's temp was okay. This second nurse had been sent down from obstetrics to assist the regular staff on the third floor. "Unless someone up there has a baby," she said, then laughed: "They wouldn't dare...."

(The nurse left at 4:20. Jane asked for another cigarette and a sip of ginger ale.

(4:35. I described for her the type of question I meant, referring to her statement today about Rembrandt supervising the preparation of his canvases so they wouldn't yellow, and the one that he'd illustrated calendars. And had he himself, as she'd mentioned in yesterday's session, actually painted portraits as advertisements for tradespeople? The same questions, I said, could apply to any facet of the material, whether social, economic, political, family, professional, etc.

(Jane began to have a BM. Then:

(4:42.) I'm trying to have a BM, but I'm getting that it was real tricky about drying varnishes in the sticky salty air. He even sometimes tried to use the warmth of the candle, without getting it to close—and that was real tricky so as not to drop any of the hot wax, you know.

(Long pause at 4:45.) I don't know, Bob. It doesn't make any sense to me— in answer to your earlier question—but it seemed he did something with glue and the whites of an egg.

(When Jane paused I explained briefly that what she said did make artistic sense, though it was probably incomplete: That she could have referred to Rembrandt's use of some form of tempera, perhaps as a priming coat. This would have inevitably cracked if used on a flexible ground like a canvas, but could have served well on panels, which he also used for smaller works. The tempera wouldn't yellow unless an oil or oil varnish were added to the mixture, as explained earlier.

(I told Jane I wasn't asking that she go into all of those details in her materi-al. I just wanted to show how one statement could lead to many questions. And so did this one:

(4:56.) The quality of the oils was never the same. Sometimes they were good and sometimes not. You could never keep them at the same consistency.

(The oils themselves, I wondered without asking, or the pigments mixed with the oils?)

I was getting something earlier that was sort of funny—that if you paint-ed a portrait of a man <u>and he liked it</u>, you didn't have to worry about posterity, because that man's vanity would see to it that it was preserved—he'd guard it with his life. And that some people had an entirely different reaction—they got embarrassed the minute you started to look at them. They felt their privacy was being invaded, and some even ran from the room—women in particular—in tears.

Some were superstitious in some strange manner. They didn't understand, and felt that it was somehow dangerous to have the images of themselves in a painting, as if the artist in painting them could magically know all their secrets, and those of their families. Such people needed a calming down, and a good deal of flattery, if you ever wanted to use them for a sitting again. A bit of brandy helped.

Women seldom traveled abroad or outside by themselves. They were usu-ally accompanied by another woman or chaperone, a member of the family—

(5:02. A nurse came in to give Jane eye drops. Jane told her she was having a small BM—"I'm not quite done."

(5:06.) And then I was getting that when you came right down to it, it wasn't even safe for men to go out at night—there were too many robbers and renegades about.

(Long pause.) His oils of course acted differently in the winter than in the summer, and it seemed to him that the studio was either freezing or sweltering. He was very leery, again, of eggs turning rotten when he wanted to use them *(pause)*, and sometimes the water they used turned brackish, or was too full of minerals, so that the water itself was sometimes almost colored.

(5:11.) There was a brush-maker in town, who made hairbrushes, and sometimes artist's brushes as well if he had material left over. He heard that some people even made brushes of goat's hair, which was quite wiry, he understood. It took enough time to get preparations together, so a man had hardly any time left to paint at all.

Some men, he heard, even tried straw to make brushes, but it was too brit-tle.

(5:15. I gave Jane a sip of cold coffee. "Let me have a cigarette and see if I'm done or not," she said. She was through with her BM but hadn't been cleaned up yet. "Well, you hit it on at least one point." I said. I told her that I thought I remembered reading that goat's hair had been tried in brushes; that, indeed, just about every kind of hair one could think of had been tried at one time or another.

(I explained a bit to Jane about how difficult it must have been in those days to do anything. Just assembling workable tools and pigments and grounds must have been something. Quality must have been elusive indeed. "And yet look at what they accomplished."

(5:18.) I was getting that they bartered a lot. Also that he did some experiments briefly with red berries—briefly—I don't know what kind. But they didn't work well, anyway. They stained enough but they were flat. He couldn't mix them. He tried boiling them, mashing them.

(Long pause.) He tried mashing certain flower petals, too, and that didn't work.

(From two doors down the hall came a drawn-out ascending cry: "AAAAAAAAAAAAAAAAHHHHH...." Kathryn, an old, old lady. I knew how she looked, sitting askew in her chair beside her bed, legs crossed and twisted to one side beneath her hospital gown. She's been there since about the time Jane began delivering the Rembrandt material. Sometimes she'll cry or utter her seemingly mindless, childlike litany for an hour at a time, over and over. Jane seemed to pay her no attention.

(5:24.) It's just that he kept an eye out for any natural food that was brightly colored—doing different experiments—but most of them failed. Besides that, of course, he could only experiment with foods in season....

(5:26 PM. "I can't remember stuff I gave you before, so I could fill in on it, before they come in to clean me." Jane said. "I didn't know it was so late.... You want to come over for just a minute and help me move my legs out?"

(Lately, since she's been going to hydro every other day, Jane has regained some motion in her legs. Now as she lay on her back I gently exerted a little pressure on her heels; and her knees flexed enough so that she could move each foot down the bed for another couple of inches. Something she couldn't do last month, say.)

SESSION 958 (DELETED)
JUNE 21, 1983 2:37 PM TUESDAY

(I got to the doorway of room 331 by 1:35. Three nurses there kidded me about being fifteen minutes late. "I'm older now," I said, referring to my little birth-

day party there yesterday, and they all laughed. I didn't think negative thinking on my part was involved—but I did on theirs. Jane was good. She was already being fed by an aide. They were almost finished.

(By 1:45 I had her reading sessions 955, 956, and the couple of pages of 957 that I had typed. We were alone and she was on her back. Her new catheter was working fine. The air conditioning was on. It was actually getting too cool in 331. Even Jane noticed it, so I turned it off and opened the window. The day was warm and sunny. "Let me know if you get anything," I said, checking my notes and the mail in between turning pages for her.

(She was through reading by 2:15. I had plenty of time to read the prayer with her, but there has been so much activity around the time I arrive each day that we'd gotten out of the habit. A lot of this results from the necessity for someone to feed Jane. Before, she could be alone as she received her nourishment steadily, through the nose feeding tube.

(Finally:) All I was getting was a little tiny bit—something about that he used his kids, but he found it most difficult to do so. He couldn't really treat them in the same way he treated models. They would want to jabber and talk, or ask about their allowance or whatever, and sometimes the younger ones pleaded to be let go for some other diversion. Children, after all, were not simply little dolls, or even little grownups, though he thought that their characters were somehow set when they were young. Their patterns were not yet filled in, but even in the darkest of clothing children's faces did possess a rosiness that was vacant in the faces of men and women, a kind of <u>rosy vacancy</u>, he used to think.

(Long pause at 2:42.) He usually had models for about an hour at a time, and in wintertime had to be taken out if the models took off their heavier outer garments—cloaks or whatever—and settled themselves down to work.

Portraits were his mainstay. There were often people, though, who wanted paintings of their houses or estates, but these did not inspire him. Landscapes, it seemed, lacked the human qualities that intrigued him so in people's faces and forms, so he kept returning to the human figure and its most intimate environment.

(Pause at 2:45.) Religious pictures by themselves always intrigued him also *(pause)*, for these allowed him to touch upon the characters of men in almost Olympian fashion. He was no intellectual. He <u>felt</u> his way through life, and let pondering come afterward.

(2:48. "That's all I was getting right then," Jane said.

("Okay." I lit a cigarette for her while she was still on her back. She lay quite naked, smoking, "dipping" her cigarette in the ashtray I'd positioned on her abdomen. We always set the ashtray on top of a piece of foam rubber—both to keep

it in place, and to isolate any heat it might transfer to Jane's skin otherwise.

(I read several letters, without answering any of them. The mail seems to be heavier than ever, and I'm falling behind. I haven't wanted to contend with it recently. Some of the letters are excellent testimonials to our work.

(3:38.) I was getting that he had to be very careful in the wintertime because the soot from the fireplaces collected on everything. Sometimes he tried to use chunks of charcoal straight from the fireplace, but it was too soft and wouldn't retain its form.

(3:40. A nurse came in to do Jane's "vitals."

(3:44.) The only other thing I got was that he wasn't pleased with watercolors. They didn't have enough volume. And they were hard to control. He liked good life-sized paintings that seemed to suggest life's commotion, and each time he did a new portrait he felt that he understood more about men—

(3:46. The phone rang. Wrong number. Then a nurse came in to give Jane her eye drops.

(3:50.) If anything, light was brilliant, and there seemed to be <u>prisms</u> of light everywhere. He also tried to suggest these prisms of light in his paintings, and he devised ways of suggesting these prisms, or that he had <u>captured light</u> in prisms that never actually showed in the canvas at all.

These prisms were like points of light that made their own patterns *(repeated at my request).* They had to agree with the painting's subject matter, but at the same time they served as their own kinds of surfaces, forming patterns within patterns: angles of a face echoed in a mountain, for example, or even in a piece of paper simply thrown upon the floor, or a curve of cheek echoed in a mountain scene outside a window. They were parts of a painting's construction that were complete in themselves, that is, even if you didn't recognize the subject matter—if that were possible—then the prisms of light would still form patterns that would unite the painting's surfaces and hold them together. Some painters of tempera did this exceedingly well. Such prisms of light could appear in the skies also, even though the sky was perceived as dark and threatening, still light would illuminate it. The same ideas of course apply to water, where the prisms of light seem quite natural—particularly if the waves are seen in glimpses of moonlight, for sparkling water carries many reflections.

In a way the water itself is composed of prisms of light, ever moving, the same methods apply to a mirror, of course, or any pattern of reflection upon reflection. Again, all this exists regardless of the painting's subject matter, yet fully in keeping with it.

(Now, as she's done before, Jane suddenly switched to speaking for Rembrandt in the first person.)

I have never gotten the same effects with watercolors. Perhaps I am too heavy-handed for them.

(Pause at 4:00.) Nor can you pile up color after color with watercolors as you can with oils, nor can you apply glazes, which have always intrigued me.

(Long pause.) I have been very careful with all of my sketches, but still some have been lost, and it is not unknown for apprentices to steal a forgotten sketch or two, and take it home, to sign it with his own name, or to forge mine. I am forever making sketches for paintings, and discarding them, until finally I approach what I have in mind.

(4:05. When Jane paused I told her the time. She was still on her back, and getting warm now with the air conditioner still off. The day was turning darker and more windy.

("It was hard to get that prism-of-light thing straight," she said. "I don't even have a chuck under me, do I?"

(I cut one in half and put it under her. She had a cigarette while I looked through a new American Artist. *As she smoked Jane said that she came up with a mental image of a heavyset man with a big nose that had a wart on it. She saw this individual in profile. "Just the kind of thing he liked to paint. I was also getting that he liked hats, to frame the face and set it off—particularly dark ones." And of course, I explained, Rembrandt is famous for his paintings of Dutch burghers in their black hats. "With glints of red, I think," she added.*

(4:32. It was comparatively quiet in the hospital today. So far, I read the day's material to Jane and she asked if it made sense to me. I said yes, but that I'd like to study some of Rembrandt's paintings relative to his "prisms of light" material. I added that such ideas could also be ascribed to the work of the Impressionists a couple of centuries later—artists like Monet, Pissaro, Seurat, Sisley, and so forth. Historically, could it be said that Rembrandt's ideas concerning prisms contributed to the distant developments of the later 19th century? Certainly, within the realms of an overall artistic consciousness.

(4:37. Nurses came in to turn Jane. She'd had a tiny BM. I don't think that one of them, Sharon, who used to work at Artistic in the early '60's, was too happy with that fact, judging by the remarks she made, even if in a joking manner.

(4:45. A third nurse came in to take Jane's blood pressure. All three were gone by 4:47.

(I read our prayer with Jane. From a few doors down the hall came the familiar cry, "AAAAAAAAAAAAAAAAAHHHHHHHHH," uttered in its ascending scale by Kathryn, the elderly lady patient. [I'd heard one of the nurses refer to her by name, but asked no questions.]

(5:15 PM. I left 331.)

SESSION 959 (DELETED)
JUNE 22, 1983 2:30 PM WEDNESDAY

(Jane called me at about 10:00 last night to say that she already knew what Rembrandt would talk about tomorrow—today—his house and the city he'd lived in.

(Today is a beautiful, warm. sunny day. Jane went to hydro this morning. Her lunch tray was there when I arrived at 1:20 PM. My wife asked if I'd seen Peg Gallagher's article in the Star-Gazette *this morning. I'd brought a copy of the article to show her, although it didn't contain anything we didn't know in general terms.*

(The nurse, Jean, fed Jane and after she left, Jane, who was still on her back, read Session 957 that I'd finished typing this morning. Jane's buttocks are healing in remarkable fashion—in an amazing way, I told her. Talk about the wisdom and knowledge of the body....

(When we were alone I lit a cigarette for her. Jane's delivery was the fastest yet by far, as though she'd been waiting all the while to get going. At times I had trouble keeping up with her, even with my abbreviated way of taking notes. She lay quite naked on her bed, smoking and speaking.)

The houses in Amsterdam were built very close together, with often one attached to the other because actually there was so little room—land—and this one place he lived in is kind of difficult to describe.

It was like the row houses we have now in developments, one attached to another, or with very little room in between.

This one place I'm sort of half-seeing. It looks to me like you first went downstairs. There were steps leading down. Like a tenement in New York, then you came to a door and a landing. The place was made up of quite a few levels. Way down on the bottom level was, I guess—it looks like laundry rooms?I'm seeing tubs *(long pause)*, at the very lowest level. The windows were up high. Then only a few steps upward there was a fireplace and a stove of sorts. I think it burned wood or coal—you could burn either in it, I think. They didn't have many trees or lumber themselves, so it had to be imported one way or another. And they had quite a few great big tubs, and—I don't know what they were used for—and there was an alcove off that area with a wooden tub that was used for bathing.

(2:37.) Then at ground level there were two large parlors, each with a fireplace, drapes with a window, which looked out to the street, the sofas and chair and so forth. And I don't know what you call them—there's a name for it—where you hung stuff: standing units instead of being built-in like closets. They also kept blankets and other stuff there also. Wines.

Off one of those parlors was a large alcove, where Rembrandt slept with his wife. You couldn't call it a bedroom. It had draperies across. There was also some kind of a cradle in there where the youngest child slept.

Outside, adjoining that, were some more stairs. Maybe four or five, and another room that was used for storage or sleeping. I think there were straw cots on the floor for sleeping, four or five of them. And on the next level was Rembrandt's studio. It had the one entrance from the rooms I've just spoken about, then from the other end it had a very steep stairway going down to the street. People who came in that way didn't go through the house.

His studio was actually quite large. It took over the entire top level of the house. It had two long narrow windows overlooking the street, with drapes—and I don't know, I was getting a kind of dark maroon velvet. His easels and boards and canvases were stored up there. The floor was unfinished; it had great big, wide wooden boards.

It seems to me that he also had—I don't know if I'm right—an oil wick lamp that was very undependable. It would sputter and go out, and smelled, and gave out—I don't know—little tiny black specks. I don't know what you call them.

He also had a straw cot where he slept occasionally, himself. And some tall—I don't know what you'd call them—something like backdrops, I guess—

("Could be. Backcloths?")

He had those too, but he'd use these as backgrounds for portraits. He had several tables with drawers where he kept his materials for oils and so forth, and a wooden box—or several of them—that were partitioned off where he kept brushes and palette knives. This also reminds me of something like the pencil boxes you'd have in school when you were a kid, only larger.

If I didn't say so, the room had a fireplace. And there were rolls of different-colored carpet that he rolled out in case he wanted to use them in paintings—you know what I mean?

("Yes.")

He had different sketches tacked to the wall in some places, and then he had different kinds of draperies on different parts of the wall, in case he wanted to use those in paintings.

(2:50. "Am I covered good down there?" Jane asked. "What time is it?" She wanted to be sure she had a chuck underneath her in case she had a BM.)

By now we're several stories above the street, and you could look out and see the ocean. You could look down and see boats—ships—with sails billowing out, so I assume it was an ocean.

("Canals?")

("No.... ")

And along that same street there were a lot of shops, but it was still fashionable, you know, and some of them were a level or so down. They would be cellars to us—the windows had to be up higher so the light could come in. All the space was utilized in the houses and shops, and often the same space would serve several purposes.

And the shops did have those signs out front, with the pictures of what they represented, because a lot of people couldn't read. The streets were very narrow, and rather dark, really, because the buildings were so stacked.

People that were wealthy often had houses further inland, to which they traveled by carriage. *(Pause.)* These were usually estates of one kind or another, very neat and enclosed by fences. I think the fences were more like stonewalls, not too high, because there was a shortage of lumber.

(Long pause at 2:58.) Those estates were quite drafty. The very fact that the houses in Amsterdam were so close together protected them from wind and so forth.

("Would you put that [cigarette] out for me?")

I don't know what kind of light they had in the town at night, but they had lamplighters to take care of something, and I think they had town criers to take care of important news. I'm not sure of this, but the shops, a lot of them, seemed to be devoted to just one thing—as if a man sold fish he didn't sell anything else, or bread or pastry or whatever.

(Long pause at 3:02.) And the stoves I mentioned in Rembrandt's house had huge ovens, though often they used the fireplaces to cook in, especially when they had kettles of water boiling in the wintertime.

They had an awful lot of chimney sweeps, men or boys who cleaned chimneys. That trade was one that was always busy. The salt from the ocean even clung to the insides of the chimneys. Rembrandt often covered up many of his paintings with cloth just to keep them clean.

(Long pause at 3:05.) I'm not sure, but it seems to me that surgeons were also dentists, and their offices opened right off the street just like a tradesman's, you know. There were numerous fish shops, and they salted many of their foods—like salted herring and stuff like that.

(A one-minute pause.) I think the streets were of brick or cobblestone. They were very noisy because of the sounds the horses made.

(A two-minute pause.) They did try to keep the streets clean by pouring bucketfuls of water on them and then sweeping them. In other words, they had street cleaners.

The women usually wore hats or bonnets—really to protect their hair from the salty air.

(3:12. "I don't know—I guess I'm done—I mean pooping," Jane said, when I suggested she take a break. She'd kept up a rapid delivery the whole time. I'd had a time keeping up with her, but had managed it with but a few exceptions—times when I'd had to ask her to either repeat the material or to wait a moment until I caught up. But it was a lot better than having to transcribe from a tape later, for instance.)

The town had a good number of fishermen—and the unmarried had small shacks way down by the docks at the waterfront.

("Could I have a sip of something to drink?"

(3:18. I lit a cigarette for her. The room was very quiet and pleasant. The air conditioner was on low, and I'd opened the window a few inches. The curtains lifted in a good breeze.

("Was 'wardrobe' the word you wanted earlier?" I asked.

("I don't know, but it was heavy. You could drag it around."

("From what you say, it seems like the house was a split-level kind of deal."

("Yes—")

Oh, there was one thing I forgot. He seemed to have a large oval mirror in a wooden frame that sat in his studio. The legs were rather elaborately carved, and the frame had scrolls around it. He could tip the mirror back and forth in its frame. Actually, it was pitted in a couple of places, the way I was seeing it.

Actually, a lot of the time he'd go downstairs after a piece of furniture he wanted, and have his apprentices drag it upstairs to his studio. And he liked good materials in his draperies, so you could see the folds—nothing that hung limply, without body.

(Long pause.) And also, if you were any decent kind of artist at all, and did portrait work, you were almost assured of a living—that was the only way people could get a likeness. And on several occasions—more than that—he'd paint a person when they were very young, and then again in later years. Some people would commission paintings to be done on anniversaries or birthdays or whatever. It seemed always a matter of mixing art with commercial work, pleasing the patron as well as himself, and the fact was that he did find peoples' faces intriguing. Each one was different, so he didn't have to prostitute his art, so to speak.

(3:29.) And all through this I got the feeling that Rembrandt was trying to give a general impression of the place he lived and the environment where he worked. I started getting vague impressions about it last night.

They had snuff shops, where all the guy sold was snuff, and elaborate boxes to keep it in—snuff boxes.

Oftentimes the physicians, though, sold pillboxes of various kinds, and often they made more money selling these than they did from their profession.

(Long pause.) At various times during his lifetime, they had theaters, with stages and everything. These were closed down by town officials, only to pop up again. The cheaper ones were on the waterfront, frequented by sailors and the like, and so-called loose women. He stayed out of such places himself. It was easy to get in a brawl, or get robbed.

If I'm right—I guess I'm right—beside the physicians there were shops where they sold medicines of just about every kind, to cure almost every ailment, and most people tried these shops before they visited a physician. The doctors bought many of their medications at such shops, too, but at a discount—and if a doctor sent a patient to a particular shop, he'd get a kickback from that particular store. As a result, most people used home remedies. You could never be sure of the quality of the medicines in any case, or know whether or not they were poisonous. Too many men felt indisposed, took the doctor's remedy, and promptly fell down dead, so the people had little faith in physicians.

There were a few odd shops where you could purchase wooden legs, or teeth—

(3:38. A nurse came in to take Jane's temperature rectally, but said she'd be back when Jane was cleaned up. My wife was still on her back.)

If at all possible the proprietor would fit you with a wooden leg himself—or call in the physician to do so, in which case the physician would give the proprietor a cut. That's my word: cut.

(3:43. Jane was taking a pause of several minutes. "I've just been giving you the miscellaneous stuff that surrounds him," she said. The material had been coming through so fast that my writing hand was getting tired.)

(Jane said she gets weighed tomorrow.)

(3:47. She was given her eye drops by a student nurse, who also took her pulse and blood pressure, then left us.)

It's no big deal, but I also got that the salt air rotted out things like steps in his house, so that they were always patching up things—

(3:50. Two nurses came in to change Jane. She ended up on her left side, facing me as I sat beside her bed. Yesterday I'd remarked that "Rembrandt would have been in heaven" if he'd been able to work with the quality materials—paints, brushes, canvas, and so forth, that we have today, and take for granted. Now today I said, speculated, about "how grim" life must have been in those days, considering the problems everyone must have had with sanitation, medicine, warmth in winter, pollution, and so forth. I also noted that 300 years from now people could well feel the

same way about our own times, with our wars, famines, problems with nuclear arms, and so forth, so I wasn't making any judgments about one era being that much better or different than another.)

But Rembrandt wouldn't have been as happy as you think he would to just buy his paints in a tube at a store. He felt that you should be close to the materials of your art, that preparing your own materials was part of your art. Any fool could go buy paint in a tube and set himself up as an artist.

("I'm surprised at that," Jane said. That material had come through with a bit of disdain, and almost as a rebuke to what I'd said yesterday, I thought.

("But I'm not," I said now, nor did I think I was contradicting myself. "I've even had such thoughts myself. You know I've messed around with pigments—tried heating them to change their tone, and so forth, and experimented with various mediums. Some artists still do prepare their own materials to some extent. I still prepare my own grounds, as far as applying them—and choosing them—goes.

(4:25.) I also got that Rembrandt liked to paint all over his canvas at once. It gave him the feelings of its design much better.

(I'd written the same thing in the opening notes for the 949th session, 10 days ago, but Jane told me after the session today that she didn't remember the passages.)

He hated the look of a bare canvas to start with, and he could never understand building up one side *(? part?)* with color, and so forth, while leaving the other side vacant, or nearly so.

He always enjoyed curves and avoided straight lines. He liked to end up with the feeling that the colors <u>flowed</u> in the paintings, gradually, one turning into another so smoothly that the eye followed without distraction.

Time was <u>looser</u> then than now. A man did certain things according to the demands of his profession, rather than because it was the time to do any particular thing—that is, the time followed the action. Someone would say, "I'll meet you when my chores are done," say, instead of, "I'll meet you at 6 o'clock." Pacing your movements by the clock seemed far too rigid.

(4:30–4:32.) Paintings were hung in a house or gallery—therefore he thought they should be painted inside, since no one ever viewed a painting from outdoors.

The candlelight in the studio was as natural to a painting as sunlight is to a flower. A painting viewed outdoors was immediately dimmed in the light of the sun, and its brilliance faded away. Painting always dealt with an interior rather than an exterior world, even if one was doing landscapes, since no eye saw the landscape in the same way.

(4:40.) I was getting that there wasn't any such thing as dress shops, only tailors and dressmakers. You bought the bolts of cloth and the dressmaker would

make the suit or dress. You couldn't go anyplace and buy the thing ready-made.

("*What did the poor people do, who couldn't afford that kind of thing?" I won-dered when Jane paused.*

("*They made their own.*"

(*I wondered whether that was possible. Surely many of those people hadn't had any particular talent or ability to make clothes, say. How had they protected them-selves in cold weather? Had they worn rags?*)

They used a lot of wool. And inland there were a lot of farmers that dealt with dairy products, and some of these had sheep. Most households had spin-ning wheels of one kind or another, and if you were poor you just made your clothes go further, or patched them, or darned designs on top.

(*4:50. I put a small piece of foam rubber between Jane's feet, to relieve the pres-sure of one against the other. I mentioned that I seldom had to do that anymore, so much easier has it become to adjust her position. I also said that it was now much easier for the nurses and aides to turn her—meaning less painful, of course. She agreed.*

(*At 5:05, as I was getting my stuff together preparatory to leaving for the day, Jane remarked, "This one is different than the* Cézanne.*"*

("*That's good," I said.*

(*Then she laughed. "Then I got from Rembrandt: "That's because Cézanne didn't have a family."*

("*Cézanne did have one child, a son, but for the most part he lived alone, sep-arated from his wife and son.*"

("*Rembrandt meant the whole family thing," Jane said. "You know—the kids running around, the home, the hearth, and so forth...."*

SESSION 960 (DELETED)
JUNE 23, 1983 4:25 PM THURSDAY

(*See my own notes for more details re today's events.*

(*This morning Pete Harpending had called. He explained to me some details about putting the house in my name only, though he hasn't actually initiated any pro-cedures to this end yet. He also explained the arrangements he's made with a woman lawyer in NYC, re getting action on the Frederick Fell matter and royalties.*

(*Pete had also suggested that it might be a good idea for me to write to Yale, concerning our bequests to the library there. He's going to make the changes in our wills that I requested; to be sure our goods go to Yale University Library specifically, rather than to the university itself. I'm also to leave the house abstracts at his office, pending his work on converting the deed to my name.*

(Jane, of course, was most unhappy when I mentioned the house deed changes. I don't know whether she'll agree to go along or not. Tears came to her eyes. We'd earned the house together, she said, and of course she's right. I tried to explain that the change is only a precaution so that excessive medical bills won't cause us to lose the property in the future. She gets alarmed as soon as I begin to talk about such subjects. I explained as best I could that the whole thing is a matter of paperwork. No matter what a piece of paper says, it doesn't change anything as far as our own relationship goes, which is all that matters. I'd rather not do anything like that, I said, adding that when our situation works out for the better, and we're together as a team again, we can simply revert to our status of earlier years. More paperwork. I said Pete hadn't mentioned anything about divorce proceedings this morning, and I hadn't asked.

(He did say that the law firm he'd contacted in NYC could be of great help to us in the future if any questions arise about legal aspects concerning royalties from Prentice-Hall—and Fell—and medical bills.

(Jane was doing well when I arrived at 1:15. She was a bit upset, though, since she'd been weighed this morning and had lost half a pound. She's eating well, though. The nurse, Jean, fed her lunch. She had a small BM early in the afternoon, and was cleaned up by 3:10. "You need some prune juice," Jean said.

(I should have added, above, that I still don't understand all the legal ramifications pertaining to either the house being put in my name, or the divorce necessity. The lack of an intimate background in the law is a distinct handicap here, I've discovered, for when Pete goes into detail about such matters I find that I only partially grasp what he's saying. He does a lot of work in the fields relating to our own challenges, though, so I trust that he knows what he's talking about. The irony of it all, it seems to me, is that we have to contend with such prospects in spite of our having an excellent insurance policy. "It's all a gray area in the law," Pete has said more than once, and I agree.

(Jane had been turned on her left side, facing me, after being cleaned up. She was blue about the house business as various nurses and/or aides came into 331 to check her vital signs. I tried to comfort her. We had a discussion about articles I'd read recently, mostly scientific in nature, and how our ideas related to them. One of them concerned how the pregnant woman can tolerate the fetus, when actually it's half "alien"; why doesn't her body reject it, as it would an organ transplant? There must be many reasons, many of them outside science. I came up with one idea, possibly within science, to explain why the fetus could live; I plan to write some separate notes about this. But the scientist featured in the article hadn't mentioned anything about the egg and sperm being conscious; nor had the idea been forwarded that the

analogy with a transplant might be in error.

(I also mentioned to Jane that I was still very intrigued by the 954th session, in which Rembrandt had described somewhat his after-death experiences. I said I'd like more material on those states, if possible.

(Down the hall a woman repeatedly called out, "Nurse, nurse," in a strong voice, over and over. I hadn't heard Kathryn, though, with her wordless drawn out cries. Sharon, one of the aides, told us that the third floor was turning into a geriatric floor for "sickies"—patients from the psychiatric center next door. It seemed possible, since more and more I've become conscious of the increasing number of the very elderly people in the rooms surrounding Jane's.

(After getting her eye drops at 4:00, Jane said my talk about the excellence of the Rembrandt passages had encouraged her. She was still thinking about the house implications. "I've got a poem for you," she said. "It's not very cheerful, I can tell you that:"

> *My omissions bang at my door,*
> *each one drearier than the one before*
> *until I shout "Begone from here," while I whiten with fear and*
> *my heart huddles in a corner.*

(She'd come up with that piece because a few minutes earlier she'd plaintively asked me how she could get herself "into such a mess." Meaning her physical condition. I'd tried to briefly explain my ideas that the condition was forcing us to adopt a wider, more inclusive view of reality. Much could be written here. Then at 4:20 she said, "I've got a little more —"

> *It clutches a handful of flowers,*
> *stems stuck in a glassful of hours.*

(Then at 4:25, as she finished her cigarette, I learned that my remarks about Rembrandt's afterdeath reality had struck a certain spark, somewhere. In the first person singular:)

I thought, sir, that you were more interested in my colors than in my wit, or in those experiences I may have had that belong largely to myself alone.

My paintings exist. They are their own evidence. And where I am each portion of consciousness speaks for itself and yet for others also, for consciousness is also its own evidence.

My paintings, even, possess their own kinds of consciousness. They are aware of themselves in a way most difficult to explain. They possess their own identities. *(Pause.)* I do not mean to say that they <u>mimic</u> what you think of as ordinary consciousness—simply that their consciousness is of a different kind, possessing its own organizational framework.

A painting is quite aware of its own identity. To an extent, there is a give-and-take between the portions of any painting and the perceiver, even though the perceiver is not objectively aware of such interactions. The colors themselves are aware of themselves, and are pleased with their conditions. They are aware of the interworkings of a painting, and of their positions within it.

(Pause at 4:32.) Anything you can possibly conceive of possesses its own awareness of itself. In a dimension in which I exist, all of these variations are quite obvious. A painting is aware of its future and its past. *(Pause.)* A painting knows the artist who created it, for it emerges from his own living conscious mind, and he cannot but help endow his work with his own characteristics, though they may operate at levels he himself cannot perceive.

A painting itself knows when it is finished or completed within the terms of its existence. *(Pause.)* A portion of any artist knows his relationship with all other artists, and understands how his own work fits into another, vaster artistic creation. Any artist knows that the painting originated itself, seemingly springing from nowhere—and in an even wider framework it can be said that the painting created the artist so it could possess its own kind of life and consciousness.

Each part of any dimension interweaves with all other parts, and the actions of your mind keep originating new realities, and again, it can be said that those realities created the artist, again, knowing that the artist would then objectify their life.

(Long pause.) I created all of my own experiences, even as they in turn created me, and that process now continues. In a fashion it can be said that from my own perspective I keep my own paintings alive, while at the same time they refresh my life. What I experience is certainly life, but at a different scale than I had ever objectively known before.

No canvas is truly empty, but is alive with possibilities and probabilities that impregnate the canvas before a line is drawn or an undercoating applied.

(Long pause at 4:43.) The mistakes a man makes in living itself appear in different form in his painting—but there they are redeemed, becoming a part of this larger creative framework in which mistakes are automatically corrected, or in which mistakes correct themselves, living up to the full potential of the probability they may have missed earlier.

All paintings exist of course whether or not they were destroyed in your

realm of reality. The same applies to all works of art. The children you did not
have in your reality exist within their own worlds of probability, fulfilling their
own potentials in their own ways.

(4:48. *"I stopped for a minute," Jane said, "because I got chilly again."*

(*"I was wondering," I said. Hospital people had fixed the air conditioning system so that it was much more efficient. Now when the register was set at "low" it
didn't take long for the room to cool down, even with the door open. And Jane lay
unclothed in her bed. I was already chilly.*

(*"Give me a cigarette and I'll see if I get anything more," she said. "But I was
thinking you could bring in a copy of* Dialogues, *so I could show the nurses your
drawings and the poetry—but," she added emphatically, "I don't want this place to
get too homey."*

(*"I take it that someone was sort of upset about my remarks earlier about
another reality?" I asked Jane. I meant, of course, when I'd asked for more information on Rembrandt's "present" reality. I'd never thought to have such a personality
respond to any of my own thoughts in such a direct manner—even though that
response was mediated by a world view.*

(*"Not mad," Jane said, "or sarcastic or upset—but he wanted to respond
directly."*

(4:55. *"I had something else," Jane said as we talked. "It's poetry—"*

> *The pages of my mind*
> *turn one after another.*
> *I read them with amazement.*
> *Sometimes I read the end*
> *before the beginning.*
> *Sometimes I leaf through*
> *the paragraphs and sentences, and*
> *dream up living illustrations.*

(*"Here's another little one." Jane said after a moment.*

> *"Will nobody come to help me?"*
> *I cried, and nobody came.*
> *"Will somebody please help me?"*
> *I cried, and someone came*
> *to help me carry my packages.*

(*"That's all. I don't know whether that's too opaque or not," Jane said. "It means that if you don't expect anything you don't get anything, so when the person asks for nobody, nobody comes. When you ask for somebody, your expectations are higher, and you get the help you want."*

(*Down the hall, an older woman was still calling out in a new—familiar refrain: "Nurse. Nurse. Nurse...." Then Rembrandt speaks.*

(5:00.) It is not that I put a life of art above all others. It is simply that I am most familiar with that pattern of existence.

All artists from all earthly ages form their own <u>assemblage</u>. They trade their secrets back and forth across the centuries, so you can read the history of art as you think of it backwards or forwards. It makes little difference, for the interrelationships exist within their own timelessness.

That timelessness is an invisible ingredient in every painting, however timely the subject matter may appear to be.

Nationalities do not really matter as far as the inner communication of artists is concerned. Through their art such artists speak to each other even though they possess different languages. Painting, of course, is a language of its own that needs no translation.

Sometimes I do see a spacious academy with green lawns and shrubs disappearing off in the distance. I know I am within the atmosphere of a vast academy, an academy of knowledge that opens its doors to me when I am truly ready to enter, and that I will naturally assign myself to whatever level of reality *(pause)* <u>will fit me</u> most easily. This is my interpretation of the library, except that here I know that worlds are formed of form and color, and I and my many selves twirl like honeybees about delicious nectar.

(5:10.) That is, I feel myself attracted more and more to certain particular aspects of consciousness toward which I seem to naturally gravitate. *(Long pause.)* I have an inordinate fondness for my Rembrandt self, however, so in my mind I carry that image. Knowing that I have had other images. I grow full with reality's fullness, yet hunger to know still more of this endless universe of consciousness. It comforts me and challenges me as well.

No simple explanations of heaven or hell will do *(long pause)*, and here <u>torment</u> finds no place. It appears to me now that the various elements of the Christian faith, as I knew it, actually represent stages of consciousness, each one interacting with the others. All the stories of the Bible seem to represent the various trials or dilemmas of any given stage of consciousness—a child's <u>primer</u> that <u>means what it does not say</u>.

(5:16.) In the same fashion a painting is what it does not show, for each color or line or object in a painting is there because of those lines or curves or objects that are absent. The elements of a painting thus gravitate toward themselves, as now I feel myself gravitating toward the strange academy that exists because I perceive it as such.

Yet its existence is still not dependent upon my perception. I enjoy, sir, dealing with puzzles as I enjoyed the paintings' interrelated designs.

(5:20 PM. "That's it for the moment," Jane said.

("It's very good, Hon," I said. I should have noted earlier that when I'd asked Jane for more material on Rembrandt after-death reality, I'd wondered how much it resembled William James's "atmospheric presence." I think that Rembrandt's reference to the "academy," and other assorted remarks, may have come through today partly in response to those wonderings.

(Jane's delivery had been steady and intent for the most part, in spite of the interruptions, the noise and confusion around us in the hospital. I still want to get from her material on the states of consciousness she's "in" when delivering the Rembrandt material, information on his particular world view, and other related data. I'd also like to know what Seth thinks of this latest creative venture of hers.

("Yes. I thought it was good," Jane said. "I think there's things there that Seth hasn't said. Give me a cigarette, and read the prayer, then you can go...."

(Come to think of it, I thought as I got my things together, we hadn't heard Kathryn sounding off all afternoon. I suspected that she was gone.)

SESSION 961 (DELETED)
JUNE 24, 1983 2:20 PM FRIDAY

(Jane went to hydro at 8 AM today—her first time on the new routine; so early, in fact, that she didn't get any aspirin or Darvoset before going, until at the last moment. She was doing okay when I arrived, though. The nurse Jan was feeding her. There were several nurses in the room at times. Once the phone rang. It was Jean, a nurse who had attended a going-away party for a couple of other nurses at Lib's last night. Jean reported that she had a hangover, and everyone laughed. Jean said she was still in bed. The nurses who were present laughed at this, since they'd all attended the party too, but had been up working since early morning.

(Kathryn's room was empty, I'd noticed as I walked down the hall to 331.

(Jane measured Jane's urine output in the Foley after lunch. It was up to 300 cc's, she said, which was good.

(Jane said amid the usual routine that she felt she could kick her legs back and forth if she were sitting up, but that she couldn't do it while in bed. I've been helping her move her feet down each day, an inch or two at a time, until I feel the resistance. She hasn't yet quite attained a right angle bend in her left leg; the right one is

more contracted.

(Margaret and Joe Bumbalo visited her last night. In fact, they got there soon enough to let Margaret try to feed Jane a bit of supper when the nurse was called out of 331, but the effort hadn't been very successful. ["We'd have stayed longer," Margaret told me the next day, "but we had to leave to go see someone else." "Oh, that was plenty long enough," I said, for Jane had told me that she'd been quite tired out by the hour-long visit.]

(Jane had picked up a line or two of Rembrandt material last night. "Let me have a cigarette, and I'll start with that." she said. She lay nude on her back. The day was bright and beautiful; I'd turned off the air conditioner for the moment. Jane's delivery was as good as it had been yesterday.)

The phrase, God made man in his own image, or likeness, always intrigued me. Did God then somehow execute a self-portrait, but using some dazzling cosmic art and mathematics? Did he create all possible versions of himself, both masculine and feminine, and then were his powers so magnificent that he endowed each living portrait with breath and life?

The same would apply in one way or another to the world itself, for surely it appears to be some spectacular cosmic landscape, with all versions of nature produced, each one filled with splendor of life—and moreover, able to reproduce itself. This is my own version of physical reality, at least.

I have had periods in which the world seemed incredibly small, aglow, tiny as a raindrop. And then on other occasions the world seemed impossibly vast and multitudinous, so that one could never take in all of its splendors.

I do not consider paintings completed until they are framed, but after death—

(Jane broke off. "Am I covered down there, Bob?" She meant that she felt she might have a BM, and she wanted to be sure there was a chuck in position underneath her hips. To make sure she was adequately protected I cut a chuck in half and worked it beneath her.)

It seems as if life also had <u>its</u> frame, though it was invisible, and suddenly the self finds itself <u>unframed</u>, ready to know itself in a completely new context, or to take part in larger realities that are somehow more elastic.

(Pause at 2:27.) It is as if the soul stretches in ways it did not earlier, and then suddenly snaps back into itself again for some kind of physical experience, and that this process follows for some indefinable time. The word "time" is not appropriate, really, but certainly the soul experiences different kinds of time. Each one seeming more logical while one is so involved.

Time, I know, can enlarge or shrink, or run backward or forward, but in any case in a fashion the very experience of time is misleading. There is only a timelessness, from which endless times emerge.

(Long pause at 2:30.) In some worlds I am sure I do not exist, and my paintings are absent. Yet even in those worlds my paintings and I are implied—they merely form a part of existence's large underpainting, so they exist but in different form.

The same is true of historical sequences: Each one is implied in every other. And each one is somehow dependent upon those events that do not show themselves but remain latent.

(Long pause at 2:35.) I feel like a giant enclosed in the form of a mouse, knowing I am more, and ready to take on my true structure.

("That's all for this minute," Jane said. She was having a small BM. "But not much of a one, though. I took some prune juice this morning, too, but I keep having these tiny itsy-bitsy things. Oh, give me one of those chocolate-chip cookies."

(2:45 PM. Jan and Mary Ann came in. They left Jane on her back for a bit longer. I lit a cigarette for her. The session was over for the day; somehow the routine events of everyday care swamped everything else. Jane said she'd really "been into it" with the session. I could tell that she had.)

SESSION 962 (DELETED)
JUNE 26, 1983 3:33 PM SUNDAY

(No session was held yesterday, although we'd hoped to get one. The day was very upsetting. Among many things, Jane was concerned because her catheter was leaking; she dreaded having it replaced. We almost got down to something from Rembrandt's world view at 3:00, but a nurse came in to "do" Jane's teeth. So it went. Down the hall a man kept calling out "Amen, Amen, Amen," over and over. Kathryn was gone, though, taking her wordless vocalization with her. Jane hollered in pain when Georgia and an aide turned her on her side. There was often so much noise in the hall outside 331 that Jane and I had trouble conversing above it, what with people shouting, talking, laughing, calling, pushing carts and wagons and trays of supplies. Hardly the peaceful atmosphere we'd always insisted upon at the house for our work. Now Jane and I try to work amid all the hubbub and let it slide off us. I doubt if a single nurse or aide or doctor or LPN, interrupting us, comprehends what we're up to—that Jane may be in a trance, that I'm sitting beside her bed, notepad in hand, for a reason. I think we're doing well under the circumstances. It shows what you can do when you have to, as they say.

(Today, I learned upon arrival that Jane had been having much trouble with bladder spasms and a leaking catheter. The word from her doctor was that the

catheter may have to be removed. By 3:10 the nurses had cleaned up Jane following her BM. They left Jane turned on her left side, facing me; for the moment she was actually quite comfortable.

("Obviously," I said, "the body is trying to get rid of the catheter—something it doesn't want," I said. and Jane agreed. I was concerned about her having to void in the "fracture pan," though. That hadn't worked too well at the house. We anticipated interruptions today also, but decided to try to get something down.

(I was having one of my old-time "eye things" as we made ready, but didn't tell Jane so she wouldn't be upset. It wasn't very strong; I could still see to write. This phenomena has come to me very seldom in recent years, and didn't last long now. Jane had been picking up a little from Rembrandt's world view. Her delivery was good. And again it was in the first person singular.)

It might seem that I am rather self-contained, but that is a trait of the Dutch. We avoided foreign influence far better than many other countries, and if someone like the Spanish tried to invade us, we simply paid our dues to a different landlord and went our way.

I did not see the work of very many foreign artists, though a small exhibition once came by ship *(pause)*, and though kept covered, the canvases were nearly ruined by the damp salty air, so you could actually see the specks of salt ingrained.

I do not remember the name of the artist, nor am I sure of his nationality. [One] painting was of a bullfighter and a bull, however, so the artist may have been Spanish.

I found my world so full I did not feel the need to compare my work with artists from other lands. *(Long pause.)* It is true we lived in a time of tumult, but by the time we heard of one war it was over, and another one begun.

Women's and men's fashions changed quicker. Merchants always carried with them sketches of the latest fashions, particularly from France, and tailors and dressmakers were always in a dither, trying to copy them. I was somewhat of a fashion plate myself for some time, for after all I did deal with the public, and did not want to appear out of place. I also gathered quite a wardrobe of costumes for my models to wear. These I kept in a wooden wardrobe and shook them out to let them air before they were used.

(3:42.) Many artists kept such a collection, and oftentimes we traded back and forth.

Now I seem to wear whatever suits my fancy. The clothing just appears as my thoughts change. In summertime I used to look for occasions to study my naked body, the better to understand the human form. In winter it was far too cold and damp for such endeavors.

The artists in one area often shared models. There were but a few good professional ones. They were also the bearers of gossip, however—

(Pause at 3:46. "Just a minute...." Jane seemed uncomfortable as she lay on her side with her legs drawn up. She flexed her arms and moved her feet as much as she could. My eye interference was clearing up. In fact, I'd forgotten about it as soon as Jane got into her delivery.)

—And many would report to one artist the subject matter and progress of another artist's work.

(Rembrandt had referred to this once before.)

My wives did not mind if I had naked female models. They managed to pretend the women were not human at all, but fleshy <u>dolls</u>, with no private lives of their own. At least in some strange manner, they seemed to consider the models as inanimate. Indeed, they were not, and many an artist fell prey to the beauties of the models they used for work.

I myself was always faithful. I had children enough without raising illegitimate ones—

(3:51. Ruth, a nurse, came in to take urine specimens and to check Jane's Foley. "Your urine has been kind of thick lately," she told Jane. "There may be a blockage. They haven't gotten much on the day shift." She tried flushing the tubing with a syringe, but it didn't seem to help. She left to get another kind of syringe. Jane felt all right at this time, though.

(3:59.) Anyway, Bob, when Ruth came in Rembrandt was saying that making love to a model was a <u>professional hazard</u> *(with some humor)*—and it was known also that such models could be carriers of a dread disease. He supposed he was somewhat of a hypochondriac. He always feared he was coming down with one malady or another, and collected all sorts of potions or remedies, meant to cure this or another ill.

Artists' studios were notoriously foul-smelling, smelling of *(long pause)* zincs, coppers—

(4:01. Ruth was back. The larger, more powerful glass syringe she brought worked good enough to get a small specimen of urine for testing before she began to irrigate the tubing. Her attempts at irrigation didn't help, though; since the catheter appeared to be blocked, she left sterile water in it to see if that would help.

(4:10. Jane resumed as soon as Ruth left again.)

Bob, the rest of that was: —and other metallic pigments.

(Long pause.) Some of the models also had their own wardrobes, because you rented the clothes as well as the model. And the models were jealous of each other, and did a lot of backbiting.

He usually asked his models to remain silent. He was particularly secretive with them also, because they carried tales back and forth—some true and some not true.

(Long pause at 4:14.) Artists had the reputation of being loose with women, so he was particularly prudent. His own feelings were ambiguous toward models, because you needed them as an artist, and because they had ruined many a good artist's name.

He understood that doctors had somewhat the same difficulties with women patients, so many doctors demanded that a member of the family be present when they examined a female—

(4:17. Jane broke off because she began having bladder spasms. She still lay on her left side, facing me. The catheter was blocked. A different nurse came in to 331 to take my wife's temperature rectally, her pulse, and so forth. Down the hall a ways an older woman with a strong voice was calling out periodically, "Nurse, nurse. nurse."

(4:30. I read our daily prayer with Jane while we were alone.)

(4:32.) He envied their knowledge of the body. They fascinated him for that reason. Yet he was dubious of their ministrations, and sometimes wondered if they were not driven by greed rather than by any great compassion for man's plight.

(Spasms at 4:34.) The doctors were the most fashionable of men, in a manner of speaking. He often noticed that their hands were not as clean as they should be, however *(long pause)*, and he wondered often about their practice of using leeches so frequently—

(4:37. Eye drops. The nurse checked the Foley to see if it was still blocked. It was. "We'll have to take it out," she said finally. The staff had already received permission from Jane's doctor to do this, if necessary. Jane, of course, wanted to get rid of the catheter and return to a more normal routine of voiding.)

(4:51.) The little bit I was getting was that doctors made good patrons and purchasers of paintings, though, so he tried to keep on good terms with them. The artist was truly a part of his community in those days.

Few artists tried to paint out of their heads. They needed models and apprentices, and people to buy their paintings and so forth. He always felt that he was <u>needed</u>, and he always had work piled up ahead. After all, beside his supplies he had his other expenses and a family to support.

Now looking back in retrospect, his earthly life seems most cozy, his ups and downs insignificant—though then sometimes his troubles weighed him down most heavily.

(4:55. Jane began to have more bladder spasms, and I pressed the button to summon a nurse.

(5:00. Two nurses came to remove the catheter. They wanted to know if Jane had used a "fracture pan" at the house. I said yes. They asked me to wait in the hall for a few minutes. "First we take out the balloon." I heard one of them tell Jane, "then the catheter itself...." I carted a folding chair into the hall outside 331 and worked at answering a letter or two. I was back in the room within fifteen minutes. Jane was free of the catheter. However, we hadn't talked for more than a couple of minutes when she suddenly began to release urine in a steady flow. Fortunately it was caught by the underpad, which began to partially absorb it. Once again I pressed the call button.

(5:17.) I don't know where this came from—or why— but I got that twice during the year they began to delouse the house with tar.

("With tar?" she repeated, puzzled. How would that work?")

("By odor?" I guessed. "I thought it would take more than that....")

(We had no chance to explore the question. The nurses returned. I mentally filed away the question of delousing with tar along with our unanswered queries about dry ice and China: still to be investigated. "Every time I think of dry ice I think of China," Jane had said today.)

ROB'S NOTES
MONDAY, JUNE 27, 1983.

This morning our neighbor's dog, Gus, died. He's dead by now, I'm sure, at 9:20 AM. At about 6 AM I was wakened by strange sounds in the neighborhood. My bedroom windows were open and I thought I was hearing someone beginning construction work, for instance. These sounds were loud, high-pitched, and had almost a metallic, scraping quality to me as I lay in bed. I sat up briefly and looked out the window opposite the foot of the bed. I saw that Joe Bumbalo's garage door was open; I thought that maybe Joe was beginning some project around the house, since he's always doing something like that. Usually his garage doors aren't open until later in the morning.

I was tired so I went back into a fitful sleep until 6:35. I was shaving when I thought I heard a noise at the back screen door. It was Joe, I saw as I peeked out. I hurriedly put on my shirt and went to the door. Joe had left, but I called to him in the road and he came back. "Gus is dying," he said, "and I need some help getting him in the car to take him to the vet...."

"I'll be glad to help." I buttoned my shirt as I accompanied him across the road. His wife Margaret was in the garage. So was Gus. He lay in a pool of urine at the foot of the step leading up into the den from the garage. "He can't get up any-

more," Margaret said. "He smells awful. He's been making the strangest sounds I ever heard, the poor old guy."

So that was it. Margaret said Gus was alert, and so he was, trying to look at me by cocking his eyes in my direction without evidently being able to even move his head. His legs were sprawled out akimbo, yet he looked as if he'd just lay down as a dog will do—only now he couldn't get up, this was the end. "Oh, that's too bad," I heard myself saying several times. Already I felt the beginnings of emotion tugging at my insides. Gus was old. One had only to look at him walking about this spring to see that here was an old, old dog, that he wasn't going to live out the summer. I'd even expected him to die last winter, when Margaret and Joe had been in Florida for several months.

As it happened, I'd fed Gus this weekend. The Bumbalos had gone to their cottage on one of the lakes upstate, and asked me to feed their dog Friday and Saturday nights; they'd returned late Sunday—last night. Gus had eaten all right, for I'd found his dish empty in the garage when I'd gone back to feed him on Saturday night. He hadn't been anywhere in sight, though; I'd taken it for granted that he'd struggled up the hill to the Merrills, where Marion Merrill often fed him when the Bumbalos were away. I'd caught one glimpse of Gus Sunday afternoon as I'd driven away from the house on my way to see Jane in the hospital. He'd been laying in the Bumbalo's backyard, the sun catching on his reddish-brown coat as he watched me pull away down Holley Road. He was quite deaf, and had arthritis. He'd had skin cancer last year. He couldn't walk very far at a time, and could no longer wave his tail up in the air. It hung limply, yet he could still wag the end of it in a brief, friendly gesture.

"John's in Binghamton," Margaret said, "otherwise he could have helped us. He's going to feel bad about this. Old Gus was his favorite." John is their son. He's 40 years old, and unmarried.

Margaret had fallen a few weeks ago, and cracked her pelvis. She was getting around now without a walker or a cane, but still had to watch herself, and she couldn't do any lifting. Joe had told me at the door that he couldn't lift Gus by himself. They wanted to get him into the trunk of their Buick, so they could take him to the vet and have him put away. "The vet will be there by 7:30," Joe said. He'd called him.

Gus lay in an awkward position at the foot of the steps into the den, for the materials we wanted were piled up in a corner of the garage next to the door to the den, and in back of Gus. By stretching across him, though, we got what was needed: a folded sheet of dark green plastic, a piece of rope, a white quilted blanket. Joe planned to leave the trunk lid up, but I suggested he tie it down enough so that it was still open a foot or so, enough to give him some visibility in his rearview mirror while driving. He agreed. He put the plastic on the floor of the trunk. He also hand-

ed me a pair of gloves and found a pair for himself. We didn't know whether it would be painful for Gus to be moved or not. I also thought that an animal that was hurt could turn on the person trying to help—but nothing like that developed. Joe and I lifted Gus up easily and lay him in the same position on his belly on the white robe. He did have a strong odor, evidently having lost control of his bladder. His hair looked lifeless and matted and wet, but his eyes seemed clear. Without protest he let us lift him in the blanket, as in a sling.

We deposited him in the trunk, which was quite deep in the Buick, a new car. There wasn't a whole lot of floor space in there, to my surprise, and we ended up with Gus's head wedged against a bulkhead. "Sorry, Gus," I said. as I moved the blanket on top of the plastic, easily enough, so that he had room to stretch out in a natural position. All of these careful, caring motions we were going through, to take Gus to the doctor to be put to sleep, to death, I thought.

And what else could you do? I wondered. Here the dog was completely helpless. You could just let him lay there and die, I thought, but it seemed cruel. Wasn't that what "nature" intended, though, I wondered. Gus hadn't emitted any more of those strange sounds, though—not since I'd been up. When Jane and I had watched our cat, Willy, die there on the living room rug, right at our feet, it had seemed the right thing to do—neat and clean, and quickly over. Here Gus wasn't going that way. By his choice, I thought, and obviously there was a lot none of us knew about death. I was particularly vulnerable to this kind of thinking because of the material on Rembrandt that Jane was coming through with these days, as she lay in her hospital bed. A few days ago she'd delivered some especially terrific material on Rembrandt's account of his afterdeath experiences, and as I worked with the Bumbalos and Gus now the gist of those passages kept returning to me. If those experiences were true for Rembrandt, involving the survival of the soul, or spirit, then obviously they were true for every other living creature, in those terms. Gus would be going on to something far better, then. I remembered that Seth had said there was no such thing as a cat consciousness, or a dog consciousness, or for that matter a human consciousness. There was only consciousness. The Rembrandt material was bearing such statements out in its own unique way. As Jane said the other day, there are things in the Rembrandt sessions that Seth hasn't said.

While the Bumbalos made ready to get going, I stood at the trunk of their car, looking down at Gus as he lay half covered by the quilted blanket. He was quite peaceful. What did he know, or sense, of what was going on? Joe had tied down the trunk lid to a degree, but I had a clear view of the dog. I felt my emotions of sadness and questioning rising in my throat. Margaret was talking. She sounded quite fine, but I could tell she was deeply upset: "Poor old Gus...." They still had to take him to the veterinarian, but my part in the drama was about over. I didn't know whether they were going to stay at the vet's, while it was done, bring Gus home for burial, or have the body disposed of. I didn't ask. I knew Joe was nervous.

"Well, thanks for helping out," Margaret said as I turned away. I didn't dare look at them. I felt like crying. I managed to acknowledge their thanks in what I thought was a normal voice, but I started to walk away, across the road toward our house. I heard them get in their car. Joe was driving and he started it up. I heard them back into Holley Road, as usual. My eyes brimmed. Joe drove down toward the corner of Holley and Pinnacle as I reached our back porch. Gus was gone. For good.

I was crying by the time I got inside the kitchen. I hoped Joe and Margaret would make the trip okay—which wouldn't be easy, if they felt like I did, I thought. On the other hand, I thought the necessity of what they had to do would sustain them at least until they returned home. I remembered that it had kept Jane and me going okay when we'd had to take our own dog, Mischa—who bore a striking resemblance to Gus—to the veterinarian to have him put away because he, too, had lost the ability to walk....

But I cried more for Gus than I had for Mischa. whom I'd loved dearly. I'd also cried more for our cat, Willy, than I had for Mischa. Jane had talked about Mischa just yesterday, remembering a photograph of her and I that my father had taken shortly before our wedding in December 1954. Mischa had lain on the kitchen floor beside us, ears cocked. I believe staring up at us as we'd talked and joked that evening, sitting at the kitchen table.

But I do think I've learned to be more vulnerable to my feelings these days, and can at least express some of them a little more easily. Probably some of that stems from one's growing older and shedding earlier inhibitions, and some from the work Jane and I have done, and are doing. Trying to delve into even the idea of other realities is bound to open up one, to lead you to consider facets of reality quite ignored before, in those days when physical reality seemed to be it, and one had the "time" to consider ideas of immortality in the physical sense. Jane will feel bad in turn when I tell her of Gus's death. I don't know whether to let her read these pages or not. Maybe later, after she's gotten used to the idea that Gus is gone. I do plan to take them to the hospital with me today. I had a rough time trying to get breakfast after leaving the Bumbalos. Cereal, cherries, toast and tea. I forgot to bring in the morning paper, as I often do. The old habits serve to mask other feelings and emotions. I knew I didn't really want breakfast, but still I ate some of it. I turned on television and watched a little news. I planned to call our lawyer after breakfast. I thought of writing an account of Gus's demise, like this, but didn't know whether I would or not. The tears came several times. "Goddam it, Gus...." Our cats eyed me at times, then chased each other through the rooms.

At about 9 AM, when I looked out my studio window, I saw the Bumbalo's car sitting in their driveway just in front of their garage. No one was about that I could see. A half-hour later, when I looked again, I saw that their car was gone.

The day was beautiful, cool and bright and sunny. But if Jane was right, if Rembrandt was right, then the light and color I saw in our mundane world would pale indeed compared to the brilliant, indescribable, shimmering color and feeling in the reality Gus had entered by now. But one thing I was sure of—I wouldn't be handing out to Gus any more dry cat-food snacks at our screen door. And as Jane had written in one of her books, "If I could explain that cat's death, then I could explain everything." I saw Margaret and Joe at noon when I left to drive down to the bank, to our lawyer's office, and then to the hospital. They were cleaning up after Gus. Joe had taken the soiled blanket and plastic sheet out in back of the house, and was going to burn them on the stone patio there—only the items were so wet he was afraid they wouldn't burn. "Oh do it tomorrow, Honey," Margaret called to him as she talked to me. "Lay 'em out in the sun and let them dry out first."

I could tell Joe didn't want to wait.

"The veterinarian told us he could run some tests on Gus," Margaret said, "but he didn't think they'd do any good. I think he had a ruptured bowel. There was blood all over by the time we got him there, and he was in a lot of pain. So we had it done...."

When I backed my own car out of the driveway I saw that Joe had succeeded in setting afire the quilted blanket; he kept poking at the little blaze with a stick, turning the burning fabric. Margaret was sweeping the garage, I think. "That's okay, Gus," I thought as I drove down Coleman Avenue, letting the car cruise down the steepest part of the hill in second gear, as I usually did. "You did good, Gus. You did real good." He'd given much and asked only a little.

POSTSCRIPT
JUNE 27, 1983

At about 10:00 tonight the phone rang. I hurried to it from the couch, where I was having a snack and watching television before going to bed. I thought it was Jane, but it was Margaret.

"Say Rob, you know Dutchess, Wyckoff's dog?"

"Sure. I haven't seen her for a few days. I thought they all went to the lake, with school being out."

Actually I didn't know whether school was out yet or not. But I hadn't seen Wyckoff's beautiful young female collie, Dutchess, for several days; she was always coming to the screen door for a little handout of dry cat food. Like Gus used to do.

Like Black Dog, as I call another dog, still does on occasion. Dutchess was very shy and high-strung, and I'd spent weeks last year luring her to my door so I could have the fun of feeding her.

"Well," Margaret said, "Dutchess was poisoned here a few days ago. She's dead. They found her before she died and took her to the vet, but he couldn't do anything."

I was astounded.

"So I'm wondering if something like that happened with Gus," Margaret said. "I know he was going to die, but...."

"You mean you think Gus actually died of poisoning?" I asked.

"Well, he had some of the symptoms. A distended abdomen, that smell, and so forth. The vet did a post on Dutchess. They don't know what kind of a poison it was yet, though. Maybe somebody put out rat poison, and she got into it. No," she said in answer to my question. "Gus wasn't examined that way. He'd already been cremated. It's too late—they do that right away."

Dutchess, then, is the second young dog of the Wyckoff's that's been poisoned to death within two years. Jim Wyckoff—whom I've never met—was very bitter, Margaret said. He thought someone on the hill was out to get him and his family. Their house has been robbed twice also, within the same period.

"But I can't imagine anybody on the hill doing that to animals," Margaret said. "Besides, there's lots of other dogs running around loose, and nothing happens to them. So I don't know."

"Wouldn't it be awful is somebody is poisoning dogs?" I asked.

"Terrible," Margaret said. "I can't imagine it."

We agreed, though, that we didn't really believe that Gus had been poisoned. The impending signs of his death had been too obvious, too close. Coincidence? What does one mean with the use of that word, anyway? But there was the question of where Gus had been for the two days the Bumbalos had been away. He'd eaten the food I put out in their garage for him, but except for that one glimpse I'd had of him laying in the sunny backyard, he'd been out of everyone's sight. The Merrills, up the road, hadn't seen him, Margaret had learned. Yet Gus had actually looked okay to me when I'd seen him lying in the sun. Doing just what one would expect an old dog close to death to do.

"Well," Margaret said, "I just wanted you to know."

"I'll tell Jane. Don't forget, though, Margaret, about another dog...." I said that because earlier in our conversation I'd come right out and said that I hoped she and Joe, and the Wyckoffs, would both get new dogs. Selfish of me, of course, but I wanted to see the activity of the animals in the neighborhood.... And because this afternoon Jane had given some great material on animal consciousness while delivering Rembrandt material. See the 963rd session.

ANOTHER POSTSCRIPT.
JUNE 28, 1983 9:45 AM.

Margaret Bumbalo called me this morning to say that the veterinarian had told her that Gus had definitely not been poisoned. He was very sure and responded without hesitation to her question. She'd called him back after learning of the Wyckoff trouble with Dutchess. Gus, he said, had had a condition known as "fly-blown" in the profession. This was brought about over a long period of time. Flies would bite the dog and implant their eggs under his skin. Because Gus's hindquarters were growing progressively more defective, he couldn't evacuate properly, and get rid of the toxins the fly's desposits built up in his system. Eventually his colon had been affected, and finally ruptured.

The vet asked Margaret if the Wyckoff's vet knew yet what kind of poison had killed Dutchess. There's a well-known poison for rats called D-Con that causes the symptoms Dutchess had, he said. Margaret told him the Wyckoff's didn't know yet. They are having the necessary tests done to isolate the poison. They've also contacted the police, who are very concerned that there's poison evidently out in the open in the neighborhood, and are trying to track it down. The Wyckoffs left for their cottage today, but Margaret will be seeing Jim, she said, and will let me know what transpires.

(A note: This morning's paper carried the news that a nurses' strike will probably take place at St. Joe's. Margaret wants me to tell Jane that if necessary she'll come down to sit with her. Margaret was a nurse.)

SESSION 963 (DELETED)
JUNE 27, 1983 3:30 PM MONDAY

(This morning was extremely upsetting and hectic. See my own notes, plus the attached Gus material, as I'm already thinking of it. Gus, the Bumbalos' dog, died early this morning—or, rather, he was assisted toward his death by a veterinarian after he lost the ability to walk. I helped Margaret and Joe get him into their car, and so forth, to take him away. I ended up so bothered by this that I wrote seven pages on the episode this morning. I didn't get anything done toward typing the two Rembrandt sessions I have yet to do.

(Steve Blumenthal called at about 11:00 to tell me that Seagull's, in Elmira, will have the voice-activated tape recorder I ordered a month ago, within a few days. Or that I can let Steve fill the order and cancel with Seagull's—which I didn't really want to do. Steve is also fired up with enthusiasm about marketing transcripts of

the ESP classes Jane used to have. Last Saturday night when he'd visited with Tracy I'd asked him to send a copy of his best cleaned-up Seth/ESP class tape to Mike Appel, to get Mike's opinion as to whether the tape was of good-enough quality to consider marketing a record of class material.

(I called Pete Harpending to tell him I'd drop off the abstracts for our house, on my way to see Jane this afternoon. Then in ES&L I met Jean Sweeney-Dunn, before I got to Pete's office, and explained to her that we were having the house transferred to my name to avoid possible legal hassles in the future over medical bills, and so forth.

(I should have noted earlier that as I was eating lunch Seagull's called, to say that they would have the recorder in stock within a few days, so I didn't cancel the order.

(On my way through the emergency room at the hospital I met Ken Wrigley, and told him Jane's catheter had been removed, yesterday afternoon. However, the first thing I discovered when I got up to Jane's room was that she had a new catheter inserted. Her doctor had called in last night and ordered its use, although the urine tests hadn't shown any sign of infection. A nurse we hadn't met before was feeding Jane. She—Jane—had been to hydro this morning, and seen her doctor besides. When we were finally alone for a few minutes I explained Gus's death to Jane. I'd brought my material with me, and she read it as she lay on her back.

(Jane had also been weighed this morning, and had lost another half-pound. She refused to go back on the feeding tube. As we talked about everything—the house, money, lawyers, her weight, and so forth, we decided that we'd just have to continue with our prayers and our trust in Framework 2. Otherwise we could spend all of our time contending with such worries. Jane felt okay by now, although last night for an hour or so she'd felt strong spasms after the new catheter had been put in place.

(After lunch, and following her reading of my material on Gus's death, Jane said that she might have some information on animal consciousness. I was surprised, since I hadn't expected that at all. We went through the regular routine of temperature taking, and so forth in between our efforts to hold a conversation. Down the hall the same woman was again calling loudly for a nurse. Jane was feeling quite good, everything considered. She was still on her back. I didn't know whether she was going to give anything herself on animal consciousness, or via another source.

(It was a relief to just sit quietly beside her bed, taking notes, to just let everything else slide away. I believe [without checking] that this is the first entire session Jane has delivered for Rembrandt in the first person singular.

(3:30.) Dear sir. You have touched that part me that was so fond of animals—and as I lived in town *(pause)* my experience with animals was limited.

There were horses, cats and dogs, but the farmers' land was further inward. I was very fond of cats and dogs—and for that matter, pigeons; and sometimes I kept pigeon, in a poor sort of a cage, outside my top windowsill.

I cherished cats and dogs, since they asked so little and gave so much. Indeed, sometimes when I was alone I talked directly to those pets we had, and I knew that in their ways they understood what I said.

For my [present] edification, several cats and dogs of whom I was fond have appeared to me, taking the semblance of their old selves, I am sure only to please me.

(3:36. "Just a minute," Jane said, waiting for a spasm to pass.)

Actually they gravitate, as I do, toward the levels or stages of consciousness that serves them best. (Long pause.) Animals have a certain kind of yearning for the earth, for in life they possess a greater sense of belonging to it, so often they return many times, in various shapes and forms, and frequently they return to the places they inhabited before.

(Long pause.) They learned to love the earth in a different fashion than man does, but their way is very powerful. Your friend Gus, I imagine, will spend some time returning to the Holley Hill location, with his senses renewed again, even though of course he is not present in physical terms.

In a way most difficult to explain, animals <u>know</u> places in the same way that they <u>know</u> people—

(3:42. "Excuse me, Bob," Jane said, "but is that chuck in place? I've got to go." I cut one in half and worked it underneath her.)

—That is, to animals places have their own personalities. It is not that animals do not distinguish between animals and people, only that animals <u>know</u> a place in the same way that you might know a person. They understand physical existence in an entirely different fashion than you do, and they love the land. The land loves them in return, for the land is not just land, but possesses its own conglomeration of consciousness, to which animals respond as you might respond to another person.

In the same way, animals may take a dislike to a certain place, though overall their entire disposition is friendly, open, and certainly nonhostile.

(3:49.) Gus knew he was dying quite before it was obvious. He prepared himself in his own way, so that a main part of his consciousness settled down to rest before his actual death. He possessed that love for places that I mentioned, and so a part of his consciousness will linger in the old neighborhood.

(A one-minute pause at 3:51.) I had a few carrier pigeons that I trained myself, and I enjoyed the idea of their flying up in the sky when I could not.

What I said about cats and dogs applied to all animals—

(3:53. An aide came in to take Jane's temperature but couldn't because Jane *hasn't been cleaned up yet. Another aide gave Jane her eye drops. Jane had a cigarette while I read her some of the material. The aides had told us that the nurses are having a meeting right now with hospital management, negotiating to prevent a possible strike.*

(Jane said the material today added dimension to the idea of Rembrandt as a human being. I said that we were so used to thinking of him as an artist that it seemed that was all he'd ever done, for 24 hours each day of his life; we forgot that he must have had many other interests in life. Jane said that as we talked she had an image or impression of him, then, at a window, wearing a floppy white nightcap, releasing his birds to fly out over the canals of the city.

(4:08.) I kept up my practice of keeping a few carrier pigeons right up to the time of my death.

On several occasions while I was alone, in your terms, it almost seemed to me that I saw land and water below through the carrier pigeons' eyes. The experience momentarily made me dizzy. For I did not know if what I was experiencing was real, or whether my imagination was playing tricks on me.

I had some flying dreams also, when I was alive in your terms, and once or twice I seemed to awaken still clothed in my nightgown, and to my horror I looked down seemingly wide-awake far above the land and the water, and climbing ever higher into the nighttime sky. Then without warning I felt a severe jolt and woke again, this time in my bed, to find myself severely sweating. I did not understand at all what had happened, and it was only after death that I understood the meaning of such experiences.

I believe that all people travel out of their bodies almost as a matter of course, but the usual earthly training does nothing to prepare an individual for such experiences. Now I know that animals have out-of-body travels also, but they take them quite for granted, since in certain ways their consciousnesses are more mobile than man's.

(4:14. "Just a second—I'm trying to see if I'm done or not," Jane said. The sky was getting very dark. I gave her some cranberry juice. "I've got something else," she said as we discussed the material. "It's rather strange, though...." With a laugh: "Why is it I always feel __comforted__ after giving some Rembrandt material?"

(4:17.) I am aware of your scientific advancements. All of them at one time or another lived in man's imagination, even in my time.

As television has had its effects upon man's consciousness, even though it originated seemingly from his own mind, so that same medium to some extent has its effect upon domestic animals also. This applies particularly to cats and dogs, and even house birds, according to their dispositions.

First of all, animals at one time were not __used to__ hearing sounds that came seemingly from nowhere. At first, then, many house pets were disconcerted by the voices on television, when people seemed to speak, while their senses could not locate the speakers. Before too long, however, the house pets began to take such experiences for granted, and tried to manipulate their consciousnesses in such a way as to make such occurrences more understandable. They activated certain electromagnetic centers that they had not previously used to any degree. They react to the <u>emotions</u> of the actors, for example, in the television dramas. They make a distinction between the actors' emotions, however, and the emotions of people in the room. They have learned to stretch their own capacities, however.

Earth consciousness itself is forever changing. It changes at every generation, whether or not it seems to be. Animals in life know ahead of time when earthquakes or storms will occur, and in their own ways they have learned to distinguish between the sensed emotions of the actors and those of the observers. But they are far more aware of your television programs than you may have thought.

(4:29. Jane paused. "Every once in a while I almost get one of those spasms," she said, "you know?" Down the hall, the same woman we've heard often before was calling out for a nurse, over and over.

("Yes," I said. "It's very interesting material. I used to think our cats would lie there and not pay any attention to the programs we watched on television, beyond reacting to a sudden loud noise, say. However, Jane reminded me of the way Mitzi especially would seem to follow motion on the screen, occasionally rising on her hind legs while she pawed at the screen.

(4:30.) Had I lived in the country, where animals were more numerous, I would have painted them frequently—doing portraits of a different kind, for each animal has its own character, and animal portraits done with understanding could be a diverting *(long pause)* and fascinating as portraits of people are.

Animals do not have to ask who or where God is, for they possess their own understanding of their places in nature—

(4:35. Dawn and another aide we hadn't met before came in to clean up Jane, take her temperature, and so forth. When they were through Jane lay on her right side, facing the window. She'd been on her back all afternoon. I moved to the other side of her bed when she wanted to give some more material.

(5:00.) Everything possesses its own kind of consciousness, whether or not this is apparent to you. Even the images on your television screen have their own kind of electromagnetic awareness.

(Pause.) In ways quite indescribable they are aware of those observers who view them, so that a certain kind of communication happens between the

images on the television screen and the viewers, whoever they may be.

It is strange how limiting ordinary vocabulary is, in any language, when it comes to describing the vast realities that do exist—yet communications happen, of course, regardless of words, at certain realities where comprehension is almost instantly available.

(5:06 PM. "That's all," Jane said. "Basically, I'm uncomfortable with my toes." The aides had left her in a position on her side that I'd never do, with one foot lying on top of the other, exerting pressure. In this case Jane's left foot was pressing down on her right. I was able to shift them slightly and insert foam rubber wedges in a way that relieved the pressure. Jane would be turned on her back for supper.

(I told her I thought today's material was most evocative indeed. Even that on this page alone is worth much thought. I'll check the Rembrandt sessions to see if I'm correct in thinking that today's is the first Jane has given in which she used the first person singular throughout.

(I read the prayer to her before leaving 331 or the day.)

SESSION 964 (DELETED)
JUNE 28, 1983 3:58 PM TUESDAY

(It had rained heavily throughout the night and most of the morning. It had started in again by the time I stopped at the post office to mail a copy of Emir *to Saul Cohen at Prentice-Hall; they may reconsider their decision not to publish the book. Along with* Emir *I mailed to brother Dick for safekeeping a number of* Rembrandt *sessions.*

(Jane was feeling good when I arrived, eating lunch with Pat, an aide, feeding her. The hospital was quiet today—so far. Sure enough, the woman down the hall began calling loudly for a nurse.

("The dreams of the human race are responsible for its evolution." So ran a quotation from Seth, presented by Maude Cardwell in Coordinate Point International *for May 1983. There was more Seth material on evolution. I wondered whether I had Seth's position on evolution all wrong, before realizing that he was referring to that concept as we visualize it in our reality. That is, he left us room for it should we choose to view reality in that fashion.*

(Jane's catheter is working all right, and she has no bladder infection. She began to have a BM by 2:20; at the same time she read the rest of my Gus material, *Session 961, and the first two pages of 962. "I feel something on Rembrandt," she said then, "but I can't do it when I'm pooping...." We waited.*

(The head nurse, Mary, brought in an in-house bulletin revived by the hospi-

*tal; it contained reassuring messages about the impending strike by RN's, see the news-
paper article [end of this session]. I told her that we see no problems for Jane and me.
NY State law very strictly governs the procedures to be followed by hospitals in case of
strike actions. Also see the letter sent by the hospital to all employees, re possible layoffs.*

*(Jane was cleaned up by 3:40. She lay on her left side, facing me; I lit a ciga-
rette for her. She said she "felt something" from Rembrandt. Five minutes later an
aide came in to take her temperature and check her blood pressure. Jane occasionally feels as though she may have a bladder spasm, but they do not develop. Finally she
told me to move my chair over beside her bed. And once again she began speaking
for Rembrandt in the first person singular.)*

Now that I am not alive in your terms, I am intrigued by the idea of space
from the earthly artist's viewpoint.

The fact is that the earthly artist is trained to see only certain kinds of
objects or entities or realities, but in greater terms no space is empty. On the
other hand no reality is <u>cluttered</u> either. Realities move through each other without bothering each other in the least.

Sometimes when I was alive I used to think that I caught motion out of
the corner of my eye, or sensed a person or an object where there shouldn't have
been anything, and I think now that on those occasions I was trying to see other
realities than my own. It seems to me that knowing this, an earthly artist could
somehow suggest these other realities by the clever use of design and transparent lights against opaques in the backgrounds of the paintings, in the folds of
garments, the designs of a coverlet, or whatever.

In such a way it seems that he could cleverly weave patterns so that the
observer's eye—

*(4:03. LuAnn, a nurse, came in to give Jane her eye drops. "Did you miss me?"
she asked Jane.*

*("Yes, I missed you," Jane said. After LuAnn had left Jane said, "She's one of
the big ones in the strike—she sits at the bargaining table...." I read the last part of
the material to my wife.)*

—would be led to make a kind of <u>double use</u> of space within the painting.

If the method were done with expertise then the observer's eye <u>would
seem to see</u> what it could not actually see. It would sense motion and moving
forms, and yet there would be no sense of clutter or disorder.

*(Now there was a lot of noise and clutter in the hall outside 331. Elevator
doors are only a room or so away, and people congregate there, often not silently, while
waiting before those orange doors.)*

That method would work in painting skyscapes, where one could freely use the designs of clouds and so forth, not being diverted by many objects as such. There the artist could suggest the wind's patterns, and other spaces within spaces, without having to be distracted by the number of objects that one must use in, say, a still life.

In another way, artists have used angels and cherubs and so forth to suggest these other realities, by giving them an earthly kind of form. The method I am thinking of would be less obvious, for in a fashion the observer would be left to form his own images of these other realities. They would not have to conform to a conventional angel shape, for example.

When I sent my pigeons out, I used to watch their wings and how they moved, and I wondered exactly how an <u>angel's wings</u> would work, lifting such a sturdy creature as an angel, who seemed to be as heavy as any man.

(4:14.) You could suggest that same upward motion in the background or the skyscape without ever actually painting wings, but by suggesting upward motion so that the designs of clouds themselves suggested interwoven patterns, perhaps of ascending values.

You were speaking yesterday of animals, and certainly no painting shows animals with some kind of angel's wings. In my earthly time animals were not supposed to have souls. To paint a painting from an animal's viewpoint—now <u>that</u> would be a strange wonder indeed!

(4:17. Someone screamed down the hall a ways. I couldn't tell if man or woman. There was a heavy thump, as though someone fell. Jane paused.)

Objects seemed to move, to animals, where to you they might appear stationary in an animal's reality, if so full of odor and sense that no painting without those ingredients would have any reality at all. If there are other than human artists, then these artists would work with canvases that somehow combined sense and smell, translated perhaps into color *(pause)*, as if an artist on earth drenched his canvas with perfume. For through their nostrils as well as their eyes the animals filled out their picture of the world.

(Long pause at 4:20. "What time is it? Jane asked. I told her. "Let me have a cigarette. He was getting into stuff that was awfully difficult to describe," she said. "I hope it's clear."

("It's very good," I said. "It's another case of once you hear it, you wonder why you didn't think of it yourself."

(The heavy rain seemed to have stopped for the moment. I turned off the air conditioner and gave Jane some Ensure. I'd looked for the half-and-half mixture of cranberry juice and ginger ale she'd had left after finishing lunch, but someone had taken it away; it's supposed to help clear out her bladder. Jane talked about her youthful poem about Tippy the cat going to cat heaven, apropos of the Rembrandt mater-

ial today, then she got into a discussion of the poem on reincarnation she'd written as a teenager, the one Father Ryan had changed. Then she recounted the episode in which Father Ryan had burned her set of books on The Decline and Fall of the Roman Empire.

(4:37.) The knowledge of such issues is bound to change an artist's work for the better, particularly if he is spontaneous enough to give his brush some freedom, for in his inner heart he understands that other realities also exist.

I can see evidence now in my own work of such unknowing knowing, where I succeeded in making evident realities that had escaped my own physical eyes. It pleases me to pass this knowledge on for others to you, as before I passed on what I knew to my apprentices.

(Long pause at 4:40.) Who is the artist within the artist within the artist? I wondered about such questions when I was alive, on those occasions when my hand and my brush seemed to know more than I did, or as if some greater artist than I took over my brushes for a while. I thought of myself as a creator, of course, and so was endlessly led despite conventional religion to wonder what greater artist had created me so that I could then produce my own creations. My only answer was that God is the medium in which I exist. I suppose if I had to think of a name I would call God "The Giver," and I feel my own reality <u>afloat</u>, as it were, in this great medium that surges through the universe and supports all realities.

(A one-minute pause at 4:44.) I truly loved my families, and it seems to me that a man must love if he is to paint, for no great art can thrive on hate. So this medium of life that I sense is first of all a lover of its own creations, and it creates out of some gigantic or cosmic love quite beyond our usual understanding. It must give then, without asking anything in return, for its own creations are its own reward. Even in life I had no use for doctrines of the devil or his cohorts, because for all its difficulties the world kept on happening, as if kept alive by some giant love.

I loved to paint, so I imagined that feeling multiplied a million times, and then I <u>seemed</u> at least to get a glimmering of understanding as to the nature of the Giver.

I suppose man's wars are his growing pains, which will one day vanish— for in all my experiences since death I have never encountered torments or devils or the like, nor have I ever found any breed of comparable characteristics. Even a painting of dark storm clouds is filled with creativity, so even in the midst of earthly sorrows those sorrows rest securely within the great medium of the giver.

It has been said that artists are not philosophers, but they are, of course.

(Sneeze at 4:52.) They philosophize with paint rather than with words. They form their realities and structures of thought through color and line, and thus comment upon their realities.

(4:53 PM. "That's the first time I've sneezed since I've been in here," Jane said as she asked for a Kleenex. It had been a good one. I gave her some Ensure. I read the prayer to her at 5:00 before leaving for the day.)

AK-UAZE I

Elmira, N.Y., June 28, 1983

St. Joe's nurses set to strike

By KAY BLOUGH
Staff writer

Negotiations between St. Joseph's nurses and the hospital administration broke down Monday night, three hours after the nurses filed a strike notice effective at 7 a.m. on July 11.

Karen M. Maune, spokeswoman for the New York State Nurses Association, said the session, which started at 3 p.m., was ended by the federal mediator about 9:30 p.m. No new session has been set, but both sides said they hope to settle at the negotiating table.

"There was no significant movement," Maune said.

Douglas said the talks mainly centered on economic issues.

The nurses are required by law to file a strike notice at least 10 days before going off their jobs. During the intervening time, the hospital is required to implement an emergency plan.

The nurses have been working without a contract since Dec. 31.

The results of a strike vote taken June 7 among the 200 nurses represented by the nursing association are clear in the filing of the strike notice. Results had been closely guarded until Monday night.

"The strike vote was affirmative," Maune said. "We got authorization by at least two-thirds of our bargaining unit or we wouldn't have filed the strike notice."

Maune said the nurses have tried several options to tell the hospital their concerns about pay, shift rotation and mandatory overtime are serious.

"Unfortunately, we saw what happened at the (negotiating) table, and that was virtually nothing," Maune said.

Douglas said the negotiator recessed talks when the nursing association refused to drop their first-year wage demands below an aggregate double-digit percentage.

The nurses' last demand was more expensive than their previous demand, Douglas said. He pointed to similar wage increases recently settled with other nurses across the country, saying those agreements "parallel approximately 4 percent for this type of settlement."

But, Douglas said, "We're cautiously optimistic."

ST. JOSEPH'S HOSPITAL

555 EAST MARKET STREET
P.O. BOX NO. 1512
ELMIRA, NEW YORK 14902
TELEPHONE 607 733-6541

June 28, 1983

Dear Employee:

The New York State Nurses Association, representing the staff Registered Nurses at St. Joseph's, has notified the Hospital that the nurses intend to conduct a strike starting Monday, July 11, 1983. I am sure that you are concerned about the continuity of care for our patients, and about the effects a strike may have on your own employment situation. I, of course, share these concerns, and therefore I am taking this opportunity to share some of my thoughts with you.

We will be meeting with the Medical Staff, the Director of Nursing, and the Nursing Management Staff to assess our patient care needs, according to the provisions of the Hospital's Strike Plan. There may be a need to reduce the staff temporarily if we are forced to close certain patient units. Please be assured that your department head will be communicating with you on a regular basis to keep you informed of the status of this entire situation, and of any factors that may affect the functioning of your department.

I am sorry for the concern that I know this situation is causing for you and for your fellow employees. I want to assure you that we are attempting to resolve the issues confronting us through every available reasonable measure.

Gratefully,

Sr. Martha Gersbach
Administrator

SESSION 965 (DELETED)
JUNE 29, 1983 2:37 PM WEDNESDAY

(Jane went to hydro this morning, and did well. I was able to move her feet down a couple of inches after lunch. Several nurses and aides were in 331 when I arrived. They furnished a very pleasant interlude, laughing and joking, kidding each other about everything under the sun, including their weight and so forth. I did wonder how they had the time to do this, but they didn't stay that long. Jane said they often congregate in her room around noon. There was talk about the impending nurses' strike but nothing vehement.

(Things were pretty quiet in the hospital generally, and Jane got an early start with her material, working it around the usual routine of medications and so forth. She lay on her on back.

(Once again, as he has often these days, Rembrandt spoke for himself through his world view.)

I enjoyed the bustle of the city, and I considered myself a city man.

It was far easier to purchase supplies, for one thing—and if you were a painter you needed customers and patrons, so it was best to live where the population was thickest.

In the backlands there were some itinerant artists who traveled from estate to estate, doing portraits of the landowners and their families, but how they managed to carry their supplies with them in some semblance of order is beyond me. Sometimes such artists lived for several months with one family, doing the portraits of the entire household—but it took a long time for supplies from the city to reach them, and everything was more expensive then because of the transportation required. Such artists were also given to painting landscapes. Sometimes they painted a portrait of the estate itself as well as the family members. Such paintings were indeed held in a place of honor, and given from father to son and so forth, staying in the family.

(Pause.) I believe that some such artists worked in temperas, and that they dealt with dry colors, which were then moistened so that they could be carried more easily from place to place. For myself, however, I preferred the city and the company of my own family, for the itinerant artists were usually unmarried, or they had to leave their families while they traveled alone. A lonesome existence, I should think.

I believe that such artists traveled in the same manner throughout the Danish and the Swedish lands. To me it almost seemed as if they had no country of their own, and were creatures of the outdoors, for certainly they had to love travel, and the estates were very far apart. In winter such journeys could be quite perilous. Horses and carriages took a good deal of money, and often such artists traveled alone on horseback, carrying their supplies in saddlebags, and were therefore at the mercy of the wind and rain and the blizzards.

It was certainly true that wolves roamed the backlands also, so those traveling had to keep an eye out lest they become a wolf's meal. That was not for me, dear sir.

(Pause at 2:50. Some of this material awakened old memories. I meant to mention it to Jane after the session, but neglected to do so. Early in the sessions with Seth, we were told that I had been a traveling artist in Denmark in the 1600's—coincident with Rembrandt's lifespan, then. Seth also said that eventually I gave up the roaming life to settle down as a wealthy landowner. Little material, actually, came through on such episodes, though I found them evocative.

(Some of today's material also touches upon thoughts I often have of different courses I could have followed in this life. I tell myself at such times that if I had it to do over again I might be much more of an outdoor person—living and painting as much as possible in the outdoor life, as opposed to my largely interior existence now. Such ruminations may stem from reincarnational memories of the Denmark period. I don't know, and haven't given any time to trying to more seriously learn if such connections and "hangovers" exist.

(The mention of wolves in the European lowland countries is also very interesting, since these days we're so used to thinking of that whole area being so heavily populated that such native wildlife has long been squeezed out. I suppose that in the Dutch backlands in the 1600's there was much open, even wild, country....)

Nor could I stand being so weighed down with the heavy clothes needed by such artists to protect them against the cold. To have no hearth of one's own seemed a pitiful life indeed. So it is true that I remained well-fed and warm. On the other hand, I had more time for painting—not wasting my hours by traveling all over the place—and building up routines that suited me so that I could paint in peace.

I did not paint the most miserable or destitute men, the most disdained, those to be found in taverns, half-drunken, by the waterfront. Some artists, I hear, specialized in just such subjects. Most, if not all, of my portraits were of people obviously well-fed, those who bustled about in business or profession.

(2:53. Jane paused at a sudden clatter in the hall outside 331. There was a small storm of nurses, aides, visitors, patients, carts, and so forth going past; momentarily I could hardly hear her speak.)

The days of ordinary men are not mundane or trivial, for in their ways they carry tragedy and joy both, in a balanced fashion, managing to forge some kind of peace amid an often disruptive world. The people I painted were ordinary men and women, poised between life and death as all men are, yet finding satisfaction in life's daily ways. People always had their favorite ornaments or toys or beloved objects or buttons, for however trivial such things may seem they brought a childish pleasure and a certain delight. So I tried to include them with my portraits whenever possible. Does the writer not love his pen, or the seamstress her needle? So I tried to include objects that were in one way or another precious or useful to the persons involved.

(3:00. Jane asked me to turn off the air conditioner and light a cigarette for her. "Funny," she said, "but I could feel his distaste for riding horseback in all that winter weather."

("It gives you a different perspective on life in those days, doesn't it?" I asked. "Especially when you think of those wolves."

(She laughed. "Yeah—and he was a man who liked to be comfortable. Well-fed and comfortable.... Oh hey: I got that Rembrandt saw several traveling circuses that came to town by ship...." And she was off again—this time speaking for Rembrandt.

(3:03.) The circuses had attractive girls who attended to the animals and did some of the acts. The whole thing excited him greatly, especially the animals. They had clowns whose faces were painted with white chalk....

(3:05. "That's all," she said. She began to have a BM while she talked and smoked.)

The people would talk about the affair for months—the circus.

(I thought the session was over for the day. Jane's delivery had been fast and steady, comparatively; I'd hoped that with our earlier start today we'd get more material than usual. But she'd done well. Peggy Gallagher visited and we talked about the nurses' possible strike.

(4:15. By then the aides had cleaned up Jane, and she lay on her left side facing me. And we weren't done yet.

(4:33.) Another thing I was getting was that they had jugglers—down in the street—you'd throw down money from your window. I was sort of seeing an image of a juggler, and he had a beaded shirt on with real puffed sleeves up at the top, but very narrow trousers, or whatever you call them.

I was just getting that from that top window he liked, he could participate in the life of the city—the narrow streets, the shops. They had smithies, where they put shoes on horses. They had milk in cans in carts. They, the cans, looked like aluminum, but couldn't have been. They were of a good size. They must have been certainly a gallon or two—I was getting it visually. A lot of women made their breads every day, but there were also a lot of bakery shops.

(4:40. "I've got to wait a minute," Jane said. "It always takes a while to get

comfortable after being moved around...." She'd really hollered when Lorrie, the aide, had tried to get her feet in a more comfortable position, so that one didn't press on top of the other: "Excuse me, Lorrie, I know it's not your fault."

(I'd been surprised at Jane's correct use of the word "smithies" for some reason. The dictionary verified this. We had no idea of what the aluminum-like metal of the milk cans might have been. I rank this intriguing question along with those about the dry ice/China, and delousing the house with tar, and the canals of Amsterdam.

(Because of this note, I took a minute to consult our encyclopedia re Amsterdam. It gives a most fascinating account, which I can barely refer to here, but can use for future reference. [The one thing not given, and which I really wanted, was the population figure for Amsterdam in the 1600's.] But Jane will be pleased to learn that Amsterdam has often been called "the Venice of the North" because of its system of canals. These days they total more than 40, ringing the city in concentric circles. Many ancient buildings still exist, including the town hall, built before Rembrandt's time, and one of Rembrandt's houses itself. The city was a cultural and business center in the artist's time, and still is; book printing and diamond cutting were two of its main industries, etc. All in all, the description reinforced my own strange feelings of nostalgia for a place I've never seen.

(The city's present population is around 850,000, which means it must have been considerably less in the 17th century. Along with questions about the city itself, then, would go those concerning the "backlands," as Jane had put it. I'd like to know about things like the wildlife—the wolves, say—in those days, and the itinerant artists.)

The children weren't allowed to play on Sundays, and they dressed very stiff and formally then. He even had trouble painting on Sundays; it was so against the temper of the times. The family used to sit in a parlor, talking quietly. It was a very somber day.

(Long pause.) Sunday mornings in particular the women and children went to church, again dressed in dark clothing, and anything frivolous was frowned upon. Children got punished with a paddle. The father of the house was supposed to do this—and while he knew it was his duty, Rembrandt couldn't bring himself to hit with any force at all, and the children knew this.

Actually, He was glad if they were slightly unruly on Sunday, to break the heavy serious aire *(spelled).*

(4:45 PM. "I'll wait and see if I get anything in a minute," Jane said, but this was the end of the day's session. I fixed her feet somewhat by propping them apart with small pieces of foam rubber.

(I read the prayer to her at 5:00. "Sometimes it seems so impossible," she said, her voice nearly breaking.

("What's that, Hon?"

(Her eyes were very red and irritated looking. "To get back home, and walk decently enough so I don't need all this...." She indicated her bed, the dressings, and so forth. "And in a fairly short time. I don't know how all that can be done."

(I didn't either.

("Oh—I didn't say this," Jane said as I made ready to leave, "but all the houses I saw there had steep peaked roofs. They might have been made of slate.")

SESSION 966 (DELETED)
JUNE 30, 1983 3:43 PM THURSDAY

(I arrived at 331 much later than usual—1:55. At 11:30 I received a long call from Steve Blumenthal, regarding the possible marketing of ESP class tapes. Steve talked about a lot of money being involved, but I'm very cautious about the whole thing. There are also many legal questions to be resolved about permission from those on the tapes, and so forth. I told him everything would have to be resolved through lawyers, and gave him Pete Harpending's number. I added that I have no time at all to do anything with this idea—which I brought up myself—and that I dare not get involved in any more projects. I said I'm starting to feel a bit harassed, and will not allow that to continue.

(Then on the way to the hospital I stopped to pick up Jane's voice-activated tape recorder.

(At the hospital, I learned through nurses and aides that in the event of a strike Jane's wing of the hospital would be closed and she'd be moved to another wing—just what I was hoping wouldn't happen. We like the setup we have in 331, and want to maintain it as long as we're in the hospital. This includes the staff that takes care of Jane, of course.

(Many of the people at the hospital are upset, for notice has gone out that if certain portions of the hospital are closed, layoffs will inevitably result for the duration of the strike. I said I didn't really think a strike would happen, but that it would go down to the wire before the two sides agreed, as much of the staff in Jane's wing would be moved as a unit as possible, to maintain continuity of care, we've been told.

(Today I obtained from Georgia, an aide, the letter that the hospital mailed to all personnel on June 28, concerning the strike eventuality. It's been inserted with the 964th session for June 28, the day it was mailed.

(Jane was weighed this morning, and was very pleased to learn she's gained a pound. Her weight is back up to 76. Her doctor was pleased also. [He said the doctors don't know anything about the strike; no one has told them anything.] I messed

with the recorder for half an hour after arriving at 331, but didn't get to use any tape. I've already learned that it's a more complicated mechanism to use than I'd expected.

(3:00. Jane began having a BM. There was much noise and confusion in the halls. Jane read the 964th session and part of the 965th, as well as other material I had for her to look at. Jane hadn't been cleaned up by the time the session began, but she told Sharon, an aide, that she didn't want to be moved off her back yet. Sharon said she'd be back; she also promised to bring in her copy of the letter the hospital had sent to all employees, so I could copy it for these sessions. It will be the same letter Georgia gave me.

(I should correct a mistake I made earlier in these notes—I didn't get Georgia's copy of the letter until the next day, the 1st of July. Sharon was the first one I asked for a copy. Georgia had her copy with her and gave it to me, saying she didn't need it back. This will clear up any confusion that might results weeks or months later in these notes.)

In my time, frames were most elaborate and very heavy, so when a painting was completed it almost seemed only half-done until the frame was in order.

Apprentices did most of the work. The frames were very heavy, and usually required at least two men as they placed the canvas onto the frame *(?)*. It was very important that no moisture seep between the two, and the frame itself was stained and varnished many times.

(This paragraph isn't clear. As far as I know, there's no way moisture is going to be kept from a canvas placed in a frame; both components are exposed to all the vagaries of humidity, dust, pollutants, and so forth. The situation is a bit different when watercolors or pastels are framed under glass, and the back of the frame is sealed. Maybe Jane can give more on this later.)

I did not particularly like showing my work in galleries because I feared the paintings would be marred in the traveling, and simply to carry such paintings up and down stairs required much care, unless you at first took the two apart. I did not like to do that, for the less you touched the back of the canvas and the frame the better off you were. No one ever thought of selling a painting without a frame, however, and I think that some purchasers ooed and aahed over the frame wore than they did about the painting itself.

Of course, we tried to keep the wood for the frame from warping, and kept unused portions covered to protect them from the damp salty sea air. There were also a few shops that repaired frames, for the artists were usually too busy. I could never take the interest in the frames, however that I did in my painting but I knew they were indispensable to the purchaser.

A good deal of time had to pass between each layer of varnish, so that it was completely dry and not sticky before the next layer was put on. The varnish in particular <u>smarted</u> my eyes. If you had a cut on your finger the varnish smarted there also. At times I tried to work with gloves. But found them—

(*3:52. A nurse came in to give Jane eye drops. As long as we had been interrupted I cleaned Jane's eyeglasses. Jan, a RN, stopped in. She didn't have a copy of the letter—RN's didn't get them, she said: Maybe Georgia would let us see her copy of the letter.*

(*4:07. Sharon came in to clean up Jane and turn her on her right side, facing the window. She agreed to bring in her copy of the letter. Sharon, an aide, hoped there wouldn't be a strike.*

(*4:22. Jane asked me to sit on the other side of the bed in case she resumed dictation. "I'm just not very comfortable," she said a few minutes later, though, and I doubted if she'd be giving more material. I fixed her feet with pieces of foam rubber, which helped. I answered a letter from a fan, concerning Seth and Alice Bailey, while waiting to see what Jane would do. And it bothered her: "See," she said, half crying, "I haven't done hardly anything today—"*

(*4:45.*) All I was getting was that he felt he had to compete with his frames even before they were put on—and every artist had to take those frames into consideration as he painted.

(*Long pause. "What are you thinking about?" Jane asked.*

(*"Nothing. I'm trying to avoid thinking."*

(*"Oh...." And when Jane resumed it was to let Rembrandt come through his own world view.*

(*4:53.*) Still, I found a fine freedom as I felt the oils flow freely through my brush, and on those occasions I felt that I was flying as surely as any bird.

(*Long pause at 5:00.*) I was getting something about he enjoyed trying to paint the effects of wind—for the wind suggests a power that is not visible in itself, and only its effects betray its presence.

(*Long pause.*) I enjoyed that great feeling of motion. Wind in the trees seen through a window, fascinated me. Though in the main part of Amsterdam we had few enough trees indeed.

I suppose I imagined the life force was like a wind that blew through the universe, filling all creatures with life. It seemed to me it had a murmur that was inaudible in usual terms. But that it possessed some sort of sound to which all creatures moved, as to a strange rhythm. (*Long pause.*) Would such a sound possess a color? It seemed to me that certain shades of violet, deep violet, suggested that particular kind of motion. I have seen that color also in the waves and in the sky on tempestuous dark nights—a deep staining violet.... a royal purple as it were, as if the entire earth were heir to royalty.

(5:07. Jane lay so still I thought she was drifting off to sleep, even though her eyes were half-open, as she used to do. But no: "I was just waiting to see what came through—." During the last paragraph of material there had been much noise in the halls outside 331.

(5:08.) I never tried to be a great painter, but sometimes I felt my paintings quiver with their own greatness, and I was mystified and taken aback, and wondered what it was—that force—that filled some of the paintings and gave me my very life.

Sometimes one of my own paintings would seem to talk to me, and in my sleep I often dreamed that we conversed. Sometimes in dreams I asked one of my portraits what color <u>gown</u> or apparel he or she desired. If I got an answer I would follow through on the reply. Once completed my portraits sometimes seemed almost as alive to me as their models were. Though not living, they seemed to possess the better parts of the people themselves, suspended as it were in space. If people lived up to their own portraits, what splendid people they would be!

(5:15. "That's it for the moment," Jane said.

("That's a pretty good line," I said, referring to people living up to their own portraits, and we both laughed. Another one of those ideas that is obvious once mentioned. "Give me a cigarette and I'll see if I can get more." Jane said.

(5:20. "Now I got something that surprised me:)

That Rembrandt actually painted several pictures of women that didn't sit for him. He saw their faces.

I don't know anything about it except the women had shaded bonnets, deeply shadowed. Their faces almost seemed to appear out of the shadows. He was quite startled and mystified at the time.

("Well, the images were obviously strong enough for him to paint them," I said when Jane paused. "These days people do that all the time—that is, work without models. It must have been quite unconventional then, though. Even I do it.")

They were profiles, and one at least had folded hands. And there was something strange and intriguing about the folds of the dresses where the hands appeared—they seemed to possess some kind of mystery, and were evocative of some color he'd never seen. I'm not sure, but that's what I got. I think one was framed by a window. He felt as if the face appeared from nowhere.

There were two such paintings. And I think one had a cupboard, and the cupboard seemed to have that strange kind of shadow, that to him at least it seemed quite mysterious. Both paintings seemed to possess an odd secrecy, as if he'd caught some different reality unawares.

(Pause at 5:30. There was much noise in the halls.) In at least one of them

the face was turned to the left. No one ever commented about it.

There was also a death scene he painted. This time the person was a man, and in the way it was painted he thought—

(Jan, a RN, stopped in to say good night. After the interruption I read to Jane her material from 5:20.)

—that other faces appeared in the shadows that he hadn't intended to paint. They weren't complete, yet features definitely were suggested. I think in the painting there was also a candle, and that these odd features seemed to happen in the shadows from the candle, and the dying man had a nightcap on his head.

(5:34 PM. After a long pause we realized that the session was over. We'd let Jane's cigarette burn out in the ashtray—something we seldom do. She wanted to be turned back on her back. Jane was glad to "get that much."

(I explained that I couldn't pinpoint any particular work by Rembrandt that would fit the information she'd given, but that that didn't mean anything. This observation led me to mention a group of questions I'd had for some time now— principally concerning paintings by Rembrandt that hadn't survived into our time, or for that matter were quite unknown. They could have been lost in a number of ways—through fire, theft, neglect, accident, etc. They could have even been obliterated through someone painting over their board or canvas surfaces, not realizing or caring about their original value.

(I read the prayer to Jane at 5:40. There was much noise, clatter and confusion in the halls now.)

DELETED SESSION
JULY 1, 1983 3:45 PM FRIDAY

(Jane called at 10:25 this morning to tell me that Frank Longwell had visited her last night. Via the Ryall brothers, Frank had relayed the news that in her latest book the actress Shirley MacLaine had devoted two pages to our work in very favorable terms. We haven't seen the book, of course. The information reminded me that perhaps two weeks ago, when I had supper with the Bumbalos, Margaret had let me borrow a woman's magazine containing excerpts from the MacLaine book. We hadn't been mentioned in that article. I remember telling Jane afterward that I thought some of the statements she'd made—the actress—about reincarnation had sounded too simplistic, even dogmatic. But I suppose we'll track down a copy of the book. It hasn't been mentioned in any of the mail we've received, although I'm a couple of weeks behind in opening it.

(I took with me to the hospital the letter we received from Eleanor Friede, re a possible publication of Emir by Ten Speed Press. Jane read the letter, plus an article about Ten Speed in Publisher's Weekly—very favorable—plus Session 965 of the Rembrandt material and the start of 966.

(She went to hydro this morning, and did well. We tinkered with the voice-activated tape recorder, but so far she's been unable to work the unit by herself.

(After lunch and around the various regular ministrations she receives, we talked about the Rembrandt material. I said I was finding it evocative in a way that the James and Cézanne material hadn't been, while at the same time I respected and admired those two works greatly. [I still read from Cézanne several times a week.] The Rembrandt material, however, is ranging widely, touching upon many facets of not only the artist's life in Holland in the 17th century, but upon the city of Amsterdam and its environs. The picture that is emerging is quite different, extremely interesting to me, at least.

("Those people in Amsterdam must have accepted their world just as we do ours," I said. I was thinking of how it might have been pleasanter to live there, then, than we might have supposed; at the same time, though, I wanted to come to grips with the thought—even a strange fear—of being thrust back into that world. Surely it would be horrendous to one used to living in the 20th century. What did they do about sanitation? How would you dare even drink a cup of water?

(But then, I said to Jane, one living in the 1600's wouldn't have felt any such squeamish reservations, because, of course, they'd have no basis for a comparison with anything different from the life they knew. How obvious and trite these observations were, I thought, yet I wanted to record them as part of my reactions to the material. I haven't asked Jane what her own reactions are; she hasn't said much.

(Naturally, many questions about the artist and his times have come to mind. I've already noted my musings about paintings by Rembrandt that didn't survive. Today I explained to Jane a little that I remembered about his domestic background: How, in between the death of his first wife and his taking of a second, he'd hired a housekeeper who'd eventually had him in court for, evidently, breaking a promise to marry her. I wasn't at all clear on the details, but told Jane I'd look them up in a certain book I had. The settlement of the case had cost Rembrandt some money, I thought. The disgruntled woman had been named Geertje Diercx, I thought, guessing somewhat at the spelling. Could she have had a French background, with a last name like that?

(Also to be elaborated upon eventually, should Jane want to, is the question of the way she receives the Rembrandt material. I believe that two main methods are involved, playing like counterpoint to each other; Jane's own verbal translations of what she mentally sees visually, and the material she relates in the first person singu-

*lar, as though it comes from the artist directly; actually it stems from Rembrandt's
world view. I don't think either one us is under any illusion that Rembrandt himself
is speaking directly to us, that in whatever fashion he peers "down" at us as we sit in
that hospital room....*

*(There are obviously many fascinating questions here. One could start, for
instance, with the nature of the visual material Jane receives—its completeness, its
color, its depth and perspective, its accompanying sound effects [if any], and so forth.
Its odors and memory; the way it can range about, focusing upon an individual or
a house or a city....*

*(Jane had a BM as we talked and discussed mail, and so on. She was cleaned
up before 3:30, and ended up lying on her left side, facing me as I sat beside her.
From down the hall came a familiar, strong female cry, "Nurse; nurse; nurse...."
There were by now also a number of other sounds in the halls outside 331. "I'm just
waiting," Jane said. I was very surprised at the material she began to relay through
Rembrandt's world view.)*

I called the woman Gerda *(my phonetic interpretation)*. She was the housekeeper and watched the children, as you say, between my marriages.

The matter in question was similar to a breach-of-honor suit. She made a
good-enough companion, and I gave her a few trinkets. She put more store in
them than I had—that is, she took them as promises of some kind. It did not
occur to her that I might marry again. She was fond enough of the children, and
had few relatives—I believe a maiden aunt.

She acted as head housekeeper. Of course I treated her kindly enough, and
never suspected that she misread my motives, or thought that I would care for
her in any permanent fashion. Her hair was brown. She was portly enough, and
around her waist she wore the various household keys—

*(3:52. A nurse came in to give Jane her eyedrops, but since she lay on her side
my wife decided to wait until she'd been rolled on her back later in the afternoon.)*

When my affections were awakened by my second wife, the housekeeper
flew into a temper and refused to hand over the keys to the new lady of the
house. It was an unpleasant situation. She threatened to throw the keys away
rather than give them up, and I wrested them from her—though without undue
roughness. This so angered her that she brought the suit against me.

I was told that she returned to live with her maiden aunt, who dwelled in
another small town—that is, smaller than Amsterdam. It also bordered on
water, however. I think the aunt took in boarders, and the woman in question
took over the main kitchen duties.

I did indeed pay her a small sum, so as not to seem ungenerous. She had
been well paid—

(3:58. Temperature time, and so forth. The lady down the hall is really hollering for a nurse. She's not in our section, or mod, our nurse said. Jane was finishing a cigarette. "All I was getting was a little bit—"

(4:13.) She was vindictive, however, to have me brought before the court to begin with. Later I missed a few items from my various collections. Not expensive, but not cheap either, and I wondered if she had taken them. Perhaps not, but we never found the items.

The times were difficult for unmarried women beyond their youthful age. They had to stay on with their families, or live with relatives, turning into maiden aunts or sometimes acting as nannies, but unless they had some money of their own they always must rely on one kindly relative or another, and that is how I explained Gerda's behavior to myself. Surely she wanted to change her estate. Not at my expense, however.

Some men I know would have paid rather large sums just to stay away from the court's procedure, but I would have felt cowardly acting in such a fashion.

(Pause at 4:20.) Also, I knew a few of those men who sat in judgment. They were kindly disposed toward me, and knew I would not make the woman false promises.

(4:21. "How long have I been in this position?" Jane asked. I told her just about an hour. She wanted to go back on her back. I finally pressed the call button to get her moved. I retired to my other chair to work on mail while a couple of aides repositioned Jane. "Okay," she said after she'd been made comfortable and all had left, "come on over."

(4:35.) All in all it was an unpleasant episode, but the main point in my favor was that I had signed no legal papers making any promises at all. She could have stayed on as head housekeeper if her temperament had not betrayed her into making such false statements. Some unmarried women did find excellent positions, if they were lucky, as head housekeepers, trusted by both the master and the mistress of the house. They were often named in the families' wills. Thus they were able to collect a small cache of their own.

(Long pause at 4:40.) There were several women I had vaguely considered as wives between my first marriage and my second, but my feelings were not strong enough to really drive me into action, and while I dallied, trying to make up my mind, other men spoke and the women married.

Husbands were usually, though not always, a good deal older than their wives—and it was of course unfortunate that so many wives died in childbirth. The doctors seemed unable to prevent such tragedies. It was not unusual for a man in his 50's to marry for the second time, choosing a girl in her teens, and if he was well-situated her family was indeed pleased, and considered the marriage a great success.

(Long pause.) I was plunged into the deepest mood of melancholy after my first wife's death, and I hired Gerda as housekeeper almost without looking at her, but satisfied with her references. She had held such positions before, and apparently without any difficulties.

(Long pause at 4:45. The woman down the hall was still calling for a nurse. There was much noise in the hall beside that, also. Elevator doors are perhaps 20 feet away. A heavy white draw curtain shields the door of 331 from the stares of passers-by, but not their voices. I knew a hospital employee was standing in front of the elevator doors when she yelled out, "I might be going on a couple month's vacation." Referring to the incipient nurses' strike, of course.)

I was completely taken by surprise when Gerda made her accusation, but I held no bitterness toward her. I was too busy to hold such grudges.

(Long pause.) It is true I may have indeed felt differently had she been young and beautiful, but her youth was past and her disposition, all in all, not that pleasing. A <u>truly</u> clever woman in such a position could become so indispensable to a family that she was remembered in their wills, and therefore able to collect a small fortune, or according to the circumstances become mistress of a house of her own.

(Long pause at 4:50.) There were also situations known to me whereby the housekeeper of a family gave birth to a child fathered by the head of the family if it were known or suspected that the wife was barren. Such a woman was well paid <u>for her labors</u> *(humorously and louder)*, though she could never claim such a child as her own. It must have been difficult for such a woman to watch such a child grow in close proximity without blurting out the truth. Sometimes the truth was suspected by the community, but if so no lips spoke the truth, and respectability was preserved.

(4:55.) If such a child was a daughter then the process might well be repeated, hoping that a male child would give the father a son. From doing portraits I learned the backgrounds of many such families, and when painting the sons or daughters I need not wonder why there was little resemblance to the mother, but only to the husband in question. As convention demanded, of course I held my peace, and pretended not to know what surely everyone suspected.

(4:59. Jane took time out for a cigarette as she lay on her back. I told her the material was very interesting, that even a seaport like Amsterdam must have been like an enclave for the natives in those days. The observant artist wouldn't have any trouble discerning any blood relationships. "I've got to find out what the population

of Amsterdam was then," I said again.

*(The woman down the hall was still calling for a nurse. Jane said she was get-
ting something on population, but that first she had to put out her cigarette. "I can't
smoke and do the material together," she said—whereas she'd done it all the time
when giving the Seth material. There was a lot of noise in the hall.*

(5:05.) I do not mean to imply that women were not held in honor, for
they were even under the circumstances I have just mentioned, as long as the
conventions were followed.

There were loose women, whores, who frequented the waterfront, and no
respectable husband had better get caught visiting such women. They seemed to
have their own positions outside of well-bred society. They loitered in certain
parts of the town, but did not show their faces in good society. Young men of
decent families had better not be found in their company, and such women did
not possess the—uh—ambiguous stature that was in keeping in some other
societies.

*(5:10. The woman was still calling for a nurse. I learned more strike talk out
there before the elevators.)*

They never achieved high position, for example, as French women did, of
such persuasion. They did not become the confidantes of men as I understand
they did in France. It was usually unheard of that they married into good families. Their children wandered the waterfront and on occasion begged in the
streets. Some such women did collect small fortunes from sailors, but they never
moved upward through the strata of society.

Their children were usually poor urchins indeed, living in huts or even
doorways down by the waterfront, collecting handouts from the sailors, or bothering travelers as ships pulled in.

We did indeed have many small-businessmen, and many shops, that were
run by husband and wife, with all the children and family members taking part.
Such was considered a most respectable and honest enterprise.

Thus young boys learned their fathers' businesses, and many well-run
enterprises continued for generations.

There were usually soldiers of one kind or another who seemed to live a
life apart from normal life. I knew little of them. On some occasions young boys
were expected to join a regiment, at least for several years, but in times of peace
the military were almost invisible, at least as far as I was concerned. I often wondered about the relationships of those on shipboard. Again, they seemed to live
a life apart, and from what I understand from captain downward they made
their own society. They were indeed a motley breed, and when they were on
shore they frequented the waterfront neighborhoods, and generally did not

appear in so-called good company.

The Germans seemed to hold the military in high esteem, as did many other countries. Some artists painted scenes of battle, but I cared little for such affairs. There were tragedies enough in everyday life without depicting life's goriest conditions.

<u>Now there were</u> honest fishermen and such—Dutchmen with small boats, and these men were indeed respectable enough, having wives and children. The boys often learning to fish as the fathers did, while the women learned to clean the catch and then to sell the fish in markets of their own run by the family. Or else they sold the fish to other fish shops in town. There was no dishonor in being a fisherman. All in all, we kept our homes and streets quite tidy by the standards of the times.

(Long pause at 5:27.) There were streetcleaners with huge brooms. These people were held in poor repute, however, and perhaps some were the sons of the town's prostitutes. But in any case they performed a service for the town at large.

(Long pause at 5:30.) The churches were usually Lutheran or some kind of reformed this-or-that, plain and unassuming, though often exceedingly strict. I still liked the Roman church's tales of saints, however, and had seen *(long pause)* some rich paintings, I believe Spanish, of Roman churches with their decorations of gold and their many statues. Such opulence both fascinated and dismayed me.

(5:33. Jane had a cigarette. "I was pretty well lost in some of that." She also said she'd been picking up that the old people were accorded a place of honor in the community. They all lived together: grandparents, parents, children, and so forth.

(5:36.) It would be unthinkable for a young married couple to have a house of their own. They lived with the parents of the bride or groom, and moved only when a goodly number of children had arrived, because space was so limited.

(5:38 PM. I told Jane I had to get ready to go, since I had shopping to do, etc. Her material was excellent, I said. I read her the prayer before leaving. The place was quiet as I walked down the long hall.)

DELETED SESSION
JULY 2, 1983 4:00 PM SATURDAY

(Jane went to hydro this morning. She was good when I got there at 1:10, but worried about her catheter, which she felt was leaking. There was some sediment and

mucous in the tube, although it isn't plugged up. By 3:00 she was having a cigarette before having me ring the call bell. Finally LuAnn, a RN, and an aide did change the catheter. It went well. They left Jane lying on her back.

(Jane's material to follow results from our discussion of that on page 90, for June 30. She'd quoted Rembrandt about the problems of keeping moisture from canvas and frame, and since that material wasn't too clear I'd mentioned that perhaps more would come through on it eventually.

(Actually, the first portion of today's work is a repeat of what Jane began to tell me before I was ready to take notes. Down the hall, that same woman was calling stentoriously for a nurse.)

I was getting images—that his house, like a lot of the other ones, had a steady problem with leakage. This is stuff I'm seeing rather than stuff he's saying. The water would come down almost in a steady small stream. And you had to be particularly careful that you didn't put your canvases and frames and stuff on that side of the room. Otherwise they could be literally, slowly soaked and ruined. And when I got that I also saw rain barrels. And then I saw some kind of white, smooth collars the women wore, like linen, so they must have had linen. But that moisture thing was what he was referring to in that other session.

Also, that we have no idea how busy those households were, at least for the women. They were almost like small factories. The women did needlework. I'm not sure what material the blankets were made of, but you saved them from generation to generation.

Cooking was a real chore, 'cause they did everything from scratch. And they ate a lot of fish because it was so available, and they salted a lot of fish and a lot of meat.

(4:05.) Some of them also had herb gardens on windowsills. Because there was so much water around they really appreciated the land they had, and they loved to have a small garden out back on what land they did have, and they liked to grow flowers in windowboxes also. Once the available land was taken up, like in Amsterdam, it was taken up. You just didn't go on building houses, and so property was considered extremely important. If you were a man of property it really meant something.

People might rent out a room. But they had no apartments as such —you know, like apartment houses. There were inns *(long pause)* for visiting travelers. Both expensive and cheap ones, and the cheaper ones would often just provide huge rooms where people slept in their clothing, and they might serve ale and a broth in another one.

They drank ale quite a bit, as a matter of course, but few people got drunk. They also drank wines. They were considered respectable beverages.

People rarely drank water by itself.

(4:10.) According to the—I don't know how to say this—according to the financial condition of the time, dishes and mugs were pretty expensive as a rule. They were also handed down from family to family. *(Pause.)* I was wondering what the very poor used, but I didn't get anything on that. If a dish broke you glued it—you didn't throw it out. As a rule the people really cherished the objects they had, entirely different from our ideas of discarding something for a better model or something like that. So the objects in a painting or still life really had meaning. The same applies to children's toys. Huh? I got that they had tops—you know, for kids? That were cherished, and they had fine music boxes for adults.

(4:15. Sharon, an aide, came in to take Jane's blood pressure. Being only an aide, she couldn't irrigate the catheter. Jane still thinks it's leaking. This is the <u>new</u> catheter, the one LuAnn just inserted. No sooner had Sharon finished than LuAnn returned, to irrigate the catheter. Her syringe didn't work well, and she left to get a larger one, a Thomas. Jane and I hope that irrigation is all that's necessary. I lit a cigarette for her.)

I also got that Rembrandt thought the Dutch had as good mechanical ability as the Swiss. The children really treasured their toys. If anything went wrong they were repaired—they weren't thrown out.

(4:35. LuAnn came back with all the equipment she'd need. The Thomas syringe didn't help either—the new catheter was already blocked. Jane was most unhappy at the prospect of having another new catheter put in place; last time had been quite uncomfortable. None of us knew why the replacement wasn't working properly.

(4:55. But LuAnn and her assistant did well, putting in another new catheter with little discomfort on Jane's part. Jane felt much better. She had a cigarette....

(<u>Yet by 5:05 Jane was leaking again</u>, around her second catheter for the afternoon. She was whimpering in frustration by now. We couldn't help wonder at the troubles the staff was having. I was also aware that since Jane was so intimately involved in this process, an unwitting or unconscious adversarial relationship might be functioning. I asked her to be patient. Maybe the new catheter was okay. Maybe the new leakage was a reflex action, I said, and would automatically clear itself up. Jane agreed to try."

(I read the prayer with her. Then as I was getting my stuff together to leave she said:)

They had glassblowers then.

(5:15 PM.)

DELETED SESSION
JULY 3, 1983 4:36 PM SUNDAY

(In last Friday's session for July 1, Jane gave some of Rembrandt's material on the troubles he had with his housekeeper. She came through with the data following my own description of what I recalled reading about that affair, and some other aspects of Rembrandt's life. Last night I read a little in the Time-Life *volume I have on Rembrandt and his times. It seems that Jane's material fits in very well for the most part, and where it doesn't jibe completely may be a matter of elaboration still needed to clarify her material. I made a few notes on what I read and went over them with her today in 331.*

(According to the record, then, Rembrandt did hire the housekeeper, Geertghe Dircx [I'd misspelled the name originally], in between his two marriages. As a result of the court action, however, Rembrandt paid her a yearly sum of 200 guilders for some six years, I believe. Speaking through Jane, Rembrandt declared that he "did indeed pay her a small sum...." I took this to mean a one-payment lump sum, although the material doesn't actually say that. This may be a point to be cleared up as this material unfolds, in the same manner as the problems with moisture and leakage in the artist's studio were resolved.

(Jane had relayed the note from Rembrandt that Geertghe returned to another small town after the trial. The book names a small town, Gouda, wherein the woman was confined to a house of detention or correction in 1650, noting also that Rembrandt may have been responsible for this. No details are given.

(There is another point that needs elaboration, and I may have mislead Jane here. A study of the Time-Life *volume tells me that Rembrandt may not have <u>remarried</u> upon the death of his first wife, so as to not lose an inheritance income from a young son by his first wife. According to the history, he simply took up living with his "second wife," who bore him two illegitimate children, and remained with him until her own death at age 37 in 1663.*

(In the session for July 1, however, Jane has Rembrandt remarking that he hired Geertghe "between my marriages." I must admit that for many years I'd taken it for granted that Rembrandt had remarried following the death of his first wife. It would be interesting to let Rembrandt "himself" comment upon all of this. The history uses words like "apparently" when referring to many of Rembrandt's familial adventures. I'm not sure, then, whether historically Rembrandt may not have remarried after all, though it "apparently" isn't likely that he did because of the financial problems.

(Clearing up such confusions may be most instructive in themselves. Jane didn't go into them today. However, she did give material relative to some other points I

described this morning, namely, concerning Rembrandt's pupils or apprentices, where they worked, and so forth. I also described his famous "Night Watch," his etchings, and a few other things in case Jane wanted to comment upon them I mentioned one of his houses, also.

(I might add that Geertghe Dircx was confined from 1650–1655. The volume on Rembrandt's life doesn't reveal what may have happened to her after that.

(Late last night Jane called me to say that her catheter had been changed <u>five</u> <u>times</u> after I left yesterday afternoon, and on into the night. Each one kept leaking, until finally one seemed to be inserted right. Four RN's worked on her. All in all, the changes went well, everything considered, Jane said on the phone; she sounded tired and relieved, and slept well. We want to get the lowdown on the catheter troubles from Jean, a RN. Jane said that as she was told, there are series of passages into or involving the bladder, like sinuses, and troubles with these were involved last night. I thought I knew anatomy, but that news was new to me. I asked one nurse to explain but she seemed embarrassed in an odd way, and I didn't pursue the matter with her.

(The afternoon grew quite dark and windy as it progressed; it was also very hot out, and Jane went through her usual routine of vital checks, a BM, and so forth. See my own notes. We even heard thunder, but saw no rain. Jane ended up on her left side, facing me. It was then that one of the nurses discovered that a couple of bandages had been left off the ulcers on her back. Sarah replaced them. All in all, not a good period for efficient nursing service, we'd say. The staff has decided to irrigate Jane's catheter every day as a matter of routine, however, in an effort to prevent future complications.

(I'd been working on mail during the afternoon. At 4:30 Jane said she had "a few things" if I was ready.

(4:36.) I was just getting that they got up very early in the morning — around 4:30. Some of his favorite apprentices stayed in the house, and the youngest of these would start out like servants almost, they'd light the fires, get out what materials were needed for the day.

Then he got up and had breakfast with the family. They usually had a warm meal, an oat porridge and homemade bread. If there were pigments to be prepared they were prepared then in his studio.

It is true that for some time he had rooms apart from the house that he used for teaching —

(4:40. An aide came in to urge Jane to drink some more Ensure or other liquid, since the staff wanted her to take in as much liquid as possible.

(In the Time-Life book, I'd read that it was said that at one time at least Rembrandt had so many pupils that he'd rented a "warehouse" to house them all.)

I'm getting this visually, so it's sort of hard....

I was seeing sort of a barnish place. Underneath they kept the horses that were used with carriages, I believe like taxis. They may have been publicly owned. I'm not sure, stalls and things, and he could smell manure, for example, a lot of straw around. Right next door was a large building *(pause)*. I think it belonged to a furniture manufacturer, and part of it was used to store completed work and supplies also. *(Furniture or art?)* It also contained several large rooms, and these Rembrandt took over. The most he ever had at one time was about 27 students. According to circumstances some of them lived there, or some of them lived at home—that is, he had a few local students. They also ran errands, and so forth.

(The Time-Life *history says, "By the late 1630's Rembrandt had many pupils; at least 50 Dutch artists served their apprenticeships with him." Some of these became very well known in their own right. The 50 number must be very speculative.)*

They did odd bits of commercial work, for which they received payment—not from him, but the merchants involved. He always had a painting in progress at this location, at least one or two, and several at home. The boys had to supply their own canvases and paints, and they learned to mix colors as they watched him work. Some older boys acted as tutors to the younger ones, passing on things he had showed them. In all cases they paid a fee to <u>him</u>, though this often varied.

On some fine days he would send the troop of them to sketch outdoors, and to begin work that could be finished in the studio. He also had them paint portraits of each other, and of him.

(Pause at 4:48.) They vied for his attention, and often there were small jealousies, but he tried to be just and fair. Sometimes these were boys of wealthy patrons, and sometimes they were sent by their parents from other towns if they'd showed ability at home. They knew how to use their own kinds of slide rules *(?)*, and each usually had their own boxes of pigments and brushes—boxes that they treasured immensely, either given to them by their parents or made by a carpenter, and these boxes were highly treasured.

Each boy had a small cabinet in which to keep his supplies of bottles and small boxes. *(Pause.)* Sometimes as many as four or five of this number stayed at his house. And these were considered highly lucky by their fellows.

(4:55. I turned off the air conditioner, since both of us were getting chilly. It still hasn't rained, after all the fuss. Jane wasn't very comfortable as she lay on her left side.)

They usually had biscuits and maybe warm ale or milk in the middle of the day. The largest meal was supper time. A good number of the boys stayed at boardinghouses, where they were supplied a room and the large meal of the day. Apartments as such were unknown. Rembrandt ate with his family with the large meal, and he always saved tidbits for the dogs. It seemed they always had one or two mutts.

(*Pause.*) He had to pay rent, though, for the rooms above the stable, and pay on his own home as well. After dinner he socialized with his family and friends, then he went back to work for several hours.

(*"That's all I was getting right at this minute. Most of it was visual," Jane said. "The horses seemed to be owned by the city, the way the city now would own vehicles. I don't know where the carriages were kept. They even had horses that were kept for fire—to use getting to a fire."*

(*I read her the prayer, and left at 5:07 P.M.*)

DELETED SESSION
JULY 4, 1983 4:00 PM MONDAY

(*This holiday day was very hot and bright. Jane looked good, scrubbed and clean as she lay on her back waiting for the lunch tray. She was a bit unhappy because she'd lost a pound, though, she said. I told her I'd seen Shirley MacLaine on the TV news this noon, plugging her book; we weren't mentioned, nor did I expect that we would be. SM is to be on again tomorrow. I'd tuned into her interview quite by "chance," since it's a station I rarely look at at noontime.*

(*Jane went through her regular routine. She was cleaned up from her BM by 2:45. Had her blood pressure, pulse and temperature taken as the afternoon passed; eye drops; caught up on her reading of the last two sessions, as usual. And she read the literature I'd brought in on* Pau D'Arco Roxo, *the South American herb that is supposed to be beneficial in treating numerous illnesses, including rheumatism. One makes a tea from the bark. It's said to help relieve chronic pain also. The story of how I learned about* Pau D'Arco *from a fan, and obtained some from a supply house, is on file. I brought the first jar of tea with me, and to my surprise Jane drank her first cupful right away "Anything, if it'll get me out of here," she said. To me it tastes like wood chips. I said it would be of use even if it merely stimulated her appetite—one of its touted virtues.*

(*The recommended daily intake is three cups, but Jane had only one. I plan to bring it is to her room each day. We may be somewhat handicapped trying to get her to take more because I'm not there over a long-enough period. But we'll see. We don't want others in the hospital to know about our new routine, until we learn more our-*

selves. I can see how Jane could take two cups daily, if she takes in a cupful when I arrive, and another before I leave. I too have begun using the stuff.

(I read the portion of yesterday's session that I haven't typed yet, and when I finished Jane expressed concern that the catheter might be leaking a bit. I hoped it wasn't; she looked concerned. She was still on her back when she began her material. I'd turned off the air conditioner.)

There were quite a few seamstresses in Amsterdam, and in most other towns as well.

The wealthier women had their own seamstresses *(pause)*, but the less affluent went to the seamstresses' shops. And the well-to-do seamstress had other women working under her.

(Long pause at 4:02. Jane now felt definitely uncomfortable, as though she were going to have a bladder spasm—"almost as if I were going to have one of those things"—but it didn't happen.

(4:03.) There were also women who just specialized in lace-making, and each class of people had their own kinds of seamstresses and tailors. He understood that some of the whores on the waterfront wore very expensive finery, and that some such houses had their own seamstresses and dressmakers right on the premises. If the whores were visited by any other seamstresses or had any work done by them, then the seamstresses certainly told no one.

The tailors also had their shops, usually for men alone, though again the very wealthy often had their own tailor, who would either come to them at a moment's notice, or who lived in the same house, in the servant's quarters, yet with a status apart from that of a servant.

(Long pause at 4:09.) He himself had a practice of visiting such shops, and if someone were dissatisfied or refused to pay the tailor, and if he liked the material, then he would often buy it from the tailor for a much lower price. *(Pause.)* If the clothing fit <u>him</u> he would use it. And if not he added it to his collection of wardrobes *(pause)*, in which case he could study the material itself, in case it should some day be appropriate for one of his models.

(Long pause at 4:12. Jane's delivery was somewhat slower than usual today. Usually she keeps me writing at just about top speed.)

As for himself, he knew several splendid tailors, and in sudden bursts of great enthusiasm he would go out and purchase attire for himself. It is true he did not always have the ready cash available, but charged the garments to his account and when the day of accounting came he was often hard put to pay the balance.

(Long pause at 4:15.) The very poor often did errands, or provided other services in return for a seamstress's work. *(Pause.)* Wives ususalsy kept their chil-

dren's clothes after they had grown out of them, so that future children as they came along could wear them. If it were not for that practice, then undoubtedly many children would have gone unclothed.

(Long pause at 4:18.) He often studied various versions of the color white, comparing, say, the white of milk to the white of linen, to the white of a flower petal, and was amazed that these whites could be so different while still bearing the same name. Even bleached-out ashes had a white look, and of course white changed as it reflected other colors. *(Pause.)* He painted strips of white—that is, using lead white he painted many strips, and then studied them in all different kinds of light to see what made them warmer or colder. He was interested in seeing if you could ever contrast white with white by alternating warm and cool shadows.

He often studied people's clothing also, for it was dyed, and he wondered how to duplicate in paint *(pause)* those shades he admired in clothing.

(Long pause at 4:24.) Whenever he had the opportunity he questioned both tailors and seamstresses as to the nature of the dyes used to produce the colors, and he tried various crushed flower petals himself. When left alone, or dried, some dissolved into the finest dust.

(Pause.) On some occasions he did indeed have to pay off some debts with paintings, but this was not so unusual for the times. And while he did not like the procedure he did not feel that it went against his honor, either—for the paintings, he reasoned, had far more value in all than whatever items it was he had to trade them for. An artist's life was deeply involved with the community and with the world at large, and a good artist was respected by society, and held generally in excellent esteem.

(4:29. I turned on the air conditioner for Jane, and lit her cigarette. She continued to give material as she smoked—something she's seldom done in these sessions, as noted before.)

I was getting also that there were furriers—from the cheapest to the most expensive, used for exterior clothing mostly. The furs came from trappers, of whom he knew little, though he had on one occasion watched this one furrier choose from a trapper that selection of furs he wanted, and watched the trapper lay the pelts upon the counter. It was a good selection, from rabbit, bear *(pause)*, mink and even wolf. There was even talk that some unscrupulous trappers trapped squirrels and even cats, and tried to change their appearances in order to convince some ignorant peasant that they came from better breeds. Actually the peasants had a good sound knowledge of pelts, but people with a peasant's background living in the city often lost the knowledge their parents had, while not yet acquiring the wily nature of the doubting city dweller.

(Pause.) Some sailors tried to sell all kinds of pelts, saying that they came from great exotic animals from other lands, having dyed the poorest of ordinary pelts, hoping to cheat some greedy passerby with his own greed and ignorance.

(A one-minute pause at 4:36. When she resumed, Jane was speaking directly for "Rembrandt" through his world view.)

We had silver and gold, used by gentlemen for buttons, and often these were misrepresented—of a poorer quality than they were supposed to be, or converted from cheaper metals.

Buttons and all such items were saved and reused time and time again, and women often saved a variety of thimbles, which were highly valued for their usefulness and also for the decorations they often held. The same was true for pillboxes and snuffboxes. These were highly valued and individualistic. I collected snuffboxes myself, and pillboxes as well.

(Long pause.) I often had to go to housepainters' quarters, searching for various kinds of brushes, or for certain varieties I did not myself possess, and here again it was rumored *(long pause)* that disreputable men even killed certain kinds of dogs or birds to produce their brushes. *(Birds?)* Even goats' and horses' hair were used at times. Sometimes the thickness of a brush was composed of fine brush hair intermixed with cheaper bristle hairs inside. To purchase a brush meant to examine each hair carefully, and that I did.

(4:46.) Sometimes I would make a mistake, though, and find the hairs of a brush falling out in the middle of a painting, sticking to the wet oil like glue, until I had to fish it out myself. I taught my apprentices how to choose good brushes, and how to check the quality of their material. Sometimes I would use wood for frame-making only to find that I had been given green wood instead. *(Pause.)* The same manufacturer often made housepainter's brushes and artist's brushes as well, and if you had a clever and quick-enough mind, you could make some excellent purchases.

Almost every window had a windowbox of flowers, and I always remember those windowboxes when I think of Amsterdam. If no land was available the windowboxes also held kitchen garden, specializing in healing herbs for poultices and for teeth.

I also wondered if <u>teas</u> *(spelled)* could be used in my own work—perhaps as staining colors, but they were too acidy, and I was afraid that they would eat away at the canvas itself.

(4:53. Jane asked the time. She thinks she's been "close" to bladder spasms a few times. Her catheter tube looked clear, however; it had been irrigated this morning.

("There seem to be three ways I get the material." she said, possibly elaborat-

ing upon some of my own speculations in the session for last Friday, July 1. "One through me, one through him, and one is just there." They're all related, then, and could be studied both separately and together. [They already are, obviously, through this material itself.] In my own musings I hadn't made the distinction between Jane's own material and the material just being there. Note that after break she went back to delivering the material herself.

("He also tried to crush flower petals," she said as we talked, "to see if he could use them in his paintings. There was a particular rose color he liked, but they often just turned to dust." She's mentioned this subject a few times before in the material.

(With a laugh at 4:58:) At one time he even had the idea of trying to include the petals of certain flowers in his paints to see if he could capture the <u>odors</u> of the flowers themselves. If you painted roses you would smell them also. But the experiments didn't work, and he discovered shortly enough that the flower scent died when the flower did.

He'd seen cooks, though, throw together packages of herbs to put in soup to give it flavor, and he wondered what other ingredients he could use in his own paintings to excite the senses of the observer. Making the observer almost sure that he or she actually <u>heard</u> the wind rustle through the painted branches, or smell the sea air in the painted waves—to no avail.

(5:01.) Yet, he realized, if you truly excited one sense, then surely to some extent all of the others must be activated, so a good painting should activate many senses, even if it only dealt with vision alone.

(5:03 PM. That was it for the day. Jane coughed, and I turned off the air conditioner. She'd been very interested in the material, she said. I read the prayer to her before leaving a few minutes later.)

DELETED SESSION
JULY 5, 1983 3:25 PM TUESDAY

(I reached 331 at 1:10 PM. Jane was okay, but getting restless as she lay on her back waiting for the aspirin to some with the lunch tray. Her doctor had told her she might be moved to another floor if a strike takes place. He also said he'd be seeing her only once a week from now on, unless she asked for him. He still wants her to use the feeding tube, but Jane refuses.

(Last night Jane had called me, late—about 10:45—to say she'd been picking up more Rembrandt material. About how he painted his flesh tones, and some other things. I was very interested.

(Peggy Gallagher visited at 2:10, right after I'd finished feeding Jane her

lunch; the aide had been called away to attend a meeting of personnel concerned with the possible strike. When the aide returned she told all of us that Jane's wing will be closed between Friday and Sunday—the strike may start Monday—and that Jane may be moved to the 6th floor. The latest is that now the aides and others don't know whether they'll stay with the same patients or not.

(Peggy told the aide, Shirley, that she worked for the Star-Gazette, *and asked some questions, which Shirley answered—she's against the strike—but she couldn't contribute much hard information.*

(Jane didn't have a BM. Just this one change in routine meant that we were able to begin dictation a little bit sooner. As we made ready for the material we could hear that familiar female elderly voice down the hall, strongly calling for a nurse. And at times, almost like musical counterpart, we heard an elderly male voice, repeating the same name over and over. There was mental deterioration involved there, though.

(Just before we started I gave Jane a start on her daily cup of Pau D'Arco Roxo.*)*

In a way, the best way to do flesh tones is to pay them hardly any attention at all, but apply yourself to those areas that surround the flesh.

Artists who struggle to duplicate flesh tones alone often end up with flesh that looks like a porcelain doll: rosy and artificial—yet also contains a cold, marblelike white.

Indeed, the flesh contains all colors. I studied it endlessly, but always against varying backgrounds. We want contrasts, of course, but not harsh ones, and we want to give, certainly, a semblance of life. It goes without saying that however we paint we cannot produce life itself, and I am sure that the very earliest artists must have wondered why the likenesses they painted did not come alive. I used to wonder endlessly about that myself, for no matter how animated a painting was, it remained a painting, and I could not even breathe my own life in it if I wanted to.

The face should seem to emerge from the background almost as if it surprised itself, even if the expression is one of calm serenity. We want it to appear as if we have <u>caught</u> action, and pretend that in the next moment the eyes will move, or the lips or the head.

Uneven strokes of the brush produce this quality better. Even strokes are far too harsh, and tend to lead to a feeling of stiffness. The strokes should be short, also, and always more curving than straight.

(Pause at 3:34. Jane's delivery was intent, steady, and obviously this time it was coming through Rembrandt himself.)

One of my students once said, as a joke, that some of my brushstrokes looked like small wiggly worms, and without knowing it he paid me a compliment, because he meant that the strokes seemed alive. *(Pause.)* I should think that artists even in the far future will always wonder about the likenesses that they paint, wondering why they cannot produce life itself. Through a wife a man can produce a living son—yet in that respect a painting is sterile. The child shown throwing a ball into the air will never catch it, no matter how long you wait, staring at the picture. Yet the painting must give the impression <u>of</u> motion, so that you are at least tempted to wait for the ball to return through the air down to the child's hand.

In terms of association, it is impossible for me to <u>think</u> of a likeness without wondering why I cannot give it life, and it seems to me that in one way or another every artist is really trying to produce life. What a valiant, triumphant, and yet futile attempt!

The sepias are very important in suggesting flesh, for they also suggest the earth and the fruits thereof. In the shadows or material surrounding the flesh there should also be some dark green glimpses, but not continuous. Small but uneven strokes, alternating with the tiniest smidgeon of lead white, and when that is dry—

(Long pause at 3:42.)—I'm trying to get the color — it should be covered with a very soft transparent burnt orange.

(Jane looked quizzically at me as she delivered that last line, and I nodded affirmatively, since I thought the burnt orange she mentioned fit in very well with Rembrandt's approach to color in flesh.)

All of this done with a very quick hand, so that it seems you have painted a <u>glimpse</u> of flesh, and therefore suggested the flesh's motion.

I mentioned painting the eyes before *(page 24)*, and the whites of the eyes should contain the same glints as I have just mentioned, as if they are catching the same glints that are there even as moonlight catches the light through the clouds.

(3:44. There was much varied noise in the halls. Now Rembrandt makes some remarks that I believe apply to Jane's production of this material. However, they could also be interpreted as referring to his "present" activities....)

The kind of work we are producing now allows associations the greatest play, and does not cut them off as convention dictates, according to liner conventions. The mind is far freer to roam through time, its own emotions or desires connecting to all others with like interests or persuasion. It is indeed like learning a new mental language that uses words, but in a strange fashion goes beyond words so that it is only partially dependent upon them.

There is a connection between what I am saying and the short uneven brushstrokes of which I was speaking. This is quite a natural way of communication, however, used for example by children long before speech is developed. Even then they speak in small vowels and syllables that again bear in their way a connection to the short uneven strokes, as if a painting transformed vowels and syllables themselves into strokes of paint, so that you have a kind of painting language that exists quite apart from the painted subject matter.

(3:49. Jane has a cigarette and some herb tea. She wanted to know if Rembrandt's material on painting flesh was legitimate. I told her it was excellent. It gave me the strong urge to try it myself, but I have no time at this time. I've been wanting to return to painting for some while now, especially since the Rembrandt material began coming through.

(Dawn, an aide, came in to take Jane's rectal temperature, her pulse and blood pressure, and to talk about the strike. Things were quieter out in the halls now. Jane remained on her back.

(4:12.) It goes without saying that the lips should never appear to be a straight line, any more than the nose should.

With all of these suggestions, however, the model must be taken into consideration. If lips that appear straight are a model's characteristics, then you may have to use slightly larger brush- strokes, or slightly more even ones. The same applies to landscapes. Curved uneven lines suggest the liveliness of nature—the curve of a hill or a cheek or an apple—and even the straightest tree looks false if it is painted with a series of long even strokes. Nothing is truly straight in nature, and long harsh brushtrokes suggest an unyielding quality, or a stiffness.

To suggest severity or primness, however, you can use longer, stiffer strokes, thus using the general ground rule backwards for your own advantage.

In a way the color of the skies contain the same colors that flesh does, only in different proportions, so a flat blue sky seems lifeless and unreal, whereas clouds give it life, and the suggestion of breezes can be approached, again, with short uneven strokes that suggest quick eddies of air.

(4:18.) The sun itself cannot be shown adequately unless it be contrasted somehow with shadows and eruption of air, for at no time is even the stillest of air that quiet. The sun or moon are best suggested through their effects: rimming clouds appearing out of shadows, but never fully seen. *(Another questioning look.)* For that matter, profiles always seem *(pause)* more evocative than full-face images.

(Long pause at 4:20.) Half-smiles are far more attractive than full ones, as a general rule, though again you must take the model also into consideration. *(Pause.)* Warm tones are extremely important, but never appearing by themselves alone, but always amidst shadows or cool colors. This way the values take

care of themselves.

(Pause.) What I have said applies even more faithfully to the painting of women's flesh, faces, and smiles, unless of course you want to suggest a characteristic heaviness of manner or severity of disposition. Even then dark colors should be transparent whenever possible, so they do not give a flat lifeless quality. The shadows should always seem to move, so that your backgrounds possess their own vitality, and therefore add to the seeming motion of the model's.

Study people's expressions and how quickly they change. How many are characteristic, and never forget that gestures themselves possess their own kind of life. Gestures of course are indicative of motion, but overdone they appear untidy, or suggest tumult. You must also be careful about folk sayings, for example: green suggests envy, or sometimes greed does. Society's general understanding of colors, then, is important, as of course its understanding of gestures is.

(Long pause at 4:29.) Brooms suggest diligence, tossed clothes untidyness, so the objects in a painting, besides adding to design, should also help carry through the painting's theme, or the characteristics of the model.

Generally, children will move faster than adults, so with them it is possible to portray more gestures than with adults, for real children seldom stand straight, with their arms rigidly at their sides, and my own knowledge of my own children can attest to that.

Never use garish colors by themselves, but suggest them by bounding them about with dark transparent colors—otherwise the effect will be one of artificiality, and that in a painting must be avoided at all costs. You and the observer of a painting must play a sort of game. Both of you know that the painted branches will not bend; yet they must <u>appear</u> as if they are about to do so. So in all cases paintings should contain a strong hint of anticipation, a feeling of secretive motion about to occur. At the same time it should not leave the observer frustrated. His emotions should have a chance to complete themselves by the unity of a painting's design. This particularly applies to paintings with tempestuous subject matter, as violent death or storms at sea. If they are not done properly, from an understanding of the principles just mentioned, then people will want to run from the paintings as they would from such subjects come upon in real life.

The viewers' emotions in such cases are not esthetically satisfied, and can seem to be attacked instead.

(4:38.) Even war scenes in a painting must somehow creatively find justification, and provide a feeling of completion, no matter how violent the actions within the painting itself seem to be.

(4:40. Jane broke off dictation to have a sip of ginger ale. She had gotten some

of the material in images—some of it quite clear, she said, as when she'd glimpsed the sun through clouds, or saw a landscape outside a window. As she talked now she picked up from Rembrandt that "he didn't like stylized landscapes with castles, say. He turned away from them because they were too artificial."

(Since she was still on her back she had a cigarette. Then she saw a painting that Rembrandt almost remembered—was it Spanish? She picked up that he never used black by itself. It was too dead.

(I applied some lipstick to her, and then read the prayer to her, since it was later than she'd thought it was. She seemed hesitant about ending the session, though, so I asked her if she wanted to continue. She said yes.

(4:49.) We had fine maps. I used to look at them and try to imagine the many lands they portrayed, with their actual mountains and valleys and hillsides and villages.

I would even try to paint in my mind some gigantic canvas that would suggest the great variety of the world with all its peoples. It seemed as if there were a million different varieties of flesh tones, from Chinese to African, and I tried to paint many strange faces in my mind. I thought that in one way an excellent portrait suggested every other face on earth, while still being its own individual self. It was an impossible venture, a heroic enterprise. But somehow I hoped that one of my paintings in a way stood for all of mankind, as if one hillside implied all others, and one small waterfall suggested all the great waterfalls of the world—and yet was done so that one must draw the <u>implication</u> at least of the importance of rainfall over the entire planet.

The biblical story of the flood always fascinated me, for it made me think of power—the power of nature, and how it was used or misused, and that reminded me of the power of emotions. So I tried to keep track of my own, to see how they influenced my painting, and how in turn my paintings might influence my emotions. I could become quite desolate at the end of a poor day, when I felt I had not approached my best. On some occasions I even wondered why I ever considered myself an artist at all, so below my hopes did my efforts fall.

As far as my painting was concerned, I was exceedingly stubborn, however, and so I always began again and still again, trying to create a feeling of heroic completion, even though I knew the effort was futile.

Sometimes I began a painting and did not complete it for years, because the original inspiration had vanished. Then the day would come when I would remember it, and be seized again by the old vision. Then sometimes I finished the painting with no difficulty at all, though years had passed since I last touched it.

(Pause at 5:11.) Some of my apprentices at times have become so angered by their own incompetence that they attempted to burn their paintings, but I always held them back. A painting begun is begun for a reason—one that has nothing to do, even, with the models or the patrons. For a painting has its own impetus, and if you do not feel that impetus, which is something like a hunger, then your paintings will possess no life. A canvas is made to be covered. Sometimes you can stare at an empty canvas, and immediately envision *(long pause)* a painting that wants to be painted. You may experience this as a sense of urgency *(pause)*, even with sexual overtones, as if you were driven to create the painting's particular world.

I cannot bear to look at bare canvases unless I am ready to paint them. *(Pause.)* It seems impossible, of course, that one painting could ever suggest the entire world, yet I do think that artists really try to do that, using all of the techniques and knowledge they possess. I have painted valleys that I knew must exist somewhere, though I know I have never seen them.

(Long pause at 5:18.) No one item should overwhelm a painting, of course. For a creative completion would not then be possible, and such a painting leaves the beholder vaguely dissatisfied.

(Long pause at 5:20 PM. "I'm just waiting," Jane said.
(Finally: "Is that it?"
("I guess so.... Let me have a smoke and you can go.")

DELETED SESSION
JULY 6, 1983 2:35 PM WEDNESDAY

(Jane went to hydro this morning. She had her hair washed also. There's lots of strike talk around. Jane read Peggy Gallagher's article that I brought in from the paper this morning. She also agreed to go to hydro each day now, with Debbie and Darlene, who told her that if they could get enough patients who wanted to go to hydro, that that department might remain open during the strike.

(Before the session we talked some more about Rembrandt's tangled personal affairs, and how he'd mentioned being married twice, whereas the Time-Life *book declares that he married but once. I also explained some things to Jane about Rembrandt's great painting,* The Night Watch, *and added that the history in question states that the housekeeper who'd taken Rembrandt to court had been confined for some six years. See the session for July 3, for many more details.*

(Jane still lay on her back when she began speaking for Rembrandt in the first person singular. Her pace was very good.)

In many ways, I would find it an almost lonely existence if I lived as most artists do in your time, for when I was alive I was accustomed to the companionship of family; and artists in general, particularly in Holland, were considered most necessary to the community at large.

My work, obviously, was not done in isolation from my time, but grew out of it. Even artists of somewhat meager abilities were in demand, for if people wanted likenesses of themselves or their families then they had to visit the artist's studio, and it was to the artist they must turn.

Through the years I grew familiar with many, many families, of course, sometimes painting a child and later that child's children. (Pause.) A sort of clientele resulted, so that through the years the same family would have family portraits done in young and old age. So it was almost impossible for an artist to think of himself isolated from society. And of course this colored his work and his ideas about it.

There were also group portraits of many kinds, often because people could not afford a portrait of one person alone, so several friends or members of an organization would band together and order group portraits.

(Long pause.) There were itinerant artists with less talent who went door to door, or canvassed the poorer neighborhoods (pause), so that such families would almost always have a treasured portrait of a grandsire or other member of a family. Some artists specialized in children's paintings, and since many children never grew to adulthood parents were most anxious for such portraits, so that they would have some likeness of a child in case it was taken by disease at a later date.

(2:45.) We were as much a part of a community as any physician, and liked far better.

Local politics at the time varied a good degree from town to town. I was indeed married a second time, but due to the confused local politics (pause), I was married by the Lutheran church, but in a ceremony that was not legal in civic terms.

I took advantage of a community situation of politics and religion that actually existed very briefly, for I believe that later the religious and civic ceremonies became one and the same, so it is not quite fair to call my two sons illegitimate, and no one treated them in that manner. My second wife was considered very much the respected good wife, and my sons bore no dishonor. Such a circumstance did indeed allow me to continue receiving my first wife's inheritance.

(See the session for July 1 and the one for July 3. What Rembrandt was actually receiving was the income from his young son's inheritance. Upon her death his

first wife had left her half of their joint estate to their son. The wife hadn't foreseen that Rembrandt would run into serious financial difficulties in later life.

(Or had she? The Time-Life *history says nothing about this quaint possibility. But it seems that she must have known of the artist's spendthrift ways, having been married to him for a number of years. Why couldn't she have resolved to save something of her estate for the boy? Interesting. Her will also specified that if Rembrandt married again her sister would inherit her share, and with it the interest.)*

I did not consider that any chicanery was involved. Oftentimes local laws might vary from town to town in many respects, so it was possible, say, to avoid debt by briefly taking up residence in another locality. I had nothing to do with the fact that Gerda was sent to a house of correction. I believe that some items were found missing from a house where she worked briefly after she left me. When I heard of it, I was reminded of the items that could not be found from my own quarters after her unfortunate exit from my house, but I had nothing to do with her confinement, nor was I asked any questions about her behavior on that instance.

(2:52.) I had told several people of the missing items, however, and so when Gerda was confined to the institution it was possible that gossip may have formed quite a false picture of the entire affair.

It was also rumored at the time that Gerda had borne me an illegitimate child, for later the rumor came to my own ears, and I promptly disavowed it. I heard nothing of her after she left the house of correction. I did believe she had a maiden aunt in some obscure village, and I assumed that she went there.

(3:55. I turned the air conditioner off for a bit. I gave Jane a sip of herb tea and some coffee. [She takes a cup daily of the tea.] She had a cigarette. I had to laugh, I told her. It almost seemed that here three centuries later Rembrandt was trying to set the record straight, whereas in the Time-Life *history, those authors had also tried to set the record straight. If Rembrandt, speaking through Jane, was correct, or largely so even, it made one wonder how often and to what extent other historical "facts" aren't facts at all.*

(I also wondered if civil and religious history in 17th century Holland could verify Rembrandt's statement about the split of brief tenure between civic and religious law and marriage. Most interesting.

(Jane said she'd also picked up from Rembrandt material to the effect that some of his students simply took off—he knew not where to—with some of his sketches, also that some stayed with him for seven or eight years, and that he grew to be as fond of them as he was of his own sons. Resume in the first person at 3:10.)

Artists were often called upon to do portraits of wedding parties, and also to do group portraits of certain political events.

Members of various guilds often came for group portraits as well. It was known that I had many Jewish friends, and the Jews had many connections through their banking interests in many capitals of the world. Often because of this, I was given commissions by wealthy patrons from other countries, including Italy, and it was my good relations with the Jews in general that kept me out of financial difficulties for a long time. They even stood beside me when I was beset by other creditors, and on several occasions Jewish bankers bailed me out by lengthening the period of my loans.

(Long pause at 3:14. There was much noise in the halls.)

My fortunes were uneven. I might be in financial difficulties, for example, when on the next day a wealthy patron would commission a painting, and on the basis of that commission I could get a loan. *(Pause.)* I did overextend myself finally, it is true, but I always kept some property *(long pause)*, and I was certainly never destitute. In my later years there was a Jewish banker who undertook my financial counseling almost entirely—that is, he managed my money for me, and gave me an allowance so that I would not be tempted to overspend. For this of course I was required to pay a fee, but it was fairly reasonable, and I also gave him several paintings as part of his payment. Of these he was exceedingly proud.

(3:20.) His likeness also appears in another painting of mine, a group portrait. I believe I painted him as a cavalryman. Artists had to be men of business to some extent. There was no way out of it, and I think I vacillated, having both the qualities of a miser, alternating equally with great moods of generosity and fits of overspending.

(Pause at 3:23. Jean, a nurse, and Georgia, an aide, came into 331 to say goodbye for the day. Georgia doesn't feel good; she has an ulcer. She's been noisy and joking out in the halls. "The worse I feel the noisier I get," she said. "I don't like to not feel good."

(Jane and I discussed the many interesting aspects of today's material. She said Rembrandt would really have been surprised at our present alienation from society, as artists. She also suggested that I bring in an art book on Rembrandt's paintings, and leaf through it as I held it up for her, to see if "Rembrandt" had any comments on any of them. "If he does, okay. If not, okay," she said. I told her I'd thought of doing that, but hadn't mentioned it because I didn't want to push her.

("It must be great to have an overview like that, though," I said. "It stands for some kind of new development, an enlargement of what you can do—"

("But not a literary one," Jane said.

("No, but it's different," I said. "A larger perception of not only an individual, but a time." We began talking about Rembrandt's famous painting, The Night

Watch, which is some 12 x 14 feet in size—after having been cut down by a couple of feet on each dimension, I remember reading. I didn't particularly expect Jane to discuss the painting, though—nor was I at all prepared for Rembrandt's opening statement after break.

(3:38.) I produced a smaller version of *Night Watch* in my studio. It was nearly identical to the painting with which you are familiar. Only when I had completed that version did I begin the larger one, which was done in my other quarters, next door to the stables, in the rooms I mentioned before. These were very large, and to a degree unfinished so that dripping paint, for example, caused no problems. And its high ceilings were made for such a big canvas.

I only had help as students helped me with the vast bulk of the canvas itself, for it was very heavy and hard to handle. Also, some of them helped in mixing colors, but only after I coached them, and was certain that the colors met my strict requirements.

At the time I did the painting I had no student that I trusted enough to do the underpainting, or whose talent was thoroughly capable of the task. The main difficulty I had with such a large work was the placement of the canvas so that the light would shine where I wanted it at any given time. It was impossible to have the whole painting illuminated at once in any even manner with the candlelight. We were often annoyed when drafts blew the candles out, of course, and the students were busy enough keeping the candles lit, and seeing to it that the candles did not drip upon the canvas itself. Students served as candleholders, particularly when I was working on the faces themselves, so as to hold the lights steady.

The placement of the candles was highly important, of course—something you do not have to consider. Instead of letting the sunlight in, we kept the drapes closed so that we had better control of the sources of our light. Paintings done by daylight, or out of doors, always look poor inside. I always did my final paintings indoors, where the observers would later see them, and I am convinced that that practice worked highly to my advantage.

Even landscapes were shown when completed indoors, so if they were painted outside they showed to poor advantage in a parlor or studio.

(Long pause at 3:49.) We always kept buckets of water nearby in case of fire, for we had all kinds of materials and fabrics and dropcloths that could catch fire, and we used the water to douse the small fires that resulted. Fire could be quite a hazard, and many an artist also found a canvas ruined when he or a student held a canvas too close and scorched it in the flame. I also feel that the use of candles partially accounted for *(pause)* the excellent flesh tones that I managed to produce. *(Long pause.)* This particular area was barnish, so that there

were many drafts. *(Long pause.)* It was so damp that sometimes I imagined that the building was above some hidden streams of water—

(3:55. Bobbie and LuAnn, nurses, and Cathy, an aide, came in to see Jane, check her blood pressure, temperature, pulse, etc. I was writing these notes, my head down, when Bobbie tripped on the cord for the call bell, and fell heavily at the foot of Jane's bed. We all cried out in reflex actions, of course. The woman just missed hitting her head on the bed and the floor. I was all set to jump to her assistance, but she said she was okay except for a bruise on an arm. She was embarrassed.

(Jane ended up on her left side, facing me, when they were through ministering to her and had left. The air conditioner was on and I felt chilly. The day is much cooler. Jane hasn't had a BM today, nor did she have one yesterday. She's quite comfortable.

(We discussed the material. In her own way, I told her, she'd talked about a work of Rembrandt's that was completely unknown today: a smaller version of The Night Watch. *I've mentioned being curious about unknown works by Rembrandt. I added now that I didn't even know if any of his sketches for the large* Night Watch *still exist, let alone any for the smaller version. I only know that I haven't seen reproductions of any such material. What happened to all of it? It's said that Rembrandt made thousands of drawings, and that obviously many didn't survive.)*

DELETED SESSION
JULY 7, 1983   3:08 PM THURSDAY

(Got there at 1:10, after stopping at the bank to get money to pay for having the car's rust spots fixed next week. I'll lose the car for up to a week, and will take the taxi to the hospital. Jane went to hydro, as she'd promised. She also got weighed, and lost half a pound, in spite of all her eating. Both of us slept restlessly last night. I brought some Pau D'Arco *herb tea to her. She began a small BM at 2:15. By 3:00 she'd read the sessions for Monday and part of Tuesday's, and I'd read to her the rest of Tuesday's session and that for Wednesday. Many layoffs at the hospital have been announced, preparatory to next week's impending strike.*

(Jane was still on her back when she began dictation. This time she gave the material for Rembrandt, rather than as the artist.)

First I was getting that he also collected mirrors—all different kinds. Some were in the warehouse, some in the studio, and others scattered through the house. Wherever he was, if there was a mirror available he tried to study his own face, to learn more about heads in general.

Some people were delighted by their own likenesses when he painted them. Others were unhappy, but he noticed that almost all people were some-what disconcerted when they saw the finished product. He felt the same way himself when he did his own self-portraits, for each one seemed to reveal anoth-er facet of his personality than the ones before, as if each one were a different version, or as if he'd changed in some indescribable way. The change didn't have anything to do with age, say. Those changes he understood. But the ones he spoke of were more like transformations, as if he changed from one person to another between portraits. He knew of course how various expressions altered the face and features, but the alterations that always astonished him seemed <u>dependent</u> upon the features, of course, yet also independent of them.

Outdoors the quality of light was always changing, giving, he supposed, a thousand alterations between dawn and dusk. In one moment a field might be sunny, and in the next with a darkening of cloud the same field could take on a threatening cast. That much was clear. The transformations that seemed to hap-pen in his portraits, however, while they reminded him of the various moods of nature, also seemed to be of a different sort. It was almost as if his own features changed so completely that they belonged to someone else—sometimes even being reminiscent of a woman's face rather than a man's.

(3:17.) On other occasions a sly secret, childish enjoyment seemed to emerge from his own face. Sometimes his forehead as he grew older was obvi-ously wrinkled, and yet on other occasions it appeared smooth. At one time he used to think that a portrait should display or express a person's overall general temper, or disposition, or characteristic. As he continued to study his own fea-tures and the features of other people, he realized that the elements of personal-ity were far more evasive than that, and ever-changeable. The face was hardly ever still, even in repose.

(Pause.) It was indeed its own field of action. He had known, of course, that few faces were really symmetrical, but he discovered that the truly sym-metrical would be a poor topic for painting—or, indeed, any art. It would become boring too quickly. There had to be a difficult-to-achieve balance between mobility and stability in doing portraits, and the older he grew the more he thought that this could best be accomplished by those uneven, short strokes of the brush, and with colors that had a reflective quality, so that the use of transparents was vital.

(Pause at 3:25.) Some children's faces actually possessed an odd glimpse into the child's future appearance. Both the very old and infants had wrinkled foreheads, for example. The infant's wrinkles vanished. But still he *(Rembrandt)* was possessed with the wrinkles of the old and the young—the ways that they resembled each other, and the ways they were different.

(Long pause at 3:28. LuAnn, a RN who is involved in the strike negotiations, came in to give Jane her eye drops. "We're down to 15 patients," she said. "They're clearing us out." Meaning that the hospital was removing and resituating patients in our wing into other wings, preparatory to closing down sections of the hospital.

(3:29.) In any case, each time he did his own self-portrait, the results made him feel as if he'd painted another, different person. It was the same feeling, he felt, that—

(We had another brief interruption, someone asking a question of Jane, who said she'd like to stay on her back for a bit longer if possible. "Shit," Jane exclaimed when we were alone again.)

—was shared by sitters when they saw their own portraits. Some of them used to say that it was as if he had painted a part of themselves that they had not known before. Some even felt that though the resemblance was nearly perfect, still the painting was more like a portrait of someone else who had the same features, so he always remembered that the face itself displayed constant motion, continual change, and that with each change the colors and the values and the features themselves rose and fell, twisted and turned, forming new angles, curves, inclinations and hollows.

(Pause at 3:34.) When he did landscapes he felt that he was doing a portrait of nature *(long pause)*, as if nature itself was a gigantic sitter while he was a tiny artist, awkwardly trying to paint the features of a personage so vast that his canvas could only portray the tiniest natural characteristic at any given time.

(Long pause.) In other words, he tried to paint the face of nature when he did a landscape, and each different landscape showed that odd transformation that his own face showed with each new portrait. Nothing, it seemed, was truly still, but always in motion, even though the motion be the gentlest possible.

Feathery brushstrokes help suggest that kind of soft action, he felt, that soft motion, as in the spray above the waves.

(3:40. "Okay. I'll have something to drink again," Jane said. She had some herb tea and a cigarette. "It's funny. I can feel him working up to make certain points, but sometimes I don't know what they are until he gets there."

(The halls outside 331 did seem a bit quieter, as though there were indeed only 15 patients left. That total would apply to our "mod," or section. I told Jane that I'd noticed quite a few empty rooms on my way down the hall today, yet they weren't all empty by any means.

("It would be nice if they gave us some notice before they moved us," Jane said. I turned on the air conditioner. She was cleaned up from her small BM by 4:30, and her vitals had been taken. When I paid the gal who collects for the TV service each week, I learned that Jane probably wouldn't be going to the 6th floor, as someone else

had told us on previous days. But our friend didn't know where my wife would go, either.

(I read the prayer at 4:55 PM.)

DELETED SESSION
JULY 8, 1983 4:00 PM FRIDAY

(The hospital was very quiet. There was little strike talk among personnel. Jane still doesn't know where she will be moved. I took the morning's news article about the strike with me so she could read it; along with the session material I typed this morning. By 2:00 she was having another small BM, and was cleaned up by 2:35.

(Peggy Gallagher and Jean Sweeney-Dunn visited—it turned out that the two knew each other well. Jean doesn't think the strike will happen, that the hospital has too much to lose. I think there will be a strike, but probably one of short duration. By the time the visitors left Jane was unhappy at the time lost before she could do some dictation. Jean asked Jane to try physical therapy in the near future, and Jane said okay.

(Jane was still on her back at session time. I turned off the air conditioner for a while. The day was partly cloudy and windy, not at all hot. At a slower pace and with many pauses:)

A good painting will have a <u>theme</u>, or it will make a statement, even though the artist himself may not consciously know what the theme or statement is.

This is a kind of natural eruption; so that once a painting is completed it has the look and feel of inevitability, as if it always existed as it does now, or as if it followed some natural inevitable flow.

(Long pause at 4:03.) The painting should seem as if it has completed itself, so that you cannot imagine it existing in any other fashion than it does. *(Pause.)* The painting itself will tell you when it has spent itself, or when it attains its sense of inevitability, and then the painter should leave it alone, for anything he adds after that point will be superfluous. Certainly he need not be able to state a painting's theme in a sentence, for if he could do that he would not need the painting. A painting's theme can only be stated by the painting itself. No verbal explanation can substitute.

(Pause.) Any explanations about a painting can never really come close *(pause)*, and no painting really needs an explanation. The painting then speaks for itself, and makes a statement that can be made in no other way. It is as if the artist's <u>view</u> of life *(pause)* can only be stated in visual terms.

Whatever critics say about a painting does not matter, for the artist is inside his painting as he paints it. It is almost as if when painting an artist becomes an inhabitant of another inside world. No matter how objective the objects within a painting seem to be, a painting's statement is as natural as a plant *(pause)*, and in the same respect a painting's statement grows even as the plant does.

It obviously does not grow through time and space as the plant does, yet in some inside dimension of existence *(long pause)*. The painting continues to complete itself, on this other level *(long pause)*. The painting puts down roots that tie it to the time that it was painted, and yet also sends forth new shoots in an inner dimension in which it is given a different kind of growth—a growth that transcends time while yet being a part of it.

(4:16. Jane's delivery has; been very intent, if slow.) Such a painting also becomes a part of the artist in some way that it wasn't as he was painting it. The finished version is compared in this inner dimension to all other versions of itself that the painter might have executed instead. This process goes on continually, stirring up new springs of creativity, serving as a basis for other paintings even though consciously the artist may be unaware of this.

(Pause at 4:18. "Well, that much came together," Jane said. "Some of it was hard to get."

("Was that just you talking?")

("No, it was direct," she said.

("It didn't come through in the first person, so that's why I was asking." I'd wondered whether the material was "just there," as Jane had said it sometimes was, or whether she'd been aware that she was picking it up and relaying it for Rembrandt through his world view. In any case it was excellent, and full of the potentials inherent within probable realities, I thought.

(From the hall: "It's time to turn Jane—"

("Just as I was getting some more," Jane said. Sharon, an aide, looked in, saying she'd give Jane a little more time before turning her. And now for Rembrandt "himself":

(4:27.) I am still learning where I am, though where is not the best word in the world to use, if you will forgive a pleasant pun. For I am not in any particular world as you think of them.

I am beginning to sense a new splendid kind of art, though I cannot describe it very well, since it is so new to me, and I am not completely aware of it. I am aware of a very definite feeling of anticipation—and I do feel: my emotions for that matter are rather vibrant.

(Jane put out her cigarette at 4:30.) I sense a kind of art—

(*Sharon and an aide came in to turn Jane. My sense of the material of the moment was that although Rembrandt has been deceased for some three centuries, he speaks as though he died but yesterday. There's a collapse of time, or an absence of it, reminiscent of some of his much earlier material.*)

(*4:45. Jane began speaking slowly once again; she seemed to almost grope at times for the material.*)

The kind of painting I am speaking of uses space and time in the same way that an earthly artist uses consciousness.

(*Long pause.*) He begins with a certain kind of a threshold (*long pause*), then he mixes time periods again in the same way that an earthly artist mixes colors. (*Pause.*) He translates what you think of as minutes or years into a sort of visual terminology. (*Pause.*) It is as if a woman crocheted minutes or years instead of crocheting with thread or yarn, looping together space and time to create new visual patterns, producing colors far more brilliant than any earthly artist could duplicate.

The kind of artist I am trying to speak of (*pause*) can translate evenings or dawns into visual patterns, though while I am on the subject I should mention that we are dealing with visual patterns that are alive in this inner dimension. You could not see them with physical eyes.

(*Long pause at 4:53.*) Instead of values as you think of them in connection with painting in usual terms, this new artist works with an almost limitless number of perspectives.

(*4:55.*) These perspectives are power packed. Their vitality is far beyond normal imagining, but past, present, and future become legitimate elements within the painting at once. (*Pause.*) The past leaps out of the future. It takes exquisite—

(*4:58. "Read me back the last two lines," Jane said finally, after a long pause, almost as though she'd lost her way. "I stopped in the middle of a sentence...." Then, after I'd done as she asked:*)

—understanding and balance to manipulate such issues in these inner visual patterns.

If this material is coming through slowly, it is because of the nature of the material itself—because trying to describe it is extremely difficult.

(*Long pause at 5:00—Jane lay so quietly, eyes closed, that I thought she might have fallen asleep. Then: "I'll have to wait a minute, and have a cigarette. I can feel him, or me, searching for a way to try to make the stuff understandable to us—"*)

("*Okay.*")

("*Oh—one thing I got just as I said that:*")

Rembrandt wanted to make sure that we realized we still were dealing with images and visual patterns, even though an inner vision was involved.

(5:05.) I just can't get this clear, but like now when you draw a picture of a house you can only paint the inside of it or the outside of it, or whatever, but this other-world kind of artist would only have to paint the outside of the house and the inside would appear as well, appearing in a different kind of space than we perceive. I got that clear.

(5:06 PM. That was the end of some excellent material. I explained to Jane it was strongly evocative of a TV program called Entertainment Tonight *that I'd "accidentally" tuned in to last night while eating supper on the couch. A long segment of the show had revealed how computer operators can now create three-dimensional-appearing objects on the screen—objects that have never existed in "real" life. It was explained further that not only can this be done with objects like balls and houses, and so forth, but with human beings as well. In the planning stages are projects to make movies with images of real-life actors—Marlon Brando, say—that the actor in question never made. The recreated images of the said actor will act out his or her role just as they might in real life—yet it will all be an act of creation on a computer screen.*

(The show had sample footage of the creation and movement of various objects, fitting together and moving through each other in different ways, but would not release any of the experimental work involving "people." I tried to explain to Jane how I thought that what I'd seen was at least a pale echo of what Rembrandt meant.

(I read the prayer, then left by 5:20.

(Jane called me late—about 10:30 PM.)

DELETED SESSION
JULY 10, 1983 1:58 PM SUNDAY

(No Rembrandt material came through yesterday—Jane missed for only the second time since she began this project on June 9. In other words, she's had 30 Rembrandt sessions.

(We missed because yesterday she was moved out of 331 and back into her old room, 350, in Rehabilitation. The move was very stressful. "I really feel trapped here," Jane said through her tears, and I didn't feel much better. I was also angry with her and myself. "Well, it takes a while to get into a fix like we're in," I said, "like a lifetime...."

(I've made extensive notes on the transfer, and it isn't necessary to use them all here. The upshot of it all is that Jane doesn't care for rehab, nor do I; I even suspect that the feeling may be mutual on the rehab staff's part. There is some sort of changed

or charged atmosphere in rehab that was missing in that of 331, and both of us feel it. Obviously, personnel must be involved. Coupled with that situation is the situation of the strike: Everyone is upset. It's easy to spot omissions or deficiencies in service or performance, although some of those may stem from the process of the transfer, and people having to get acquainted with Jane, and vice versa. Both of us hoped the strike wouldn't come to pass so a move couldn't be avoided—especially one back to rehab. Jane had called me at 10:30 AM yesterday and told me she was slated to be returned to the old department. She cried more than once that afternoon, her eyes as red as I've ever seen them. For some reason, as though they're offended or moralistic, the help in rehab keeps insisting that my wife remain covered, instead of being allowed to lie nude and more comfortable on her mattress.

(The staff was obviously shorthanded, and I fed Jane supper last night. This didn't stop them from trying to change Jane's dressings twice daily, as opposed to the once-a-day routine she'd settled into at 331. A call to the doctor was necessary to straighten that mess out. I have notes on all of these little imbroglios.

(No sooner did I get home last night, at about 6:15, than Steve Blumenthal called. He and Tracy had planned to visit Jane tonight, whereas I'd thought they were to come next weekend. I put that off out of sheer weariness. Steve has talked to Pete Harpending about possibly marketing class tapes, but I haven't yet. Now the visit is set for next weekend.

(Actually, we'd been left alone in 350 yesterday for long periods of time. A lot of activity—moving beds, people, and so forth, had gone on around us. Having a session just hadn't worked out, and I'd answered a few letters. The time went fast. The TV gal turned on the set late in the afternoon, which helped. I kept hoping everyone and everything would relax somewhat as the days passed, no matter how few we spent in rehab. Jane read the session material I'd brought in, typed. She hadn't taken any of the herb tea I'd brought in. I was pretty unhappy myself: "Well, I don't know if it matters much where we are." I simply didn't believe we needed the hospital lifestyle any longer; yet saw no way out of it for some time to come. I thought—and have for some time—that one could come to accept such a manner of living almost unknowingly. It could insidiously manifest itself, and in so doing satisfy many facets and goals of an individual's life. One may not plan for things to work out that way, but once manifest they could become extremely difficult to dislodge. "I didn't get anything done today," she said, half-crying. "Maybe you will tomorrow," I said as I left.

(The atmosphere in 350 was much improved today, Sunday, I noticed as soon as I arrived. Jane wasn't wearing a gown. A nurse from 331 was feeding her lunch, which had helped. "These people are offended if I'm not covered," she said. "I think they're embarrassed. At 11 o'clock last night they insisted I wear a gown."

(They had given her a shower this morning, since she hadn't gone to hydro, and *she'd hardly needed that. It had also been very uncomfortable. I told her to refuse it after this. The staff is shorthanded. The halls were relatively quiet. The strike hasn't been settled yet; I'd brought in the short article from the paper for Jane to read. I also read to her parts of an article about Shirley MacLaine that had arrived yesterday in the National Enquirer. It dealt largely with the actress's hectic personal life. "If we're really mentioned in her book," I joked, "it may be a mixed blessing."*

(See my opening notes for the session on July 1, 1983.

(Jane seemed to want to get right to work, to make up for missing out yesterday. She lay on her back, nude except for the corner of a sheet thrown loosely over her hips.

In my time few people went to the hospital, except as a last resort.

Either that, or the ill person had no family to take care of them in the home. Women seldom went to the hospital for childbirth, and while it was fashionable later for physicians to handle childbirth, usually mothers-to-be were taken care of at the home, and the birth itself was attended by midwives. The entire affair of childbirth was considered almost primarily as a woman's arena.

No one in my time would think of sending a woman to a hospital to bear a child, for hospitals were for the very sick and the uncared for, and no one considered that a pregnant woman was ill in any fashion. *(Long pause at 2:00.)* Perhaps the midwives of the very poor were less efficient than those in the mainstream, but even the poor would never consider sending a woman to a hospital to bear a child. Childbirth was considered entirely a family matter also, with all the female members of the family involved, preparing for the new arrival, crocheting dolls or other toys, and making garments.

The richer families often had portraits done of the mother holding the baby, and such portraits were highly treasured. If the child later died, the family still had its likeness, and if not, of course, the painting was often given to the child when it matured. Some artists specialized in painting such portraits, and were sometimes jokingly referred to as "birthing *(spelled)* artists." They would often make contact with a family when a young couple married, and keep in steady contact, waiting for the first signs of pregnancy, and then without hesitation they would try to get a commission to paint the unborn child. If the child were stillborn, some unscrupulous artists would demand a fee in any case, for the time they had invested.

There were also some men that were called "vulture artists," for they hovered around the bedside of those seriously ill, trying to convince the family to have a final portrait of the beloved family member painted. There were stories about such artists, with fake tears in their eyes, parading about a dying person's bedside, eyes glistening with greed.

Such men were certainly in the minority. They were particularly detested by some physicians, who were bent upon <u>receiving their own fees</u>, and did not want the extra burden of an artist's commission to water down any amount that might have been promised them.

(Pause at 2:11.) Of course, many doctors also scurried to get their fees from a patient before the patient died, in case after death there were too many other debtors that might drain the family's purse.

Several more generous versions existed, as some artists specialized in doing graduations, marriages, and whatever. If they heard a marriage was about to take place, they would quickly contact the family, pressing to paint a group portrait of all those involved. Sometimes a person in a group portrait liked the work so well that he later gave the artist a commission for a larger personal portrait.

(2:16.) Many artists, myself included, kept props of various kinds to serve as background, rather than painting a person's actual surroundings. *(Long pause.)* A good deal of the people wanted their portraits painted as if they were at some exotic location, as a king's court, for example, and the artist would simply rely on his imagination, and that seemed to serve the sitter as well.

Physicians themselves often commissioned self-portraits—that is, portraits of themselves, which would later be placed in their parlors so people could see that they were men of substance. Sometimes they wanted paintings showing themselves with a smiling, satisfied patient, obviously cured of all ills, and so it went. As with any lucrative profession, there were those who misused it and betrayed people's trust, but most artists were men of fine character, who honored their profession. Rather than short-changing anyone, many artists had trouble collecting their money —and again, with group portraits a wise artist made sure that one person was responsible *(pause)* for the fee.

(Long pause at 2:25.) There were also costume artists —

(Phyllis, a nurse who took care of Jane in 331, came in to turn Jane on her right side, facing me as I sat beside her. Phyllis had brought a new foam-like bandage material that she wanted to try on Jane's nose where the bridge of her glasses had rubbed it raw. We talked about the strike, and national elections, and so forth. Phyllis and her husband live in Wellsburg, outside the town on Comfort Hill Road— beautiful country. After she left us Jane had a cigarette while lying nude and waiting for more material.

(3:06.) They specialized in costumes from other lands or from earlier periods of history. The paintings of the costumes were all-important, while characterization lagged well behind, and sometimes the features held only a small resemblance to those of the sitter.

At various times such paintings were admired or despised. A doctor's patient often inquired *(long pause)* as to what artist *(long pause)* the doctor knew, and the doctor might then refer his patient to the particular artist he mentioned—and if the patient were wealthy sometimes the artist was expected to pay a fee to the doctor in return for the new commission.

(Long pause at 3:11. "I'm just waiting.... What?" Jane asked when I laughed.

("I was just thinking of how thoroughly the artist was integrated into his society in those days," I said. "He and his abilities were just as much in demand as a farmer or a doctor or a shipbuilder or a tailor, or anyone else. It must have been great. I hope they appreciated it. Art must have been as common as your next-door neighbor. You didn't have to go to a gallery to see it unless you wanted to. Here certain people were born with certain abilities that fit right in with their times...."

(Jane lay half-dozing, waiting. "I do want to add just one thing," I said as she looked at me. "That art in those days—and maybe up pretty close to the present—was male dominated. There must have been many talented women artists, at least potentially. What did they all do?"

(3:19.) What you say is largely true.

It seemed almost preposterous to think of a woman as a professional artist. Women were almost completely identified with their roles as housewives and mothers. Besides this, much physical labor was involved in the preparation of canvases, particularly large ones.

(Pause.) Many gifted women made a practice of producing small watercolor sketches *(pause)*, honoring a child's or husband's or other relative's birthday. That kind of art, however, however good, was considered quite apart from a professional's. I did some watercolors, and I knew of other professionals who produced some also. I must admit that I did consider them as woman's or a student's medium.

(3:25 PM. After Phyllis told us she was leaving for the day I read the above material to Jane. Shortly thereafter other people came in to do Jane's vitals. My wife gets weighed in the morning, and she'd worried about this. She goes to hydro also, so she wonders how all of that activity will fit together with breakfast. I told her to let the staff worry about that sort of thing. She had a couple of cigarettes.

(At 4:38 Jane told me she'd picked up that Rembrandt had tried to become more interested in landscapes, but that he just couldn't do so—he was much more interested in people's faces, and the way their expressions changed, and so forth. She told me these things after she'd been lying there dozing, seemingly out of the mood after having her vitals taken.

(Bea Dibble brought the supper tray at 5:00. She didn't stay, though, and since no one else came in I fed Jane. No one had brought the aspirin Jane was used to taking with supper. She ate well enough, I thought, and then had another cigarette. I

read the prayer to her while we were alone. When I left at 6:20 she thought she was getting ready to have a BM.

(Jane called me at about 10:00 PM.)

DELETED SESSION
JULY 11, 1983 3:06 PM MONDAY

(The day was hot and brilliant. I took the car to the garage for bodywork early this morning, and am supposed to call Thursday to see when it'll be done. I took a taxi to the hospital and didn't get to 350 until 1:35. Jane's room was hot, even though the air conditioner was supposed to be working. She was in the midst of a large BM, and the odor was strong so I opened the window wide.

(I'd had to sign in at a desk in the emergency room, and get a red sticker for my vest. There were only four pickets at the main entrance to the hospital. I looked down the long hall leading to Jane's old room, 331, as I headed for 350, and saw that it was deserted.

(Jane went to hydro this morning, but didn't get weighed after all. She's been expecting her doctor but he hasn't showed up yet. The rehab area is rather hectic, with more beds being moved, a swarm of strange faces moving about. Much noise. Jane was practically nude, though last night one of the aides had said, "This isn't a nudist colony, you know." Her hair hasn't been combed or her face washed, so I did those things now, and she had a cigarette. All in all, she looked good and events seemed to be more under control.

(Amidst the strange faces I saw several that we knew—women I'd thought were RN's. A couple of them had Jane cleaned up and turned on her right side by 2:30. When we were alone Jane read the rest of the session for July 7, and the first part that I had typed for July 8. Then I showed her some of Rembrandt's work in the Time-Life book on the artist that I've been using as a cursory reference. I had to hold it up for her as she lay on her side, so I leafed through the pages having to do with his Night Watch, *and several group portraits especially. I felt a surge of emotion as I came across the pages containing enlargements of the main characters in the* Night Watch. *Even as I stared down at them upside down, I felt that powerful charm and intrigue they always roused in me. To me this was a sure sign that this was great art, even in these small reproductions. "Thrilling to look at," I told Jane as I explained some of it to her. "One of the great achievements of the species.... And to think of the conditions under which it was painted...."*

(Even so, once again I was surprised by Jane's opening remarks through Rembrandt's world view:)

I am delighted, of course, that so much of my art endures, and I am certainly pleased that you find it so inspiring.

I wish that I knew then what I know now, however. The kind of multidimensional art that I have tried to describe applies even more to portraits than it does to any other subject matter. *(Long pause.)* In my portraits I dealt with a model of a particular age and time. The kind of art I am referring to, however, manages to portray a person as he or she exists not only within but beyond the usual confines of space and time *(all quite intently)*.

It is as if each face suggested an <u>entire army</u> of other faces and figures, each fully vital *(intently)*, each revolving in a strange fashion about the core of being. *(Pause.)* There is an immense, largely unsuspected field of existence in which each personality has an opportunity to grow and develop. So in a fashion the face of one person can suggest his kin, both past and present, with all in your terms <u>moving around</u> time, orbiting it. Such a personality never loses track of itself, however, but revolves around itself as if on a silver leash.

(Pause at 3:14.) In the kind of painting I am trying to describe, then, one face contains a multitudinous number of other faces that are usually not seen in physical life, you must remember I am still learning, and still only sense the limitless dimensions of this new art. It is as if all my life were a preparation, however, for that work I hope to embark upon very soon *(all intently again.*

(Long pause.) In such work the face of the old man and the infant are <u>simultaneously one</u>, each alive and vibrant. *(Long pause.)* The colors that you see in my old paintings indeed do appear almost dark and dismal in comparison with those colors that I see sparkling all about me. It is as if an artist's paintings come alive, possessing their own will and volition.

It goes without saying that I am indeed only a student at this time—yet another larger part of myself is teaching me, and I can sense a limitless number of self-portraits, each portraying new facets of my own identity. And that identity reaches out to include so much more than I wonder now at my old ideas of the human soul and personality.

What is fascinating is my ever-renewed zest and vigor, a vigor so vast that it continually astounds me.

(3:22. "Okay, I'll have a sip of something and try to get more comfortable," Jane said after that very emphatic delivery. "It's real hard to get that, without sounding trite, without using just a string of superlatives. But there are only so many words around, and there's only so much you can do with language."

(I lit her cigarette. "One thing I wanted to add," she said, "was that I wanted to stress that he was still thinking about images, about an inner visualization." In answer to my question she said she hadn't glimpsed any of the vibrant or supremely

beautiful living colors Rembrandt had referred to at times. Yet, she said, in connection with the portraits he described she had seen "beautiful loops of color impossible to describe."

(Jane still lay on her right side. Since she expected people to come in soon to turn her, she had me cover her backside with a corner of a sheet.

(3:48.) The painters in my day were far more involved with their society than you imagine.

They dealt with people as much as they did with art, and it was difficult to tell where one began and the other left off, I was deeply engrossed in the lives of many of those who became my sitters, and in my time it was unavoidable that each painting became a social comment, or made a social statement.

There was far more diversity in dress and costume in one city than exists in your own time, at least as I understand it. Almost everyone wore a particular kind of uniform or costume depicting his or her social situation. There was a great richness and diversity then in hair fashions, costumes, and attire in general. Dress itself was therefore far more important than it is in your time.

(Long pause at 3:55.) In the book that you have been looking at (pause), much of the background of my paintings have lost their liveliness. You are correct in believing that the paintings were not as dark as they seemed to be. (Long pause.) It seems to me also that in some instances, unfortunately, some painting has chipped off, and perhaps been repainted, though the overall patterns have remained true.

(I didn't ask "Rembrandt" which paintings he might be referring to. The most prominent ones I'd shown Jane had included, The Night Watch, The Syndics of the Clothmaker's Guild, The Return of the Prodigal, The Jewish Bride, a portrait of Jan Six and one once thought to be of Titus, one of Rembrandt's sons, and Jacob Blessing the Son of Joseph. Several of these, according to the authors of the book, are painted in very thick color. This could have been chipped or damaged over the centuries. I think it remarkable that many of them survived at all.

(Long pause at 3:59.) The darks had far more glimpses of light than now appear.

I often bartered some of my ink washes (a few of which I'd also showed to Jane today) to various tradesmen for their goods, and this was also a habit characteristic of my times. We did a good deal of bartering. Even doctors often accepted various kinds of goods for their fees, and various kinds of—

(4:01. "Hello. Jane, I'm Sister Mary Lou—I'm your charge nurse for tonight." A youngish woman wearing a white uniform walked into the room. "Would you like your liquid tears now?" Jane agreed. After this interruption she began relaying the material herself.

(4:03.) I was getting that paint chipped off of paintings he did of waves, showing the moonlight on waves.

("I don't remember any paintings he did of waves," I said when Jane paused. Not a single one, to the best of my knowledge. Jane agreed that she didn't either.)

It was very thickly painted, like the other stuff, and it was sold to a tradesman—somebody from Venice. Could have been a very wealthy merchant. No—it was a wealthy physician. He simply doesn't remember the name. *(Jane laughed.)* He was simply much better at faces than names. I don't know why, but I got a jovial reaction to that.

I don't know how this fits in, but there was a very famous market at the time in Venice, where tradesmen and craftsmen brought their wares. It was almost like a community in itself, and some of Rembrandt's paintings ended up there. They also had exotic birds there, and parrots and some other kind of bird that talks. These were lesser works that wound up there, only three or four.

(Long pause at 4:10.) He often sent notes by carrier pigeon.

(4:13.) I was also getting that squab was one of his favorite meals — and only once or twice did he find it ironic that he loved the pigeons so, and yet would eat squab.

I was also getting that there were a lot of pigeons, and their droppings were on all the buildings. He still found them lively, and liked them because they were so sociable.

Other artists might feel differently, but he could never imagine himself a recluse, his art was so dependent upon commerce with people.

(4:15. Peggy Gallagher visited. We talked about the strike, although there was nothing new there. Peggy told us people had called her from Chicago who wanted our address; she hadn't given it to them. No one tried to see me at the house this evening at home.

(It would be interesting, I told Jane, if someday we could get more information on the paintings Rembrandt supposedly did showing waves. That he could have tried his hand at seascapes, for example, was a reasonable enough one, since after all Amsterdam was a seaport. I thought I remembered sketches he'd done of water— placid canals, perhaps the shoreline, etc.

(I read the prayer to Jane at 4:55.)

DELETED SESSION
JULY 12, 1983 2:38 PM TUESDAY

(The day was, again, very hot and bright. I was a bit late getting to the hos-

pital by taxi—1:35. There were four nurses picketing the main entrance. I signed a petition for one of them—in fact, one of those who had first put a gown on Jane when she'd been moved to 350. I don't know her name.

(Jane was okay, lying nude on her back. She looked much better than she had her first two days in 350. The room was warm but bearable. Someone had opened the window wide and tied back the curtains, since the air conditioning seemed not very effective. I washed her face and changed and cleaned her glasses. She finished reading the session for July 8 and the first four for July 10, as well as Peggy Gallagher's article on the strike from this morning's paper. I'd found an article on Shirley MacLaine in the latest People Magazine, *and brought it in, but Jane didn't want to read it. I'd also brought in one of Jane's little house paintings, done in August 1977, and hung it opposite the foot of her bed, on the same nail I'd driven into the wall during Jane's previous stay in 350 in late '82 and early '83. I'd also moved a card from Sophie Fordon, containing an oil pastel of a tree in Arizona, from 331 and taped it to the wall near Jane's painting. I plan to bring in more art for the room.*

(All of the people at the nursing station for C3R looked mighty busy as I walked by. Ron, the male nurse Jane likes, helped take care of her last night. He brought in a floor lamp that gives a softer light than the bank of examining lights arranged on the wall over the head of Jane's bed. Jane ate supper okay last night and slept well, she said. I asked her if she'd been weighed as scheduled Monday morning. "No, and it's fine with me."

(So far there haven't been any more conflicts about nudity, even from those who mentioned it yesterday. By 2:30 I'd read the rest of the session for 7/10 to her.

("I was getting from Rembrandt something about what you'd just read, about women artists," she said to begin the session. Then:)

Perhaps I spoke too hastily about women's connection with the arts. My memory is not too clear on that issue, and it seems to me I do recall a kind of primitive folk art. I believe it originated in Denmark and spread to Holland. In these cases women produced some small miniature paintings—portraits of their children or other family members. They were treasured mainly for sentiment's sake. They were never compared to the work of a professional artist. They existed in different realms. In most cases, for example, the perspective was out of focus. The figures were stiff, and the portraits were done from a full-face view.

I do not know how extensive such folk art was—only that it did exist. These are comments on the material given earlier *(in the session for July 10).*

What I wanted to do was to make some further statements about what I have discovered concerning dying *(spelled).*

When the person dies, he or she actually grows out of the earth's framework, and is placed in an entirely different context. In a way, the malady of the dying could truthfully be called "growing pains," as the personality bursts out of the frame that earlier held it to an earthly existence.

You step out of the times and places you have known into dimensions that were always present but hidden earlier. It is as if the perspectives within a painting moved within themselves. When you are living in usual terms you can paint a picture depicting a road going off into the distance. When you die it is as if such a road not only appeared to exist, but did in fact, so that you could travel into a new distance that before only symbolically made itself known *(all quite intently.*

(Long pause at 2:47.) Even when an artist does a portrait of a given person, he somehow feels that in some strange fashion he is creating that person all over again and giving him a reality within the painting that he did not possess before. After death, it is as if you do indeed create your entire personality over and over again, while still retaining full knowledge of who and what you were before.

Perhaps death just involves an innumerable series of self-revelations, in which you grow to know yourself in ways that earlier you could not imagine. It is almost as if you grow into an entirely different kind of species, while always retaining knowledge of your ancestry. You can even go back, so to speak, to visit yourself, as I am doing to some extent right now—

(2:51. "Bob, am I covered down there?" Jane asked, "cause I'm going to have a BM." I said she was, that a chuck was in place. "But it's better to do it than not," she said, and she did. I told her it was good material.

("Fascinating, that going back," she said.

("Sometimes you might see things you wished you hadn't," I speculated. "Sometimes you might not be able to stand it...." But we agreed that everyone had many things they'd like to look in on. "I suppose that even the worst crimes would seem different, though," I added. "Even murder would be seen as a transition, since you'd know it wasn't an end—"

("Also," Jane said, "you'd get to find out what you had in common with the person you'd killed." A most interesting point.

(3:05. I pressed the nurse's call button. Amazingly, in five minutes she was all cleaned up by a very efficient and nice aide, who also got the chuck out from beneath my wife's back. After the aide had left I cut another chuck in half and put it under Jane, just in case. Jane had a cigarette and some ginger ale, saying she felt more Rembrandt around. The day was hot, no doubt about it. Room 350 couldn't compare to 331 for comfort. A blast of brilliant heat and sunlight came in the open window. More hot weather is predicted for tomorrow, we heard.

(3:30. Jane's pulse was taken but not her blood pressure. The nurse turned her

on her right side, facing me. I helped her get comfortable, but not too successfully.

(3:49. "Oh let me have a cigarette and I'll see what I can do...."

(A male nurse, Mike, came in to give her eye drops. Neither of them was embarrassed that she was nude. But Jane was so uncomfortable from the pressure on her right shoulder that she couldn't concentrate upon getting the material: "I know I have some more Rembrandt material there...." Finally:

(4:12.) I was surprised to know that I had died.

The experience seemed strange and familiar at once. It seems to me we have a knack for death —that is, we seemed to know how to do it, and it becomes as natural as birthing, even though physically the body births no more.

I do not know exactly how reincarnation works. I have heard exotic tales about it from some of the merchants who came to sell their wares from foreign lands. Some, having traveled most broadly, were familiar with many bizarre customs. I considered them in the same light as fairy tales. I am <u>somewhat</u> aware of reincarnational existences, although they do not unduly concern me. I am not focused in their direction. I imagine that they are fully concentrating on their own experiences, and are only dimly concerned with mine. I know we are related, though the manner of that relationship is not clear. It is as if you discover you have an entirely new and different family of many members: you sense an odd kinship. I am content to know that such relationships exist, and there is a certain sense of anticipation.

(Long pause at 4:18.) I imagine I will meet these selves someday. *(Long pause.)* I am not speaking of an earthly day, of course, but of some imagined future, when the terms of that relationship will become much clearer than they are now.

How many worlds do we populate? I wonder—for sometimes it seems to me that with all these sensed selves I could populate an entire world and still have innumerable selves left over.

(Long pause at 4:21.) So far, though I do not meet people in your terms, I have hardly been lonely. I sense so many personalities about me that I feel surrounded by friends and companions, even though we never directly speak. I know that when I am ready those meetings will happen. I think I was so involved with people in my lifetime that I am dealing now with other aspects of art that requires more contemplation, more understanding, than I could ever apply to my art by itself when I lived my life.

(4:25. "Okay, I'll stop," Jane said.

("That was very good, Hon." Her delivery had been soft but steady. I'd had to ask her to repeat a word occasionally. She was still uncomfortable lying on her right shoulder. "And I feel there's more there." I tried to help Jane get better situated, but

my efforts didn't seem to do much good.

(4:28.) I am convinced that somewhere my paintings exist as symphonies. And I am still intrigued by the entire idea of creativity.

I always thought while alive that there was something childishly naive about an artist, as if he were imitating some greater artist *(long pause)*, playing with the blocks of creation while hardly knowing who was doing so. *(?)* I interpreted much of that in religious terms, considering God as the unseen creator, and the artist the ambitious child who was saying, "Look, my father, I will follow in your footsteps, and create as you have done." I still believe the analogy is still valid, for while I have not visited with any God in religious terms, I am constantly aware of the presence of some benign energy or force or power which carries me along, or fills me with vitality as the wind fills the seaman's sails.

It is as if on earth artists *(long pause)* try to use the entire world as a model, hoping somehow to recreate it on canvas, or as if they are given some entirely different task to perform than other men.

(Long pause at 4:44 PM. "That's it for a minute," Jane said. It was hot. Jane asked me to put her on her back, which I did. She had a cigarette. "I felt a lot of material there, but I was so damned uncomfortable I couldn't get it...."

(I said I'd often had similar ideas about the purpose of the artist in physical life—to demonstrate to the world that there are other realities and meanings in life beside the "basic" ones of gathering food, making shelter, and so forth. Otherwise, why artistic activity at all, since one can't eat it, or keep warm with it? Why are some human beings born to be artists?

(I added that it could turn out to be quite ironic that eventually it would be recognized by all that artists had all along been offering evidence for the afterdeath reality. Evidence that had been largely ignored through the centuries. This brought up the very interesting question of the role of other kinds of creative activity. Certainly the poets and writers had been offering their own sorts of evidence for survival of the human spirit. So has religion in innumerable ways. Yet, we still cannot accept wholeheartedly the idea of survival. There must be a host of reasons for this. A simple acceptance, I told Jane, would most likely bring about such vast changes in our societies and cultures that the very idea of the change itself had come to mitigate against change....)

DELETED SESSION
JULY 13, 1983 3:42 PM WEDNESDAY

(My own notes for today's events at the hospital run to three full handwritten

pages, so I'll only summarize them here. Jane had been involved in another hassle with nudity. "What if a cleaning man comes into the room?" Pam, an aide, had asked this morning. Jane had gotten several things straight with her doctor this morning, including the nudity bit, not being given a shower on Sunday when hydro is closed, and so forth. Pam and others, however, later asked the doctor if he minded if they used a canopy on Jane's bed, a metal frame device to hold a sheet up off her body. Jane was waiting for the frame to be brought in when I arrived. She was obviously upset again. I put in a call to the doctor's office in an effort to forestall the canopy being used.

(Yesterday the temperature had reached 99 degrees, but today was cooler and Jane's window was closed. Jane's doctor had said she could go back to 331 as soon as the strike was over, and that she'd "be there for a while." My wife can't wait, and neither can I any more.

(The doctor is starting a calorie count tomorrow, and taking blood for testing. While I waited for the call Jane read the rest of the session for July 10 and the first part of that for July 11. She lay on her left side. She talked constantly about the nudity problem. She wanted to look at the Time-Life book on Rembrandt that I had with me, but thought she couldn't do it while lying on her side.

(3:10. Pam and an aide [who was black] brought in the canopy—a poor affair that I saw at once wouldn't work. When they had it in place and a sheet pulled up, three-quarters of Jane was still exposed. I said with some heat that I had a call in to the doctor, letting them know my feelings in no uncertain terms. "My wife isn't doing this to bug people, you know." And more. "This is ridiculous." Right away the aide backed off, disclaiming any responsibility. Pam said the male porters were embarrassed. I said were you going to keep a person covered for 24 hours just because men might be in the room 15 minutes a day? She had no answer.

(3:30. The doctor called, evidently from his house. After I explained the situation he suggested a sign on the door: "Check with the nurse's station before entering Jane's room." I said good. He also mentioned a fan. Jane can't be turned very easily with the canopy frame in place.

(I held the Rembrandt volume for Jane at enough of an angle so she could look at some of the illustrations and glimpse portions of the text, especially about the artist's early life, his physical dress and appearance, and so forth. I also checked some dates about Rembrandt's places of residence, as he moved between his native city, Leiden, and Amsterdam. At first I thought Jane's material—and my memory—were in error in thinking he'd spent his professional career in Amsterdam, but this wasn't the case. He had spent his first years as a professional in Leiden, however. Jane was especially interested in the reproductions of Rembrandt's first self-portraits, both in oil and as etchings.

(Jane hadn't had her face washed yet today, nor the catheter irrigated. I washed her face. She was on her back when she began dictation for Rembrandt.)

Your book reads: "He was ugly, and he knew it," end of quote. Untrue. I was not handsome in conventional terms—

(3:43. Mike, a male nurse Jane likes, came in to give her eye drops. He wasn't embarrassed. "I'm not if you're not," he'd said the other day.

(After he left Jane said that as soon as she'd read the passage referred to above, she'd felt an emotional charge from Rembrandt. "So that's what got you going," I laughed. Actually she'd misquoted the sentence. It reads: "He was homely...." I mentioned this after the session was over.)

—I was not handsome in conventional terms, yet my face was striking in its own fashion, and in many of my self-portraits I purposely exaggerated one feature or another, to see its effects on the facial characteristics—purposefully causing the features to all slump down in an avalanche of flesh. Or to squeeze other features together until they seemed to disappear, or to purse my mouth and lips into the tightest pucker to see the face in that fashion, or to study the facial motion in many ways.

I thought that only by knowing my own face completely, in all of its circumstances, gyrations, wrinkles, smirks, smiles or grimaces could I learn to understand how emotions moved the facial characteristics—so that in painting other faces I believed I must know my own in all its moods.

Often as a small boy I would stare into the mirror, screwing my face up as much as I could, screwing my lips and nose, twisting my features, taking certain thoughts and seeing what <u>expression</u> they made upon my features. I laughed loudly, sobbed, told jokes, and watched my face change with each display. I found that the most fascinating of pastimes. I pretended I was a woman and tried to smile a woman's smile. I turned coquettish and watched what I did to my features.

When I was punished as a child, sobbing loudly <u>with real hurt</u> I would nevertheless rush to the mirror to study my tearful face. So I dared show my face more than other men, in all of its moods and vacillations. I did not pretty myself up for posterity.

(Long pause at 3:53. Jane's delivery for Rembrandt has been quite emphatic.)

As my own children grew, I made endless sketches of their faces and their moods, and would often even rush from the dinner table to sketch a tiny angry face.

(3:55. A black lady came in to take the water pitcher. I ran out into the hall a moment later to ask her for ice only—no water—but she was already out of sight.)

My sitters on the other hand always wanted to preen and smile, <u>thrusting</u>

forward those social formations that the face takes when it wants to please observers.

People often wanted to hide themselves from the painter, even though they themselves had requested a portrait. They wanted a surface glossy view. They hid their emotions and tried to make their foreheads smooth, unwrinkled and trouble-free. I never stood for such nonsense, for I knew that in their hearts they really wanted me to see through such manipulations, and they actually hoped that I would see the real person they were hiding, and so I usually did.

(Pause at 4:00.) Many artists settled for far less, of course, and there were even those who treated the face as if it were nothing more than another design, almost geometrical—

(4:01 PM. An RN came in to take Jane's temperature. We thought she must be one of the supervisory personnel, since she was older and obviously still working despite the strike. She left to get ice cubes for the Ensure. Jane had a cigarette.

(I'd known all along that things were too simple. No sooner had I finished these notes than the RN returned with a male worker who carried another canopy frame. He inserted it into place in the bed frame, but even with the new position Jane was still half-exposed. He also banged her knees against the metal tubing while putting it in place.

(I was angry and Jane was speechless. I told the nurse in no uncertain terms that the doctor had just given us the word that the canopy wouldn't be used. It would act like a tent over Jane, I said, keeping heat in even if the sheet didn't touch her. Once again I said it was ridiculous. I had the feeling I was talking to an inanimate object, but the RN said she'd check. As soon as they left I took the sheet off the frame. With the window closed, the curtain pulled, and the air conditioner on, the room was barely comfortable. It faces the west and the sun beats in during the late part of the day.

(At 4:40 I put in another call to the doctor. Ten minutes later I heard a female voice in the hall call out. "Janey, your doctor wants to talk to you on the phone." Our phone hadn't rung; it gave a busy signal when I picked it up. I worked on these notes. I'd explained the situation to the doctor's nurse. I hoped that now he was talking to someone at the nurse's station, C3R.

(For once I was right. At 4:55 the RN came in and took away the canopy frame. Jane hadn't said anything about it during the second episode. I purposely refrained from asking her what she was thinking. Ten minutes later the same RN was back, asking if I could stay to feed Jane. I apologized that I couldn't, since the taxi would be waiting for me at 5:30. It wasn't until some little time later that I came to regret my action. I could have called and had the ride home postponed until I called in again. "Boy," I said to Jane, "you've got to stay on top of things every minute.

Otherwise they get by you...." She agreed.

(I read the prayer to her at 5:05, and left at 5:20. I still don't think the nudity thing is settled.

(Jane called me around 10 PM.)

DELETED SESSION
JULY 14, 1983 3:24 PM THURSDAY

(In the session for July 12, Jane quoted Rembrandt as saying that he was surprised to learn that he had died. While shaving this morning a question popped into my mind; I wrote it down to read to Jane this afternoon: "If Rembrandt was surprised to know that he'd died, did he also perhaps feel grief or sadness at leaving behind those he loved—or friends, his work, even his historic times? This would apply to others too, of course." For I'd found myself ruminating that perhaps grief at death wasn't only experienced on our side, but over there, too....

(See my own notes for more details. I took a taxi to work. The day was brilliant and very hot. Jane lay nude on her back. The window of 350 was closed but the room was fairly comfortable. Jane almost had a confrontation, she said, with Ann O'Neill this morning over the nudity thing, but evidently that possibility had dissipated when Ann checked the doctor's instructions about a sign on the door. All who enter 350 are to check at the nurse's station first. [Ann O. is the head nurse on the day shift.] Jane had blood taken this morning.

(I'd hardly been inside 350 when Ann and two others came in at various times to tell me that two visitors from the west coast were waiting in the rehab lounge. Jane knew it, of course. I must have walked right past them. I'd brought in Jane's acrylic flower painting of November 4, 1976. She'd done it the day before Willy died, while he lay on her lap. I hung the painting on the last available nail—Jane can see it from her bed when she lies on her right side—then went to see our visitors. One of their names was vaguely familiar.

(They were very nice people—the man lived in Elmira 20 years ago, the woman had written last year—but I couldn't help wonder why total strangers would go to a hospital to see someone who was obviously not well. Roll with the ups and downs of life, I told myself, though that isn't always easy to do. They didn't stay long, and left a dozen red roses. They're beautiful. As they left the man, Jim Olsen, said, "Tell your wife that she changed my life." What're you gonna do?

(Peggy Gallagher came into the lounge just before the visitors left, and I sent her in to see Jane. We talked about the strike. After Peg left Jane began to have a BM. She read the portions of the two sessions I'd brought in as usual. I explained my ques-

*tion about Rembrandt's surprise at death to her. She also read Peggy's article about
the strike from this morning's paper.*

*(Jane was cleaned up very efficiently from her BM by 2:58. She had her tem-
perature taken at 3:00. I cut a chuck in half and placed a piece of it under her for
additional protection, if necessary. She'd been asked if she wanted to go on the commode this morning, but had decided she wasn't ready to do that yet.*

(I'd brought in a copy of If We Live Again *to go with Jane's* Dialogues. *I
thought she might like to show it to some people.*

*(The commode question may have come up as a result of my talk Monday
morning with Jean Sweeney-Dunn. She'd called wanting to know if Jane could start
therapy while in hydro each morning. Jean feels that* Jane can walk again *if she can
loosen up her knees. An alternative is knee surgery, as a last resort, if desired. Jean
said she'd drop the doctor a note about beginning therapy, and about sitting up a bit
each day. I don't know whether she's contacted Fred or not.*

*(The room was getting stuffy so I opened the window, though I kept the cur-
tains three-quarters drawn. Jane had a cigarette at 3:15, as she lay on her back. So
far things seem the calmest they've been in 350, since the transfer. Jane and I discussed
the question I'd come up with about Rembrandt's surprise at learning he'd died.)*

Again, I suppose that everyone's experience is different. I was not <u>used</u> to
seeing either of my wives, who had died some time before, or my children, so it
is not as if I was yanked from their loving arms, or thrown from the warm
bosom of my family into death. Then, I imagine, I would have felt the greatest
sadness, and tried and tried to return. As it was, I did keep returning to my old
reality, like a fly lighting on a windows ill—but to me my old rooms looked
amazingly cramped and small. *(Pause.)* There was no doubting it—I had literally grown away from them. Now and then it seemed that I <u>was</u> for a moment
sent back to my old self, as mentioned somewhat previously, when I did find
myself as my old self, then once again my rooms seemed dear and precious.

I would snap to, to find myself dozing or daydreaming, with only a vague
memory of where I had been or what I had been doing. I would rub my brow
and yawn, shake my head and go back to my painting. Then the "I" that I have
become would rouse, and I would be out of the room again and away from my
old self.

(3:30.) I knew that my wives and children had a new reality *(long pause),*
and that if we wanted to meet we could indeed do so. On the other hand, in an
odd manner, it seemed as if we <u>were</u> together in some fashion I could not decipher. As if we knew each other so well and had become part of each other—

(3:33. A worker brought in some ice water. I read the last paragraph to Jane.)

—that we almost had a deeper relationship than any ordinary meeting could establish. For that reason I did not seem lonely in usual terms. It was as if we had fulfilled our relationships in a way we could not have earlier. We were so much a part of each others' *(long pause)* marrow that an ordinary meeting in earthly terms would actually diminish the strange closeness that we felt.

All of these experiences, I'm sure, would vary according to an individual's circumstance and the nature of their earlier relationships, if certain persons have their own purposes that involve entirely different kinds of decisions and activities.

(3:38.) One thing I do know is that after death you never feel alone, whether you are with someone or not—and there is always the feeling of support, as if you are being lifted or carried psychologically.

(Long pause at 3:40. "Okay," Jane said.) Another matter that you wondered about: I painted several seascapes, though my memory is not clear. I remember being in a room on a second or even third story. I believe I was by myself, perhaps visiting someone on a brief vacation. I had brought some supplies with me, however: smallish boards that were easy to handle. They were already prepared and primed. I looked out the window and saw the moonlight on rushing waves. There may have been a few ships, but they were not in my painting. I was struck by the design of the waves, and the glints given to them by the moonlight. I think I worked three nights by candlelight. I also used my palette knife almost exclusively. The paint was very thick, but glistened with transparencies. It may have been that I rushed or made some error that I did not know, for later I found that some of the paint had chipped—

(3:45. Madeline, one of the nurses who had taken care of Jane last year when she'd been first admitted to St. Joseph's, came in with her tray cart to give Jane eye drops. The day was beautiful, the sunny atmosphere in 350 quite pleasant.

("Every once in a while, though," Jane said when we were alone, "I have a feeling I'm going to have one of those things." She meant bladder spasms. "But I have them irrigate it every day—the catheter...." I thought she might be on the way to having more catheter trouble, as she had before the transfer. I explained to her that I may get the car back from the body shop tomorrow morning; I'm to call the garage at 10 AM. Now the room was getting too bright, so I pulled the curtain closed. I read Jane the material from 3:40.

(4:06.) I did another—again on vacation—this time with my family when we visited the seashore, again on another brief vacation. It was a small resort. *(Pause.)* It was warm. I couldn't sleep. Quite uncharacteristically I dressed and walked down to the seashore. Once again I was seized with the feeling of the ocean's mystery. This time the moon did not shine as brightly, and part of the ocean seemed to disappear in a sparkling gloom, illuminated only by specks of

white. I tried to produce a wash sketch so as to keep the view effectively in my mind, and when we returned home I painted a larger oil version *(pause)*, which was later bartered to a haberdasher. *(Pause.)* I do not know what became of the painting, but I did see it once in his rooms, and saw again that portions of the waves had chipped—and *[that]* he must have had someone else retouch them. It was a good job. But not done as well as I would have, but I said nothing.

There were also small resorts along the canals *(evidently of Amsterdam)*. Sometimes the water was smooth as glass, clear and transparent, while other times the canals were sluggish and filled with filth. All such resorts were usually crowded, however.

(Long pause at 4:13.) Some artists lived full time in such environments, always painting the tourists, producing picturesque paintings that showed little insight or ability. Others, however, did excellent work, and studied the water in all of its moods and phases. I still liked working in my studio best of all. I had a variety of ladders so that all portions of a canvas were readily available. Again, however, I always returned to portraits and people, though I tried to use what I had learned—imagining, for example, that the wrinkles in an old man's forehead moved back and forth like waves, filled with motion. I also produced at least several small portraits of my children, but these ended up in my wives' estates, passing to their relatives. *(Long pause.)* It seems to me, though I am not certain, that my memory becomes stronger if I think back on those times for your benefit—and for mine.

(4:20 PM. Jane had done well, her delivery often quite positive. We talked about a number of things. "When I left the house to come here [last April] I thought I'd be here for just the weekend," she said."

("So did I."

(I held up If We Live Again *so she could look at the table of contents, the essays, some of the poems in various sections of the book. After a while she didn't want to read any more: "It makes me sad." She wished she could use a tape recorder, since she's been playing with the idea for a poem. "You can always dictate poetry to me," I said.*

(I told Jane that every so often lately I'd found myself speculating about how Rembrandt might have painted a seascape. Once the idea was implanted, it seemed quite natural that he might have tried a few such paintings, I added. My thoughts had been triggered not long after Jane had begun her dictation, for the artist, through his world view, had made references to moonlight on water, and so forth several times.

(I read the prayer to Jane and left at 5:20 to meet the taxi. I had supper with the Bumbalos. Jane called me later that evening.)

DELETED SESSION
JULY 15, 1983 4:38 PM FRIDAY

(I picked up our car this morning from the garage—had it cleaned of rust and painted, it looks great—and so was able to get to 350 by 1:10 PM. Jane had gone to hydro this morning. Also weighed—down to 73 pounds; she has to take in at least three cans of Ensure daily. 1200 calories yesterday. She hasn't been given the results of the blood test yet.

(She lay nude on her back. The day was another very hot and bright one, but her room wasn't too bad with the window closed, the shade drawn and the air conditioner on. She almost had a hassle with the aide feeding her breakfast, about being covered; the two of them ended up doing breakfast in silence. Ron, the male nurse who is embarrassed by nudity, had fed Jane supper—she's been covered then—and a different nurse, Phyllis, whom Jane likes, had given her lunch today. Jane's catheter had been irrigated after supper last night, but she doesn't think it's working very well.

(Her face hasn't been washed today, so I did that. Nor has her hair been combed. The strike goes on.

(2:15. Jane remembered and dictated to me a poem she'd created last night. [She'd also mentally written a couple of others, but couldn't come up with them now.]

> *How unassuming*
> *walking is. Sweetly greased*
> *ball-bearing joints*
> *move as silently as squid.*

(Jane wanted to look through the Time-Life *book on Rembrandt again, so I held it up for her and turned the pages as she read. She was getting more and more concerned about the catheter. Mike, another male nurse, gave her eye drops at 4:04, and she told him about it. He said they'd check it this evening, irrigating it. And now* Jane *was embarrassed if she had a BM tonight and Mike, who said he was to be her nurse this evening, had to clean it up. Her temperature was taken this morning, but no other vital signs through the day. She worried because she hadn't gotten any Rembrandt material today: "I don't know why I haven't gotten anything yet today...." I said the general upset had a lot to do with it. She'd read the rest of the session for July 12, and the first page for July 13. I'd read her the rest of the notes for July 13 and all of July 14.*

(We spent some little time searching the volume on Rembrandt for a passage that Jane said had referred to his keeping a diary. I didn't remember any such material, and eventually she said she must have misinterpreted something she'd read. Very

little direct material from Rembrandt survives other than his art; seven letters, I believe.

(When Jane did begin delivering material for the artist, it was easy to tell what portion of the Time-Life *book's text and illustrations had "set her off," one might say. I thought it quite amusing.)*

I was not blind when I was alive to the petty jealousies of some men, who envied me my estate *(long pause)*, and whose petty jealousies caused them to do me injustice whenever they had the chance.

Just after my first marriage *(to Saskia in 1634)*, for example, I did indeed purchase some fine coats lined with furs *(long pause)*, and if I may say so myself, some of our furnishings were quite elegant. There were those who said *("wait a minute," Jane said, and coughed at 4:43)* that I entered into society only by virtue of my wife's higher status. There were even those who intimated that some of my wealthy patrons came about in the same fashion—that my abilities were overvalued *(long pause)*, so that I owed my abundance because of my marriage.

There is no doubt that the marriage was fortunate in many ways. My wife was beautiful, we were in love, and she did indeed bring an excellent dowry besides. My ability, however, spoke for itself, and it was by merit of that ability that I received many fine commissions that I did *(quite emphatic, almost strident at times)*. We moved in good society. There was no reason why we should not. I was far from the scheming artist, however, or the scheming husband—and I was convinced that my paintings would have been just as appreciated whether I had a wife or no.

(4:48.) A good number of my commissions were given by *(pause)* men connected in one way or another to Spanish nobility, and some of our furniture originated in Spain also. *(Long pause.)* If the truth be known, I liked their furniture better than their art.

As far as my religious ideas about Christ were concerned, I never blamed the Jews, as Jews, for Christ's death. *(Long pause.)* I held the Jews in particular favor, and in my way I tried to pay them back for Christianity's poor treatment of them through the centuries. *(Long pause.)* Christ himself was a Jew, a fact that seems often forgotten, and whether he actually lived and died was, in a strange manner, beside the point, his plight seemed symbolic of mankind's own triumphs and tragedies.

(Long pause at 4:55. In this material, then, at least one individual who's died, in our terms, still cannot say that Christ existed in physical terms. There must be many reasons for this. The fact that Rembrandt cannot declare the reality of Christ is one of a number of observations he's made through Jane that set up definitions of his afterdeath reality. Whether or not he moves into other kinds of reality, and per-

haps larger ones, it would be very interesting to compile a list of those hints and clues he's given us already that do declare his current reality. I assume that such definitions or areas would vary with the individual.

(If Rembrandt hasn't met Christ, then, or at least verified his existence, neither has he met any other god. He did speak of encountering an angel immediately after his resting period following his death—but here again, the nature of the angel requires more elucidation.)

He was supposed to be a king, and it seemed to me that this represented the fact that true nobility had little to do with wealth, but with a man's soul. I believe that Christ represented, again, man's triumph and tragedies. I portrayed him as vulnerable, taken from the cross, and painted myself beside him also because I believed that the story represented each man's plight, including my own.

(4:58. "That's it for now, I guess, Bob. I'm glad I got something," Jane said. "I'll have a cigarette and you can read the prayer." However, as she smoked she said she might get some more Rembrandt material—on the artist and art critics.

(5:12. I thought she was through for the day. The supper tray came. Jane asked me if I'd feed her. Then she said, she'd get some more Rembrandt. She quoted a line of it—something to the effect that one who wrote about cooking wasn't necessarily a great cook. I yielded to the temptation. 350 was quite pleasant and cool and we were alone. Jane ate well enough. No one brought her the aspirin she usually takes with supper, though. She had a cigarette.

(6:08.) Food critics often do not know the first thing about good taste or good cooking—and critics of art most often cannot paint themselves.

In a strange way they are overeducated for their task, having lost the fine instincts that most children have. Instead, their minds are filled with rules and regulations, prejudices and misconceptions. *(Pause.)* Usually they understand little about true design, and less about the nature of color. They live off of other people's work, producing nothing of quality by themselves, and if it were not for the artists the art critics would all starve.

During my lifetime I suffered often at the hands of such men. Often they seemed to misread my motives on purpose—and on <u>some</u> occasions at least they seemed filled with malice. This even applied to *Night Watch* in some circles. Nothing could content such people, and by the shrug of a shoulder or the lift of an eyebrow they could dismiss an artist's work as if it were nothing. This sort of thing was particularly prominent in the so-called better social circles, for the poorer people valued art for its own worth, and did not particularly expect the artist to have any great reputation.

The trouble with a great reputation, of course, is that there is always someone ready to rip it down. It is true that I was sensitive to such instances, but it seemed to me unjust that a man who knew relatively little about art—

(6:14. Mike, the male nurse, looked in, and Jane asked him for some aspirin. I read the last few sentences to her.)

—could destroy an artist's reputation often simply because he was the darling of some wealthy socialite. I could not understand the motives of such people.

There were indeed some critics who were kind to me and my work, and sometimes critics battled among themselves as to who was the most serious artist of the time. Often Rubens was held up to me as a superior artist. He was older, and held in great renown—but I was not competing with him or with anyone, and I did not like my name linked with another artist, no matter what I might think of another artist's work. My work was my own.

I rode clear of all early influences, and forged my own path. I knew this instinctively. Most art critics, I thought, were in the same category as a man's debtors; they chased after him and gave him no peace.

I did think that my work was often misunderstood — and sometimes I was congratulated for having qualities that I did not possess, and for which actually I had little respect, so often my art was valued for the wrong reasons as far as I was concerned.

(Pause at 6:22.) There was indeed a strange relationship between debtors and art critics —

(The aspirin and vitamins came.)

—for if the art critics were unkind and degraded a man's work, then the artist's debtors were afraid that the artist's popularity was over, and they would begin to hound him for what he owed. If the critics smiled favorably upon the artist, then the tradesmen's faces are wreathed in joviality, and he can charge to his heart's content. Sometimes, I thought, the two were in league with each other, so nefarious did the critics seem.

Even if he did not care a whit what the critics said, he had to pay attention, then, for their opinions often regulated the prices in the marketplace. One artist might be in favor for a year, while his fortunes changed completely in the next. It therefore behooved the artist to take all of this into consideration, but still go his own way—and so I did.

(6:30.) Provincial artists did not have such difficulties. Critics left them alone, thinking them beneath their notice. In a fashion, then, they had more freedom than the artist who already had a reputation. Even some of my own students were envious of my work—they flattered me to my face and spoke against me when my back was turned. They would applaud a work when they spoke of

it to me, and sometimes I would hear them degrade the same work when they spoke to someone else—a sad affair indeed. Yet all in all I went my own way, and at the very heart of the matter I did paint more for myself than for any other reason.

I did many uncommissioned paintings; many uncommissioned portraits, because I was so intrigued by a particular set of features or by a person's overall character or temperament.

(Pause at 6:35.) The market value of a painting could change dramatically in a year's time, so the artist could never be sure of his income, no matter how prosperous he was. That is why I squirreled some money away, both in the cash of the day and in collectibles. In later years they stood me in good stead.

I always had friends, however—Jewish ones in particular, so I was never lonely, even in the years before my death. I went to many auctions as a buyer, and unfortunately I saw some of my own paintings auctioned away—always with pangs of torment. But all in all everything was unimportant except for my painting itself, which always brought me reward and comfort.

(6:39 PM. "Well, let me have a cigarette and then you can go," Jane said. "That seems to be the end of that piece. There doesn't seem to be anything new there—"

("But he talked about the most important things of all," I said. She agreed. And she felt glad that she'd done something today. I read the prayer to her before leaving at 6:50. Later tonight she called me.)

DELETED SESSION
JULY 17, 1983 2:51 PM SUNDAY

(When I got there shortly after 1:00 Jane was on her back in bed with a sheet half over her: Ron, a male nurse, had fed her lunch. I took it off her, and she began a BM soon afterward. The window was closed and the curtain pulled. The room was comfortable, but there was quite a lot of noise in the hall. Jane had been given a sponge bath in bed.

(Steve and Tracy Blumenthal visited her last night, but didn't mention tape marketing. I saw them later, and they gave me a demo tape that I'll check out and play for Jane also. Steve is to see Pete Harpending, our lawyer, this coming Friday. He has many ideas about marketing class tapes; I tried to caution him not to get his hopes too high. He knows Vincent Canby, the New York Times critic, and also has connections with a vice president at MGM in Hollywood. I asked him to have that individual write to Jane. He is to send the tape to the Vice President. I also gave Steve

Harry Winer's address to relay to MGM, since the vice president in question knows our work and is interested in Oversoul Seven *as a film. I don't know how much interest there is in any of this. These varied projects seldom work out. Steve talks about large royalties for us.*

(I told Jane I might be late getting to the hospital Monday afternoon: I've lost part of a filling in a tooth [on Friday evening] and want to see Paul O'Neill as soon as I can. I also have to call the garage about cleaning the car battery and repairing, or at least checking the makeshift tie-down wire I fashioned to hold the battery in place on its tray.

(Jane was given her vitamins by 1:30. Then Rose and another aide began cleaning her up fifteen minutes later. I went into the lounge to do mail, and fell to talking with the cleaning woman, Alexandra, about her childhood in Russia. I cut Jane's fingernails and toenails after she was cleaned up; she was still on her back, so she read the newspaper clipping about the nurse's strike, and the session for July 14— all I'd done this morning. Her eyes are very red and irritated looking.)

Poets have their own ways of thinking, which I do not pretend to understand, but artists have their own way of thinking, and that way was native to me since my childhood.

It was as if I didn't know what I thought of a particular person until I painted whoever it was. The same thing was true of myself—that is, I painted myself innumerable times, and each time I saw myself slightly different, or understood a different phase of my own character. In its way painting was always some kind of revelation: I always learned from what I had painted.

This applies to objects also, as if my painting of them showed them in a different light than usual. They attain a strange unity within the painting that they did not seem to possess outside of it, so I learned that the <u>act</u> of painting undeniably organized the world in a different, unexplainable manner.

I grew through my painting, therefore. It was as if the painting itself had a unique consciousness, so that it taught me as I might teach a student, except that it spoke no words.

(Pause at 2:59.) Once I had painted a person it was as if I had captured a portion of their personality, or as if I knew something about them of which they were consciously unaware. I am convinced that my paintings themselves taught me how to paint, and I was aware of that odd give-and-take. Sometimes it seemed that I was painting even when I wasn't, and that every bit of my experience was somehow or other turned into my art and used. *(Pause.)* There must be something different in a man's temperament, to be so specifically oriented in visual terms. I don't believe that any man can be an artist unless he does have that knack of visualization. It forms its own kind of language, working with

images instead of words.

(Long pause at 3:04.) There are people who can copy nature very well, but who lack this native visualization. They do not learn by what they paint, and there paintings seem lifeless, or soggy. You do not even have to reproduce nature <u>that</u> faithfully, but allow the painting itself to construct its own kind....

(3:07. Jane's voice drifted off. She lay so quietly, eyes almost closed, that I thought she'd fallen asleep in mid-sentence. Rose came in to take her temperature, and Jane roused. But she hadn't been asleep, she said. I read the last paragraph to her.)

(3:12.) ....of nature. I felt sometimes that a nature existed within nature itself, and that it was the artist's task to discover or uncover that hidden nature.

On occasion I felt frightened *(pause)*, wondering how other people got along in the world if they could not understand it through painting. When I was very young I used to worry that I would lose my gift, and be like other people, who almost seemed blind—not that they didn't see the world, but they seemed blind to its true characteristics.

It was as if their eyes stopped at the very outside core of other people or of objects, so that they never perceived nature's true motion. To me, my paintings possess their own inner mobility, as if they were about to come alive in any moment. I even felt that way when I was very young, and I felt sorry for others who did not possess that kind of gift. If my painting went well, everything else seemed to fall into place. And if it did not then nothing else could really content me.

(Long pause at 3:17–3:19.)

When I was young there was never any question in my mind about what I would be when I grew up. I always thought of myself as an artist, and did countless childish portraits, even with <u>crayons</u>. Then I felt as if somehow I controlled a part of the world—the part that I painted.

This part of me was very strong also, and I used to question older artists about it. They did not seem as <u>vividly</u> aware of visualization as I was, however, and their work had a primness, as if they tried to make the world too neat, or did not allow it its own mobility.

(3:22. "Okay for a minute," Jane said." I gave her some Ensure; she's supposed to drink five cans a day, but hasn't been able to get down that much—an effort to halt her weight loss. Jane's eyes were very red, as red as I've ever seen them. I cleaned her glasses. "Are you ready for more?" she asked me.)

(3:32.) My first wife *(Saskia)* loved to rearrange furniture, and through watching her I understood that while I was fascinated with nature, still I was driven to rearrange it.

I really had no quarrel with nature, yet just the same I had to rearrange everything, and in my paintings I tried to transform nature into something else. Sometimes I would just change the color of an object, but in any case painting an object put it in an entirely different relationship with all other objects—each painting, faithful enough to nature, still rearranged all its parts, and formed a new dichotomy. I seemed to know how to do this even when I was a child, and I also seemed to know that the more I painted the more my own paintings would communicate with me. Painting is its own teacher.

(3:36. "I'll have a cigarette, I guess," Jane said. Her delivery had been steady and intent, very well done. I cleaned her teeth, which hadn't been done yet today. She worried about how her hair looked. I read the material from 3:32 to her. A new nurse came in to check her out: Ann, who'd cut her chin executing a jump from a diving board. Jane's right eye was running, so I patted it with a cold cloth, which seemed to help.

(4:00.) I tried to get these ideas across to my students.

Actually, all I did was to introduce a student to his own paintings. You cannot paint heavy-handed. Regardless of your ideas of what any particular painting should be, an artist has to be free enough to allow the painting its own freedom. Some of my students wanted to be painters without actually ever feeling the joy of painting itself. They were so earnest that they could not playfully tune into the painting, the models, or even themselves. I knew that that kind of student would never make a good painter. When I tried to explain, they usually just kept staring at their painting, then back at me, but you could tell that they didn't really seriously have the slightest idea of what I was trying to say.

There were other students who allowed their paintings too much freedom. They were always changing their minds when a painting was half-started, and they might then go back and repeat the same errors. I knew they would not make good painters either.

(Pause.) Paintings could be bought and sold, of course, but even when I had sold a painting and had not seen it for a long time, I could remember all of its characteristics. I felt that I was invisibly connected, even, with the paintings I had sold. I used to imagine that if I wanted them back again, somehow or other they would return to my rooms.

(Long pause at 4:07.) At the same time an artist really has to love nature in all of its ways. It is true he seeks to rearrange it, but he does this lovingly. On our living room table I often used to keep a few small brushes, with materials for a wash. As others conversed I would watch their faces, and often do several small washes. Sometimes I would incorporate these into paintings. Often I would just keep them to compare them with others I had done.

A painter paints all the time. Even when he is not touching a brush to canvas, he is always thinking of painting, and of this odd communication that exists between the artist and his work.

(4:10. "I think that's all right now," Jane said. Soon afterward an aide came in to give her her eye-drops. Her eyes were so red looking that I gave her her sunglasses to wear for a change. These helped.

(4:36.) Sometimes it seemed to me that I had a different kind of faculty—as if my seeing was truer than other men.

I wondered if some men possessed such a gift while others did not—but I had noticed from a very young age that I took in details far better than most people, and I felt a certain kind of visual excitement. I rarely spoke of this to anyone. On occasion I used to patch up one eye and just use the other, and then I would reverse the process—

(4:39. Sister Mary Lou, the charge nurse for the night, looked in on us. She brought word that Sister Leslie, from hydro, wanted to be remembered to us. I read the last paragraph to Jane. I told her the material sounded remarkably like my own reality, that I'd always been aware of my ability to see and remember detail in a manner that even my artist friends didn't seem to have.

(4:43.) You said you had a memory for visual detail—and that is one of the things I was speaking about.

Many other people appear to use words to trigger their memories. They rely upon verbal patterns and associations. The artist, however, organizes his memory in a different fashion, so that images serve instead of words, and even his associations are visually organized: one image will remind him of others, for example.

It makes me think that the artist's brain is organized in a different manner than usual. Certainly he seems to <u>possess what he sees</u> in a way that other people do not. *(Pause.)* I think that through his painting the artist finds a new kind of balance, putting images together in such a way that they seem to balance by themselves, and yet there are points of visual balances that are pertinent within the painting even though they do not appear elsewhere.

It is not that artists create an artificial world....

(Jane paused, eyes nearly closed as she lay on her back. Just as I wondered whether she was dozing she woke up with a start.

("Did you start to go to sleep?"

(She nodded. "Right in the middle of a sentence.... What was I saying?")

....but that they create a world that is alive in a different fashion. They do not mimic life. Their whole knack of organization, however, for a different kind of creative framework in which different rules apply than apply elsewhere—and those rules have to be discovered by each artist, and it is even possible that the same rules are <u>different</u> for each artist. Certainly my own work was my own, and the truth of my images possessed is by no other, so between them, artists of all times and places must be embarked upon some mysterious task that cannot be put into words.

(*4:51. "I don't know whether there's more or not," Jane said. I'll have a ciga-rette...." Then, "Do you want to stay and feed me? If you don't it's all right," she said as I laughed. I was tired. I read her the prayer and left soon afterward. She called me later that evening.*)

DELETED SESSION
JULY 18, 1983 4:44 PM MONDAY

(*I didn't get to 350 until 2:00 because I had to see Paul O'Neill about getting a tooth repaired. There is what I think an amazing little story connected with seeing Paul that I plan to write up elsewhere. I discussed it at length with Jane.*

(*Jane was nude on her back, having a BM. The odor was strong enough to make me open her window. She went to hydro this morning, but wasn't weighed as planned. I was most pleased to see that she is able to extend her arms out at least three inches farther, suddenly, than she's been able to do for many months. No pain. My wife looked strange to me, straightening her arms that much; they looked almost spindly. Now we hope the effects show up in her legs. We don't know what has led to this increased mobility. My hope is that it's the result of increased knowledge that her psyche has been absorbing from many sources, including our own changing attitudes and beliefs. We'll see. I told her enthusiastically that I hope the motion continues to grow.*

(*At the same time, Jane was upset to learn that Pete Harpending had called me this morning, suggesting that he get busy seeing about having our income from Prentice-Hall converted to my name. [He hasn't done anything about putting the house in my name yet. I don't blame Jane for feeling as she does. I said that it was only paperwork, but also that we were taking other people's word that such acts are necessary. Personally, I have no idea as to whether we should follow through with these changes. I told Jane that perhaps we should get a second opinion, as in medical questions: but this may tell us no more than we already know——which is precious little.*

(*Pete had nothing definite on the F. Fell matter. Vacations with the NYC law firm have interfered here, he said.*

(*I am somewhat puzzled and upset by a letter we received today from Arizona, concerning the recording of* Seth Speaks *and the* Nature of Personal Reality *for the blind, but evidently without any sort of permission. I plan to write Prentice-Hall in an effort to learn more about what our position should be. At first Jane said forget it.*

(Jane read what I'd typed on the session for July 15, and I read the rest of it to her as well as the session for July 17. People cleaned her up from her BM by 3:20 and turned her on her right side. No vitals were taken during this time, yet Jane said she had interruptions each time she felt like getting some Rembrandt material. She was turned back on her back at 4:30. Now her legs moved farther down than they have been, although not as much as her arms are extending. But this is encouraging.

(I lit a cigarette for her. Then: "I may get some...." I put out the cigarette when she was ready to begin dictation in the first person singular.)

When I was alive I wondered and prayed and tried to have faith. Now I do not need it—faith—because I know that there is a supreme deity, and so strongly is this impressed upon me that I actually feel no need to discover the nature of that deity.

I am so certain *(pause)* of the existence of such a being that to seek it out would almost imply a lack of faith, or a doubt *(all with quiet emphasis and surety).*

I do not believe one meets God, or a god, or a deity in the same way that we meet other people on earth, nor do I believe that any introductions are necessary. It is as if I exist in an entire medium of revelations that reveal themselves in their own order. I am certain of a relationship that exists between me and that deity, a relationship that fulfills itself, and is fulfilling itself, constantly. Sometimes I imagine that deity as a continuous, eternal motion, consisting of dazzling colors that pulsate—but colors that are alive and aware, that....

(Long pause at 4:50.) .... have emotional realities of their own, and are remarkably well-disposed toward me, revealing themselves in such a way that I should never be frightened or ill at ease. These colors are unbelievably comforting and supportive. I suppose they are my version of what the deity is, for I feel that this deity would most kindly take whatever color or shape or size that fit our own temperaments, and suited us best.

I do not believe that this deity has a superlative human form, though I do believe that it could take that form—

(4:59. Rhonda, an aide, looked in to say hello, interrupting Jane's inspired and excellent material. I'd known it was going to be exceptionally good as soon as Jane began speaking. It contained new things. Yet as soon as Rhonda spoke her friendly greeting, Jane was able to answer her in the same manner, as though she hadn't switched realities in any fashion. She has responded in the same way to innumerable interruptions ever since she began giving the Rembrandt material. I don't think she

could have done so as easily if she'd been in Seth trances, though her "recovery time" from Seth is also rapid. Perhaps the necessities and realities of Jane's hospital environment have simply led her to create a new version of her trance abilities, one that functions easily amid the comings and goings of so many others. Jane goes in and out of the Rembrandt mode as easily as she breathes, I think. And as Rhonda walked out of 350, I wondered: Did she really understand what we were doing? Did any of all those people? For each interruption found me sitting beside my wife, pad open and pen in hand.)

—as if to fit our needs. This existence is so vibrant of itself, so mysterious and yet so supportive, that it is impossible not to know that <u>somehow we are in the midst of</u> some inexplicable presence. I suppose you could say that I am aware of being in the deity's attention. I do not now think of God as masculine or feminine, or indeed in any human terms. I think of this presence that I sense all about me as "the majesty"—a term that leaves room for many interpretations and definitions, so I feel comfortable with it.

(Long pause.) I believe that the whole world is held in this deity's attention, and indeed that everything the human population does is known to this deity. I do not feel the existence of any hell, or torment or damnation.

(Long pause at 5:00.) I do not sense a devil, or the existence of demons, or the necessity for punishment. Those ideas simply vanished in the light of this new kind of knowing. I certainly cannot really describe what I really feel, but it is as if *(pause)* a deity artist was painting millions of portraits at once, and millions of landscapes, each endowed with their own kinds of life and consciousness, and each able to reproduce themselves in their own ways. *(Long pause.)* If a human being tried to paint a portrait <u>with his consciousness alone</u>, using no brush or color *(pause)*, then he would have some small indication of what I mean—for consciousness is a medium in which, or with which, this deity forms the universe. He puts his own consciousness into each creature, yet he does not entirely lose consciousness of himself either. Perspectives have no meaning unless the consciousness perceives them.

(Long pause at 5:06.) The deity, moreover, endows each consciousness with its own self-awareness and with the ability to create according to its kind. I am sure that other men might think of the deity as a superlative mathematician, or whatever, according to their own interests and preoccupations.

Again, I do not feel that in ordinary terms we can come face to face with God, for that reality would be so vast *(long pause)*, that we could lose ourselves in it forever, and I am sure that such is not the deity's intent. Its intent seems to be to create within us some superlative consciousness, some awareness better than we have ever known. How I know this I do not know.

(Long pause at 5:10; one minute.) Eternity seemed to be an impossible term to me when I was alive—yet now I understand that in one way eternity passes in the twinkling of an eye, and yet lasts forever. Surely that seems like a contradiction. Yet it is the truth. *(All of this material has come through with an intent sureness on Jane's part.*

(5:13. "I'll wait a second, I guess," Jane said, "and have a cigarette. I think that whole thing came from something you wrote in your notes this morning. I felt an emotional reaction when I read them. I'm glad I got something, though."

("I was wondering," I said. Jane actually referred to the note I'd inserted on page 148 of the session for July 15. It had to do with the area of Rembrandt's after-death perception—that is, my speculations about this. She'd read it this morning; then I'd read the balance of that session to her along with that for July 17. "It's obvious now that the area of his reality encompasses much more than I thought it did," I said. "I think the material's excellent."

("Well, you can stay and feed me, and I'll try and get some more," Jane said. I agreed, since I'd been late getting to the hospital today. The supper tray came soon. She was through eating by 6:10, and having a cigarette.

("Whenever you're ready get your pen out."

("I'm ready."

(6:12.) When I was alive, perhaps because of my training in perspective, it seemed that life also followed some of those same laws.

They seemed to make such sense, but where I am, for example, parallel lines can and do meet. I used to think that perhaps there were a certain number of intersections, in which one reality was connected to another. In usual life, I thought in terms of heaven, so I used to wonder in what dimension heaven existed, and I wondered also if our souls resided in heaven while our bodies were earthbound. These questions in their own way are apparent, I believe, in many of my paintings, and in the questions I used to ask that I mentioned earlier: do angels' bodies have form?—

(6:15. Bea Dibble, an aide, came in to use the phone to call her husband. Then Jean Knapp, an RN supervisor, came in to pick up the supper tray. "Where were we?" Jane asked when we were finally alone again. I read the last paragraph to her.

(6:25.)—Volume and form? In what kind of space do they exist? Does that kind of space have its own laws, independent of earth, or are they connected?

Now I realize the seemingly impossible is true: All realities are connected at every conceivable point. There is no place or space in which all realities do not brush against each other, leaving no trace. *(Pause.)* I can be aware of myself being in more than one place at the same time. I can be where I am, so to speak, and back in my old studio, and be conscious of myself to one extent or another in both locations. The very word "location" suggests a placement in space. Yet I see now that the very word "space" is a designation only, signifying a certain stance that consciousness takes.

(Long pause at 6:30. Several people, a doctor among them, were talking about cancer in the hall just outside our door to 350. Every time a woman asked a question the doctor would go into a lengthy explanation. This exchange had been going on almost since the two women had left us following supper. I'm not sure it bothered Jane as she gave her material, but at times it was so loud that I had trouble hearing what my wife was saying. I also enjoyed the subject of conversation.

It seems that one would be loose or unsupported or disoriented without the usual kind of space to operate in, but such is not the case. The same applies to time.

(Long pause at 6:32. The conversation in the hall continued.)

When you utilize earthly methods of dealing with space and time it is as if you chose to use one technique only in a painting, ignoring many others that were available. I am not sure of this, but I suspect that before we are born again we undergo a certain kind of schooling *(repeated at my request)*, or take a refresher course in how to operate in ordinary physical reality.

Again, when I look back at my old life it does seem incredibly small and cramped, unless I adopt the self that I was for a while—in which case the bustle of traffic and the hustle of family life once again seems full of experience *(pause)*, and indeed fills my consciousness. Certainly when one is alive day-to-day living does indeed seem to take up your entire thinking time. The world seems very vast *(pause)*, but once outside of that context you have all kinds of room for other experiences. It's as if you can hold more much more, in your mind at once *(pause)*. You find whole areas of your consciousness virgin and unexplored—

(6:39 PM. People came in to turn Jane on her left side. Jane said she was glad she got something after supper. I left her at 6:45. It wasn't until I was outside the building, walking to the car in the parking lot that I realized I hadn't read the prayer to her. I think this is the first time I've forgotten to do that.

(She didn't call me later in the evening, telling me the next day that "it didn't work out.")

DELETED SESSION
JULY 19, 1983 4:20 PM TUESDAY

(Fred Kardon called me this morning after seeing Jane. He's very concerned over her weight loss from 79 to 73 pounds. He wants her to go back on the feeding tube, at least for a while; if she continues to lose weight, he said, her ulcers will stop healing. He also asked if Dr. Gibson had talked to her about knee surgery to straighten out her legs. I said possibly early last year.

(Fred also said Jane might try range of motion exercises while in bed—this from Jean Sweeney-Dunn having contacted him following her talk with me last week, I believe it was. He's also quite surprised and pleased at Jane's increased mobility, in her arms especially. I've been hoping that the daily prayers with Jane have contributed to the greater mobility, though I didn't mention this to him. I said I'd talk it over with Jane and see what we could do about halting her weight loss.

(Of course Jane refused the feeding tube. One of her fears, aside from its general discomfort, is diarrhea. I asked her to keep an open mind about whatever might help her to whatever degree, even surgery, which I hate. She maintains the mobility in her arms and legs. I told her Fred's idea of her walking again gave me some kind of hope, just as I'd felt when Jean Sweeney-Dunn had mentioned the same thing. I didn't think to ask Fred his opinion of whether Jane was strong enough for surgery eventually. "Of course, we're talking about beliefs," I said, "not joints. If you or your psyche can resolve the fear of going too far if you're on your feet, then maybe the body can start fixing itself. I'm not talking about 100% magical recovery. I'd even settle for 50%—anything so we can get you good enough so we can leave here. Hell, I want you home so you can help me get our work done...." Plus a lot of other reasons. Jane said that last night her hips were "jumping," as though they were trying to move. Another good sign, I told her. Let it continue.

(Last night I'd taken the time to listen to the Seth tape Steve and Tracy had left last Saturday night. I'd brought it in to 350 today with our recorder, and now I laid the machine on the bed beside her and started playing the tape for her. I kept it low so it wouldn't attract attention. Jane seemed to get a kick out of hearing Seth, though after 20 minutes or so she asked me to turn it off. I asked my wife to resist the idea of spending the rest of her life in a hospital bed, and cautioned against letting that become a way of life for both of us—as, indeed, it already has. I speculated that we may even have to get used to the idea that it's truly safe for her to return home; this aside from the questions of walking, and so forth.

(I also explained that Mike Appel called last night. He wanted to come up, but I put it off.

(Jane was on her back when I read the last part of the session for July 18 to

her at 2:45. "Give me a smoke." Georgia and Jan visited from 331. She's drinking down all the Ensure she can get into her, in an effort to stem her weight loss. The day was much cooler. I figured our "doctor talk" had upset her to some extent, yet her left leg was now extended more than it's been for months, I thought, with the right one moving down a lesser distance. Her feet move better also. At 3:25 she began having a BM and was cleaned up by 3:50. She ended up on her right side, facing me as I sat beside her. She had a cigarette. "I feel some Rembrandt, if I can just get comfortable...." Her right shoulder dug into the air mattress. I tried to ease her discomfort with a foam-rubber wedge beneath her upper arm. The hall was fairly quiet. I'd been working on mail, and showed Jane a couple of the letters, with photos.

(4:20.) There is one point in particular that I wanted to mention. It is this: whenever I do go back to my old rooms, they always appear to me as they did in my lifetime. I have not returned to them <u>before</u> that birth or after my own death.

I have not seen the future tenants. I have only been aware of the rooms and the city as it was when I knew it. I might see one place as it appeared to me when I was 10 years old, and another when I was 50, but so far I have only traveled in that particular manner through the years of my earthly lifetime.

Now I would assume that the streets of <u>your</u> time exist where the streets of my lifetime—

(4:25. *"I'm coming, Mrs. Butts, I'm coming...." a black nursing aide called out as she came in to get Jane's water pitcher. She sang out because of the sign on the door of 350, notifying people to check at the nursing station before entering the room. As explained in earlier sessions, the sign was the result of the hassles over Jane's nudity and the embarrassment this had caused some male personnel—and female too, for that matter.)*

—still do exist. During my wandering, no one seems aware of me, either, unless I return <u>into</u> my old self, in which case I find myself, as I mentioned, daydreaming, half-dozing or, whatever, caught in the midst of ordinary living.

I do not know if this is the case or not generally speaking. (*Pause.*) I am aware of much of your world through your joint knowledge of it, but I do not perceive it directly. I simply know what you and your wife know. This sharing of knowledge, however, only exists for as long as we are in this kind of communication. I do not try to read your minds.

(*Long pause at 4:28. "Rembrandt," then, continues to give information upon the area and characteristics of his afterdeath reality. Some of his information is quite surprising, and obviously many questions arise.*)

Instead the contents of your minds become available. In one way or another you have given consent (*long pause*), or the situation would not exist as it does.

It may be, I suppose, that the greatest balance of interest in my case lies in the years of my life. I am not really interested in who lived in the house later, or what improvements were made. To me those improvements have not taken place.

(This material must be in response to a photo we saw in the Time-Life book on Rembrandt the other day. It showed one of his houses, and explained improvements and additions to its structure.)

If someone else's interest was of a different nature, then I assume *(pause)* that they might visit the years before and after their own birth and death. *(Long pause.)* I have not particularly tried to follow my paintings *(long pause)* after my death. This may seem strange, yet for me when I had finished my paintings I had indeed finished them—and since I am seeing *(pause)* a strange and new kind of art, my main interest now lies in what I may yet discover. *(Long pause.)* If ever God did have apprentices, as men do, then I must say that I believe he gave artists a particular advantage.

(A one-minute pause at 4:36.) I am aware of the technological duplications in your century—the prints and photographs of paintings and so forth—yet it also seems that such instances cut down on the very private concentrated nature that original art had in my time. It could be copied but never truly duplicated. Whatever else an oil painting was, it was the artist's private earthly statement, painted with his hands and with his brushes, with his own colors. You could almost smell the artist's sweat mixed into the oils *(all with emphasis).* Your duplications may be immaculate, but it still seems to me they must possess a sterility that would drain a great work of its direct virility and power.

(Long pause at 4:40.) When a man bought a painting in my day, he was given not only a painting but a portion of the artist himself—so that to one extent or another there was always some kind of dialogue that went on between the purchaser of a painting and the artist himself.

(Long pause at 4:42. "I'll take a break and have part of a cigarette," Jane said. She was still on her side, still vaguely uncomfortable. "Some of it was coming through good...."

("It's excellent," I said. "There's new stuff there."

("I've got this little bit more, even though I've still got this [cigarette]—"

(4:45.) Painting is, among other things, <u>honest toil</u>.

The artist's sweat is as real as any peasant's. All of this carries quite clearly in any original work. Not only the artist's personality and his temperament live in his painting, but often his very fingerprints, perspiration on his hands. He himself is stained with his own colors. He smells himself of oil, he is chemically connected with his work, and no copy, however elegant, can carry those same marks that rough yet blessed reality of man's physical toil mixed with spiritual endeavor. Paintings are intimate statements, personal declarations, and no glossy counterparts can duplicate that spiritual and biological connection. *(Pause.)* So while many people in your century view reproductions of great paintings, they are still somehow robbed of the paintings' true worth. This would be fair enough—but as I understand it, in their minds people seem to equate the reproduction with the original, while a reproduction is but a thin and distant relative *(all emphatic.*

(Cigarette out by 4:50.) All of those intimate connections between the painter and his work and the painting's owner were taken for granted in my time. A good artist would equate your reproductions perhaps to stale loaves of bread, robbed of their nutrition, and not fit for a man's table.

(4:54 PM. "That's it for this minute, I'm afraid." Jane said after a long pause. I turned her on her back. I read the prayer to her, and then we checked the TV schedule for tonight. I circled the programs she wanted to watch.

(I left at 5:15—she called me late tonight.)

DELETED SESSION
JULY 20, 1983 2:15 PM WEDNESDAY

(I arrived at 350 fairly early, after stopping at the bank to get a money order in payment for a couple of books by a medical doctor who advocates a cure for arthritis by treating it as caused by an amoeba. Who knows? I asked Jane. She lay nude on her back. She read the literature on the book, and had a cigarette. The day was cool and cloudy. We'd had a little rain, though not nearly enough. Jane still has the extra freedom of motion in her arms, and to a lesser extent in her legs and feet. I still feel encouraged about this. She seemed to feel pretty good, although she thinks the new catheter leaks a bit at times.

(I'd brought in the Safe-Universe Seth tape, but didn't play it for her right away—both because I forgot to, and because we became so involved in other discussions that lead to an earlier-than-usual start for today's session. Jane read the last portion of the session for July 17, and the first part for July 18. Then I read the last few paragraphs of the session for July 19 to her, on Rembrandt's opinion of reproductions, and so forth.

(It was obvious the artist didn't—doesn't—think much of reproductions—but what, I asked Jane, would we do without them? How many people in small towns would ever get to see an original Rembrandt, for example, or other great works of art?

They would have to travel extensively. "I can see some benefits to the situation local-
ly," I said, "in that a town's native artists would be much more appreciated if we did-
n't have all of these reproductions around. If people wanted to see original art, they'd
have to turn to the artists in town. But this would certainly make things much more
insular, too...."

("Are you ready?")

("Yes.")

We simply did not think of the world as you do.

The known world, the civilized world, was not nearly as large as it is in
your time. Besides that, you are quite correct—every town had its art and its
artists. They were an indispensable part of normal living. It is true that artists
hoped that their paintings would be seen by men of influence, but the world
view, in physical terms, was far smaller than your own. It is not possible for me
to judge—but perhaps the <u>inner</u> world view in my time was far vaster than in
your own historical period.

Many of man's dreams have been exteriorized in one way or another in
your century. You have airplanes, for example, and most of your national and
educational and artistic foundations deal with the making of your physical
plans, so that your world view becomes exteriorized.

(Pause at 2:20.) You are used to almost instant communication through
your television. This was unknown to us, of course. *(Long pause.)* On the other
hand *(long pause)* certainly my own world was more intimate, and the communication was not secondhand. You see images of people on television, but they
are images alone. You cannot talk to the people themselves, nor can they
respond as you watch them on your television screen. You have a great diversity of <u>outsideness</u>.

(Pause.) In the same way it certainly seems to me there is a great distinction between an original painting and its reproduction, and when people see
reproductions they are not seeing great art necessarily, <u>but merely an image of
it</u>, while the real guts of the original are lacking, and where the basic communication between artist and viewer is not present.

In my time many people were familiar with original art, both of good and
bad quality, but there was an intimacy present that your century seems—at least
to me—to lack. There is another point, however, that I wanted to make: in my
lifetime I painted one thing before another. I might work on several at once, but
generally speaking the paintings seemed to be done more or less one at a time
from my younger through my later years.

*(2:28. Jane paused, interrupted by a cleaning woman making a good deal of
noise in the bathroom of 350.)*

I do not know exactly when it was that I suspected something different. I think it was shortly before my death, when I could look back on a large accumulation of work—those already sold, those still in my studio, and paintings I had planned in my head. With all of that work imaginatively at least at my fingertips, I began to suspect that I had known about <u>all</u> of the paintings—including the later ones—from the very earliest moments of my career.

(More noise.) I was somehow certain that in painting one painting I was inexplicably aware of all of the others. It almost seemed as if in the past I had been influenced by my future work, so that each painting in the past was executed in such a way that it would bring about the existence of the future paintings in the way I wanted them to be .

(Pause at 2:32.) My choice of colors, my ideas of design and motion, and mostly of lighting, appear to have been <u>always</u> in my mind, assuring from the earliest years that the later works would be created exactly as I wanted them. *(Long pause.)* There are many paintings that I planned but never did execute. I could draw them into my mind at will, as if they did exist somewhere, and I had seen them. It might be said that these existed only in my memory, but sometimes they appeared to be as vivid and alive as those paintings I <u>had</u> executed in physical terms, and I did see that those unpainted paintings were as responsible for my entire work as any of the <u>executed</u> paintings were.

It even seemed that if I had painted those works physically, they would not have served the purpose that they had, but might have led me astray instead. So I think a man's work is also highly dependent upon those paintings that exist only in his mind. They are underpainting of a different kind that still adds to the entire flesh of the physical works.

(Pause at 2:38 PM. "That's it for the moment," Jane said. "I'll drink some of that junk [Ensure]—my throat got dry." Her delivery had marched right along for the most part, steady and with a quiet emphasis.

("I do feel something that he doesn't seem to get through his head," she said, to my surprise. "That he can't understand that the reproductions are better than nothing.... It's like our times are too difficult for him to really understand.... or are too far away, maybe...." She had a cigarette. The sun was out now, shining weakly through the drawn drapery. Room 350 was cool and pleasant and we were alone for the moment at least.

(At 3:25 I began playing the Safe-Universe tape for Jane. I could see that she got a charge out of it. She smiled, listening intently, staring, shaking her head. The tape's quality isn't very good, though. I'd also brought in a couple of tapes by Michael Lorimer, one of which he'd just sent us. I didn't get to play them today, though. I began working on the mail. Jane hasn't had a BM today yet. Shortly after 4:00 an

RN came in to check us out, since she was new to the case. There's been a steady flow of new people since the strike began. They may stay a day or two then disappear; we don't know where they go. Jane ended up turned on her right side. She wasn't very comfortable, though.

(I read the prayer to her at 5:00, and then left soon afterward. She called me at about 10:15 PM.)

DELETED SESSION
JULY 22, 1983　2:22 PM FRIDAY

(Jane was too upset to have a session yesterday. See my own notes for a summary of events then. Things were triggered by my visiting Jim Clune yesterday morning about supplementary insurance. He reinforced the advice we've been given by Pete Harpending, about the transfer of our assets to my name, the divorce, and so forth, and when I reviewed all of that material for Jane yesterday afternoon she became quite upset. Not that I blamed her. Even I still only half-understand why we have to go this route, but evidently it's the "smart" thing to do. I still wonder, I told Jane. At the same time, I was angry at the whole business, no denying that. I told her she'd carried the whole business of protection, via her symptoms, much too far.

(There's even a question now about whether we should accept social security disability benefits now, while working on the Rembrandt material. The material is obviously publishable eventually, I said—so if we do publish it someday, are we violating the law now by accepting those payments? I want to see Pete about this and other points Jim Clune made. [He's investigating what he can do for us about additional policies. Even if a long waiting period is involved. But it's costing us in the meantime.]

(Jane still had the increased mobility in her arms, neck and shoulders, and so forth, yesterday, and I said I hoped this motion was a sign of psychic change. She reminded me that Frank Longwell swears she doesn't have arthritis at all. I said that was fine with me—that it meant she didn't have an incurable disease, that her body could recover. Seth has said this all along, of course. As he said in the private session for April 28, 1981:

Ruburt's entire group of symptoms does not follow any established pattern. They are the result of applied stress, exaggerated finally by feelings of hopelessness, and by some relative feelings of isolation.

(Today, July 24, I'm bringing in the entire page from that session so that Jane can review it.

(Jane said all the doctors believe without question that she has arthritis, and

point to her hands, for example, as illustrations of this, of the sedimentation rate of her urine, which is very high. But even with these obvious signs, if she didn't have arthritis per se, seemingly she has the potential for recovery.

(We went through a lot yesterday. During one discussion I complained that I wasn't painting at all, and that I wouldn't go along forever not doing so, that we had to work out some sort of life wherein we could live creatively and not in a hospital. Jane said that sounded like an ultimatum. I said it wasn't.

(There were a number of factors involved in such exchanges, and all in all I thought them quite beneficial.

(Jane was weighed yesterday morning, and for the first time in some days learned that her weight had stopped dropping—in fact, she gained 1/ pounds; she now weighs 74/. This is a great relief. Her increased consumption of Ensure and food is evidently paying off.

(A couple of days ago a woman from Australia who's hitchhiking around the country visited Sue Watkins in Dundee. Sue called Debbie Harris, who's been visiting Jane fairly often in the evenings. The two came to Elmira and had supper with Debbie, who, last night brought Jane a couple of little gifts from Australia: a transparent blue scarf showing an Australian aborigine, and a baby panda. Now the panda clings upside down to the arm holding Jane's TV set over her bed.

(Then yesterday afternoon, during her visit Peggy Gallagher told Jane that a very persistent woman from Canada had been bugging Peggy at the newspaper: She wanted Jane's address, and so forth. I saw no sign of the visitor at the house, however.

(Since because of the strike the hospital staff is so short-handed, I was asked to stay and feed Jane supper last night. I read her the prayer afterward and left at 6:45 PM.

(In this morning's Star-Gazette, I read Peggy Gallagher's article saying that the hospital management and the nurses have resumed negotiations re the strike. Peggy's article was written too soon to include the news that the nurses have agreed to vote today on a possible settlement agreement. I found this news in the daily Today bulletin issued by the hospital. Jane said everyone was excited. We might know by 3:00 whether the strike is over.

(The day was cool and bright. I found the window and curtains in 350 open, and Jane nude on her back. She'd just had her catheter changed again. I'd noticed yesterday that the tube looked half-clogged with mucus. Samples of urine have been taken to test for signs of infection. Jane feels better, but still gets twinges at times. She doesn't think there's any infection present.

(Moods in the hospital are much improved, Jane said. She said Ron, a male nurse, told her that ironically enough some of the patients who were moved to new

quarters in preparation for the shutdown of certain wings in the hospital, now want-
ed to stay where they were. Jane, however, can't wait to get back to 331.

(Jane read the last part of the session for July 18 and the first portion of July
19. I read her the rest of July 19 and all of July 20. She also read Peggy's morning
news story, which was already outdated. Her slight bladder spasms continued inter-
mittently.

(I paid the TV girl for next week's service. She too was expectant about the
strike being over. "Okay," Jane said when TV had left, "I'll get some.")

I am sure I would find your world most confusing.

(Long pause.) I cannot imagine living in the midst of so many conflicting
beliefs, forms of government, and a myriad of religions. It seems impossible for
any one person to sift through all the religious questions alone, much less the
matters of politics and government.

My world was much more manageable. You seem surrounded by an amazing amount of information. *(Long pause.)* I do not understand how any one person can deal with all that data while still living a private life. Many of our marriages were arranged, certainly, but a good number of them worked out very
well, while your own method of seeking lifetime partners in marriage does not
seem to have resulted in any additional happiness. The difference in the treatment of older people, however, strikes me in the strongest manner—for in my
time a man was honored because of his age, and certainly not in spite of it, even
though he might have infirmities.

(Long pause at 2:28.) It must take an extraordinary amount of concentration to be an artist in your historical time, since there are so many diversions on
every hand. *(Amen.)* It makes me wonder how often the world has changed
character almost completely, so that the members of one age might seem completely alien to those of another. Great art should serve as an excellent communication, connecting the generations to each other, even as each painting should
be in its time and ahead of its time simultaneously. *(Long pause.)* I assume that
the beloved streets of my Amsterdam exist more or less in the same space as your
modern ones, yet there is never any conflict between the two realities—and
when I look up at the skies above the streets of Amsterdam, I never see an air-
plane, though in your times the heavens must be full of them. It constantly
amazes me, then, that our realities are so separate—and more strange still, that
these communications are possible.

(I've been meaning to remark to Jane that some information on just how these
communications take place would be most helpful. I suppose there could be many
questions involved. I also suppose the questions, since they would be asked from our
standpoint, would appear to Rembrandt as distortions. For instance, just how does

he know when Jane is receptive to his material? In what form or state is he in—something like a physical one, or not? What is he "doing" when Jane tunes in? Are his statements really feelings or reactions to our own, that Jane then delivers in linear sentences? Rembrandt tells us that so far he's still alone in his reality, yet here he's in communication with us. I include both of us, since he's also saying that he has access to the contents of both of our minds. These comments could go on and on.

(2:34. "That's it for the minute, I guess," Jane said. She drank some Ensure and I lit a cigarette for her. I could see tiny clots of mucus in the catheter tube, though the device was working all right. She still has "those feelings" relative to spasms occasionally, though. The hall was quiet, although I could hear a TV going in the lounge next door. Nobody has bothered us since the TV girl came in. "I've got a little more when you're ready," Jane said finally, as I answered a letter.

(2:48.) I imagine that I must sound extremely provincial to you—yet I must admit that I am almost scandalized by many aspects of your world, as I understand them through your knowledge.

(I should have added to my comments above that if someone in the afterdeath reality tunes into our physical reality through the contents of a human mind, that then there are many possibilities for distortions on both sides. Or if not distortions, necessarily, then an individualistic view of physical reality as well as the afterdeath reality....

(I hope that the contents of the minds of Jane and me offer "Rembrandt" some sort of balanced view of our current physical reality, since we are interested in a wide variety of subjects and actions. I can see, however, how a narrower or unbalanced view of our physical reality could offer quite a distorted view to any "one" tuning in to that stance.

(Pause.) There seems to be (pause) horrible instances of wholesale starvation in India and some other countries. In my time we had people who were very poor, and by your standards I see that our sanitation (pause) was very inferior to your own. All in all, however, we did not have a staggering number of displaced persons. The Dutch in particular have always been industrious, tidy, and in their ways ambitious. We certainly had social classes, yet it seems to me that on the whole we fit more people into our society than your world does (all emphatically).

We had all kinds of guilds, of course, but they were far different than your unions, and a man's son often followed in his footsteps, though I did not follow that course. But a man of honor could almost always find his place. We did not have the leagues of the unemployed, as you do. Again, we did have poverty, but if a man wanted to work, there was always enough work to go around. We needed all the business and products and food goods that we could produce. We did not seem to have as many people who were <u>dispossessed</u>, or aimless. There was slavery, but even the slaves had their own places, poor as they might be. They were provided for.

(Pause at 2:58. The lady brought in ice water. "I guess I'll have to wait a minute," Jane said. "I think I'm going to have a BM...." Later: "I'm doing so little it's hardly worth bothering with. I've got a little more [Rembrandt]."

(3:06.) During my lifetime I had no clear idea of what was happening in India, while your communication puts you in touch with all portions of the planet.

I have the <u>impression</u>, however, that there are fairly large population shifts in very short periods of time *(long pause)*, with resulting armies of refugees— while our populations were far more stable. *(Long pause.)* I can tune into the conditions of my own lifetime, of course, and my own work, far easier than I can into conditions in your own time. That information is indirect at best, so I may be misinterpreting some of the aspects of your world, and judging them overharshly. Such of course is not my intent.

(A one-minute pause at 3:10. I'd say that so far at least Rembrandt's comments on our current physical reality have been quite accurate.

(3:13. "That's it for now," Jane finally said. She drank some Ensure. I asked her if she'd mind an occasional comment from me while delivering material. She didn't know. I haven't wanted to stick in any remarks of my own. I asked the question now because I could have answered Rembrandt more directly, above, but refrained from doing so. "So I'll make the comment now," I said, explaining to her that I thought Rembrandt's interpretations of our own reality have been good.

(Jane decided to wait on calling an aide to clean her up, since she wasn't sure she needed it. If an aide came, my wife would end up turned on her side. Her vitals haven't been taken yet today.

(3:25. Jane wanted to know if Rembrandt himself named all of his paintings. I said I didn't think so, although I didn't recall reading anything about this one way or the other. "That's what I was getting," Jane said as she smoked a cigarette. "That he didn't." I added that the titles of some of his paintings must have been obvious or automatic—Flora, say, or The Anatomy Lesson of Dr. Tulp—but that others are guesses or approximations: The Jewish Bride, The Night Watch, and so forth.

(3:32. At a slower pace:) I am pleased to see that Christianity endures, even though it is broken into thousands of fragments.

(Pause.) I thought that it was indispensable *(pause)*, that man used it as a kind of sounding board, or a framework, in which he tried to explain his experience and the connections between the body and the soul. *(Pause.)* I am also pleased to see that the Bible endures—for in the same way it also serves as a

sounding board, containing stories that are somehow fitted to man's highest hopes and most profound anguish. I thought that Christianity was a spiritual framework upon which the world of ethics and law revolved. *(Long pause.)* In my day every child knew the biblical stories by heart. They were considered morality plays of a kind, and I must say that I do not understand what could conceivably replace Christianity were it to disappear.

(3:38.) I did want to mention that I will of course try to answer any questions when you have them. *(Pause.)* There may be some I cannot answer, or I may have to think some over for a while, but you may always feel free at least to inquire.

("Alright."

(Long pause.) I am surprised that religious subjects are not used more frequently in your time as a proper subject matter for paintings; for I believe that the biblical stories alone united many varieties of people, so that they did indeed have a universal quality.

(3:42. "That's all for the minute," Jane said. "I seem to be getting it in fits and starts. I don't know, Bob—maybe you could make a list of questions."

("I haven't particularly wanted to do that," I said.

("You mean directing material that way."

("Yes. You could ask questions till doomsday. But it's really interesting. It means there's another dimension there to the material. Not that I haven't thought of questions lots of times."

(3:45. An aide we hardly knew came in to take Jane's vitals. When Jane asked, <u>she told us the strike is over</u>! The word just came in. She looked pleased and flushed. She had no other word yet, no details. The news seemed almost anticlimactic to me, although it meant a lot more to Jane; she wants to get out of 350. Right now she thought she might be having a small BM, but she didn't mention it to the aide. She had a cigarette. "I feel a little more," she said after she'd finished smoking.

(4:02.) During my lifetime, we considered anyone who was not Christian to be an infidel.

Shortly after my own death, I understood for myself how wrong that attitude was. Somehow, then, I instinctively realized that this vast universe opened its doors to everyone. No one was left out—

(4:05. Now Jane really began having a BM. Her face began to suffuse and I wondered at first what was going on. "I'm still getting more, but I can't do this and that at the same time," she said with unwitting humor. I started working with the mail again.

("Alright, I'll try...."

(4:07.) An almost exultant feeling of being welcome permeated every-

where, and I understood that each and every creature, regardless of its degree, was somehow welcome here. Not only welcome, but desired—and that no exclusions ever applied.

I had long thought, even in my lifetime, that Christianity somehow misinterpreted the Jews, but I was so used to the concept of hell or damnation that it was with a sense of shock that I understood that no hell or damnation existed. No matter how foul a man's deeds might have been on earth, here they were somehow redeemed. Such an atmosphere of loving acceptance exists in this afterdeath dimension that I found it almost impossible to imagine that I had ever believed in punishment or damnation. So certain attitudes of mine have changed, and certainly for the better.

I also understood that Christianity itself was actually a frail vehicle, that its framework was far too small to contain the reality that I was and am experiencing. This does not mean that I do not still feel a genuine fondness for Christianity, because regardless of its shortcomings I grew up in its atmosphere. *(Long pause.)* I am filled, however, with the greatest sense of acceptance, of being where I should be, and of the rightness of being who I am. I barely remember having such feelings in my early childhood. It now seems to me that all children are born with this sense of freedom—and that indeed by adulthood, however, the old sense of rightness vanishes. I am not sure why.

(Pause at 4:16.) It occurs to me that you and others are indeed trying to form a new framework large enough to contain man's experience, and that such communications as ours serve in that regard.

(4:17 PM. "That's it for now," Jane said. No one has come back into 350 yet. I've heard some enthusiastic talk in the hall, having to do with the strike being over.

("That was very good, Hon," I said.

("I'm glad, 'cause I haven't been getting anything for two days," Jane said. Rhonda came in a couple of minutes later, and with another aide began cleaning up Jane. They were done by 4:35, and I showed them how I often gently helped Jane move her feet down the mattress a bit, letting them straighten out to that extent.

(I read the prayer to Jane and left by 5:15, to go food shopping at Acme.)

DELETED SESSION
JULY 23, 1983 3:05 PM SATURDAY

(There was no in-house bulletin from the hospital today, now that the strike is over. Jane still doesn't know when she'll be moved back to 331. The staff is returning full force Monday. She began a BM shortly after I arrived. I explained to her that

yesterday when I got home I found the Dutch translation manuscript for Mass Events—*a total surprise to both of us, since we hadn't known such a deal had been made. This morning I tried to contact someone at Prentice-Hall to send a cable of approval to Ankh-Hermes, but all is closed there on Saturday. See the file that I suppose will grow out of this event, since I'll have to write both Prentice and the Dutch publisher.*

(After having a cigarette Jane read the newspaper article about the end of the strike. She also finished reading the rest of the session for July 19, and I began to read her the session for July 22. We worked around the fact that Millie Smith came in to clean her up at 2:18, followed by a porter who had to swab the floor of 350. [This meant Jane had to be covered, since she lay nude in bed.]

(The day is cool and very sunny, the room very pleasant and breezy, with the window open. A patient down the hall was hollering steadily, emitting alternating high-and-low-pitched, unintelligible cries. A couple of nurses hurried by, carrying medications; after a bit the cries ceased. Strange, I thought, how soon one becomes used to such events in such an environment. At home they would be highly upsetting. But they have definitely added new dimensions to our awareness of the human condition. That person, hollering—I couldn't tell if it was man or woman—was in distress. He or she was quarreling with physical reality, I thought, in most basic terms. The whole medical-hospital thing could be likened to a vast subculture within our society, I speculated—and one in which its members may actually be flirting with, or exploring, many questions having to do with the connections between life and death in a way that the healthy individual walking the streets, say, did not do....

(As I neared the end of my own notes after reaching 350, Jane started on her bed: She woke up from a short dream: She'd been standing on the front porch of 458 West Water St. She was walking, but wearing a hospital gown and high-heeled shoes, saying something like, "You mean there's still an outside?*" I told her I thought the dream was a hopeful sign, since her walking had been brought into the present. She still has the increased mobility in her arms especially, although her legs haven't been as free today.*

(3:00. She had a cigarette as she lay on her back. She still has "those feelings" resulting from the catheter, which she had irrigated this morning. The hall was quiet. Then the yelling abruptly resumed, louder than ever.)

When an artist is producing a painting, and makes a mistake, that mistake carries no moral connotations—and I see now that the same applies to those errors people make in a lifetime.

They are not held accountable, or judged in moral terms. They are simply shown how to correct the error. This applies to acts of revenge or murder as well. *(Long pause.)* Such people are simply shown how to project a better picture of reality, and no punishment is ever implied. At least this has been my own experience thus far.

(Long pause at 3:08. The yelling has stopped again.)

I meant to mention that I did indeed consider myself fairly sophisticated during my lifetime, and Amsterdam certainly seemed as exciting as any other place in the world. We had an excellent choir. There was even a theater group, and there were always acting troupes that made tours, and they almost always visited our city. To some extent, with a few qualifications, the same applied to much smaller cities also. As they had their own artists, they usually had their own choirs also, their own theater groups, even though many of these were religiously connected.

Some towns had small zoos, and in Amsterdam we were often treated to traveling circuses, so children could see elephants and tigers and so forth. *(Pause.)* I always went to such affairs when I could when my children were young, and I often sketched both the children and the animals. I suppose you could say that community events filled our days, and in the wintertime there was always some skating on a few canals. All of the canals were not favorable for skating, but those that were were well frequented.

The world certainly seemed as exciting to us as yours must seem to you, beside the choruses there were also opera companies, even in many small towns, and the different guilds were always holding one kind of affair or another. Artists were in great demand to memorialize such events. Some towns seemed to possess unhealthier air than others *(long pause)*, and were most likely to be visited by various kinds of plague. These seemed to come with varying symptoms, and they always seemed to come with a certain rhythm, and then disappear.

(Pause at 3:18. Jane's delivery has been steady.)

The surviving population almost appeared stronger after such outbreaks; as if the population had cleared itself out in some strange manner. We had no real idea of what caused such outbreaks. Though at various times different culprits seemed to be responsible: flies and rats and general filth. We thought that the lowness of the land might be responsible also—and that reminds me that many people *(pause)* went about the streets on stilts to keep themselves clean and to keep their garments off the ground.

(I didn't know offhand whether I'd ever heard of this practice or not. I also made a mental note to ask Jane what she knew about it. There are many rather hilarious implications here, although the use of stilts must have been seriously enough motivated. [What did old ladies do, or fat people, say?] The problems connected with manure alone in the streets must have been great. I remember that some time ago in these sessions Rembrandt referred to street cleaners.)

Various kinds of head attire and umbrellas were also used for protection against the slop jars, which were often emptied out the windows. Most towns also had a doctor, or a barber of some kind, several midwives, and one or two good blacksmiths. Sometimes illnesses swept through the horse population also, so that many carriages sat horseless.

(More yelling.) There were usually some kinds of carriages on rent, however, and some people of course possessed their own horses and carriages. In the city, though, we did not really have the room. Since the city was laid out in a certain fashion, it was quite easy to visit a large variety of shops while traveling on foot, and there were always small boys around who would carry your parcels for you for a fee. If anything, cities and towns both had more pharmacies than anything else, and though I may be exaggerating slightly, it did seem that there were pharmacies everywhere.

There were also vendors who sold their wares on the streets themselves.

(3:28.) Amsterdam was also exciting because of the many foreign merchants that came by ship, with all kinds of wares to sell *(pause)* —bolts of cloth, buttons of every description, and always novelties such as pillboxes or snuffboxes. They also sold spices and oftentimes fine rugs.

(Long pause.) Many women of wealth had their own hair stylist, and for the others there were small shops specializing in women's coiffures, hats, and collars.

(Long pause at 3:32. All was quiet outside 350.)

I never knew anyone who was bored. *(Pause.)* Certainly I was busy enough as an artist and a family man. *(Long pause.)* There were poorhouses, and houses of correction, though I was not familiar with either of these. I understood, however, that it was certainly better to stay clear of both places, and there were stories told that if you could bribe a guard you could escape easily enough.

(3:35 "I'll take a drink and a cigarette," Jane said. She finished the contents of a can of Ensure left over from lunch. She was also supposed to take another can before supper, so I got a cold one from the refrigerator in the kitchen next door to 350. I didn't see how she could take it before suppertime, though. We checked the TV programs for tonight.

(Then: "I've got a little more."

(3:53.) I should probably mention that much of an artist's prestige rested on the number of students he had, for theoretically this meant that he was held in honor by younger artists who yearned to study under his tutelage.

Besides this, however, most artists needed the income, and physical help with the work of preparing canvases, boards, and pigments. It is true that some artists, even well-known ones, misused the situation. Leaving a good deal of work to the apprentices while adding only the final touches by himself — and then of course signing his own name. The students were usually quite honored by the situation, to think that the artist found their work suitable enough to be signed by his name. It seems strange to me that you do not have students yourself, and to some extent we did feel that a good artist had a certain responsibility to teach his methods and philosophy to others. A large number of students, of course, also meant that the artist could take on a larger number of commissioned works, knowing he would have help with much of the physical labor involved. *(Long pause.)* There were also father-and- son arrangements, in which case it was often difficult to tell who's work was whose. The younger or the elder often did each other's work and then signed the name of which of them was specified in the commission.

(4:00. Ann, the RN on the evening shift, came in to say hello. She said Jane might be moved on Sunday—tomorrow—since everything is supposed to be back to normal by Monday at 11:00 AM. [The newspaper story reported this also.] "Gee, I hope they don't put anybody in my old room," Jane said, referring to 331.

(Another nurse came in to give Jane her eye drops, but left when she couldn't find any in the room. I heard thunder. Now the sky contains dark heavy clouds at 4:10, and the curtains are blowing. The nurse didn't come back, so I read Jane the last couple of paragraphs of material.

(4:25.) We had several regiments of cavalrymen who were to protect us in times of invasion—but more often than not they simply held parades on holidays or days of special designation. Some artists specialized in painting members of such regiments. Many smaller towns also had such regiments, though smaller in number. And the very smallest of towns had citizen soldiers—groups of ordinary men from all walks of life who wore a uniform and took part in parades or festivals.

In a way we were far less dependent upon other nations than you are, for while we traded, still our main means of support came from within our towns themselves—so the politics or natural disasters in distant lands did not have the same effects on us as they do in your time.

(Pause.) We were nationalistic, quite proud of ourselves—and indeed we may have been a mite overly smug, but we were overall a kindly industrious people, well respected in most of Europe.

(Long pause at 4:30. We heard the loud sound of someone pushing the medication cart in the hall; it came to a stop outside our door, but no one came in. We expected the eye drops. "I'm just waiting," Jane said.

(4:33.) I cannot imagine what it must be like to live under the threat of nuclear destruction.

Such a wholesale annihilation never occurred to us, of course, nor did it ever occur to us that man would ever have such power. One day God would destroy the world—we were taught that—but we always managed to put it far into the future. We never thought it possible that man by himself could achieve such power. In that regard, of course, we differ considerably, for families imagined their generation populating the future, and the earth itself seemed indestructible until God himself deemed to bring it to an end.

(Long pause.) Certainly your country has men of honor in it, and so must other countries. All politicians are not scoundrels, either in your time or mine. It is hard, however, to see how men of honor could end up in such a predicament. Nor can I understand how they justify their own positions.

(4:39. "I'm just waiting," Jane said again. We heard the cart moving again in the hall.

(4:40.) We rested cozily in the supposition that we would pass our knowledge down to our families, and in a way the world seemed protected—certainly in comparison to people's attitudes in your time. For your people must feel surrounded by uncertainty.

In my time even the poorest of men *(long pause)* might imagine his sons and daughters populating future generations—while your people cannot even be sure they themselves will survive for a complete lifetime.

According to the beliefs of my lifetime, even hell has its certain coziness, for it belonged in a definite place, and even possessed its own kind of order—and there was a promised life after death, even if it meant eternal damnation.

If I am correctly interpreting information about your world, then it seems that many people do not even believe man has a soul, or is even in control of his own will, so nuclear annihilation must imply the worst kind of negation to such people. Of the two alternatives, hell seems the better one.

Many of man's greatest hopes have always rested on a promised tomorrow, and to be denied that promise for whatever reasons, leaves him footless and hopeless indeed—or so it seems to me.

(4:48. "I'll rest for a minute and have a cigarette," Jane said. Her delivery had been quiet, but steady, even determined. There was much noise in the hall, with girls calling back and forth. "Any chance of you feeding me?" Jane asked.

("Maybe."

("Oh," she said, pleased. I washed her face with a paper towel, and then washed my own face in order to wake up. Jane said she even had more material— but that supper was coming. I'd seen the cartful of trays sitting in the hall. She put out her cigarette. "I'm getting a little more...."

(4:49.) On the other hand, I suppose it's possible that man might realize

that he himself commits the evil that we once thought originated from the devil.

Faced with the possibility of annihilation, man could take a nostalgic look about his planet, as if for the final time, and see it suddenly in its true light, so that he recognized all of the beauty and majesty of the planet itself. In that case, the species could almost remake itself in the twinkling of an eye, and artists would feel compelled to *(pause)* portray earth's beauty with a vitality and force that artists have never possessed before.

In the past the Roman church for centuries provided the artist with inspiration, and by my time that had already vanished. To a larger extent than you realize art became more secular, more oriented to humanity, perhaps, and less to religious values, though these did linger on into my time, but man needs the feeling of a tomorrow. He needs to feel that there is room for improvement, and it is difficult to see how any worthwhile endeavor could exist under the threat of a complete annihilation—one that sees nature as well as man destroyed.

(5:05.) We thought of man and nature as if man were one thing and nature another. I see now that both are intimately connected — yet I think that I did know that without knowing that I did. When I was alive and painting my own work.

(Long pause.) I cannot even imagine how the unit of the family could exist if a future were not promised or assumed, into which future generations could grow. *(Pause.)* This perhaps disturbs me more than anything else I understand about your historical period. I do not happen to believe that man could actually destroy himself and the planet to—

(5:10. Bea Dibble brought in the supper tray. She didn't stay. Jane seemed to hesitate. "Is that the end, or....?" I asked. She resumed right away.)

There is something about the dimension in which I now exist that tells me that such a statement actually could not occur—that such a wholesale destruction is literally not possible under those conditions *(most emphatically).* Planets might be destroyed through eons of time, for example, but following their own natures, one creature alone could simply not force such annihilation on the rest of the planet's creatures. In one way or another that particular kind of catastrophe would not be allowed to happen.

(5:12 PM. "Okay for the rest of that particular chunk," Jane said. I fed her supper, and then read the prayer to her. She had a cigarette, and I left about 6:45. She called me later that evening.

(One question has been occurring to me more and more often as these sessions progress. I haven't mentioned it to Jane yet, and am not sure whether she's thought of it also. My query concerns the world-view theory behind these sessions—that the material coming through is supposedly from Rembrandt's world view, rather from

any survivor of physical death called Rembrandt per se. [It might help if I took the time to review Jane's and Seth's materials on the world view schema.]

(Some of the Rembrandt material, however, appears to be so up-to-date that it makes me wonder about our usual picture of a world view. There are many questions. One explanation could be that even a personality's world view continually updates itself, that it's not a static thing that ceases developing at the point of death of the individual it represents. More questions: If this is so, then the world view itself is conscious and absorbing more information that Jane, say, can tap into. It could be a relay station between Jane and Rembrandt himself. Would Rembrandt know about this?

(Certainly some of my own uneasiness here stems from the way Jane and I regard tales we hear of people getting information through the Ouija board, for instance, from world figures like Socrates, or Cleopatra, or whomever. We've always laughed at such delusions. It seemed quite logical to assign such goings-on to the safety of a world view interpretation, since we've been thinking a world view is available to anyone who can manage to reach it. The concept of world-views, perhaps, may be much more flexible than we've considered. And the explanation of what Jane is accomplishing with the Rembrandt material, especially in the first person singular, may be much simpler—a much more direct contact with the artist....)

DELETED SESSION
JULY 24, 1983 2:48 PM SUNDAY

(It rained rather heavily last night, and to a lesser degree this morning. Room 350 was cool and sunny and breezy when I arrived; the window was open and Millie Smith was finishing feeding Jane lunch. Jane lay nude on her back. Millie was talking about Jane going to places like Bethany or Eicor, and I sidetracked that conversation since I didn't think it had healthy implications. Jane didn't seem to be bothered. The talk revealed Millie's own lack of perception, though, how little she knew of suggestion, etc. As Jane and I have both said many times, "You've got to watch it every minute." Yet Millie is perfectly entitled to her own world view.

(Jane gets weighed tomorrow, and is eating all she can. Millie said she has to take in more fluid, though. The talk now is that there won't be any moving of patients before next Wednesday—back to their old rooms.

(Jane read the newspaper article I brought in, on the aftermath of the strike. She also read the session for July 20, and the first three pages for July 22. Then I showed her page 2 of the private Seth session for April 28, 1981, in which Seth said her symptoms were the result of tension, etc. She said, "I've been working on the idea *that I <u>don't</u> have arthritis." She said Peggy Gallagher's article on the strike aftermath was "well written."*

(Jane still has the extra freedom of movement in her arms, but today when I tried to help her move her legs down farther, I found them to be quite resistant. In fact, her arms have gained even a little more extra motion; her legs will also open sideways more than they have been doing. See my own notes for more details about the usual routine Jane undergoes each day re medications, checking, and so forth.

(At 2:20 I read to her the last couple of pages of yesterday's session, concerning Rembrandt saying that he didn't think man would be allowed to bring about his own destruction plus the annihilation of nature itself. "I'm just waiting," she said. It was a very pleasant, peaceful interlude in 350, with the curtains blowing in the breezy sunny air—but I soon had to pull the curtains closed because of the glare. "Let me know when you're ready," I said, and began to work on the mail.

(Rembrandt's subject matter really surprised me at first; although I soon saw how it fit in with the notes I'd written at the close of yesterday's session. If varieties of the world view phenomenon operate, then "Rembrandt" can talk about these subjects just as well as about any others—and this is another of those simple observations that become obvious once one thinks of it. I think these comments are especially appropriate since Rembrandt continues to refer to his interpretations of material he's picking up from Jane and me.)

Mankind has always dreamed of a continuing life after death—and perhaps the whole nuclear-disaster concept represents the other side of that picture: the fear that instead of continued existence nothing at all would remain of man or his works.

In any case, the longer we are in communication, the more information I receive concerning the nature of your own world, so I have picked up the idea of <u>evolution</u>—and I am amazed that the concept has so influenced the schools of knowledge in your time.

(Again, another instance of the growth of the world view that Rembrandt discussed at the end of the last session. I'll add here another comment I meant to add to the close of yesterday's material. Rembrandt implied that from his viewpoint he felt that mankind would not be allowed to wreak wholesale destruction upon himself and the planet itself. An interesting statement or belief, with many connotations....

(It's also somewhat amusing to consider whether the theory of evolution has anything to do with "knowledge.")

If I am interpreting that information correctly, then it appears that the evolutionary theory has affected painting to a much lesser degree than it has the other arts. Given the popularity of evolutionary theory *(pause)*, it seems initially that the concept would have influenced painting <u>the most</u>, firing the painter's imagination to such an extent that he would have been driven to express the idea through the use of images, and then expressing through painting the many stages through which the various species have traveled, portraying these in visual terms.

(Long pause.) I would have thought *(pause)* that painting, being so visually oriented, would have found a special place of its own *(pause)*. I imagine the world of portraits being transformed as the artist tried to follow mankind through its various stages, trying to portray *(pause)* man when he was half-man, half-ape, or trying to suggest in a man's features the visual remnants of his evolutionary past.

(2:59.) If I understand my information correctly, such however was not the case. The world of literature was highly influenced by evolutionary theory, but the world of art, that is painting, seems almost as untouched as though the theory of evolution did not exist at all.

(Long pause at 3:00.) I find the theory itself rather impossible to understand, and I am amazed that it held such a sway for so long. *(Long pause.)* It seems to me that when one is painting the human form there is a kind of truth involved. The artist must have recognized intuitively that evolution simply would not work when it was stripped down to its barest philosophy. The truth of anatomy would actually be violated if evolution was a fact. The artist is used to studying the body and its anatomy. He understands what the body can do and cannot do.

(3:05.) No visual reproduction of evolution would work. The artist's eye would immediately see that such and such a position, or temporary organ, was impossible. It <u>seems</u> that the artists *(pause)*, whether they believed in evolution or not, kept it far enough away so that its influence upon painting was insignificant. The artists apparently were not fooled—or at least at some level they realized that the evolutionary stages could not be visually shown because they did not exist as given.

The idea of reincarnation has not left its mark on the world of painting either, though again at first glance it seems as if any painter believing in reincarnation would attempt to make an artistic statement as he applied it to portraits.

(3:10.) It seems to me that the idea could vastly enrich *(pause)* portraits as the artist attempted to portray or suggest the other faces his sitter might have known. At the least, it seems the artist should suggest those other features, so that the sitter portrayed in time was still shown as wearing many faces, and to see the face shadowed by other influences.

(Long pause at 3:13. "That's it for the moment," Jane said. "I've got more, but

I think I'm going to have a BM, too. I'll have a cigarette."

("He sounds like me," I said, feeling somehow vindicated in my own ideas about evolution. I explained to Jane that in this material she'd touched upon my own visual objections to evolutionary ideas. I reminded her of the argument I used to use, of the dolphin at one end of the room and the four-footed land animal from which it's supposed to have descended, in its return to the water, at the other end of the room. I wanted a series of transitional stages lined up across the room, showing exactly how the land creature changed, step by step, into the water-based one. How it ate, when and for how long it lived, just how all those postulated changes took place. I used to laugh and say that if I had unlimited funds I'd hire some of the world's leading evolutionary experts to construct actual models, say fifty in sequence, showing how the dolphin looked as it returned to the sea, I'd even finance the building of a museum to house the exhibits, so that all could see, I used to tell Jane. My only stipulations would be that the experts constructed each model in the finest detail, so that it could be examined inside and out, and furnish with each model a detailed written plan of when each stage took place, and for how long, and why, and so forth. Maps of the changing earth would have to be included, also. I envisioned some hilarious questions arising as the sequence of models neared the shoreline from dry land. How would the change from air-breathing to the water environment look, for example? From legs to fins?

(I used to think Jane just let me ramble on, since I don't recall her saying much about the idea one way or another. I still think it's a good idea, however. I've always been surprised that extant museums haven't mounted such exhibits on their own, at least on a much more modest scale. I used to think that if they were well done they might help quiet some of the criticism of evolutionary theory. Now I think that the model-makers would have enormous difficulties showing in visual, three-dimensional terms, the stages involved from land to water, say.

("I think you're coming up with some extremely original ideas here," I told Jane. "Here Rembrandt is saying that the longer these sessions go on the more he learns from us. That's backwards from the way psychic stuff is usually presented in the literature, isn't it? It makes you wonder what can be accomplished this way...."

(Jane put out her cigarette. She was having a small BM. She received her eye drops. I worked on the mail. We talked about the Rembrandt material on art and reincarnation. Again, I said it was quite original. I was pleased that painting had largely "escaped" evolutionary implications especially. His reasons for this made intuitive sense to me. "I do think that some of my own sketches show the reincarnational idea, though," I said. "That one I did of your mother, from my dream, and some others. Also, I've always felt that some of the heads I like to paint in oil have a reincarnational basis." Jane nodded. "But I've also always felt that what I've done is so

minute in comparison to what it's possible to accomplish," I added. "Compared to what I wanted to do...." And still do, in painting. Sometimes the yearning to do this is like an ache.

(Jane got her eye drops, and told an aide that she was through having her BM. No one came in to clean her up, though. I worked on mail. Finally, tired of waiting, she said she had some more material.

(4:38.) In my time artists must have been held in greater honor than in your own, since any good artist would have given the theory of evolution the boot—seeing that it would not work out.

In visual terms it was impossible to suggest or reproduce the so-called stages that were required in the evolutionary process. Indeed in wonder, seriously, if there was something drastically out of order in the working of Darwin's eyesight—or perhaps he was weak in mental visualization. I don't believe that any person with clear visualization could have originated the theory, or taken it seriously. The accumulation of information in your historical period is so vast that no one man could ever hope to embrace it *(pause)*. No one person, it seems, can be a true master in every field of endeavor, while in my time a man could master his profession or his trade, and know it from the inside out. *(Long pause.)* Even with the religious restriction the world of my time was not as mapped out. In a fashion perhaps men felt freer to speculate because so much of the world was still unexplored and mysterious.

The extent of your scientific development did not at first seem too surprising to me, since I thought of it in mechanical terms — the invention of countless new gadgets — and I did not understand its philosophical connotations, or the direction in which it obviously led the scientist. The Dutch, like the Swiss and the Germans, always had a love of gadgets and liked mechanics. I always thought that such leanings simply represented good energy, ambition, and an almost childish fascination with tinkering. Now I see that science and your theory of evolution joined hands, and so the entire idea of a nuclear annihilation must have come out of that uneasy marriage.

(4:50. Excellent, Rembrandt, I thought. I heard the supper trays in the corridor.)

I see also how it completely changed the idea of the family, and to some extent robbed both parents of their rightful honor. It also must have dampened man's enthusiasm, for he thought so poorly of himself that I do not see how he could trust his own works. I must say I am indeed pleased that such ideas were not reflected by the painters or artists of the time—and in that regard art certainly retained an innocent integrity.

(Long pause at 4:53.) If I understand my information, again, painting

turned away from outward visual objects into an abstract phase. This might have been because the artists felt they could trust the integrity of the exterior world no longer.

(Pause at 4:55. "I hate to say it," Jane said, "but you better press the call button. The smell is getting pretty raunchy." I hadn't noticed, actually, perhaps because I'd been so intrigued by the material and the answering thoughts and material that raced through my own head as Rembrandt talked, and I wrote.

(4:56.) Abstractionalism was not seeking *(pause)* a spiritualistic knowledge—at least to my understanding—but in a fashion it was breaking up the old world of solid images.

(An aide brought in the supper tray at 4:48, then cleaned up Jane. She was through in a couple of minutes. Jane was still on her back. I fed her supper—or what she could eat of it, since the meat hadn't been ground up and was too tough. I got Jane Ensure and ice cream from the kitchen; these helped fill her up. When she was through I read her the prayer. She had a cigarette and I left at 6:50.

(She didn't call me later. "It didn't work out.")

DELETED SESSION
JULY 25, 1983 3:21 PM MONDAY

(Steve and Tracy Blumenthal visited Jane last night. I was surprised when Steve called just as I got home—I hadn't expected them to come to Elmira this weekend. I didn't see them, since I was busy and felt tired too. Steve said he'd had a good talk with Pete Harpending re tapes, and so forth, last Friday. I plan to call Pete this week for an appointment.

(This morning I called Nancy Overton at Prentice-Hall, asking her to send a cable of acceptance to Ankh-Hermes in Holland, re Mass Events. *We didn't know this was in the works. See the file correspondence. This is Nancy's last week at Prentice-Hall. I hope it doesn't mean more deterioration in our communications with our publisher.*

(Margaret Bumbalo called this morning to say that Venice Palmer will be in town today. Margaret wanted to know if it was all right for the two of them to visit Jane tonight. I said I'd check, but thought it was okay.

(I should note that Jane tried to call me last night after the Blumenthals' visit, but I was in the bedroom by then, the TV was on, and I realized too late that the phone was ringing.

(On the way in this afternoon I stopped to see Diane Fife in the business office. She's to see me in 350 within the hour. I had questions about insurance.

(As I walked past the hall leading to 331, I saw that it still looked deserted, meaning that no moving of patients back to their old quarters was underway yet. Jane was on her back, just finishing lunch; Millie was feeding her. The day was very pleasant and sunny. The curtains and the window of 350 were both open. Jane began to have a BM not long after I arrived at 1:15. There wasn't an in-house bulletin today. As we talked I found out from Jane that she'd been weighed this morning—and that her weight was down to 73 pounds. She's quite upset about this. The weight loss didn't sound right. She hasn't seen Fred yet. The weight figure reminded me that once the same scale had her gaining five pounds within a week, in 331. That hadn't been right either. No one, including Fred, had believed it. Yet the operator insists that the scale is accurate.

(Jane went to hydro this morning.

(Jane was cleaned up by 2:00. I talked with Mrs. Fife in the lounge by the elevators. She's going to check further, but there seems to be some very good news: Major Medical may pay 100% of Jane's costs in the hospital, as outlined by Jim Clune in his letter of evaluation of a year ago. I signed several papers for Diane, which she will copy for me, and am to see her tomorrow with some major medical forms and a few more questions. I guess the potentially good news about costs is more than I expected, after all this time of struggle. If true, this news may influence actions Pete may take re our personal finances and marital situation. We'll see. So far, I seem to have had some success with the idea, even the belief, that given enough time many of these questions automatically work themselves out, if slowly. Our last month's bill from the hospital, as I explained to Jane after seeing Diane, will be revised in that a portion of it will come under major medical coverage. This should reduce our share of the costs under the 80%-20% split that applies to the 70-day sections of our policies.

(2:12. Jane read the rest of the session for July 22. The extra freedom of motion in her arms helps her steady the material as she reads. [As they did yesterday, however, her legs seem to resist moving as freely as they had been a few days ago.] I read Jane the session for July 23 and the last paragraphs for July 24. These readings took a while, and Jane dozed at times, I thought. She said it made her nervous, that she didn't want to sleep in the daytime, especially when I was there. I suggested she take a nap if she felt like it.

(Jane was still on her back. At 3:00 I straightened her up via the draw sheet. I read some mail. At 3:20 Jane said, "I'm beginning to feel as if I might have something." The hall was quiet. "Let me know when you're ready," I said.)

There are numerous methods of physical communication *(long pause)*, some that would have been considered impossible in my time.

You have the radio, and it is relatively dependable—<u>but only when you turn it on</u>. When the radio is turned off the communication is still there potentially. The same applies to any of your physical communications. You can speak through the telephone, but to do so you must work with that instrument. The television set works, but again, it has to be turned on first. In the same way, there are innumerable methods of inner communication that operate constantly— but unless you tune into them or turn them on, then you are not consciously aware of them. There are certain radio stations or television channels that you tune into or turn on most frequently, because they carry programs that you personally find informative or attractive. Using that analogy, the same is true of inner communications. They work through highly personal, associative patterns—you have to want to turn them on. It is your interest that activates them.

If a telephone rings you have the choice of answering it or not. *(Pause.)* When you become aware of inner communication, you have that same choice. *(Pause.)* Your deep appreciation of my work was largely responsible for these communications. Your wife wanted to give you a fine gift. She knew of your admiration of my painting.

(Pause at 3:30. Now the hall was quite noisy with a bevy of voices.)

She began to send out psychic feelers, so to speak, but mainly on a subconscious level, to see what might be available. I picked up *(pause)* her questioning, and I was drawn because your admiration for my painting formed a kind of bond between us, and your wife's gifts are uniquely suited to this kind of endeavor.

(Pause.) The communications were then activated. Your wife felt the tug at the other end of the line, so to speak, then she answered the telephone, or turned on the radio—but in inner mental terms. This also brought the communications to the conscious level of her mind. Where they could be recorded as you write down the words.

(All of this material brought back to mind the first session we had for the Rembrandt material. A small addition I might make to the notes I wrote for that first session, on June 9, 1983, would refer to the black-and-white reproduction of the Rembrandt self-portrait that I showed Jane in ReVision that day. [I explained at the time how someone has evidently subscribed to the magazine for us; I'd received the spring, 1983 issue a few days before showing it to Jane.]

(The point I want to make here is that while Jane was sending out her psychic feelers, which evidently took her a while. I received ReVision in the mail and spied the portrait in question. I was immediately attracted to the portrait, as I usually am to a reproduction of any of Rembrandt's works. I hadn't been painting myself for some weeks, nor had I been looking at any of the books on the artist that I have here at the house. I therefore ascribe showing Jane the portrait repro in ReVision as some sort of trigger toward releasing her material. I don't know how far back in time to follow

such ideas in order to make a case for timing everything just right so that I was able to show Jane the portrait at just the right time for her to begin these sessions. I think such timing could easily be overdone. It may be that once she'd made her proper psychic connections with the Rembrandt material, she simply held their activation through sessions in abeyance until a trigger was furnished—and this could have happened at any time. Other events besides my showing her the portrait could have done the job just as well....

(The portrait in question is attached to the first session.

(3:35.) This is a two-or-three-way communication, then, and as I do become aware of my reality I become aware of yours—though at my end I do not record the data as you do. I am simply content to receive it, and to make whatever comments I choose.

The longer the channels remain open, theoretically, the clearer the messages are. On the television set you have all kinds of knobs and dials to control the faithfulness of color and so forth. When inner communications are involved, there are also many shadings and tunings possible or necessary to keep the communications as clear as possible, and these become more automatic as the communications continue.

(3:38. "That's it for a minute. I'll have a sip of something," Jane said. Ensure and a cigarette.

("Well, I can see that the material came through in response to some of my own musings—"

("In the session I just read," Jane said, meaning that for July 22, of three days ago.

("—although I didn't mean it that way." I said I hadn't expected her to go into that subject today. "It's very interesting. It brings up some questions about the world view thing. This sounds more immediate than a world view. Do you know what I mean?"

("Yes...."

(3:45. Rhonda, an LPN, looked in briefly as we talked. Ten minutes later I turned Jane on her right side. She was quite comfortable; she seemed to lay there half-asleep, her eyes half open. I answered some mail. At 4:20 I put a wafer on Jane's lower teeth, to help her eat supper better. These seem to help.

(4:29.) As I told you, there are various kinds of communication possible.

Using the methods we are *(pause)*, then patterns of association operate strongly. My own curiosity about one subject or another serves to tune me into your knowledge of the subject, and when you ask me questions I am led to examine my own situation with your question in mind. So to that extent I gauge my answer to the question itself, so it is important that I understand your question properly, but I do not look down upon your world with some omnipotent eye—and indeed, there is little need to do so.

(Long pause at 4:32. It might be interesting to learn, sometime, just how Rembrandt does perceive Jane and me, say—as energy fields at times, or....? My hunch is that at times he may glimpse us as individuals, similar to his own perceptions of himself. But so far I haven't interrupted Jane's deliveries to ask questions.)

I am still, of course, drawn to my own work, and to my times—but I also view them far differently than I did when I was alive, and even my attitude toward my paintings has changed.

I still think more or less as a painter does, but a painter in an entirely new situation in another dimension of existence, so that my perception is indeed enlarged and more elastic than it was before.

I do not particularly feel curious as to where my paintings are. It is enough to see them in my mind's eye as vividly as ever. *(Long pause.)* I still feel as if my paintings and I taught each other, and that to some extent I am where I am because of my work—that this applies to executed paintings and those that I envisioned but never painted. To some extent I am aware of your own work. Certainly I am aware of your interests, and those of your wife.

(Long pause at 4:38. Jane's delivery had been quietly intent, and continued to be so.)

Certainly I am Rembrandt, but I am no longer the Rembrandt who lived in that studio, since I have changed so much since then. That old Rembrandt is held dearly in my mind, however, as the self that I was. So in that regard I am Rembrandt and I am not.

(4:39. Now that made sense to me.

(Rhonda came back in with her noisy medicine cabinet on wheels. She gave Jane eye drops. My wife lay on two chucks, the upper one of them extending way up under her shoulders. "She doesn't need that one." Rhonda agreed when I asked her if it was necessary. I helped her get it out from under Jane, and then the two of us lifted Jane up toward the head of the bed more. Our efforts worked well. Jane was on her back again.

(4:47.) On the other hand, some of this is very difficult to pinpoint.

It has occurred to me since our communications began that they happened in their entirety on one afternoon as I dozed and daydreamed in my studio back in my lifetime.

As sequences go, the communications are not yet finished, and the impression I have of their happening during the daydream may or may not be valid. It is simply a feeling that I have, and I am communicating it to you.

(Quite pragmatically:) After death you can indeed go back, and influence

your own life *(pause)*—a very tricky endeavor, but true nevertheless. I know that I have returned on occasion to find my old self painting, and dissatisfied with the color being used I would whisper: "No: use this or that color instead," — and my old self would do so.

I am still intrigued by the new kind of painting I told you about earlier—a mysterious yet vaster kind of painting, certainly, than any I have ever known. *(Long pause.)* I think that after death people do redouble about themselves, in that....

(Long pause. Jane lay quietly; I thought she might be dozing. The material above made me wonder if, out of all her various experiences, she might be able to say that any of them reflected such a return of her whole or larger self to her physical self, perhaps with a bit of advice or a helpful comment. She would have had to become aware of the experience from her viewpoint, of course, rather than from that of her larger self. This might dilute any awareness. I think of something like this as separate from her "library" experiences.

(She started. "Read me back that last material, Bob.")

....They return, offering advice and counsel to the old self, who may then interpret such experience as a complete daydream, while still receiving the benefits. In this way the future certainly influences the present.

(4:56. "Okay for a minute....Guess I'll have a cigarette. I finally felt I was really getting into it."

("Some very intriguing stuff there. I'd like to give it some thought...." I could hear the supper trays in the hall.

(5:00. As she smoked and we waited for supper Jane said, "I'm getting just a little more—that daVinci was in contact with many minds in the future—you know, the stuff about airplanes and all of those other inventions...."

("Whose minds? His own, or—?"

("Many different minds," Jane said. "And something about daVinci being fiercer in his imagination than Rembrandt was. And that daVinci would get bored very quickly, while Rembrandt never got bored."

("I guess I can see what you'd mean there."

(5:06. "....that daVinci could become very petulant, and was always seeking more excitement, while Rembrandt wanted to explore what was around him as much as possible. Then I had an image of Rembrandt laughing, saying that daVinci would have gone crazy in Amsterdam, and that daVinci liked to be where there was gossip and intrigue, while Rembrandt avoided gossip and intrigue as much as he could.... DaVinci would have considered the Dutch really smug—he didn't have much use for industry or tidiness, either."

(A bit strange, I thought—daVinci not having much use for industry, consid-

ering the scope of the material he'd picked up from various minds: He'd tuned into many mechanical devices that would require an industrial foundation for their production....

(Bea Dibble brought in the supper tray. It smelled good.

(5:09. "Oh shit," Jane said, "Are you ready for this? While Michelangelo was a giant-sized artist he had a child's emotions, and he—uh—almost looked for hurts and insults, but his talent was gargantuan, and Rembrandt considers him the greatest artist of all. But he wouldn't have wanted to live his life either—Rembrandt wouldn't."

("Somehow what we're getting is Rembrandt's view of these two artists."

(5:12. "Ready for supper?"

("Yeah. I was also getting that Rembrandt thought Michelangelo was overly emotional—he somehow invited anguish, and worked it out through his painting."

("I could see that."

("I was getting something else but I lost it.... I don't feel particularly hungry—just hot. I didn't realize you were going to stay."

(It's worked out that as long as Jane's in rehab, I stay to feed her supper. The staff is still quite shorthanded. Each day since the strike ended we hear unfounded talk that in a day or two Jane will be moved back to 331. Now this is supposed to happen on Wednesday.

(5:17. Jane told me as she had a cigarette after supper that Rembrandt didn't think much of Cézanne as an artist. He was upset about what Cézanne did to the human figure. I agreed that I could expect that opinion on Rembrandt's part, since Cézanne's treating the figure as an object was contrary to what I thought were Rembrandt's deepest feelings about human beings.

(Then Jane came through with dictation:

(5:48.)—and while Rembrandt wasn't given to landscapes, as many artists were, still it seemed to him that if you painted landscapes they should look sturdy enough for a man to walk upon, rather than the way Cézanne painted them—so hazy that it looked as though they were filled with holes that wouldn't support even the hopping of a rabbit. *(Pause. Cigarette out.)* And he didn't think too much of the colors, either, finding them also too hazy and pale. The world as Cézanne painted it wouldn't hold together *(half-laughing)*, but would fall apart. In fact, everything looked as if it was falling over. He admired the man for his spunk, and so defying the usual rules of painting, but that was all.

("Okay, I'll have some ice cream. I still get feelings I don't like in that catheter. It was irrigated today." I read her the prayer, and checked the TV listings for tonight. Jane said she could get more on Rembrandt; it was going that well today, if I could stay, and if Margaret Bumbalo and Venice Palmer and Debbie Harris weren't to visit

this evening. I left at 6:15. She didn't call later.

(A note: While eating a late supper, by "chance" I tuned into the Phil Donahue show on TV. His guest was Shirley MacLaine, talking about her book for an hour. I watched it for three-quarters of an hour. We weren't mentioned, nor did I expect that we would be.)

DELETED SESSION
JULY 26, 1983 4:04 PM TUESDAY

(Jane didn't call last night. The day was clear and warm and sunny in 350, with the window open but the curtains closed. Jane lay nude on her back. She saw Fred this morning but doesn't think he knows she lost weight—though he asked her if I'd talked to her about the feeding tube, following his call to me. He wants her to drink "a sugar thing" tomorrow morning; then, Jane said, they take a blood test to check her absorption of nutrients. Fred thinks her trouble lies in the intestines. Yet he told her that even if the absorption rate is impaired, they wouldn't be doing anything about it.... I don't know whether this means they can't do anything about it, Jane couldn't respond very well, or what. It represents another of the imponderables that it seems we're always dealing with these days. I asked Jane to try to remember to ask about the results of the tests, and I'll attempt to do the same.

(2:00. Jane read the first seven pages of the session for July 23, and had a cigarette before I turned her on her right side. No one had cleaned her teeth or done her hair yet today, so I did. Neither has she received her aspirin, although she's asked for it twice. Rehab is evidently still not well-balanced; now the talk is that Jane will go back to 331 tomorrow or Thursday. The in-house bulletin seems to have disappeared since the strike was settled. Today we saw two of the RN's, Susan and Jackie, for the first time since the strike; we'd known them from the previous time Jane was in rehab late in '82 and early in '83.

(The paperwork proliferates. Diane Fife called to say that Major Medical will be billed by the hospital. This might be a great relief if all goes well. I signed the two major medical forms I'd given her yesterday, and another form. I'll get copies of all forms I signed tomorrow when I see her in her office at 1:00, when she will copy Jim Clune's letter. She told me that a portion of last month's bill for Jane should be assigned to major medical, and if 100% of this is paid it should result in lower costs for us for last month, since the 20% share we're responsible for under the 70-day portion of our insurance plan will be reduced.

(Margaret Bumbalo and Venice didn't visit Jane last night also, Margaret told me in a call this morning, but plan to do so tonight. Debbie Harris did see my wife,

though.

(This morning I wrote Prentice-Hall about the affair of the Dutch translation of Mass Events.

(I read the rest of July 23 to Jane, and July 25. She looked hot and unhappy, not very comfortable on her side. Rose irrigated her catheter. Others took her vitals. I turned Jane back on her back at 3:00. Jane fretted because she hadn't come through with any Rembrandt material yet. "I got hot and tired, I guess," she said. Her eyes are very red. I closed the window to make the weak air-conditioning more effective; as the afternoon hours pass the descending sun begins to beat strongly against the one window in 350. Jane began a small BM at 3:40. I opened some mail, and checked the evening's TV programs for her.

(Jane was intrigued by the material she'd given at the end of yesterday's material, involving Rembrandt's comments about da Vinci, Michelangelo, and Cézanne. She finished another cigarette. As she delivered material for Rembrandt this afternoon, I found it quite interesting to consider that our own knowledge was being reflected through the Rembrandt world view. I was pleased that our wide interests were proving of value in an unanticipated way. This certainly gave added value to those interests, the files maintain, and so forth. At times I've wondered why I keep the files going. Obviously they serve a number of purposes. Among them would be that each bit of information I collect serves to keep us in touch with our world that much more effectively. And not only do they serve as valuable reference material for any notes I may write for our own work, but they often point up ways in which Jane and I disagree with what's going on in our world. Often an article or news event or whatever will serve as a takeoff point for what I think is a better interpretation, a more original one.... Our magazine subscriptions have been of great value here.)

I did not particularly mean to comment on the works of other artists, but your knowledge of their works sparked my own curiosity. I will add only that the energy in some of Picasso's works is amazing. Some of the canvases are charged with excitement and energy.

(Rhonda came in with a pill of Synthroid for Jane. She had to grind it up and add some ice cream. Jane has already had her morning dose of Synthroid, so this means that Fred has added to her intake; he'd mentioned doing this to Jane earlier, I believe. Jane took it without protest.

("Interesting," I said, "that he would pick up that about Picasso from us."

("I was just getting something more when the interruption came."

(4:11.) I am astounded and scandalized, if I understand this information properly, at the huge amounts of money that the works of dead artists bring—my own included.

It seems to me that the dealers simply grow rich and fat as kings *(long pause)* on sums *(long pause)* that are simply outrageous. The entire structure built around galleries and museums is utterly surprising to me. Truly in my time no one but kings could amass such fortunes—and never did the artist amass such huge portions. It all seems quite apart from the artist's own intention, or the nature of art or painting itself—a complete culture, built upon the works of dead men. No wonder you need so many museums and art tours, for no one but the very wealthy could afford to purchase such paintings. I see man's greed is still as strong as ever.

(4:16. "I'll have a cigarette," Jane said after a long pause. "I think he's thinking the whole thing over: He just can't get over it."

("Well, I can say that he's right in his assessment of the whole situation," I laughed. "In case he wants to know...." After some hesitation I added, "Some of this is making me wonder if we're dealing with a world-view situation per se. Know what I mean?" I was unwilling, even afraid, to proclaim that we might be in touch with Rembrandt himself, whereas the world-view idea was quite acceptable.

("Yes," Jane said. "There's more give-and-take in it."

(This could also depend on what our conception of a world view is, I thought. There may be more variety of response and participation than we'd considered. Jane finished the cigarette she'd started. Rhonda and Eleanor came in to clean her up. They had to turn Jane on her side. "Jane," Rhonda laughed, "you do a neat job. I'll say that." Jane ended up back on her back.

(4:40.) I am not sure that I understand your world-view concept. It seems to me that if this were a world view, you would pick up only the attitudes *(pause)* I had toward life while living—but my comments upon your world, and the interactions between us that occur, lead me to believe that something more is involved. Or it may be that even in life my curiosity was so strong that it leapt outside of the usual context and was therefore more easily activated when the opportunity arose.

The nature of your world comes to me in snatches, usually with quick images, but it is not an overall kind of view at all. In a way it is piecemeal, and I must patch it together.

(Long pause at 4:44. All of this is very interesting. I'm not sure, not having read it lately, but I don't think Rembrandt's idea of a world view coincides with that of James, for example, since James refers to his afterdeath environment. Rembrandt's would fit in with Cezanne's, however. These comparisons require some thought. I also think that Rembrandt's ideas in this area will soon enlarge.)

I seem to be aware of issues in your lifetimes that are rather immediate, though I have glimpses of past events also.

(Long pause at 4:46.) I am intrigued by the invention of acrylics, and cer-

tainly would have experimented with them had I the opportunity in my past. (*Pause.*) I am certainly pleased to know that my work, or most of it, exists in your historical period—but the uses made of it in the galleries and so forth, and with the dealers, strikes me as nefarious.

While we are communicating, other portions of my consciousness go in a different direction entirely. It is as if I try on realities to find those that suit me best.

(*A one-minute pause at 4:50.*) I suppose it is with some sadness that I view the world of photography and movies and television, for the multiplicity of images makes it almost seem that painting and the human figure become less and less immediate, and less necessary. So what must the artist do when the market for his work is so small, even though the reach of physical communication is so vast? Right now I can only ask the question.

(*Long pause at 4:54. There are several answers to Rembrandt's question, though I can only touch upon some of them here. It may be that his reaction of sadness at the state of portrait painting reflects material he's picking up from me. This would be based upon my own feelings of sadness or of things not done, pertaining to what I feel are possibilities of my own that I did not fulfill for many reasons. My own choices led me to follow my own courses of action, and painting portraits, as much as I wanted to, became but one interest I developed. As I grew I began to have many questions, and these meant that I had many other interests. I began to see my painting as but one way of expressing some of those questions. I also think Jane may have some feelings that I left certain talents unfulfilled, so Rembrandt could be tuning in to those. I would like to add that there are a number of successful portrait painters active today—and they receive very good money indeed—and that the field is still there for anyone who comes along with unique gifts and focuses upon those goals.*

(*I think the urge to paint, to make images, to recreate the world through one's unique gifts, is so strong, so innate within certain individuals, that it will always be with us—at least for the foreseeable future—and that the expression of these abilities through art is bound to stir deep emotional responses among viewers. For the images presented, if they are alive, will echo universal knowledge and feeling.*

(*I heard the supper trays in the hall.*)

It still seems to me, though, that the market should be there for a good portrait, for the painter can uncover portions of the human personality that the camera can never show. (*Long pause.*) I do not even believe that it is proper to use photographs as an aid in painting either portraits or landscapes. For then you are not really in touch with your subject, but only a facsimile.

(*4:57. "That's it for the moment," Jane said. "I was almost getting something else, but it wasn't quite strong enough." I told her that I almost broke in, above, to tell Rembrandt that he need have no worries about art not being necessary. [Hence my sticking in the comments after 4:54.]*

(5:00. "I was just getting that maybe he overreacted—" Jane began, when the supper tray arrived. I fed her. I was getting tired. While she was eating Jane said, with a touch of humor: "I was getting from Rembrandt that he thought it was a wonder you could ever get any painting done in that room at 458—you had so much light he didn't see how you could control it."

(Actually, I couldn't control the light, of course, and ended up blocking off a few of the windows of the porch, those facing the house of our dentist, Paul O'Neill, or the east side. The porch had tall windows on three sides, so when we moved into that apartment in 1960 I naturally took over the porch as an artist's studio, following the tradition of the more light the better, and so forth.

(I never learned, however, that I hadn't carried the control of light far enough; I should have blocked out more windows. I remember being particularly bothered by too much scattered light when I painted the second portrait of Jane as she stood up for me before the windows. I carried the painting quite successfully so far, going by what I saw before me, and then stopped working on it. I felt frustrated because I couldn't see before me the contrasts of light and dark I wanted. They weren't there. I didn't know how to depart from the visual evidence before me to try to achieve what I wanted. I was afraid I'd spoil what I had done. Today the portrait is just as I left it, with much of the cool underpainting still visible. It hangs in our living room. For a long time I'd stored it in a little room we had available for odds and ends on the third floor at 458, thinking that it was an unfinished job.

(After she'd finished eating and was having a cigarette, Jane said something about Rembrandt mentioning that Seth knew of these sessions—something to the effect that they were all saying the same thing, I believe. Jane also said that she had picked up from Rembrandt that these sessions were definitely different than the "usual world-view thing."

(I left Jane and room 350 at 6:20 PM without even reading the prayer. I was really tired—I felt as though it would be an effort to drive home, let alone get supper. Lately I've been missing the nap I used to get for half an hour before supper, since I stay these days to feed Jane. I didn't see many signs of activity in the long hall leading down to 331 as I walked past it on my way to the elevators.

(Jane didn't call later.)

DELETED SESSION
JULY 27, 1983 5:05 PM WEDNESDAY

(The day was sunny and warm. I got to 350 after seeing Diane Fife in the business office and getting copies of the papers I signed, as described in the last session. Jackie Felice, an RN, told me that Jane had another ten minutes to go before she could have anything to eat; she would be free at 1:20, in other words. Early this morning Jane had been given two cups of white glucose to drink. This very sweet substance was to be excreted through her urine, which all morning has been collected and measured in her Foley bag. The bag rested in a pan filled with ice cubes beneath Jane's bed. On a table lay the collection schedule for the urine, evidently for successive tests to measure the amount of absorption of the urine, hour by hour. I have the copy of the form that was left in the room. Jane didn't even get aspirin this morning, let alone breakfast. Jackie collected the last container of urine at 1:25. The lunch tray came.

(I began feeding Jane, but she soon broke off eating to have a heavy BM. She had a cigarette. She seldom resumes eating much after a smoke. I went out to the station to get some aspirin to mix with ice cream. Jane said that now the talk is that she'll be moved back upstairs to 331 on Friday—so the departure date from rehab continues to be put off.

(Last night I fell asleep on the couch after supper. Margaret Bumbalo and Venice had visited Jane during the evening.

(The curtains in 350 were pulled closed, the window was open a crack. Before lunch Jane read the rest of July 23. "I didn't realize you were upset about the Rembrandt sessions," she said.

("I'm not. I just have some questions, that's all. That's the way it'll work out—I figure we'll just go along and see."

("I've had some thoughts too," Jane said, "but I figure there's no use worrying about it. I just said to hell with it, and went ahead."

("Good. Me, too."

(Jane ate little for lunch, after missing breakfast. She took in no Ensure. It seems she's bound to show a weight loss when she's weighed tomorrow. I felt somewhat discouraged and resigned. The urine test is to show how well she does or doesn't absorb nutrients. My suspicion is that the eating-absorption challenge is one that grew out of past beliefs, designed to protect herself from a number of worldly and psychological conflicts. We have much insight into these challenges now. I believe I also know much about my own role in all of this. Jane ate a little more, and was finally through lunch at 2:30. She had another smoke as we talked and I worked on mail. Half an hour later she was cleaned up from her BM, with three people helping.

(Jane ended up on her right side. and I held up the first three pages of the session for July 24 so she could read them. At 4:00 Rhonda came in with her vitamins. At 4:10 Jane asked me to put her back on her back and get another chuck in place. She quickly began another BM. She had a cigarette while I read her the session for July 25. Her bandages became soiled this time. While this was going on Margaret Bumbalo called to invite me out to dinner with Venice and her husband. I declined, feeling somewhat upset, and tired, and not wanting the commitment.

("It seems all I've done today is shit and get cleaned up," Jane said with some humor. At 4:25 I pressed the call button. Rhonda, Susan and Jackie came in at once and cleaned her for the second time. Jane ended up still on her back.

(The supper tray arrived at 5:00. I yawned. Jane wasn't really hungry, so I let the tray sit on the bed-table when she said she might get some Rembrandt. The tray was still covered; the meal would stay warm for some time. Jane's delivery was the slowest I remembered it being for the Rembrandt material.)

Any spark of greatness to which I may lay claim is in relationship to my work.

What I am in relationship to these communications is a bridge personality, a term which I believe you are familiar with. *(Pause.)* There is a three-fold relationship between you, your wife and myself *(pause)*, and that relationship helps form the bridge personality, which is like a psychological connection, of course. <u>Through</u> that connection I am also aware of your relationship with Seth *(as Jane had mentioned late yesterday).*

The bridge personality that we have formed is, relatively speaking, a lesser one than the one created by Seth and you and your wife. You might say that Seth devotes himself to the art of consciousness, so that his greatness lies in the formation of his entity itself—while, relatively speaking, mine is far more physically attuned.

(Long pause at 5:10.) Painters have their own visual language, yet these communications deal primarily with words. There is no one kind of communication between the living and the dead *(long pause)*, but instead multitudinous connections. *(Long pause.)* The art of consciousness utilizes all of them, endlessly forming new relationships.

(Long pause at 5:14.) I know I have had and have more lives than one, for example, yet those others are not as pertinent to our communications. *(Long pause.)* You are interested in the painting Rembrandt, and so you have contacted the Rembrandt portion of me. That much is pertinent, regardless of how many existences I may have had, so with our communications those other personalities fall into the background, and I come into the forefront.

(Long pause at 5:19. I can note, however, that from our own standpoint some

of the other portions of the Rembrandt entity might be of quite a lot of interest to us. Each of the other personalities must have a bearing upon the Rembrandt personality, for example. In larger terms, a study of the personalities making up the Rembrandt entity, or however we define that concept, would also be of interest, although such an undertaking might be a very large one. I can see how its ramifications could be practically endless.)

I have the knowledge that Rembrandt had *(long pause)*, but I have full freedom to develop now as I choose.

(5:20. "I'm just waiting," Jane said after a long pause. "That's it for the minute, I guess."

(5:22. "Okay. Maybe you'd better start supper...."

(6:32. "If you want to stay I think I can get something interesting," Jane said after she'd finished eating and had a smoke. "I know you're tired—we can get it tomorrow—"

(I hesitated. "Well, do you want to do something for half an hour?"

("Okay. Just a minute."

(I got my pad and pen ready.)

You have been a partnership in many unconventional communications, and they have all differed in certain respects.

They have different starting-off points, depending upon the time of your lives in which they happened, and the particular issues that sparked them. *(Long pause.)* The James monologue, for example, was little concerned with your own world, because James himself was too involved with issues that were highly personal, and that dealt with the question of melancholia. During his lifetime he tried to hide that melancholia from the world. He was also dealing with matters of doubt and faith that exist in any period of time. And it was up to you to make what connections you wanted to as you related his material to your own world.

His interests, however, were primarily ones of a moral conscience. You are also concerned with matters of doubt and faith, and this formed a core of interest that helped make the communications possible.

Again, however, your wife knew of your fondness for one of James's books, done in his lifetime, so it was also her love for you that provided the impetus, as in the case of our own communications.

This also applied in your Cézanne material—but once again, you picked up Cézanne at a point where he was concerned only with art and painting, and other relationships with people were shunted to the background. He was not interested in your time period—

(6:42. Rhonda came in to pick up the supper tray. I read to Jane the last few sentences of her material.

(6:43.) That portion of his personality was also attracted to the portion of your personality that is tempted at times to devote itself exclusively to painting and to nothing else. Cézanne had the nature of a recluse, however, while you simply love solitude and the time to work. You ask too many questions that art alone cannot answer, and those questions serve to open up new channels of communication, so that your talents and your wife's work beautifully together in that regard.

All of these communications, then, emerge from different points of interest or concentration points within your own personalities that then reach out, attracting other personalities of like interest, or personalities whose interests complemented your own at a certain <u>portion</u> of their lives. You are always dealing with the <u>art of consciousness</u>, but using various techniques and methods that hopefully, overall, will give you a greater view of the nature of consciousness itself.

(6:46. Rhonda returned, to give Jane aspirin.)

<u>In a fashion</u>, and only in a fashion, you are also creating multidimensional paintings, composed of your own personalities, and personalities in other dimensions of activity—who then are empowered, if they want to, to look back and comment upon your own work.

(Rhonda came in with something for Jane to drink. I didn't note down what it was—probably ginger ale.)

Those communications bring about action, of course—a psychological action in your reality and in the realities of the personalities involved.

(Long pause at 6:50 PM. "Okay," Jane finally said. "I don't think we're going to get any more. But that's what I felt...."

(I read the prayer. Then we went over the TV programs for the evening, and I circled the ones Jane wanted so the aides or RN's could get the right channels later. I left at 7:10 PM, telling Jane to call me if she could manage to get someone to dial the number.

(I'd told Jane that the material after supper was especially interesting. I'd always been aware of the obvious fact that Jane had produced the world-view books involving James and Cézanne because of my own interest in the works of those two individuals, and that she'd done so out of her love for me. And now Rembrandt.... Once again, I wondered whether any world-view books would exist without the impetus—at least on surface levels—that I'd extended for her to work with. Naturally, she too is very interested in the overall questions posed by these three works. Each of the individuals, each in his own way, deals with questions of moral conscience, of doubt and faith. Each, while living in our terms, sought to penetrate as far as possible into the world around them—after death they continue to seek that

additional knowledge and awareness that they intuitively know is there.

(At times I've also wondered about Jane producing her own work: The World View of Jane Roberts, *for the material for such a work is always in existence, according to Jane's and Seth's separate statements. It's sure that Seth expresses a portion of Jane's world view, but it would be most interesting to compare her own production of such a work with Seth's material.)*

DELETED SESSION
JULY 31, 1983 4:03 PM SUNDAY

(This is the first Rembrandt session in four days. Much has taken place in the interim, and to list everything in any detail would take pages. Even to summarize events would be too much for this manuscript; recourse can always be had to my daily notes, to letters on file pertaining to Pete Harpending, Tam, Frederick Fell, Norm Hassinger, Prentice-Hall, Danny Stimmerman, and so on.

(Up until yesterday Jane remained in room 350 in rehab, despite all the daily talk about moving her back upstairs to 331. She continued to receive good and not-so-good service, to react for and against various people who took care of her. She went to hydro every day except today. She got weighed and actually gained a pound, to her surprise and relief. The weather continued to be hot and sticky for the most part, although we've had some good rains, too. 350 is still too hot and uncomfortable for her generally. More often than not I'm the one who turns Jane on her side or back when she needs repositioning. I've stayed to feed her supper each night. I've answered some fan mail. Debbie and Elsbeth have visited Jane. Jane still has the extra freedom of motion in her arms, but her legs remain relatively tight, compared to the way they were for a few days there, after her arms began to move better.

(Jane has been still bothered by the whole catheter problem. Even with daily irrigation the tube still contains mucus in the urine at times, and she feels twinges that could be the precursors to bladder spasms. We have heard nothing official about the urine tests Fred Kardon ordered, nor have we asked. [I have asked Jane at various times to ask Fred—or someone—but she hasn't; and I have grown lax in this area.]

(On July 28 I dug out Jane's wedding ring from the bedside table drawer, and put it on my own little finger to take home. Jane hasn't been wearing it lately because she fears it will slip off her finger while she's in the whirlpool, and get lost. Of course, my taking it home meant she wouldn't be wearing her—our—wedding ring at all. Why not? I asked. "It's been <u>29 years.</u>" So now I was to keep the ring home until she got back into 331. I felt the pull of emotion, talking about the length of time we've

been married. It was a feeling similar to the one I get every day when I drive past our apartment house at 458 West Water. And I believe that Jane felt similar stirrings when I played the tape Danny Stimmerman sent us—of his reading some of Jane's poetry from If We Live Again *on a radio show in San Francisco last month. Some of it was well done. It was more penetrating emotionally than we'd suspected at first.*

(My meeting with Pete Harpending on Friday, July 29, lasted from 9:25 to 11:15. I was tired from talking, covering a wide range of subjects, everything from insurance questions to Frederick Fell, class tapes, John Nelson, tapes for the blind, St. Joseph's, and so forth. I'm to play the class tape Steve Blumenthal gave us for Pete. I also have more questions. "Catheter leaking," I wrote at the end of my notes for July 29. "The chuck is collecting urine—she'll have to have the catheter changed again, probably. I left at 6:15, after feeding her supper. Jane said she'd try to call. The awesomeness of what's happened to my sweetheart is beyond belief. She smiled bravely at me as we said good night. Jane, I love you."

(Then yesterday at 12:25 I received a tearful call from Jane, telling me that she'd been moved to room 230 on the second floor, instead of to 331 as we'd wanted. The room had no air conditioning and the TV was stuck way up in a corner where Jane, with poor vision—and double vision at that—could barely see it. There followed a series of adjustments on her part to new personnel, and calls on my part to Fred and to Admissions, stressing that we wanted 331 for her. I was promised that we'd get 331. And that night I had a vivid dream in which I walked down the hall to 331, on Surgical Three, only to find that 331 was already occupied *by others. Jane couldn't get back into her old room. I felt deceived by the hospital, in spite of their promises. I didn't even write down the dream, except in my own notes for these sessions and our daily record, but I told Jane about it. I was very intent on writing letters to Tam and Hassinger.*

(The irony of the move to the second floor was that Jane had been rather unceremoniously taken out of 350 in rehab to make room for a patient being transferred from Arnot-Ogden—who wasn't scheduled to be moved until next Monday....

(Another irony yesterday was that after I'd written my letter to Tam, concerning Prentice-Hall, we received in the mail from Saul Cohen Xeroxes of the three new jackets for Jane's Oversoul Seven *novels—and the covers are terrific. I took them to the hospital to show her. They helped cheer her. So did the personnel on the second floor. They are very nice. Jane is actually in the burn unit, which was empty at the moment. One of the RN's offered to show me through the unit's highly mechanized, technological rooms for intensive burn care, but this didn't work out.*

(Another hassle in 230 was that the call system didn't work. A technician spent much time trying to repair the system, but gave up when he realized he needed a new electrical unit in the wall.

(Today I took in to Jane an explanation of an article in the National Enquirer, *about the new porous joint replacements that are being used with much success. These are said to often last a lifetime, and are far superior to the older joint replacements that are cemented in place.*

(Today, then, Jane is still in 230. The day is very hot and breezy. The window in the room was wide open when I arrived; it's shaded somewhat by the same beautiful mountain ash tree that grows up past 331—which as far as we can determine sits just above us on the third floor. Someone has also furnished a fan for 230, and that helps a great deal. It may rain. Jane lay nude on her back. The talk now is that she'll be moved upstairs tomorrow. Jane went to hydro this morning, and has had a BM. After Gail Green had finished feeding her lunch and left, I turned Jane on her left side.

(Late last night Rhonda had visited Jane, and offered to call me for her. That had been at 10:45, and Jane declined, saying it was too late. There have been some confusions about medications since my wife has been on the second floor—people sometimes forgetting to give her aspirin, trying to use the irritating kind of eye drops Jane doesn't take any more, giving her Synthroid at different times, and so forth.

("They sure do leave you alone here," Jane said, not complaining particularly, after lunch. I thought the room was rather pleasant except for the troubles with air conditioning and the TV [the set is obviously very old and functions poorly indeed]. We have to keep the door practically shut because elevators are opposite it and the room has no curtain to pull across the doorway. We also share a large bathroom with the room next door, and have to make sure the doors to both rooms are left unlocked when the bathroom isn't in use.

(At 3:45 I turned Jane back on her back. I had to turn on a light, since heavy clouds were interfering with the daylight. Jane had a cigarette. "Let me calm myself down and I'll see if I can get some Rembrandt." She'd felt material there earlier, but had been too uncomfortable lying on her side to get it clearly. The room was quite noisy from street traffic—trucks, especially—since being only on the second floor meant we were a story closer to ground level than we'd been in 331.

(And Rembrandt began on a tack that really surprised me:)

I have become aware of your work with comic books.

(A very long pause to 4:05.) I always enjoyed storytelling, but I did it through my painting, particularly of the biblical tales and parables, but it seems to me that art has thus far missed a great opportunity.

(Long pause.) I envision storytelling of a different kind, a combination of excellent drama with excellent art—large-sized books *(long pause)*, but books done entirely by painting the story line. I envision, at least, the best artists painting these dramas without any wordage *(pause)*, without <u>blurbs</u>, as I understand

your comics have, but masterful paintings telling their own stories, and so eloquently that no explanatory material would need to be added.

(4:11.) Theoretically, whole novels could be painted, the features of the characters so masterfully executed that the use of words would actually water down such a novel's impact. I am speaking of relatively large books. *(Long pause.)* It seems most strange to me that such a venture has never been attempted.

I would never be able to write unless I could paint the letters, and did whatever design I chose, treating the letters as visual objects. *(Long pause.)* In my earlier years I always tried to <u>sketch</u> an idea in order to understand it. Verbal explanations never seemed to content me, where the visual rendition of any subject matter always seemed to express the idea far more vividly.

(Long pause at 4:15.) I also used to sketch musical notes if I heard them. If someone were playing a musical instrument, I would instantly begin to sketch what the music said, and only when I had finished my sketches did I truly appreciate the music.

(4:17. "Just a minute," Jane said.) I may not have mentioned it, it seemed too natural to me, but even now I sketch constantly. I do not know how this is possible *(long pause)*, since certainly I have left the usual physical reality behind me—physical palettes and brushes and all. Irregardless, I sketch constantly, particularly as I try to understand my environment and my relationship to it. *(Pause.)* This may be only a mental sketching, for all I know, but it certainly appears real enough to me—which is all that matters, I suppose—and I can call any of my sketches back into my mind at will.

It seems to me that your comics had a great potential that was never fulfilled. *(Pause.)* If I understand it correctly, your old silent movies used artists who were actors able to express emotion so faithfully and dramatically that it bothered no one that actual words could not be heard. So in my imaginings, as stated a few moments ago, the artist would paint the features so clearly and concisely and expressively that <u>no words</u> were needed—and in fact, words might even dilute the power of such an art.

(Long pause at 4:23.) I am not sure that I understand the nature of your moving pictures or television, yet I cannot help but compare these to a different kind of painting, but one closely connected with the art of theater, with its stages and props. In a way, any given scene on a movie or television screen is a painting of its own, with the characters themselves showing and working out the problems of a lifetime, perhaps during the space of an hour's program.

(Long pause at 4:30.) It seems to me also that the greatest of artists of your time could have collaborated with the movies or the television, producing great

landscapes to be used as background—but landscapes of majestic stature.

(*Long pause at 4:32 PM. "That's all for a minute," Jane finally said. Bobbie, the RN who had tripped and fallen up in 331 some time ago—but hadn't injured herself—came in to take Jane's temperature and blood pressure—procedures that haven't been followed lately, Jane said. Bobbie too informed us that Jane was scheduled to go back upstairs tomorrow. She left to get us some ice.*

(*I told Jane that I'd really been surprised when Rembrandt began talking about our modern-day comics. I'd never bothered thinking of comics and Rembrandt together. I said his material was good, once I'd reflected upon it a bit, because it showed a surprising flexibility—how the artist could work with currently available methods and avenues of expression. It's quite easy to put down the comics, TV and movies as not amounting to much art-wise.*

("Yes," Jane said. "I've felt the last couple of days when we weren't having sessions that more stuff of ours was filtering down to him."

("This must be a sign of that."

("I'm glad I got something."

(*The noise of traffic flooded into the room. Bobbie said supper would be ready at 5:15. Since the call button doesn't work yet, she asked me to tell someone at the nurse's station when I left so personnel would know when to come in and turn Jane this evening.*

(4:44. I don't know about anybody else," Jane said with a laugh, "but doing books of paintings wouldn't go over these days—"

("I don't know. It's an untried idea, as far as I know. It may be a very good one. Suppose it was already part of our culture? We'd accept it.... I don't know whether such a book would have 10 paintings in it, or 20 or 50...." And I thought of the series of small paintings Rembrandt had executed around the theme of the Crucifixion. I could see how a series of paintings like those could well be incorporated into book-work. Looked at that way, one could see many connections between such work and modern book illustration.

(*4:45. An aide came in to give Jane her eye drops. After the gal left Jane said she got some feedback from Rembrandt while getting the drops—relative to her comment that the book idea wouldn't work: "Rembrandt said you could have a group of subscribers for the book, and that they could charge the subscribers fees for their appearances in the paintings, if he needed the money."*

(*And that, I thought was a perfect blending of past and present: Rembrandt's way of answering Jane's objection. Surely his idea of subscribers fit in with some of his work, such as the group portraits for anatomy lessons, or the cloth maker's guild. I told her my thoughts.*

(*Then Jane received some kind of jovial comment from Rembrandt, to the effect that* "Dutchmen were never impractical dreamers, whether dead or alive…"

(At 5:30, just before the supper tray came, Jane laughed and said she was getting an idea that Rembrandt was just beginning to understand how our generalized mail delivery system was working—and that he was tying that knowledge in with his idea of painted books. She didn't say just how, though. I got glimmers in light of our own experiences with books and publishing.

(I fed Jane supper. Steve and Tracy called as we finished; they will visit her tonight. Sharon Foley looked in briefly, to tell us about her ill husband in Sayre. I figured out the TV schedule for Jane this evening, and left at 7:10. I forgot to read the prayer.)

DELETED SESSION
AUGUST 3, 1983 4:48 PM WEDNESDAY

(This is the third day since the last session was held.

(On Monday morning, August 1, I finished typing the session for July 25. Then I wrote the following note, which I read to Jane when arriving at the hospital that afternoon: "Some of the material near the close of the session for July 25 deals with Rembrandt giving hints to his artist's self as that self painted. It made me wonder if I've had similar communications from my own larger or afterdeath self. [Everybody would, of course.] What I mean is in relation to my own painting—not particularly in relation to color, as Rembrandt mentioned, but the larger view, having to do with my choice, made some years ago, to paint my heads in oil without the usual model in conventional terms. I've often wondered about why I do this so consistently. Perhaps my 'portraits' represent not only learning experiences having to do with just the sheer act of painting, but represent efforts to visually apprehend portions of myself in other realities as those portions made contact with me.... Reincarnational and counterpart selves could also be involved."

(Jane was still in room 230 when I arrived on August 1. Shirley, an aide we knew from 331, was feeding her. Jane had a BM at 1:30, and was cleaned up within ten minutes. She read the rest of July 25 —all I had typed, what with doing mail and other things. As the time passed, it looked less and less as though we'd move back upstairs today. Jane dozed. She doesn't like to do this, because she says it reminds her of when she'd drift off while at the house when she first became really ill. I remembered. I worked on mail and filled out the menu, which Shirley had forgotten. I found her in the hall and gave it to her.

(Ten minutes later Shirley burst into the room. "You are gonna move," she

said, just as I was getting ready to read Jane yesterday's session [for July 31]. I'd been trying to figure out how I should react if we found out we weren't going back to 331. Shirley left before I could ask her any questions. Jane had a cigarette. "Bring my wedding ring back," she said.

(2:40. Shirley came back. "You're going to 330," she said to Jane. Not 331. I was instantly angry to think that all our efforts to get back into 331 were foiled. I thought of really raising hell, of making calls, of grabbing people—doctors, administrators, of really making a nuisance of myself. I was ready to fight. I let Shirley know how I felt in no uncertain terms. I don't remember Jane saying much at all.

("Let's get her [Jane] up there, then we can do something," she said. "Otherwise you won't make it today. I'm going downstairs to get the name tags now. Load up this cart, will you?"

(I was really angry. I couldn't believe it was happening.

("Oh that burns me up," I exclaimed to Shirley, who obviously couldn't do anything about it. "Just what do you have to do to make an impression on anybody around here?"

("I don't know," she said. "They'll listen to you like you've got a hole in your head, then go and do as they please. But it's a nicer room, really. And you can see the tree and the TV is like you had," she added, in answer to my questions. I vowed to collar the head nurse, and Fred, about the mix-up, the deliberate slight. Did I overreact? I doubt it. "The air conditioner works fine," Shirley said. "The john is much bigger, too."

(And it did, and it is, I saw as soon as I got up there with the loaded cart. I knew the room, of course, having walked past it every day on my way to see Jane in 331 next door. It's directly opposite two elevators—which may not be such a bad thing, since otherwise a patient would be in a room across the hall. Even then, a woman down the hall was crying out rather loudly—and kept it up for a long while, while we moved.

(No sooner had I arrived with the cart and began unloading it when Shirley and Georgia showed up with Jane and her Roho mattress and draw sheet all piled on one stretcher. In no time at all they had the mattress reassembled on the new bed, and Jane in position. The move was important to the girls, too, since it meant that they were back where they were supposed to be also. "Things are a mess," several people who looked in told us. They referred to the influx of new patients into the section, or mod. A woman is in 331 next door; no one knows how long she's to stay. I told Jane that the real reason the switch in rooms bothered me was that it meant you couldn't trust people—admissions, or somebody—hadn't kept their word: "If you're dealing with people, watch out," I said. Shirley said several times, very pleased, "Never mind, Jane, enjoy the room. It's bigger and nicer than next door—and you're

back home, back home. We all are," and she laughed. Jane didn't know that she agreed with that philosophy, she said later, but we could see that obviously 330 wasn't bad at all. Shirley stayed until 5:00, although she was through on her shift at 3:30.

(I bustled about, trying to make the place as comfortable-looking as possible. The TV girl came in to turn on the set. I taped the prayer in place on the bottom edge of the TV, and the clock in place on top of it. I couldn't figure out how to tape in place the little ceramic owl Venice had given Jane, though. Several RN's and aides we knew stopped in to say hello. Jane had a little bloody drainage from an ulcer on her hip, we found—probably from being knocked during the move upstairs, she said. I stayed to feed her supper, and left at 7:10—forgetting to read her the prayer. She didn't manage to call me later that evening. Debbie visited.

(August 2, 1983. When I got home from the hospital at 7:15 last night John Bumbalo called to me that he'd do our driveway with blacktopping if the weather was clear. This morning I called him to verify his offer, since the day looked promising. I talked to Margaret, and explained that Jane wasn't in 331 after all. John phoned to say okay on the driveway at 9:30 AM. I backed the car up Holley Road to park it out of the way, and met Joe as I did so. He said, "Don't tell Jane, but I called the hospital, and she'll be moved back into that room as soon as it's empty."

(I was surprised. "What did you do, push a few buttons?"

("Sure," Joe grinned. "I'm on the board. I told them it was for therapy, and they said okay. But don't tell Jane yet."

(My surprise included the thought that here was a new dilemma—for I liked aspects of 330, too, especially its size and the tree outside the window. I told Joe the air conditioning didn't seem to work as well, though. So we'll see. Joe laughed, and I did too. If this marked a change in hospital policy, if we did get our way after all, I also suddenly felt sorry for them—and, amazingly enough, my feelings suddenly reminded me of how I used to feel sorry for opponents as a youngster, when I'd defeated them in a sporting contest, say in tennis or football or track. Strange. "Why didn't you let me know about your trouble?" Joe asked.

("It never occurred to me," I said. "I called different people and they all said okay, she could go back there, so I thought it was all set...." Of course, we don't know when—or even if—the move will take place.

(330 was very pleasant today, although a mechanic is having his troubles boosting the efficiency of the air conditioner. I told Jane I had nothing typed for her to read, and that I had to take the car to the garage for inspection tomorrow. I've written Saul Cohen.

(At 3:20 Jane decided she wanted to look at herself in the mirror. I'd kept the mirror in a drawer because she hadn't wanted to use it. She lay nude on her back as

I held it up for her to peer into. She was shocked and hurt. "I look like a witch. I look terrible," she said. "I'm grotesque," she added, her voice quavering. We had a dialogue about her looks, the beliefs that had resulted in an appearance that really shocked her so. "I thought I'd look at myself and come to terms with myself," Jane mourned, "but I'm homely. Do you think I'm homely?" I replied that I did and did-n't—that her appearance was the result, a side effect, almost, of other bargains that had been made. She agreed, but she was shocked. She cried a little. I said it was good that she used the mirror, for it could signal a change in belief that could be very ben-eficial. Jane mourned her changing face, her looser flesh around her jaws and neck [some of these effects were due to her position in bed, I explained], and her graying hair—which was still thick and luxurious, actually. I think she learned things. I left the mirror out on the bedside table. I had hopes that using it would trigger good results. Jane still has the extra freedom of motion in both arms, and in her index fin-gers to a lesser extent. Her legs haven't been as loose, though.

(At 5:00 I checked the TV programs for the evening, turned her on her back, and read the prayer. I couldn't stay to feed her, since I had to go food shopping. "I got spoiled, I guess, you're staying so late...." She knew I couldn't keep it up, since I had no time left when getting home so late. I was too tired to even work on correspon-dence. She'd been blue ever since she looked into the mirror.

(August 3. The day was hot and bright. I took the car down to the garage early for inspection and tune-up. With the doors and windows of the house open the air became pungent with the smell of tar, for John Bumbalo had coated the driveway yesterday afternoon. It looked fine, to my considerable surprise; for Frank Longwell had said it wasn't worth doing.

(Jane hadn't called last night. She lay on her back, covered up, because a main-tenance man was working on the air conditioning unit. Her catheter had been changed just before noon, for the second time in four days. Now it has to be irrigat-ed each shift—three times a day. "I was blue as hell last night," she said. I missed you feeding me—I got upset over the mirror and everything." She hadn't had any visi-tors. I fed her lunch now.

(After the guy had left I hung up the two paintings I'd brought in—one of my portraits, and the oil of the back buildings of Saratoga; the one I'd painted looking out the bathroom window of Jane's apartment on Philo Street in the spring of 1954. I had to drive a couple of nails in the plaster wall at the foot of Jane's bed to do this, but it worked well. We ended up with five pieces of art on the wall—two of Jane's, two of mine, and one by Sophie Fordon. They made a nice looking display, I thought. When I'd hung Jane's paintings on August first I'd moved the crucifix to the wall in back of her bed, where she couldn't see it.

(Jane read the first three pages of July 26—all I'd gotten typed—and John

Nelson's letter of August 1, which I'd just received. By 3:15 the maintenance man had returned twice more as he worked on the air conditioner—which he thought was now fixed. I turned Jane on her left side, facing the window and the ash tree. She told me bits of news she'd heard about people taking care of her. Gail Green had suffered a broken wrist in an automobile accident; two other gals, both divorced and with young children, were filing for child support from their ex-husbands; an aide's husband is in Sayre, facing operations for serious internal problems; the little girl who does cleaning got her job back after the nurses' strike ended, but her husband lost his and the utility turned off their gas and lights; another aide talks about leaving her husband but evidently is afraid to. And more—and all of those events involved people considerably younger than we are. Truly, I thought, sometimes the world seems full of woe. I couldn't imagine getting involved in such troubles. Not from any sense of superiority; it was just that at times I was appalled at the situations people created for themselves, all unknowing, then had to struggle against. I fully granted that each such dilemma had its creative reasons on deeper levels, and would be redeemed in one fashion or another. But I could still be taken back by the evidence surrounding us that people created their lives without having the slightest conscious awareness that they were doing so in the finest detail. And maybe, just maybe, I thought, Jane and I had done and were doing a lot better than we gave ourselves credit for.... Surely our own individual and joint redemption was implied in our actions too.

(The air conditioner was working so well as the afternoon passed that I had to move to the other side of Jane's bed to get away from sitting so close to the unit beneath the window. I worked on these notes. At 4:40 I turned Jane on her right side. She had a cigarette. I'd been wearing sandals, but I put my socks and shoes back on, and my vest. "I don't want to shock you," Jane said, "but I may have a little Rembrandt."

("I'm ready," I said, and got up to push our door almost shut. A male patient down the hall had been hollering for some time. Jane lay facing me.)

Through your wife's perception, I have been studying the light *(repeated)*, and a mystery is cleared up for me.

I could not understand how it was that you painted with the curtains opened while as a general rule I used candles for illumination, and kept the draperies closed.

The quality of light is quite different, apparently, in your part of the world than it was in mine. Our skies *(pause)* often glared so brightly with a cold white light that everything else seemed to disappear in its brilliance. In wintertime the skies were often filled with smoke from all the chimneys, and sometimes misted over by fogs, yet even then the glare was unmistakable. Even on the shortest days there was that white light, in whose cast other colors became almost indistinguishable. It was a <u>cold</u>, not a warm light. The candlelight dispelled it, forming its own warm glow. Nor did we open windows as freely as you do, for in my time we were suspicious of the air itself, thinking that it carried unfriendly vapors—and for that reason also we often closed our draperies.

Your light seems to have a much more even, friendly cast, yet of course it cannot be an entirely <u>even</u> light, and so I still wonder how *(long pause)* you can juggle the light's attributes, for certainly you cannot control it. All in all, however, your skies are friendlier and easier to the eye than ours were. Over a long period of time, I still think that our method of establishing *(pause)* a friendly warm light was more advisable and less risky.

(Long pause at 5:00.) When light is more or less controlled, as I did, then you can paint day or night, and still be assured of controlling your light, and of being in command of your own light focus.

(Long pause at 5:01.) Providing my own light also saved me from waiting out a fog or mist, for example, and allowed me to control the light-and-dark motives about which each painting must revolve. Our light seemed to dissect the walls, while yours seems to melt into the walls instead.

(5:05 PM. "That's all for the moment," Jane said. "My lips got awfully dry. I need a sip...." Three nurses came in to ask me to stay to feed Jane supper, because they're so short-handed, and we had a pleasant exchange of humor. They liked the paintings. I put Jane back on her back, and we figured out her TV schedule for the night while waiting for supper. Dynasty, Jane's favorite, is on tonight. The tray came at 6:10. After supper Jane had a cigarette and I read the prayer. I also made a note to bring in a sweater to leave in 330, and a cushion for the chair. Before I left at 7:25 I asked Jane to call me if she could.

(I'd done a small sketch of just her head and hands earlier. Jane said she'd felt stuff about light from Rembrandt this morning, when she'd studied light patterns on the wall. "I'm glad I got something," she said, as though this might signal the start of a new creative routine in the new room.)

DELETED SESSION
AUGUST 5, 1983 3:22 PM FRIDAY

(No session was held yesterday. In the mail Wednesday night I found a letter forwarded by Pete Harpending—a copy of a letter forwarded to him by Helen Wechsler, an attorney in NYC who's working on the Frederick Fell matter re ESP Power for us. It gets complicated, but all of the material is on file for reference. I called Pete this morning and secured an appointment for tomorrow morning, during which I'm to play for him the Seth class tape Steve Blumenthal made for us. The

class of January 29, 1974. Helen Wechsler had also sent Pete a copy of an article in Publisher's Weekly, *published last October 8, 1982, about the Frederick Fell Company under new management. So I took Pete's correspondence in so Jane could read it. She didn't manage to call me Thursday night.*

　　(Today, Friday, I arrived at 330 at 1:15. It was a hot sunny day, and Jane lay nude on her back. The air conditioner was set on low, and she asked me to turn it up. "Everybody's noticed your paintings," she said, as I told her that I had much to tell her about my morning's activities. I'd spent a long time with Pete Harpending and his summer assistant, Jonathan Guest, filling them in on background material pertaining to our work, Tam, Steve, John Nelson, Wade Alexander, Saul Cohen, Hugh Wheeler, Norman Hassinger, Frederick Fell, ESP Power/The Coming of Seth, *and others. I showed Pete the first letter from John Nelson, which he copied. I explained the letters I've been writing to various people lately. I asked Pete if he thought the family connection that has developed between Bantam Books and F. Fell might have a negative influence on our future relations with Bantam, when that entity learns we're trying to collect from Fell. Pete didn't know, of course. "Am I being too cynical?" I asked him.*

　　(I told Jane I'd played a little of the Seth tape for Pete and Than, who were both impressed. Pete hadn't believed it was Jane speaking, at first. He has a hearing problem involving loud noise in concentrated areas, I discovered; he asked me to get copies of the tape made so he could have one to play at his leisure at home, in quiet surroundings. At the office we'd been forced to move into an interior room to get away from the sounds of construction outside his office window. I'd explained some of the background of the tape matter. Pete tried to call Wade, only to learn that Wade is in London. Steve hasn't called Pete to reschedule his appointment. Relative to questions I had to ask Pete, see my notes in the Harpending file for July 28, August 3 and August 5. One of the questions concerned Jane's request for information about forming a nonprofit corporation. Pete checked law books on NY State and learned there was no point in our creating such an entity.

　　(Pete also called Chemung Electronics, and someone at the store said the Seth tape could be copied. I plan to have at least two copies made—one for Pete and one for Helen Wechsler in NYC. I think this will be quicker than waiting for Steve to make them.

　　(I could tell from his questions that Pete is still quite skeptical of Steve's being able to market Seth tapes in any businesslike or efficient way. I tend to share his opinion, although I passed on to Pete Jane's own assertions that she didn't think Steve would try to work any sharp business deals. In her letter to the management at Frederick Fell, Helen Wechsler has demanded a return of all rights to ESP Power *by August 15, unless she hears from them beforehand. So far she hasn't heard, of course.*

I don't think she will, I told Jane, as I tried to explain that series of events to her, along with everything else I'd covered with Pete this morning. Beginning at 1:30, I fed her lunch as we talked.

(Mary Ann, an aide, brought us some chucks, and after lunch I showed her how I usually cut one in half and work it in position under Jane before she has a BM, for added protection of the sheet and mattress. Jane has been doing well today, and had aspirin and vitamins with lunch. I read her the last part of Rembrandt for August 3, and the note I'd written about my own portraits on August 1. She was still on her back. "I sort of felt something," she said at 3:20. "I'm just waiting until I get it. I'd sure like to...")

I wanted to make a few more comments concerning myself in relationship to other people. I suppose that it has not escaped your notice that my relationships were highly important to my work, and more, that I was myself a good deal like the burghers and townspeople that were my models.

(3:25. Mary Ann hurried in and out as she filled our water jug with ice.

(3:26.) The same can be said of my social life. It was not that I pursued good society, out of false vanity, *(long pause)*, or that I engaged in social affairs simply to insure my success as a businessman. The society in Amsterdam, however, was very closely knit, and some of my most inspiring ideas came from watching people in the ebb and flow of their conversations, and understanding the intricate relationships that often united them.

Again without undue vanity, I can say that I knew Amsterdam's people well, and if I had lived later and been a different kind of person, perhaps I would have been a novelist, for I was always intrigued by what <u>showed</u> and what <u>did not show</u> in a man or woman's face, and I was always interested in the webwork of society's relationships. And sometimes—

(3:31. Sharon came in to take Jane's temperature. No sooner had she left than the phone began to ring. The caller had the wrong room number. At the same time the hall outside 330 became quite noisy—A group of people waiting for an elevator across from our open door began talking and laughing loudly. I pushed the door nearly shut, then read the last portion of the material to Jane.

(3:35.)—by those situations in which man found himself despite his own good intentions. I did, in fact—

(3:35 fi. Lorrie came in to take Jane's temperature, blood pressure and check her pulse. Jane drank some cranberry juice, which is supposed to keep her bladder and urine clear. I read her last line to her.)

I did in fact believe that all the aspects of a person's soul were reflected in one way or another in the face and figure, and that all of a person's agonies, triumphs and secret desires were everywhere written upon the flesh. In that respect, my paintings in a way could be compared to novels, for each one certainly contained a story *(pause)*, an exterior one, as in the parables, for example, or an internal story, where a person's battles and victories are more inwardly turned than outward. Even in the latter case, a person's history is everywhere written in the face and figure, in the clothing worn and chosen, and in the environment. How slyly and yet beautifully these all fit together, I used to think— and I still think the same—for in your time and mine as well man is marked by his wars and victories, and the character of soul shows in each crevice and fold of the hands and face. And the man tells his own story without even knowing he is doing so.

(3:45.) So I was always curious about society, and found it full enough to content an artist for a lifetime. Each painting taught me more about men and women—and each person that I met somehow gave me clues as to my own painting. *(Pause.)* I did not deal then merely with surfaces, though I did not neglect them—but I always tried to look beneath so that the characteristics of the soul did not escape my brush as I learned about mankind and about painting as I went along.

(3:47. "That's all for this second, I guess," Jane said after a long pause. She was still on her back. "Let me have a cigarette. Then I better turn over the other way before somebody does it for me. And I can get more, too...." Her delivery had been excellent.

(4:08. I turned Jane on her right side, facing me. The room was cold. I turned the air conditioner to low.

(4:09.) With my first wife *(Saskia)*, and then later with my second *(Hendrickje)*, I attended many testimonial dinners and affairs.

These did present an excellent opportunity to meet new patrons *(long pause.)* But that was only one of my reasons for attending. *(Pause.)* Here you found men and women in their most social of attire. It was almost as if they donned new graceful faces, along with their coiffures and finery. At these social affairs in particular you could see the two great forces: the desire for expansion and the desire for concealment *(long pause)*, and each of these two characteristics, almost opposing each other, showed constantly, particularly in people's profiles.

One side of the face would seem to contradict the other side, and from where one side the lips appeared to dip downward, from the other side the lips seemed to curve upward in a half-smile. The face's features were forever struggling along the creases and wrinkles as first the need for concealment pulled the features in one direction, while on the other side of the face the desire for expression curled the lips upward.

(4:16.) I was always struck by the face's ever-changing motion, and even in repose no face is utterly still. Added to this, party finery *(pause)*, with all the folds and flounces that each tried to echo the body's inner motion, and sometimes it seemed as if a man or woman's clothing trembled constantly, expressing the high nervousness beneath.

(Long pause at 4:18.) Business meetings, or meetings of a town council or such, were much more serious affairs, and each man tried to <u>hold</u> his face so that he looked the most serious or profound—

(4:20. Sharon came in, checking. She was surprised to see that I'd turned Jane.)

—while at the same time, almost as if to mock him, the lips would begin to curl, the eyes take on a mischievous look, or the nervous twitter of a giggle would emit from the seriously pursed lips, much to a man's horror or dismay. Here, when it was denied, man's playfulness seemed to take pleasure in showing itself precisely when the man was bound to show his most mature side to the other council members—so again the face was caught between concealment and expression, and all of these tendencies were reflected in the hands, however sternly a man might try to hold his fingers quietly. If you watched you could suddenly see the fingers flex and jump, and begin a nervous rap upon the table. Then the poor man would look down astounded, as if the fingers drumming so nervously belonged to someone else instead of himself.

Such occasions put man in certain frameworks or focuses, and he would react according to his nature. I would often find myself doing the same thing as they did, so when I let such tendencies show in my paintings, I was painting a part of myself as well.

(4:29. "That's all for now," Jane said.

("That's good, Hon." Once again her delivery had been steady and quietly forceful.

("Good," Jane said. "I can see some of it—I can see him seeing some of it— you know what I mean?"

("Yes...." I checked the TV programs for the evening, circling the ones Jane wanted to see. Tonight, in order to get the shows she liked, Jane would have to get an RN or an aide to change the channels on the set several times. Sometimes this was a difficult thing to do. Even though the little set hung right over her bed on its extension arm, my wife still couldn't reach up to switch channels herself.

(Jane also knew I was leaving relatively early tonight, since when I stay to feed her supper I'm often not through eating myself, at the house, until close to 9:00. This procedure doesn't leave me much time to do anything else—work on mail, the budget, or just think, before going to bed. But she wasn't happy that I was going. "I guess

I got spoiled," she said. "I really like it when you stay to feed me, and we look at those old programs." Our routine has been that while she eats we watch Three's Company *and* Six Million Dollar Man.

(At 5:00 I read the prayer to her. I also discussed with her the letter we'd received from Nancy Cramer Ashley. She asked if Jane, Seth or I could do an intro for the Seth workbook she'd just turned in to Prentice-Hall. We'd quite forgotten that last year she'd been signed to do the book. If we'd ever known it, that is. Tam has completed his editing of the work, and has written us also, praising the workbook highly. I told Jane I didn't know how to respond to the Cramer letter. I was displeased that no one, including Cramer, had let us know the book was in progress.

(Jane still lay on her side, with the foam-rubber doughnut between her knees, and other pieces of foam rubber cushioning the pressure of her bottom right foot against the Roho mattress, and her left foot as it lay atop her right one. 5:12.)

On the other hand, when you want to paint a portrait of a person in repose *(long pause)*, you must try to disturb the model as little as possible. Certainly never chatter, but keep your voice calm and soothing, so that the model does not feel that he or she is on stage, and then attempt self-consciously to <u>look</u> moody or sorrowful.

When the face is truly in repose, it still moves constantly, but its actions do not contradict each other. The two sides of the face are in better agreement than before, and the facial motions seem to complete or fulfill themselves, rather than set up additional tensions. This is particularly apparent in the eyes, which seem to glow softly <u>but without glittering</u> *(with emphasis).* The muscles of the hands and fingers relax also, and the face and hands complement each other.

(Long pause at 5:18.) The manner in which the artist handles the model is as important as the actual painting itself, for the person must be secure enough in the artist's presence to let his or her emotions flow naturally, and to capture the <u>flowing</u> effect, however gentle, that relaxing muscles have.

(Long pause.) To do this the artist must be in rapport with the sitter, of course, and if the artist's own temperament is too abrasive he will never be able to paint another's face in repose—for his own characteristics will make the sitter uncomfortable and ill at ease.

(5:22 PM. "That's all for the minute.... I'll have a cigarette, and have you turn me over," Jane said. I ended up putting her back on her back for supper later. I left at 5:40 to stop off at Chemung Electronics. I'd left the Seth tape there on my way into the hospital after lunch. Now the clerk told me that the copies weren't ready because their equipment had broken down. Leland, a young black, promised to have them tomorrow afternoon—which meant I'd have to leave Jane to go over to the store to pick up the tapes early; the store closes at 5:00 PM on Saturdays....)

DELETED SESSION
AUGUST 6, 1983 3:37 PM SATURDAY

(I called John Bumbalo when I got home last night, and he helped me get a fresh flea collar on Mitzi. I'd put one on Billy myself a couple of weeks ago without any trouble, I told Jane today. I also told her that after talking with Pete H. yesterday, concerning the marketing of tapes, that I'd come up with a couple of ideas myself. One of the ideas was that the original class transcript could be included with each tape—which meant that a lot of the work in that area would be already done; instead of relying upon a new transcript Steve Blumenthal might produce. I'm concerned about accuracy. The other idea is that we have ourselves original tapes that no one else has. They're down in the cellar, I said to Jane. One of them would be the tape we made for Dr. Instream some years ago—a truly original performance, I remembered. Jane had reservations about the quality of the tape by now. It's a reel-to-reel and quite old as tapes go. Steve had repaired our reel-to-reel player last year and I'd intended to investigate some of those old tapes then, but hadn't done so. I told Jane I'd check them out. It's only a thought, I added.

(The day was bright and hot, yet I felt that rain was in the offing. 330 itself was cool, almost too cool for my taste. I told Jane that I'd decided not to go over to Chemung Electronics to get the Seth tape and copies today, but to wait until Monday to make sure they were done. I didn't want to leave her in the middle of the afternoon.

(After a late lunch I read Jane letters from Tam and Norm Hassinger—both helpful without resolving anything. I told her I'd written to Saul Cohen this morning, concerning the Seth Workbook, *and to Helen Wechsler, the attorney in New York City about trying to obtain a copy of the Spanish edition of* ESP Power. *Tam was especially concerned about the drop in quality of our books published by Prentice-Hall, but it seems that the question of a quality product by Prentice-Hall isn't solvable at this time.*

(I read Jane the last few pages of the session for August 5, at her request. Then I turned her on her right side, facing me as I sat beside her. At 2:45 I began going through month-old mail. Jane was quite comfortable. The hall outside 330 was pretty quiet—there was only an occasional shout from a male patient several doors down.

(At 3:10, as she lay on her side, having a cigarette, Jane asked me if I'd ever heard of Leeds in Rembrandt's time. I said maybe. Liege? I asked. She didn't know. She said she was picking up from Rembrandt that where he grew up his father used to take him for long walks down by the canals. Some of them were in poor repair, with weeds and prickers and wildflowers growing up among and around them. She said Rembrandt used to feel the plants and flowers—and it had seemed to him that

the red, blue, and green things not only looked different from each other, but felt different because of their colors. She talked about what I took to be burdock plants.

(Discussing the Leeds question, we arrived at the conclusion that she was trying to come up with the name of Rembrandt's home city—Leiden. I said that for all I knew Leeds could be the way Leiden was pronounced in Dutch; I had no idea.

("In that same area there were the ruins of an old fortress—a castle," Jane said, "all overgrown. For some reason it wasn't accessible—you had to look at it across something—a fence or canal or something. This was in the same town." She added that Rembrandt's mother never went on the walks. Rembrandt liked the wild overgrown look of the area because usually everything in Holland was so well kept up. He enjoyed the contrast.)

Your wife picked up old memories of mine, almost as if they belonged to her.

My memories do not come neatly packaged, and it is sometimes difficult for me to know exactly what portion of my life certain memories belong to. *(Pause.)* It is even difficult at times to separate my experience <u>after</u> death from my living experience. I do not mean that I feel disordered in any way. I simply know the experiences are mine, but I do not feel the need to categorize them particularly.

For one thing—as a learning process, I suppose—I have learned to put my memories together in different fashions *(pause)*, allowing myself—<u>as far as I am concerned</u>—to remember at any point in my life events that clearly came after that point. There is no doubt that the entire before-and-after sequence is a learned response, but one that I believe we circumvent despite ourselves in life as we paint our pictures. That is, I think that in painting we definitely take advantage of so-called future knowledge, and that the future knowledge always leads us on while at the same time it may have provided the painting's original impetus.

(Long pause at 3:44, in an excellent delivery.) The entire time process simply seems to be a framework we adopt during our lifetime, while afterward we are able to use it much more freely, experiencing events out of the context in which they happened. Whenever you do this, the event of course completely changes, and is then experienced in another perspective entirely.

(Long pause at 3:46.) It personally gives me a feeling of great freedom, as I put together the events of my life, sort and arrange them in different sequences than the original happenings themselves. *(Long pause.)* I have even imaginatively painted my own paintings <u>backwards</u>, from the finish to the start—and yet when I was done the paintings were different ones than those I had originally painted, as if the backward-time motion altered the paintings themselves, or put

them in a different category.

To do this with one's own work is impressive and somewhat startling. Almost as if you began with one huge scenario containing innumerable probabilities, so that the paintings could be put together in innumerable ways.

(Long pause at 3:52 PM. "I guess that's it for the minute," Jane said.

("It's pretty darn good, too."

("Strange," she said, "almost as if you couldn't put your finger on it. I was pretty far out with that...."

(Cathy came in to take Jane's temperature and pulse. By 4:25 Jane had had at least two dreams in which she was walking, or trying to. During one of them she tried to call out to me incoherently as she lay on her side and I sat beside her working on mail.

(4:30. "I wish I could tell if you were dreaming or having a hallucination," she exclaimed after dozing again. "I've just been on this little trip all by myself...."

("I doubt if it's a hallucination," I said. "You were probably dreaming—although you could do something imaginatively, too."

(4:33. "I'm still going through these little scenarios," Jane exclaimed again. "I can't tell whether I'm dreaming or hallucinating." She grunted in vexation. "Give me another smoke. I'm still having these little scenarios."

(I thought it obvious that her scenarios resulted from the material she'd delivered today—the rearranging of events especially. I thought the dreams represented a probably crude near-conscious attempt at interpreting such possibilities. We talked about why she's in the situation she's in—the efficiency of the prayer and so forth. Jane wanted to know what's next, now that Fred seems to have done all he's able to. I said I didn't have any final answers either, as she doesn't, but that things are always in a state of change. Jane sounded like me when she said she didn't want what she's doing now—living in the hospital—to become a way of life.

(At 4:42 I turned her back on her back. I read to her an excellent letter we'd received from a psychotherapist. Such responses to our work are always cheering, especially when we're struggling with our own doubts and the prospects of an unknown future. At 5:00 Joan, an RN, came in to give Jane eye drops and take her blood pressure. Five minutes later I read the prayer. In another 10 minutes I checked the TV programs for the night, and then left at 5:25. There were a few tears.)

DELETED SESSION
AUGUST 7, 1983 4:45 PM SUNDAY

(Here is a note I wrote this morning: "Have I noted anywhere in these sessions

that I find great comfort and peace in the Rembrandt material? I know I told Jane about this feeling some weeks ago—I may have inserted it in a session then. I think some of my feelings may rest upon the combination Rembrandt expresses of a love for his physical environment while he was 'alive,' and the search he conducted through his art for the meaning of life—the intuitive and psychological, unspeakable feeling and understanding of at least some of life's deeper, more penetrating meanings.

("I hardly think it an accident that Jane is coming through with the Rembrandt material at this time, then—a time when we're trying to solve many challenges. The Rembrandt material may even be pointing a way <u>out of the situation</u> we've created for ourselves. That way may not even be evident to us yet, consciously, but in a larger perspective, seen from the 'future,' this may be quite apparent as we look back upon it. Certainly the very fact that Jane is producing such a work now is a sign of great progress. The ramifications may continue to grow.")

(I do think I have several points there. Undoubtedly the main one is that the Rembrandt material may be helping us in ways we aren't clear about—yet. I'm dealing with feelings here more than anything else, feelings that are difficult to put into words. I suppose I might have added to the note what I think is probably the key thought in all the Rembrandt material. I can't quote it exactly without hunting it out—but Rembrandt said something to the effect that "I felt my way through life.")

(I brought Jane three kinds of bobby pins and a chocolate bar today. The lunch tray usually shows up after 1:30, so one of the first things I do is feed her. The day was hot and bright, but it was cool in 330 with the air conditioner going. Jane lay on her left side, so I turned her back on her back so she could eat. She's been feeling sensations in her bladder at times, but the catheter is working okay. BM this morning. Jane showed me how she's regained considerably more motion in both index fingers. Her arms still work well, though her legs are tight. Jane said that this morning Georgia, an aide, had remarked that the oil portrait I'd brought in to hang on the wall opposite Jane's bed reminded her of me—though I'd hardly intended it to be a physical self-portrait.

(Jane also said she's quite taken with my notes about world views at the end of the session for July 27; she finished reading that session today. She talked about doing her own world-view book, as I'd mentioned. "Maybe something will come of it after Rembrandt," she said. "I wouldn't know how to start a book like that about myself. With an autobiography or what."

("It wouldn't matter at all," I said. "Just let it come." We agreed that Seth would be in any book she did on her own world view—that he'd be as much a part of her world view as she would be of <u>his</u>.

(I read to Jane my own notes of this morning. "I'm glad you feel that way," she said. Then I read her yesterday's Rembrandt material. At 3:20 I washed her glasses *and turned her on her right side. She began to talk about getting some Rembrandt. The room was cooling off. During the next hour people came in to take her vital signs and give her eye drops while I worked on the mail. Blood pressure: 106 over 70, which is very good. Finally Jane said, "I guess I can get a little if you want me to."*

("Okay." I waited with pen and pad.)

Some things are so apparent to me *(long pause)* that I take it for granted that you understand a certain issue—and then realize that I have never specifically mentioned it.

I no longer experience nights and days in the old earthly manner, though I could if I wanted to, and I think that I did immediately following my death. *(Long pause.)* I am not focused upon relationships with other people at this point in my experience, though certainly in my lifetime I studied them with great enjoyment and curiosity. I know there are others in my position who do deal with such relationships, however, and I assume that their experiences are far different than my own. Perhaps I should correct myself by saying that I am not concerned with *(pause)* the conventionalized idea of people in general, but that I am remarkably fascinated with the elements of personality *(long pause)*, or the different kinds of awareness that consciousness learns to use and manipulate. Some of this is very difficult to explain, but in our lifetimes we are very limited in our conception of personality, assigning it, for example, only to people like ourselves.

(Long pause at 4:50.) In quite valid terms, however, there are other kinds of personalities, some entirely nonphysical, and others in a way forming the very elements of earth's natural characteristics. Mountains and valleys *(pause)* have personality characteristics of their own. You can learn to know them as you learn to know other people *(all emphatically)*. Their means of communication are far different, of course. They have desires and misgivings, just as people do. They have their own purposes and interests. They are as <u>conscious</u> as people are *(emphatically.)*

(This material, of course, strongly reminded me of the old, and strongly derided by science, concepts of vitalism and nature spirits, and so forth. My hasty thought here was that as our "civilizations" grew we human beings gradually shut out our conscious awareness of a living nature, sacrificing that awareness in the interests of studying and experiencing other facets of consciousness: the scientific, the objective, even the religious in ordinary terms.)

(Long pause.) In physical terms they are extremely colorful. But more than that *(pause)*, no color, of course, is <u>precisely</u> like any other color, or identical to it, even though to the earthly senses they may appear to be the same. I am able to distinguish innumerable nuances of color that I never suspected existed

before.

(There was a lot of noisy chatter at the elevators across the hall from our door. It interfered with my concentration as I tried to take notes, but Jane didn't seem to be bothered.)

The colors stand in a certain relationship to a greater unknown spectrum, and each of these communicates with each other. They make sense as clearly, say, as alphabets do. They are units of awareness—though in ways that I do not really understand.

(Long pause at 5:02.) These can be put together as musical notes can. They are units of consciousness operating at a different scale of events, and they contain their own perspective, in which each has its place.

(Long pause.) All of this excites my highest interest. It makes me wonder at least at the possibility of a different kind of painting, which was itself alive, and once painted, contained its own momentum—an amazing concept, yet one I am bound to explore *(all with soft emphasis.*

(5:06. "I have to stop a minute," Jane said. "My throat got so dry." I told her the material was excellent. I gave her some cranberry juice. A patient in the room next door had had a baseball game blaring on the TV for some time now. I worked on a letter while Jane took a break—not realizing that she was waiting for me to finish what I was doing.

(5:20. She had a cigarette. "Well, let me know if you get any more," I said. "Otherwise I'll do more mail."

("Okay.... I guess I was getting a little more," she said finally.

(5:43.) When I was alive I felt at my peak in my young boyhood, and in my teens, in my early 30's, and only briefly and spasmodically thereafter. I am speaking now of physical peaks of health, as apart, say, from artistic peaks.

In my present existence, however, I have a gargantuan sense of excellent health, and of being at my best in all of my capacities, as in no challenge was beyond my strength. This alone gives me an immense advantage, of course—and I believe it applies to everyone regardless of their interests. Everything that I sense seems buoyant, as if nourished by unconscious springs, so that the whole universe seems to be in excellent high spirits, in the same way that young animals seem on earth. There is a supreme sense of elegance everywhere, and it seems impossible that any venture could fail.

Somehow fulfillment is built into this entire reality. *(Pause.)* It is difficult to remember the woes one felt when living, and I believe that this is apparent even in the nature of colors as I described them, for they appear so vibrant and alive that their own consciousness goes without saying.

(Pause at 5:50.) A vast acceptance—love—seems to uphold the nature of

every reality I come in contact with. It is not a man or woman's love. It is not sexual or nonsexual. I suppose it could be compared to a parent's love for a child, regardless of the sex of child or parent, but it also has gargantuan qualities of strength and durability *(long pause)*, touched, again, by that buoyancy that I mentioned earlier, and it is from this perspective that I understand that in one way or another all mistakes made in life are here redeemed.

(Long pause at 5:55. Terrific, Jane.) This is, of course, the creator's love for its creation, only the opportunities for expression here are endless, and I fall short here, unable to verbalize the dimensions of creative activity everywhere available. All of this is accompanied by the highest sense of anticipation *(pause)*, as if each moment of existence from here on would be even more precious than the last. Yet I still think that in one way or another I relate this backward to my old living self, and contact my old self, perhaps in dreams *(emphatically)*, trying to comfort myself as I was once *(pause)*, and of sending messages to that old self, and moments of inspiration that appear in those paintings—for they speak to me of my desires and intents.

(Long pause at 6:00 PM. "That's it for the minute," Jane said. "I'll take a sip of that stuff [cranberry juice]." I told her the material was excellent.

(The supper tray came at 6:29. Steve and Tracy Blumenthal called at 7:00, wanting to know if it was okay to visit Jane this evening. She said okay, though I declined to see them at the house afterward because I was getting tired. After feeding her I read the prayer at 7:30. Fifteen minutes later I left, after telling Jane to call me later in the evening if she could. It didn't work out.

(I noted on the previous page that I thought Jane's material was excellent. It wasn't until I came to typing this session on August 15 that I realized just how good it is, especially the last pages. I think it's the best work Jane has done, or at least its equal. It offers insight into many facets of life—but most importantly, I think, it offers hope and meaning in physical life itself—qualities that I believe millions of people lack. I would like to see such an approach to life as that expressed in this session widely disseminated—that is, beyond book sales, which would be quite limited even if it were published.

(One of the questions that came to me as I typed today concerned Jane's ability to come through with such excellent material while she was in such straits herself—confined to bed, and so forth as noted often in these sessions. Or was it her very condition that made the material's reception possible? Seth has said endlessly that Jane narrowed down her focus and activities in life with the idea that doing so would enable her to zero in on what she wanted to do to the utmost. Perhaps her reception of the material in this physical existence is part of the redemption Rembrandt refers to as being given to all in the reality he inhabits now. Jane's reception of the materi-

al would be her present interpretation of at least a portion of that redemption....

(I tried to briefly deal with questions of redemption in one of the essays I wrote introducing Seth's Dreams, "Evolution" and Value Fulfillment.

(Also see the well-known excerpts bearing on these ideas from the deleted sessions for January 26, 1981 and January 28, 1981.)

DELETED SESSION
AUGUST 9, 1983   5:54 PM TUESDAY

(No session was held yesterday. The day had been very hot—just the kind I liked. I'd had an appointment with Paul O'Neill. He built up a back tooth with amalgam filling. No charge, since he tried to do better on a job he'd started a couple of weeks ago.

(Also yesterday, I'd taken in to show Jane a letter that had arrived the day before from an Arthur Dogan in Vermont. He'd written Bob Monroe, author of Journeys Out of Body, *who had visited us years ago at 458 W. Water, about some visualization techniques described in a medical book. Dogan's letter made me think of writing to Monroe and asking what he knew, or could find out, about a new treatment for rheumatoid arthritis involving the medications usually used for amoebic dysentery. M.D.'s in England and this country have written a book about their ideas. I've ordered a couple of copies. A list of doctors now using the treatment is promised with the book, so I hope to contact some of these about Jane's case when I get the list. My thought, also, is that Bob Monroe might put us in touch with other people who might be able to offer something in the way of new treatment. One thing might lead to another in unexpected ways, if we're open to them, I told Jane. She agreed.*

(A note: Chemung Electronics <u>didn't</u> have the copies of the Seth tape ready last night—someone had simply forgotten to make them again. I took the tape back, and will give it to Pete Harpending tomorrow. Three trips to the store are enough. Jane was upset because she didn't get any Rembrandt material. She still has the extra freedom of movement in her arms, and the index finger of each hand.

(Jane read the session for July 31, which I'd typed this morning. She liked the summary notes I'd written for the session, covering our adventures since the session for July 27. She'd "completely forgotten" the Rembrandt material about comics and book painting. I told her that the more I thought about that material the more sense it made.

(We had a discussion yesterday about visualization techniques, sparked by the Dogan material, and I reminded Jane of they way she used to visualize the little men who moved through her body with their tiny tools, scraping away impediments and

making repairs inside her body. These had been quite effective for her. Although she wanted Rembrandt material, still she dozed —and in doing so visualized a row of little shops on West Water Street—You went into the one that could give you the kind of help you needed. That was good, I said, for it meant she was creating a setting for help that was physically and emotionally familiar to her. We'll see.

(This morning, August 9, I wrote Pete a note and put it with the Seth tape in an envelope so I could drop it off at his office on the way to the hospital this noon. I also called Steve Blumenthal about getting another copy of the class session for Jane and me to keep. I'd suggested to Pete that after he'd listened to the tape he send it on to Helen Wechsler in NYC.)

(At 11:15 this morning I received a call from Bill Kautz in Washington State. He explained how his organization had a "dedicated translator" who wanted to put Seth Speaks *into Japanese. Bill said he's written Prentice-Hall, but I'm not clear on Prentice-Hall's reaction. It was evidently favorable, since Bill's organization—a holistic health center—wants to raise $8,000–$10,000 to pay for the translation. I do not know whether they have a Japanese publisher interested. I asked Bill to send me an explanatory letter I can show to Jane, as well as a copy of correspondence from Prentice-Hall, and he agreed to do so.*

(Bill said he thinks this is an ideal time for Jane's work to appear in Japan, what with the cultural revolution, as he put it, going on over there.

(The day was pleasantly warm. Jane lay nude on her back. She looked rested and at ease. Went to hydro this morning after being given her Darvoset. She hadn't received her antidepressant last night before sleeping, though—someone just forgot to bring it to her. She did get her aspirin this morning. She said she still cries on the litter going to hydro—it's still painful for her to get lifted, rolled, put into the water, have her dressings changed, and so forth. She did have a pair of beneficial dreams last night, involving Saratoga, her walking, and so forth. She still isn't getting weighed regularly, which she likes. Debbie Harris visited last night. Jane wasn't able to call me last night. She tried a set of visualization techniques in hydro this morning.

("Do you want to take a few notes?" she asked as I worked on the mail.)

I told you it is my feeling that in a sense these communications took place one afternoon while I was half-dozing.

They could make no sense to me then. The use of unconscious knowledge could not then take place. I do not know the state of your wife's consciousness, or of your own, at that time in my own past. In any case *(long pause)*, your own conscious knowledge of such events apparently had to wait until certain intersections happened.

(There was much noise and confusion in the hall outside 330. I pushed the

door almost shut.)

Awareness of these communications conceivably could have taken place at any time *(long pause)*, but certain levels of comprehension had to touch all of our personalities before such communications jelled, or became strong enough to make sense in both of our worlds.

I do not believe that I was aware of these communications either when they first happened. 1 would have had no way to evaluate or understand them. I assume that the same is true on your parts. *(Long pause.)* At the same time, in a manner of speaking, the communications are enriched as my knowledge of my world when I was alive blends with your present knowledge of your world in your present time.

(Long pause at 6:01.) It is as if the three of us all wrote portions of a letter, the words fitting together meticulously, and yet forming a fine puzzle that had to work itself out as we each made our moves in our own realities. *(Long pause.)* It is one thing to send a letter from one portion of the planet to another, as in your mail system—but it is something else when the three individuals involved are constantly changing their alignment, position, and probable activities.

(Long pause at 6:05.) It is like trying to send a letter to a certain address while the mailbox keeps appearing or disappearing, or changes its position entirely, for all three of us are a portion of that one communication, while the position of our consciousnesses constantly alters.

(Long pause.) It is a wonder that such communications take place at all considering the changing coordinates that constantly apply. The communications could all have remained in the dream state on all of our parts, but we were all determined to bring them into some kind of actuality in the same way that the idea of a painting is changed into the physical painting itself. We did not want the communications to be *(pause)* in the realm of the probable only. We were determined to pull them out into whatever realities we could, so that they could be available in more practical terms.

(6:10. "That's all for a minute," Jane said. The hall was quieter now. I turned off the air conditioner as we waited for the supper tray. Then I turned on the fluo-rescent light behind Jane's bed, since the room was getting gloomy. I opened the cur-tains. The mountain ash tree rose up past the window. A block beyond, to the south-west, the Lake Street bridge rose over the Chemung River toward Elmira's south side. Jane liked to watch the automobile headlights crossing the bridge at night.

("I thought you weren't going to do anything today?" I asked.

("I wanted to, but I just couldn't get anything. And my shoulder hurt [she'd been on her right side until after 5:00], and I got mad at all the people coming in. Then I began to get this feeling.... Give me a cigarette."

("That's hard to understand, though," she said as she smoked. "If all of this took place in one afternoon of his life, where were we?"

("He doesn't know, I don't think," I said. "That's one of the basic questions."

("That's really weird." Jane said. I heard the supper trays in the hall, while at the same time I tried to think of a simple way to answer her question.

("Do you think sometimes when I deliver this stuff that you get in a trance too, Bob?"

("Yes." No doubt about it.

("I wondered."

(I've often been aware of being in a trance when recording Jane's material— indeed; I just take it for granted that being in that state is part of my role or function as we work together. It's very enjoyable—that smooth feeling in which time is telescoped or even seemingly almost negated as Jane speaks and I write quite effortlessly and rapidly. Our states obviously fluctuate rather easily, as when someone enters the room in the middle of a passage. For me, more changes manifest themselves as I check the time every so often, or insert a mention of something I hear or see going on while Jane is speaking.

(And therein, I thought, lay the answer to her question. I became so involved thinking about it that I didn't verbalize it to her. But our situation is as timeless, actually, as Rembrandt's is. Within that greater overall timeless state, then, it's almost beside the point to be concerned about where either Rembrandt was or we are when these communications take place. They took place, in those terms, when each of us wanted them to. For certain blocks of physical information to be passed back and forth, in narrower terms, each side set up age constraints to make this possible. Those ages were later in the physical lives of Rembrandt and ourselves, so that we'd have a certain accumulated amount of physical knowledge to play with and exchange.

(6:27.) I am aware of your rocketships and space travel—

(Susie, an aide, brought in supper. The bathroom for room 330 is also used by those in the room on the other side of the john. Someone over there had left our door locked on the bathroom side, so I asked Susie to go through the other room and unlock our door. She took with her the cover for the supper tray.

I would have found such things incomprehensible were it not for my own afterdeath experience.

In a way our communications exist as they do because of our joint interest in painting, with its mixture of the ideal and the immediate. In one way or another these communications had to become immediate if they were to be consciously acknowledged. They had to jell or solidify or happen in between realities, and yet also become immediate in your reality.

It does not matter that in the greatest terms every moment is immediate—

only that in your understanding of the terms the communications finally jelled, as a pudding might—

(6:30 PM. Three people came in. One had aspirin for Jane. As we joked about I said I'd stay to feed Jane supper. "Wait a minute," Jane said when we were alone again. "Just as they came in I was getting a block of stuff—winding it up pretty good." She laid waiting. "I don't want to lose it, either...." I said I'd do what she wanted to about dictation.

(6:38. "Well, maybe we'd better eat," I said.

("I can just see it there.... Okay, better put up the head of the bed."

(I fixed the coffee. "I don't even want to think about it," Jane said several times, "but we may be getting to the end of the Rembrandt material. I could feel that nostalgia...."

(I was somewhat surprised. Yet: "I guess that material today makes me think that, too."

(7:15. "Well, I may be wrong," Jane said as she had a cigarette after supper. "That nostalgia could have come from the material itself—my feelings about those times, maybe."

(Perhaps, I thought, but she hasn't been wrong yet about when a project was coming to a close. I was getting tired, so I didn't go into it, but I'd planned on asking Rembrandt questions about certain of his paintings—The Jewish Bride, so-called, for instance. I thought there was much interesting information we could get on his work alone.

(I gave Jane her ice cream, and she had another cigarette. By the time I left at 7:50 I was really tired. I hadn't read her the prayer. She said she'd try to arrange a call to me later in the evening, but it didn't work out.)

DELETED SESSION
AUGUST 11, 1983 4:55 PM THURSDAY

(Yesterday, August 10, Jane saw Fred K in the morning. He gave her the results of the urine tests that had been made some time ago—saying that she did assimilate nutrients well, but also that she didn't do as well with medications; she's on a rather high dose of Synthroid [for her thyroid deficiency], for example. Fred doesn't want her to give up the antidepressant at night, either, saying he doesn't want her to get "down" like she was before. From now on Jane is to get weighed but once a week. The girls who take care of her have arranged to give her breakfast before she goes to hydro, since the trays are on the third floor by 7:00 AM. The trick is to get Jane fed before her 8:00 trip downstairs.

(On August 10 I wrote to Bob Monroe, asking for his opinion on the proposed treatment of rheumatoid arthritis with the medications used for amoebic dysentery. I also wrote to Nancy Ashley re the Seth workbook she's done for Prentice-Hall. I suggested she have Tam do an intro for her book. I also sent Tam a card mentioning the idea. 'Twill be interesting to follow the ramifications here.

(Jane has kept in mind the visualization techniques we've been discussing lately, re her symptoms. She wasn't sure what portion of her body to concentrate on—or all of it—so I suggested the knees. Walking is pretty basic, I said. I explained that we ought to keep in mind that sometimes self-suggestion could have beneficial effects in an unexpected area. If one focused on knees, for example, the changes might show up in the elbows, say. All well and good, of course, and welcome. You could say the elbows responded because they were left free of any grim determined focus or demands that they improve, or else [to put this idea in strong terms here]. But if one wanted the knees to loosen up as almost a side effect of concentrating upon another portion of the body—how did one know what other portion to focus upon?

("If I get anything I'll let you know," Jane told me yesterday as I answered mail. I said okay. She asked me what paintings of Rembrandt's I wanted material on, and I had to tell her that outside of a few obvious examples like The Jewish Bride *I didn't know yet. I still had to study my books on the artist. No session developed in any case. Jane was uncomfortable much of the afternoon. She was also mad: "I didn't do anything today. And I know Rembrandt is around—I could feel it...."*

(To her added psychological discomfort. I left at 5:25, after reading her the prayer and checking the TV programs for the evening. I asked her to call me later, but it didn't work out. I was tired.

(Today, Thursday, I stopped to buy money orders on my way to the hospital. I found Jane lying nude on her left side. She was near tears. She was very blue, her emotions probably matching the rainy, gloomy day. She felt trapped: "I've got to do something with myself. I didn't want you to see me this way...." There were tears as she spoke. I quickly turned her on her back, washed her face and wiped her eyes. She didn't take her antidepressant last night, whether by her own design or an oversight on the part of staff, and I didn't know what part that nonevent might be playing in her reactions now. Maybe, I joked, we could blame it all on the weather.

(The staff is very short-handed today, although Jane did manage to get her breakfast before going to hydro, she said. Jane tried visualization in hydro, but didn't get anything. People came in as I fed her lunch, and their humor, along with the activities on television, seemed to help get Jane out of her poor mood. Her catheter is working okay, with regular irrigation, although she still says she feels a bit of leakage occasionally. She read the rest of August 3 after lunch, and the first couple of pages of August 5. I worked at answering letters. Later in the afternoon, after the staff had

taken her vitals, and Peggy Gallagher had visited, I showed Jane the Time-Life *book on Rembrandt that we've been more or less using as a text for reference. I held it up and turned pages so she could read text and see the paintings I referred to, such as* The Jewish Bride. *We'd talked about this yesterday [see the notes for August 10]. By then I'd turned her back on her back.*

(When Jane did begin to deliver her material her pace was as fast as I could write.)

I produced many uncommissioned paintings, and many times I took people off the street to use as models.

Some of these were used finally in other paintings, as character figures. I particularly was interested, at a certain time in my life, with groups of children—often my children's playmates. *(Pause.)* In one *[painting]*, the children had lost or misplaced something they valued, and they are in various positions, looking for it out in the street. There was a shop in the background where candy was sold and other sweets. You could tell that the children wanted to recover what they had lost—obviously a coin—in order to purchase some sweets.

The intentness of their search, the innocence of their desire, was what I tried to depict, while at the same time showing how that same innocent desire could also show later as greed in the adult's face, and so the storekeeper's face is seen in one of the windows as he peers out, hoping that the children will also be customers.

The painting ended up in Munich, I believe. *(Germany.)*

I was in the habit of painting any strangers' faces that appealed to me whenever this was convenient, and later using them in other works—usually in group portraits. I used my own children as models often, and in fact I did a very small series of paintings dealing with schoolboys. There were adults in the paintings also, of various characteristics.

(Long pause at 5:05.) I was trying to suggest what kind of men the boys might grow up to be, by countering the innocence of the boys' faces against the laxer *(long pause)* appearance of the adults. Would the boys turn into men like these? That was the painting's question. There were several paintings of that nature, of medium size.

(Long pause at 5:07.) I felt that I owed it to myself to do uncommissioned work whenever I felt the desire, for it allowed me to break free of the patrons' demands, and allowed me a freer stronger hand with the ideas and themes that were my own. I'm afraid I did not keep any complete record of my work in any up-to-date shape, but was always in the process of....

(Jane paused. Her voice had slowed and become more subdued; I thought she might be drifting into sleep. "You wanna read me that back?"

(I read the last paragraph to her.)

....cataloging and recataloging. I also had to watch the way I did my records. *(Long pause.)* <u>Sometimes</u> I had one set which was opened for study when my bill collectors were at the door. And then I had a private set for my eyes alone—certainly not to be shared with bill collectors.

Often, my uncommissioned work sold in any case, or became part of another painting that was commissioned.

(5:13. "I'll take a sip of something," Jane said. I gave her ginger ale. She said she hadn't been falling asleep, but had simply "lost track" as she gave the material. She smoked in silence while I yawned. I thought she might be through for the day. But: "Maybe I'll put this out and do some more. Here...." I took the ashtray off her belly.

(5:18.) There was also what I call "art vendors." I did not trust them over-much, but for a fee they would <u>rent</u> a work which would then be shown to the students of other artists so that they could study it, and there were even <u>tours</u>—some fairly well established—where an art vendor would rent so many paintings, taking them to the smaller hamlets where they would be shown for a specific time and be returned. This allowed the artist to make some money on a painting which had not perhaps found enough favor to be purchased.

One had to be exceedingly careful, however, because some paintings were lost, or stolen or mutilated in the process—and some were certainly sold, even though the art vendor came back with woeful tales that a given painting had been stolen by robbers, or otherwise destroyed by fire or storm.

I took advantage of art vendors only on certain occasions in my life, when I was in need of additional cash. *(Long pause.)*

Some bill collectors collected many fine works of art, and some paintings of course ended up for auction, and the artist on many occasions never knew who the buyer was, or what had happened to his work. Some such paintings of mine, I think, ended up in <u>Edinborough</u> *(tentatively)?* Our methods of communication were far slower of course than yours, and so often it would take years before an artist discovered what had happened to a given work of art that had come to such a fate.

(Jane's hesitant naming of "Edinborough" had at once made me think that she was trying to get at Edinburgh, Scotland. Edinburgh would have been at least a small city even in the 17th century, I think, and so known in Europe and in Amsterdam. It lies northwest across the North Sea from Amsterdam, probably less than 300 statute miles distant. It's quite conceivable that work by Rembrandt could have been transported there. But I could be wrong in these surmisings.)

(Emphatically:) <u>I did have my ways.</u> Many of my Jewish friends were lovers

of fine art, and the Jews had their own system of communication from one country to another. Often they could trace down such a missing painting, and for this they usually charged but a small-enough fee.

(Long pause at 5:28.) The Jewish Wedding was indeed produced for the members of two Jewish families of wealth and prominence who were relatives of the bride and groom. The painting gave me an excellent reputation in the richer Jewish communities. I certainly liked Jews as models, because their faces seemed to hold such a bewitching mixture of asceticism, spiritual values *(pause)*, shrewdness, and sly duplicity all at once. Their faces seemed to hold the full array of man's noblest and least noble dreams and desires *(all with dry humor.*

(Pause at 5:32.) I felt no strain between my favorites, the Jews, and my Christian orientation. I also did a painting called The Runaways, of two Jewish children, a boy and girl *(long pause)*, who were determined to marry, although they came from opposing Jewish <u>sects</u>. The painting had a romantic background, a landscape that seemed to be magical and bewitched, but touched by a hopeful soft illumination that radiated also in the runaways' faces, and glinted now and then in the soft folds of their garments. In the background there was also a gate, half-open, suggesting that their escape was assured finally.

(Long pause at 5:36.) This painting did not gain me favor, however, because of its subject matter. It ended up at an art dealer's—I believe in London—where it remained unsold for some years. I believe the shop later burned.

(5:38. "Now I'll have a sip of ginger ale and a cigarette," Jane said. "That was coming through pretty strong."

("I could tell." Her pace had again been as fast as I could write.

("I suppose it raises as many questions as answers," Jane said.

("Sure—but so what? It's very interesting." I explained my idea about Edinborough-Edinburgh, an idea I now thought was reinforced by Rembrandt's subsequent mention of London, England. Maybe we'd get more on the Scotland connection sometime, I added. I washed Jane's face for supper—but then she told me to take her cigarette because she was getting some more material.

(Fast as usual at 5:45.) Few artists would ever speak of dealing with the art vendors.

They were a group quite apart from the recognized <u>art dealers</u>, and were often used by artists who, for one reason or another, wanted to disguise their inventories. *(Long pause.)* There are many differences between such practices and *(pause)* <u>black-market art</u>? *(Questioningly, as though searching for a modern analogy)*—yet the practice did offer many artists an unofficial route for exhibition or sale.

Some of the art vendors were quite disreputable, and others were trust-worthy, but prevented from taking their place in the official art market because of unfortunate feuds or an overabundance of debt. Such practices were preva-lent, however, all over Europe, and I assume in other countries as well.

(Long pause at 5:50.) There were also very unofficial channels by which an artist's students could sell their master's minor works *(long pause)*, perhaps signed by the students, but known by all secretly to be the master's hand. An artist had to be quite diligent to keep track of his own sketches and so forth, so as to not leave himself open to such trickery.

(5:53. "I guess that's all for the moment," Jane said. Again her delivery had remained good. As I lit a cigarette for her we heard the supper trays in the hall.

("Goddamn," I said, "all of that would keep you busy, wouldn't it? Doing your painting, having classes, running a house, raising a family, watching out for trickery while you were trying to sell your stuff—how did they do it all?"

("I don't know. Fascinating."

("It's almost a new class of his painting that he's talking about here—quite dif-ferent from the usual categories of his work that everybody knows: the portraits, the biblical scenes, the groups. The storytelling work about children would be complete-ly unknown, like the seascapes he described way back in those early sessions. If any of that stuff turned up now it would cause a sensation."

("Oh, you know what?" Jane asked as she smoked. "Several people have asked me if that portrait of yours on the wall is a self-portrait of you when you were younger."

("Oh yeah? I didn't intend it to be that," I said. I was pleased that people had noticed the painting, though.

("That's what I told them."

(6:04. "You know what I just got?" Jane continued. "One of those art vendors was named Van Strumph." She spelled the name rather hesitantly. "It might have been one of the local art vendors who were one of Rembrandt's art contacts."

("Then another guy's name was something like Murdouth—Murdough—"

("Murdock?" I asked.

("The pronunciation is Murdock, so maybe you're right about calling it that. Oh—and I was getting that by profession he was a doctor, and he did this on the side.... the profession was sort of a sideline of some men who had their own business-es or professions but who traveled a lot."

("Sounds like a regular industry," I laughed, thinking that it could be a sub-culture nourished by the art of painting itself.

(6:10. Now Jane began to dictate her material a bit more formally. This was-n't Rembrandt.)

There were also art smugglers. Sometimes an artist wanted to—sometimes an artist got commissioned to do a work by a patron who lived in another country *(long pause)*, and then because of politics or whatever, it became foolhardy to have obvious dealings with anybody in that particular country—like maybe a deal had been made before the politics changed. Then sometimes the artist would pay an art smuggler himself to get the painting out of the country and into the patron's hands. That didn't happen too often in Holland, but it happened often in Italy and France.

Many times—uh—<u>Oriental rug dealers</u> were involved—and they'd roll canvases up inside the rugs to get them out of the country, the rugs also protected the paintings from the dampness if any kind of sea travel was involved.

I guess that's it for now, anyway.

(6:14. Supper hadn't come yet. We waited. "Yeah," I said, "can you imagine trying to keep track of someone in those days, of tracking down a painting? When someone was out of your sight they were really gone—unless you sent someone after them—"

("And then you wouldn't know if you could trust them," Jane said.

(Supper came at 6:20, and I stayed to feed her. Jane's liquid intake this morning hadn't been very good—only 560 cc's—and she hadn't taken in much liquid this afternoon either.

(I left at 7:55, after Jane had been turned on her left side by Lorrie and Sharon. We weren't alone and I didn't read her the prayer. She didn't call me later.)

DELETED SESSION
AUGUST 13, 1983 3:55 PM SATURDAY

(No session was held yesterday, Friday, although during the afternoon Jane told me about material she was picking up on her own. First, though, let me note that I stayed late Thursday, following that day's session. On Friday Jane told me that after I'd left she picked up that there were "double-backed paintings"—meaning that a student of a master artist would paint a picture that was then framed, and visible. But on the back of the painting would be a much more valuable work by the master himself. This was covered over; in appearance this covering seemed designed to protect the student's work from damage from the rear, whereas in actuality the covering was meant to hide the master's work. Jane said that this was another way a painting could be smuggled out of the country, right out in the open, so to speak. I thought it was pretty obvious, but she said the method was used quite successfully. Her information was a follow-up from the Thursday session itself, of course, which dealt

with the smuggling of paintings.

(*I told her I didn't understand why a student's work could be so openly taken out of a country, when a master's work couldn't, unless money was involved beside politics—perhaps lower custom fees? The information needs some elaboration.*

(*Jane was quite uncomfortable at 3:25. Friday afternoon, after I turned her on her right side; her shoulder, digging into the mattress, bothered her. "I was getting that Rembrandt made a trip to Italy and other countries between his two marriages," she said. "He made the trip all by himself, and business was involved." She became more aggravated by her shoulder as she tried to get more, and shifted about restlessly. I explained that historically there's no record that shows Rembrandt ever left Holland. There are some scanty records showing Rembrandt's dealings with a collector in Sicily [off the tip of the Italian "boot"] for paintings such as* Aristotle Contemplating the Bust of Homer, *a* Homer, *and others, as well as etchings. The records exist on the Italian's side, however; there's nothing from the artist himself.*

(*The material she came up with on Thursday night and yesterday, even though no "session" was involved, is valuable indeed, for they show that Jane's creative abilities are functioning as always. And as she herself said, she was aware of much more material than noted above. The important thing is that it was there, even if her physical discomfort interfered with her delivering it at times. Words rather fail me here, but I sense or feel something to the effect that her awareness of the Rembrandt material along with her current challenges shows how she straddles realities—a pretty mundane observation, I'd say after all. However, if she does it others must also, even if on wholly unconscious levels.*

(*We forgot to read the prayer Friday night.*

(*When I got to 330 at 1:05 today, Saturday, Jane told me that in hydro this morning her right arm had extended down considerably beyond what it usually does. She's been working with visualization, and I said that perhaps the arm movement was the unplanned result of her efforts. She's been managing to eat some breakfast before going to hydrotherapy. She had a BM this morning, but felt that another might be coming. I told her that Prentice-Hall had finally decided against reprinting* Emir, *but that they want to know the outcome of our challenges involving* ESP Power, *with a notion toward issuing a trade paperback of the book eventually.*

(*The staff at the hospital was very shorthanded today. I fed Jane lunch. And she did have mild diarrhea—two more BM's, which people soon cleaned up. She read the first four pages of the session for August 6. She felt the diarrhea was over by then, so I turned her on her right side. She said okay when I explained that I had to leave early to go shopping. She lay dozing while I worked with the mail. The day was cool and quiet. Even the noise in the halls was subdued.*

(3:55. *"Have you ever heard of Hastings on the Rye?" Jane asked.*

("I've heard of Hastings on the Hudson," I said. "Do you mean in a foreign country, or what?"

("I don't know. That's what I've been picking up...." She didn't know how it might be spelled. I said that just because I hadn't heard of it meant little one way or another. I thought she was disappointed that I couldn't verify her impression more definitely.

(Then, I told her, I made a couple of obvious connections. According to the little I remembered, early New York City and environs—Manhattan Island—had been settled by the Dutch. *The Dutch could have named Hastings on the Hudson based on a connection with their native land, for all I knew. There exists a small city named Rye in Westchester County, just north of New York City. According to our encyclopedia Rye was settled early in the 1600's. The encyclopedia lists a city of Rye in England, but not in Holland. It's of considerable interest that Hudson is an English name—and that the English explorer, Henry Hudson, was the first white man to see the Hudson River—while in the employ of the* Dutch East India Company.... *in 1609:*

(A note by Jeff Marcus, who attended Jane's ESP class many years ago with Rick Stack, the publisher now of many Seth books: "The original Hastings is in England, next to the town of Rye. Both of those are near the cliffs of Dover. Hastings & Rye, New York, although both in Westchester County, are not particularly close— with many towns in between."

(Again, this tidbit of an impression from Jane needs clarification.

(At 4:10 I put Jane back on her back.

(4:37. She began to relay some impressions more formally.)

I was getting something about Rembrandt in Munich *(Germany)*—I don't know if he was invited there or what—lecturing—but he didn't like it, and he returned home.

And on another occasion he did go down to the Mediterranean, to Sicily, where he was instantly struck by the difference in the lighting in the Mediterranean sky. It was much softer than the one at home.

He went there on business—uh—to meet a man called Cervecchio *(my phonetic interpretation)*—I have no idea how you spell it—who offered to handle his work for him in Italy, and Rembrandt wasn't sure if he liked the man or not. He was very enthusiastic—he waved his arms around when he spoke *(pause)*, and in a funny way Rembrandt found him almost over-friendly, but he did end up sending him a few paintings the following two or three years. He wasn't a comfortable traveler, though.

(Long pause at 4:44.) On a few such trips he even took one of his sons along, though the boy was only half-grown. He didn't trust Italian politics—or

French politics either, for that matter.

(Long pause.) Actually, he almost preferred dealing with the art vendors, since they were unknown to the authorities, and managed to travel around with immunity, no matter what the conditions in the country were.

(4:47. During a long pause I got up to push our door shut; there was much noise at the elevators now.

("Is that it?" I asked Jane.

(4:48 PM. "I guess so, for the minute.... I haven't the slightest idea of whether Munich in those years had a university, or what...."

("Well, it's a major German city, and always has been as far as I know," I said. "So it probably had at least one university, even in those days."

(A note: Our encyclopedia mentions only one university, one that was "transferred to Munich" in the early 1800's. This seems rather incomplete, however, since the work also relates that Munich was a cultural and manufacturing center from way back, that it had an archdiocese, museums, and so forth. It's also the home of a world-famous museum, the Pinakothek, which has in its collection more than one Rembrandt painting....

(I read the prayer, then left by 5:25 to go shopping. And I discovered I'd left the long list at home, so I had to drive to the house first to pick it up, and then head for the Acme on the south side.

(When I returned home the phone rang. It was Steve Blumenthal. Steve and Tracy won't be coming to see us until tomorrow night. Steve has more work to do on both his presentation of facts and figures for marketing Seth tapes and on the touch-control cassette player for Jane.)

DELETED SESSION
AUGUST 15, 1983 3:52 PM MONDAY

(A session wasn't held yesterday, Sunday. I couldn't find anything in my reference material at the house on the Hastings-on-the-Rye impression Jane had come up with in last Saturday's session. The few speculations I added in that session are all we have for the moment, plus Jeff's note.

(Jane hadn't received her antidepressant Saturday night. Sunday afternoon I explained to her why Betty Blair at Clune's insurance agency had reported we couldn't get supplementary coverage: I was too old, and she had a pre-existing condition. Larry Allen Hummer and a young friend had visited me this morning. Jane didn't have a very good day, and wasn't thrilled at the prospect of a visit Sunday evening by Steve and Tracy. In addition, when I left at 7:20 I'd forgotten to read her the prayer.

(Surprisingly, however, Jane had a great time when Steve and Tracy visited her,

and so did they. Some very heartening events manifested themselves. I'd say that Jane's own advancements in being able to come through with the Rembrandt material made these additional developments possible. [A few months ago, say, I'd have said that all of those developments were highly unlikely, if not impossible.]

(Steve and Tracy arrived at 330 at about 8:30 PM. He had two recorders with him—a tiny Panasonic [voice activated?] like the one we recently bought, and an older, large cassette player to which Steve had connected his version of a touch-sensitive set of controls that.... hopefully, Jane could learn to operate so she could do recording whenever she felt like it, even if she was alone in her room. The Blumenthals also had with them a paperback volume on primitive archeology in this country and abroad. They'd picked up this because of their own interest in studying the American Indian artifacts on their own property outside Ithaca. The book contained many photos of ancient inscriptions on stone, and so forth.

(As her visitors held up the book for her to look through, Jane began to pick up information about some of the inscriptions [supposedly in "unknown" languages] on the stones. She began to sing in Sumari, so turned on was she by what she was looking at. Steve recorded her songs on both sets. In the larger set was a tape of the class session for January 29, 1974, which he was bringing for me at my request last week. Jane's Sumari was recorded in the middle of this tape.

(In fact, the power of her Sumari as it came through was such that she had to hold it down lest it sound too loud in the hospital, and lead to questions as to what was going on. After the singing, she then preceded to deliver translations of the Sumari. This material was also recorded on both instruments.

(Steve had rigged up earphones for the larger of the recorders, with the idea that Jane could lay these over her ears as she lay in bed. The earphones were connected by a cloth wrapped around their wiring, which made them very flexible, but he'd adjusted the set to such a low volume that sounds were nearly inaudible. The idea was that hospital personnel and other patients wouldn't be bothered, of course.

(Steve and Tracy arrived at the house after 9:30. They'd tried to play back Jane's material for her on both recorders, with poor results. The quality of Jane's material on the tiny Panasonic was execrable, and had an echo. It was very difficult to listen to what she was saying and ignore the fact that the little machine had her voice sounding like that of a little old lady singing and talking to a pet canary. Steve explained that it was possible to clean up and improve the quality of that tape considerably, and he promised us a decent copy. I really want this, since it will make up a signpost record of another step in Jane's improvement.

(It was equally difficult to decipher Jane's material on the earphones for the larger of the recorders, since the volume was so low. I explained that Jane couldn't manage such a system, and asked Steve to convert the machine to standard speakers

with regular volume control. In addition, Steve has another set of hand controls ordered, so I asked him to incorporate those new controls with the set, rather than to try to jockey into useable condition those he'd brought with him. Possibly Jane can learn to use such controls, which require little pressure indeed. We'll have to see. Presumably she will lie in bed and press upon them with a thumb. Jane had trouble manipulating her fingers to work the touch-control device Steve had brought with him. He said the poor quality of the Panasonic tape can be greatly improved by a technique called computer rerecording.

(A similar technique will also be used to clean up some of the class tapes for marketing, if that project ever develops. Steve and Tracy gave me a copy of their plan for forming a company to do this, and promised to send Pete Harpending a copy. I haven't had the time yet to read it. Steve also promised me a new copy of the class tape for January, 1974. They left at 11:30 PM. I was dead tired. During their visit I'd been so tired at times I had trouble focusing on what they were saying and doing.

(Early this afternoon, Monday, I had a good meeting with Mr. Fife in the business office, re financial matters. I felt much relieved, since I'd been concerned about a letter I'd received from him last Saturday. He was concerned about our bill for Jane's previous hospitalization, before our insurance coverage took effect. We reached an agreement whereby I'll send him an extra $2000 to bring down the total somewhat. I'd thought the hospital would demand much more. I explained that Jane and I have royalty payments due next month [for an unknown amount].

(But I also discovered that the business office can make mistakes, even if of omission—for the people hadn't billed insurance for current charges due from major medical on a monthly basis. They were going to do it when Jane's billing stopped—whereas her billing is indefinite.... The hospital had been a month late in sending us one of the statements, also. All of these things involve considerable amounts of money. Phone calls were made while I talked with Mr. Fife. We learned that major medical will be billed right away. We also learned that checks from the Syracuse office are up to three weeks late because of _vacations_ there. I told Mr. Fife I didn't understand how vacations could be allowed to interfere with payments, and so forth. Mr. Fife is to get us statements that are up to date. I felt much better.

(3:10. Jane read the balance of the session for August 6 and the first two pages for August 7. She liked my notes for August 6, dealing with my supposition that the Rembrandt sessions were forming at least part of a redemptive process in her present life. In between visits from people checking Jane's vitals, I turned her on her left side, facing the window, at 3:30. I opened the window and turned off the air conditioner so I could be more comfortable. She wasn't very comfortable. Her left shoulder was digging into the mattress again. I was still tired, and reminded her that I'd have to leave by 5:30 to do some work at the house, unless she herself was coming through *with some dictation.*

("Oh hell," she said at 3:52, after squirming around trying to get comfortable, "I'll try to do something....")

Now that I am aware of your ideas concerning the equality of the sexes, it strikes me that I was perhaps over-prudent when I was discussing social mores earlier.

I was accustomed to ignoring certain situations of the one hand. While being quite aware of them on the other. But I had to change my own ways of thinking.

(Long pause at 3:55.) I only half realized that I was acting in such a manner—so perhaps I <u>whitewashed</u> the picture to some extent. The relationship between a young man and his father was usually quite strict, generally speaking. Soon after a boy reached puberty, however, the subject of sex was usually initiated by another older male member of the family. Often the boy's uncle, who took him aside and helped initiate the young lad into the world of practical sexual knowledge. In other words, usually the lad was taken by someone like an uncle to a house, sometimes run exclusively for that purpose. There the young man was introduced to an older woman familiar with sexual finesse, and then and there initiated into physical fulfillment. This was never spoken about again by lad or uncle, and the father, often guessing the circumstances, never gave a sign of his supposition.

Sometimes the learning process was continued for several sessions—but henceforward the young man was not expected to return once his lessons were finished. Such women were paid quite handsomely, and they were usually women of excellent intelligence, sympathy, and sexual know-how.

No such learning process was afforded to young women, however. They might speak with their mothers or sisters, but only with the greatest discretion. It was expected that when they married their husbands would then initiate them into sex's rituals.

(Long pause at 4:02.) This does not mean that a few young men were not eager to show off their new powers by grabbing at a housemaid occasionally—

(4:03. Rhonda, from rehab, came in to take Jane's blood pressure; it was very good at 100 over 60. Rhonda has been assigned to our section for tonight. She asked me if I was going to stay to feed Jane supper. I said I was so tired I was going home by 5:30. I must have looked it, for she smiled and said, "Don't worry, we'll make out."

("You see," Jane said after Rhonda had left, "she was told to ask you that, they're so shorthanded here."

(I told Jane her material today was excellent, and also hilarious—and that it

certainly looked as though it put those people ahead of ours in some respects, at least.

(4:13.) A young girl might receive a few hints from a kind aunt, but these were much more socially oriented, dealing with tips on how to flirt and not flirt at the same time, and consisted of the most surface kind of social behavior.

This gave undue advantage to the husband at the time of marriage, of course, for it seemed that his knowledge was so much greater than his wife's. In the matter of childbirth, however, and afterward, the affair was completely reversed.

Men were kept purposely ignorant of the childbirth processes. The women in the household formed their own mysterious unit, and no male was allowed to enter. Men often underwent quite strong feelings of anguish, which they kept to themselves, following their manly tradition, but once a woman was pregnant, it was as if the most important issues of birth and death were in the woman's hands.

In innumerable instances this involved childbirth itself, with midwives taking over and the man literally banished into other parts of the house. A father saw his child only later, when it was properly washed and dressed, and then formally presented to him, while the women smiled secretive satisfied smiles, presenting him with such a fine gift.

(4:20.) On the other hand, I must admit that if a child was a son the gift was considered far more outstanding than a daughter's birth. *(Long pause.)* It still seems to me, however, that despite this fathers were easier, more tolerant and natural with their daughters than they were with their sons. The birth and upbringing of a son was surrounded by many more responsibilities of a legal and dynastic manner. *(Long pause.)* The little man would soon be a big man, and perhaps one day supersede his father. Was that the reason behind such behavior? I am not sure, but I do know that the father's relationship with his son was of a much more formal nature. It is also true that young daughters seemed almost to band together with all the females in the house, as if they possessed some strange knowledge of their own that men did not possess.

I sensed this, but could never quite put my finger on any <u>particular</u> behavior that illustrated my feelings. The young females, as they played with their <u>dolls</u>, however, almost seemed to slyly remind the males that they were the child-bearers, so that a man often felt that those issues of family preservation were placed almost exclusively in a woman's hands.

There was, after all, no certain method of knowing who a child's father was, and even when a man never suspected any duplicity on his wife's part, that knowledge was always in his mind.

(Long pause at 4:29. "I'm gonna wait a minute," Jane said, smiling as she

*looked at the clock I'd taped in position on top of the television set on its swivel arm,
"then you can turn me on my back."*

*("You did good, Hon." Her pace had been excellent, as was the material. After
I'd put her back on her back I said that I'd stay to feed her if I could manage to take
a nap for half an hour. I'd been considering the easy chair back in a little-used corner of the room. I turned the air conditioner on "High," and moved around to sit
beside Jane on the other side of her bed.*

(4:45.) As the years passed, the relationship between a husband and wife
gradually became much more comfortable.

Men and women were both brought up to be quite practical in their ways,
and oftentimes a woman would help her husband in financial matters—helping
to keep his books and so forth.

Unfortunately, many couples never lived together long enough to achieve
this relaxed relationship, for women died often in childbirth, and hence a man
might marry several times, each time accumulating other family members on his
wife's side. There were always exceptions, of course, but generally speaking there
were few truly <u>passionate</u> relationships. The relationships were based on the
greatest <u>fondness</u> *(pause)* that the two people had for each other—and all in all
there were strong bonds of affection, tolerance, and understanding. A man
always knew that childbirth presented the wife with grave dangers, however,
while the women's secrecy kept him from learning anything essential about
childbirth itself.

Affection still bonded most couples together, however. Very few husbands
had mistresses, and women had few affairs. For one thing, most of society was
firmly built upon the family unit, and social life merely represented the larger
scope presented by a man and woman's family relationships. There was little
opportunity for promiscuity. Men belonged to their guilds. Women had their
sewing groups, embroidery parties and other strictly female *(pause)* classifica-
tions.

(Long pause at 4:55.) Sometimes a woman's dowry was paid in install-
ments, and only finally delivered in full when she survived her first birth of a
child. *(Long pause.)* When wives did survive several births, usually the man and
the wife had the sturdiest of foundations, and the home became a unit for the
education of one's children, at least before they were sent to school.

(Long pause.) If the family was large, a maiden aunt might act as a nurse
or a nanny, and many times the wife had some female member of her own family to aid in the overall running of the household. *(Long pause.)* So the family
was experienced in different ways throughout the years, and if one man and one
wife managed to survive for any amount of time, then they were considered the

luckiest of people. Older women were particularly looked upon with merit, simply for having survived, and the elderly were held in honor.

(Long pause at 5:00.) When I was a <u>very</u> young man, and for that period only, I visited the whores in their taverns, mostly out of curiosity. *(Long pause.)* On several occasions I tried to get into the good graces of an older woman prostitute. They generally laughed, cuffed me playfully, and sent me home, humiliated as a young puppy.

Grandmothers and grandfathers were held in the greatest esteem. Both for the years they lived and the wisdom they had accumulated. Some aunts or uncles acted as nurses or tutors to the young members of the family, and there were few families who did not have several children living, and several who had died, particularly in childbirth. Marriage was no frivolous activity, then, but the time for great seriousness, as it was the social framework in which almost everyone lived out their lives.

(5:05 PM. "Well, I guess that's it for the minute," Jane said. I told her the material was very good. Her delivery had been steady and intent. "I could tell it was filling out."

(She had me put the air conditioner on low. I also turned the TV on low, and then sat in the easy chair in the corner in an effort to take a nap. I fell asleep all right—and there followed much noise and confusion inside and outside the hospital that I only partially heard: a malfunctioning alarm at the elevators outside 330, followed by the arrival of fire trucks and police cars with their sirens and bells sounding. They all parked on Market Street outside our windows while various people tried to track down the source of the trouble. The deep sound of the idling fire-truck engines throbbed inside our room on the third floor, even. I believe the elevators didn't work for a time. All the excitement came to me as a phantasmagoria of jumbled sound. I slept, though. I finally roused after an hour. I felt better.

(When Jane's supper tray came at 6:20 we discovered that for some mysterious reason the meat and ice cream had been left off it. I told Rhonda about the omission when she brought Jane aspirin and ginger ale. I checked the TV programs for the night while Jane ate spinach and potatoes and gravy. Rhonda returned with ice cream and a weird-looking salad compote—two of them—in green. They seemed to be full of salad dressing and shredded fruit. Jane tried one mouthful. She had a cigarette after eating. I read the prayer to her, and then turned her on her left side at 7:30. She said she'd try to call later, but didn't.)

DELETED SESSION
AUGUST 17, 1983 3:09 PM WEDNESDAY

(No session was held yesterday, Tuesday. Most of the day was pretty routine. It was warm and sunny. I stopped at the bank to buy a money order to apply against Jane's old bill. Peggy Gallagher visited while I was feeding Jane lunch, and brought with her a tape from a guy in Seattle who's been bugging her lately by telephone. He wants to heal Jane. Peggy wouldn't give out our address or phone number, hence the tape. I thanked Peg. She'd recorded the healer's last telephone conversation, and played a little of it for us. After Peggy left I told Jane to pay no attention to the taped message. I thought the individual was simply using Jane because he was attracted to her work, and was now caught up in the excitement of trying to contact her because he'd heard she was having challenges.

(Peggy also told us a long story about how she and Bill had met Claire Crittenden and companion last night in Watkins Glen State Park after they'd been bicycling in the vicinity.

(I'd taken another nap before feeding Jane supper Tuesday night, and left her finally at 8:00 PM. We hadn't read the prayer.

(Today, Wednesday. I stopped at billing to give them money after I'd made a copy of the check the night before at the house. Jane lay nude on her back; the day was hot. She'd had her catheter changed last night at about 9:00—it couldn't be irrigated. Today she felt okay, everything considered. After lunch she read the nine pages of the session for August 11, and I read her portions of August 15. Then I answered mail while she dozed beside me. In fact, I thought she was asleep when she abruptly said, "I guess I'll get a little....")   ○

Looking backward at my life, as I have been doing, brought about....

(After a long pause I realized that Jane had *drifted off again. Then she started awake. "Now what the hell does that mean?" she demanded. "I got the image of a* pig—*a pig leaping over a wheelbarrow, or something. The man had evidently startled the pig. I don't know what that means...." And then she resumed where she'd left off.)*

....some more understanding on my part. I realized that in my life, on many more occasions than I could count, I did indeed feel strong satisfying moments of peace that would come upon me in the midst of almost any activity. In those moments I felt lifted up into some other dimension—but usually when I realized this, the experiences ceased.

What just happened, as your wife mentally saw the young pig running across a small wooden bridge—all of that was a memory of mine.

(Maybe we'll get to go into it further sometime—but interesting, Jane's inter-

pretation of Rembrandt's experience and the way similarities exist between the pig jumping over a wheelbarrow, and running over a bridge....

(Long pause at 3:13.) I don't know if I connected those moments with my painting—yet certainly they were connected, because when I was concentrating on my work often the same feelings would come again. The painting would become almost super-real before my eyes, as if it were magnified a thousand times. I never mentioned these feelings to anyone, but they certainly brought me great comfort in the midst of so many other bustling activities.

Painting itself teases the artist into the future, for it causes him to anticipate still another painting, and when the problems in one painting are solved they seem to leave the artist into another threshold of anticipation. Certainly the artist is *(pause)* a <u>determined</u> explorer, for each painting is like a new country, and each completed painting tantalizes the artist to do another and still another.

This must invoke a certain faith in the future, for the dreamed-of paintings almost insist upon their own birth.

(3:19.) <u>I do not believe</u>, in any case, that any artist in harmony with his own work could ever commit suicide, or be lost in the darkness of despair. I <u>had</u> thought at times that perhaps an artist could <u>lose</u> himself in his painting, becoming bewitched by it until his painting pushed everything else out of his life—but true creativity is <u>not feverish</u> *(emphatically)*. It is not the result of some nervousness, but it is propelled, I believe, by a man's trust in a tomorrow.

I believe also that painting adds a spicy anticipation to the painter's life, as he feels the thrust of probable paintings, each waiting in the background, as it were, and he knows that he literally has worlds to fill—an inner landscape that stretches further and further into a distance that is at once in the future, and yet based in the present moment in his life.

(Long pause.) Some men feel that they will populate the world with fine offspring, and many old men *(pause)* can see the results with children, grandchildren and great grandchildren, all alive in the world of the flesh. Whether or not an artist has a family, however, he knows he is populating <u>and exploring</u> inner lands of creativity *(long pause)*, producing creative portraits, perhaps of generations of unknown people—or as if he is sculpting out tomorrow after tomorrow, and clearing away old debris, hoping to uncover creativity's true source.

(Pause at 3:28. "I'll take a break."

("Very good, Hon."

("Good. I'll have a cigarette. Shit, I know I'll have to turn over," Jane said. "Yeah, I could feel that."

("Hey," she said after I lit her smoke, "sometimes I can't tell if I said something or if I didn't. Did I explain about that pig thing?"

("Yes."

(3:32. Now Jane began describing for me an image of a Rembrandt painting she's been seeing "off and on yesterday and today." Then she got into describing other paintings by Rembrandt. The accounts that follow are partly verbatim as she described the paintings and part summary on my behalf. I wrote them as fast as I could while she was speaking. I read them to her later, for checking.)

It's called *The Losers*, and features a painting Rembrandt did of Roman soldiers throwing dice for Christ's robe at the foot of the cross. It has an unusually dark and threatening sky, and focuses on this act where the soldiers gamble for Christ's robe after the Crucifixion has taken place, rather than on the Crucifixion and the cross itself.

(Jane got confused, she said several times as we talked, because she kept equating this painting with Cézanne's The Card Players.*)*

In Rembrandt's painting, the artist has included himself as an onlooker, but he wasn't one of the gamblers. I think there were five figures besides Christ.

My feeling was that he was much more interested in dramatic narrative in the painting than was recognized.

("It would be interesting to know what happened to the painting," I said, because as far as I knew no such work now existed. Jane said she'd see what she could get on this. She was also worried about people coming into 330 to interrupt us.)

Oh God, then mentally I got the words *The Graveyard Robbers*, and that was his title for another painting. And that seemed to be two guys—one with a shovel and another with a pick—and it was a night scene with the moon out, partially, and they've already apparently dug down to the casket because there's a big pile of dirt. The casket's opened, and then it shows the top portion—

("Oh, look who's here," Jane broke off to exclaim as Sharon, an aide, came in to take her temperature. Then Sarah, an RN, came in to check her blood pressure and pulse. We were alone again at 3:43. Jane's liquid intake this morning had been good—945 cc's, or cubic centimeters.

(Are your hands tired?" she asked.

("No."

("All right—I'll try to describe what I see...."

(3:48.) The casket's open. There's a pile of dirt, and one guy is at the head of the coffin. They've got the body half dragged out. I assumed they buried people with their clothes on, but this one's naked and you can see the rib bones. He's got a beard, blackish, and his eyes are closed, of course, and his head is way back in a fashion I don't believe it can get in if you're alive. And there's a sug-

gestion of some kind of dark material behind him—that they might have lined the casket with—it's almost got a dark reddish cast.

The second man is at the foot of the casket. I don't understand, bracing it like you would a teeter-totter, and the other guy's at the head of the casket, holding it, there's a light source—I guess it's the moon—and it shows on the pile of dirt and a couple of worms, and the light glints on one arm of the corpse and on a ring on one hand. The other arm is behind him and I don't see it at all—it's the way he's been pulled out—

(3:55. LuAnn, an RN, came in to give Jane eye drops.)

Isn't that awful, Bob? I can see a cart—it's long, it's got four wheels and is all gray and has a pile of material, apparently to cover the corpse—but I can't tell where it goes in the painting.... There's something about the corpse. The way the anatomy shows so clearly, that makes you think they're going to take it to a doctor for dissecting, or something. You don't see either of the robbers' faces clearly. The one guy's back is to you, the one that's at the foot of the casket, and the other guy's head is obscured by the casket itself. They both wear caps. I can't describe it—they're brown....

(Pause at 3:58.) You know those stories about there being gold pieces on the eyes of the corpse? I don't see that. There's two dark shadows around the dirt that could be rats. The ring, on the other hand, looks like it could really be gold—it's got some details on it. The lighting is more dramatic probably than I can describe.

(4:00.) The one guy's face you can see at all doesn't even look lecherous. You know, just weary, as if there's one more night's work done, or something like that....

(4:05. "I'll have a cigarette," Jane said finally. I took a break to go to the john.)

I get confused, I guess, I keep getting two images of one painting. It's called *The Hope Chest*—of a young woman; we'd call her voluptuous. Anyway, in one painting she's at the foot of the bed, and there's a very big trunk, ornate, carved with little figures, and there are metal bands around it. It's open, and she's sitting on the bed and her arm with these long sleeves comes down and hides part of the hope chest. She holds a note, and her face is like forward more than a profile, and she's been crying. There's a pile of garments on the floor, as if she's discarded them. They're very ornate and embroidered, and up toward the head of the bed there's a candle, as if the illumination comes from there.

(Pause at 4:11.) In the other painting, which I'm not seeing as well at all, she's seated at a boudoir mirror and you see her face in the mirror, and she's been crying. You see her arm with the embroidered sleeve, and this time you see the wrinkled note rolled up in her hand, and this time the chest is in the foreground

in front of her. And way to the left is a doorway, with a suggestion of an older woman standing in the shadows, as if she's the girl's mother come to see what's wrong—but she's not in the room yet.

That's all I can get on that one—but there are two versions of one painting that he did. I don't know if he started one and didn't finish it, or what, but you know the note contains some bad news, as if the young man was killed, or said t.s., or something.

(4:15 PM. Jane sipped some cranberry juice and had a cigarette. Then she had me turn her on her right side, so she'd be able to lie that way for an hour before I put her back on her back for supper. She said she'd been taken back by so many images coming to her, because she wasn't used to describing things that way. Yet, I reminded her, a lot of her material represents the translation of images. She agreed. And she wondered why in the painting of the grave robbers there weren't lanterns to go along with the moonlight.

(4:20. "The graveyard thing almost seems like another version of the anatomy thing," she said, referring to Rembrandt's famous painting, The Anatomy Lesson of Dr. Tulp.

("I thought of that."

("You know," she said, "if I did have a recorder I could work with, I'd probably use it to get lines of poetry and stuff I wouldn't want to particularly share with others to write down."

(I checked TV programs for the night, put her back on her back at 5:20, read the prayer, and left at 5:40. She called me at 9:30 PM.)

DELETED SESSION
AUGUST 18, 1983 4:57 PM THURSDAY

(Debbie Harris and Frank Longwell visited Jane last night. Jane slept well after taking her antidepressant. She had breakfast before going to hydro this morning, and could have eaten more after returning from it, but staff didn't have the time to feed her.

(The day was hazy and hot. Jane lay nude on her back when I got there to 330. The air conditioner was on high and the room was brilliant with light. I closed the curtains. "Guess what I got," I said—then showed her the package of galleys for Oversoul Seven and the Museum of Time. *The mailman had delivered them as I ate lunch, and I hadn't even looked at them. I'd been surprised, since we'd been told they weren't due until September. Jane was pleased and surprised, too.*

(Fred Kardon visited at 2:00, just as Jane was finishing lunch [which was very

good, by the way —corn chowder, rice and meatballs.] Fred wants Jane to get weighed this afternoon, and once a week thereafter. She hasn't been weighed for some little time; my own opinion is that she's lost weight. But Jane doesn't want to. She said she wouldn't care if she was never weighed. "I'm not going to change my ways," she told Fred. To me, Fred seems to be in a position from which he can do her little good. He said Jane will have a blood test tomorrow. It's routine, to check the levels of serotonin in her brain. He told us the urine tests Jane had had while in rehab showed her food absorption was normal, but that she didn't absorb medications as well—which is why Jane is on a relatively high dosage of thyroid medication—Synthroid—twice a day.

(Joan, an RN, came in and asked Fred if he wanted to see Jane's ulcers, but he said no, that he'd stop in some morning when the bandages were off at hydro time. He also said he'd be cutting his visits to every two weeks unless needed. I told him that last weekend Jane had been singing—that her lung power seemed good, but I couldn't see that this made any impression on him at all. I believe he finds Jane an enigma.

(2:22. Jane began reading the Oversoul Seven galleys. I clipped each page to a piece of the cardboard they'd been mailed in so she could read them propped up against her knees as she lay on her back. She read eight pages, and then read her Rembrandt session for August 13. I turned her on her side and read her the last part of the session for August 17 [yesterday]. We hadn't been finished long when Jean Sweeney-Dunn visited. She talked about Jane sitting up in a chair each day. "Lying in bed all the time isn't good. It isn't good for the heart, the lungs, the muscles...."

(By 4:00 I'd put Jane back on her back. As we talked, five minutes later the emergency bell sounded in the hall. Someone was in trouble. Shortly afterward we heard heavy footsteps running in the hall. I looked out: Three men—doctors?—and three nurses ran by. A couple of the nurses pushed before them a cart of closely packed equipment, including what looked like an oxygen tank. They all hurried around the corner toward the rooms leading to the nurse's station. A minute later two more nurses or aides went by, pushing what looked like a portable EEG machine. One of those running had lost a pen out of a pocket; I saw it lying down the hall, a tiny reminder of those thundering by. Another gal came along and picked it up and went around the corner. I heard a female voice talking. Its possessor seemed to be connected with the emergency, but it couldn't have belonged to the one in trouble. Then all was quiet. There wasn't a person visible the whole length of the warm yellow hall. And the episode had reminded me that we were in a hospital, and that people died here.

(At 4:30 Jane finished a BM, and I rang for help. Dawn came in right away, and told us "they" were working on a man who'd passed out. No details yet, she said. I heard someone loudly giving instructions about how to breathe. By 4:55 Jane lay *cleaned up and on her back still. I told her about receiving the new art book on Rembrandt and his times. It looked promising, though I'd hardly taken time to look at it. I described how I'd come across a passage dealing with his Protestant religion, and closely-related subjects like Calvinism and the Mennonites.)*

It is hard to remember exactly what I did believe or didn't believe during my lifetime.

My own ideas have changed so drastically that sometimes I do not recognize the familiar thoughts that I used to accept during my lifetime. I know I believed in penance—but contrary to theological concepts. I did not necessarily agree to the idea that God inflicted punishment. *(Long pause.)* I think I loosely held the idea that a man's mistakes <u>were</u> his penance, in a way: not inflicted, but brought about as a result of his lack of knowledge or understanding.

I did know that there was little light in our religions at the time. The sermons were always full of warnings about God's judgment and the pains of hell. Generally, I held my own beliefs to myself. It was not wise, certainly, to state openly any religious ideas that were in opposition to church law. Basically, however, considering myself a creator as far as my paintings were concerned, I did not believe that any divine creator would treat his own offspring so poorly, or demand of them <u>abilities with which he had not endowed them</u> *(emphatically)*. Even my experience as a father led me to the same conclusion.

(Long pause at 5:05.) It was ridiculous to punish a girl for not being a boy, or vice versa—so again I could not understand a God who created marred creatures and then blamed his offspring for his own failings. I did not believe in a God of wrath, then. I did believe that men and women both suffered many darknesses of the soul that I did not understand. I did not blame God for these—nor, again, despite Protestant doctrine, did I believe in hell or demons. I was meticulously discrete, however, as a way of achieving simple personal privacy, and also a way of not upsetting any patrons or other men of business.

(Pause at 5:08. Now there sounded a series of cries and calls in the hall—but these weren't connected with the emergency that had developed an hour ago, as far as I could tell.)

As to whether or not Christ was the Son of God, I did not know. It would be nice to believe that he was, I used to think, but then again I was led to question: What kind of a God—or even human father—would treat a son with such cruelty? It is most likely true to say that my painting was my religion—and that remark itself would have been considered heresy in my time.

Women seemed to follow the church's dogma more dutifully, as if they secretly suspected their husbands' lack of faith, and so tried to act as religiously as two people instead of one.

I suspect, however, that the women managed to form their own social groups with religion as the <u>excuse</u> rather than the true cause. *(Long pause.)* The Bible was held to be the word of God, and was held in great and dreadful awe. Still, I was struck by the drama of the parables and by the thematic structure that lent itself so beautifully to images, colors, and forms—a spiritual pageantry, I suppose: right or wrong, the carrier of great creative power.

(5:15. "I need a sip of something," Jane said. "My mouth got dry," I told her she'd done well. "Yeah, I was getting it before the BM," she said. "Then I think I was getting another idea from him," she said now as she smoked. She said she'd be giving that material. The room was getting chilly to me—Jane laughed—I put on my vest and turned the air conditioner down to low.)

(5:23.) I was, certainly, against the idea of a pope. It did seem more than a trifle audacious to imagine that any man, pope or no, could stand in the Almighty's place, to declare himself omnipotent in matters of faith and doctrine. The original *(pause)* Protestant beliefs were meant to return the individual to his own conscience, and to refuse to accept another man's word as the word of God.

In that, Protestantism was in the right direction. As various Protestant churches developed, however, the churchmen <u>might as well</u> be considered omnipotent—so surely and firmly did they leave their mark of severity upon their parishioners. One thing did strike me in my lifetime, for all my dislike for the Catholic Church and its pope. It was the fact that the church was indeed an excellent patron of the arts for centuries, while Protestantism in its very early centuries began to look upon the arts with the deepest suspicions, and even managed to banish some entirely. Dancing had to be very firmly attached to religion, or its enjoyment was prohibited. Protestantism even disliked the use of color or design or elaboration. There were certain religious themes that justified a painting, for example, and indeed I used those themes many a time. I also tried to supervent *(circumvent?)* them, however, and even in using them I tried to root them more in sympathy with man's condition.

(Long pause at 5:32.) A nude, painted for a nude's sake, could bring great displeasure, or even censorship, while a painting of a nude who was obviously a whore or a harlot <u>from a biblical story</u> was considered quite acceptable—and so many an artist's mistress appeared in the form of a biblical whore.

(Long pause at 5:34.) I was bound, also, to admire the opulence of the Roman church in its use of statuary, brilliant color *(pause)*, and I think that Protestantism made an error when it threw out that particular aspect of the Roman church's culture.

(Long pause.) Protestantism's idea, initially, was to bring simplicity back to the individual. Statues were regarded as graven images, and they were the first

art form to go. Statuary was banished almost overnight as far as the furnishings of the churches went. Some denominations still approved of park statues of honored men, but in some communities these were also barred.

(Long pause at 5:38. "That's it for the minute. I guess. I want something to drink." Jane said. I gave her a sip of coffee. "I think there's a little more there...."

(5:39.) Snuffboxes and so forth were considered legitimate only if they were categorized under the heading of investments. The same applied to certain pine buttons, or pillboxes and such.

(Long pause at 5:40.) There were two beautifully opposing ideas often held equally by the same people. One of these said that to be wealthy was to be poor in spirit, so that the wealthy could righteously be accused of gluttony and sloth. The other idea said that God helped those who helped themselves, and that to be wealthy meant that God smiled upon you with his benevolent blessing. In any case, it was not wise to <u>flaunt</u> wealth. It was always wise to express feelings of diligence and belief in the <u>economical use</u> of one's means. It did make life a trifle difficult if a man tried to make his way between those two rulings and opposing concepts.

(5:45.) I would be accused of pride were I to flaunt my collection of snuffboxes, or admitted that their beauty held any merit with me —but when I proclaimed them to be good investments, there was no problem at all. These same contradictions ran beneath much of the social structure, and, it sometimes seemed to me, muddled any idea of esthetics.

A woman who was beautiful could be proclaimed as a good and worthy soul, blessed by the Almighty for her virtue. Under different circumstances the same woman could be called to a church council for the sin of pride if she dared to show any <u>appreciation</u> of her beauty. So certainly there were as many contradictions in my time as there seem to be in yours—yet, think what <u>great energy</u> there is in man's folly.

(5:50. Jane had another sip of coffee, and then I lit a cigarette for her. "Some of those things were difficult to get because of the differences. The thing between the woman's beauty, and so forth," she said when I asked her what she meant. I replied that the material made sense to me.)

("Oh—he does have some more on it...." Jane chuckled to herself as she picked up more material. I'd been snacking on stale Planter's cheese curls—something I seldom do. I took her ashtray after she put out her cigarette.)

(5:57.) It seems to me that any religion is colored by the traits of the people who follow it, and the Dutch were always economical *(with some humor)*.

This is certainly reflected in ideas about the poor. Most Protestant sects believed that good works alone would not ensure a place in heaven, and so aid to the poor was promptly dropped by many. One belief helped—that God created poor men, and so it was almost a sin to try to better their condition, for if God wanted them born rich, they would have been born so.

The poor themselves did not necessarily favor such a belief, however *(dryly)*. It was also held by many that the poor or sick were being punished for their own sins, or the sins of their fathers, and therefore to help them would be a sin, since such interference would be in opposition to God's plan.

The poor or needy or sick were therefore considered to be doing punishment or penance for their sins, or their fathers'. The man who was rich was born to his estate through God's plan. Therefore it behooved him to better his investments *(long pause)*—and *not* to do so put him in a very poor light in churchly eyes.

All of these conflicting beliefs were woven into social law and custom, of course, so overall there was little sense in the social fabric.

(6:05.) Yet men made those conflicting theories work adequately enough. They managed to hold families and society together with far less upheaval then many other countries suffered—and that certainly was an accomplishment for any time or age.

(Long pause at 6:07 PM. "That's it for this minute," Jane said. Both of us chewed on cheese curls—surely one of our own society's more diabolical inventions, I said to Jane. The supper tray came at 6:20. By 7:15 supper was over.

(Jane's liquid intake this morning had been okay—810 cc's. No one took her vitals this afternoon. I left at 7:30 after reading her the prayer. She didn't call later.)

DELETED SESSION
AUGUST 19, 1983 5:15 PM FRIDAY

(I got to 330 at 1:10 PM. Jane was very uncomfortable as she lay on her right side with her right foot digging into the mattress. I turned her on her back at once. The day was hot and sunny, the room flooded with brilliant light. I closed the curtains. The air conditioner was on high. Jane had a BM before hydro this morning. She'd wanted some cold cereal when she got back from downstairs, but Sharon had time only to give her a couple of cheese curls. She'd also been hungry late last night, but no one had been available to feed her. She didn't get her antidepressant until midnight, when she asked for it.

(I showed her a hilarious letter I'd received from the NY City attorney, Helen Wechsler, this morning. It was dated two days ago and was a copy of her communication to Thomas Flatt, re Jane's ESP Power. We may get some action yet.

("Aaaaaaaaaaaaahhhhhhhhh...." Kathryn, down the hall, was sounding off as usual.

(Jane began reading the session for August 15 after lunch, and then she read some more pages of the galleys for Seven. *She's trying to do about 10 pages a day for the book. Today she ended up with five chapters of* Seven *checked. Her temperature today was 98 degrees. I turned her on her left side, facing the window, at 3:58, after LuAnn had given her her eye drops. I read Jane the last part of yesterday's session. Jane wasn't very comfortable. While I was reading the session Steve Blumenthal called twice. He and Tracy were in town to see Pete and conduct other business. Jane decided not to see him this afternoon. Steve said he didn't want to be "pushy," while conceding that his behavior at times seemed that way. I agreed, but didn't say much about it on the phone. We may have to come to an understanding on the subject eventually though. I believe I can see it coming. Steve said he'd left an updated version of the company proposal at the house.*

(I also explained to him that the first version had been so fragile that the ink rubbed off the pages at the slightest touch.

(I'd put Jane back on her back and she'd had a cigarette before she began dictation.)

I think I was born knowing that I could do anything I wanted, but as my living proceeded more and more, I began to feel the weight of limitations.

That feeling of being completely unhampered still remained in a fashion. It formed the basis of my painting. I began to paint quite naturally—sketch and draw—and when I indulged in those activities the old feeling of freedom always reasserted itself. My own art reminded me of those earlier feelings of creativity, and to some extent I always retained that knowledge—that basically I could indeed do anything I wanted to.

Sometimes, in fact, my own art seemed to mock me, for it seemed so complete in its fashion that by contrast I became more and more aware of my own other limitations, and the limitations of the world as a whole. I think that any artist in whatever medium draws from this same fountain of inner balance, wonder, and creativity. Some young children still possess those feelings, and you can sense the freedom of their motions and the clarity of their thought.

(Long pause at 5:23.) Animals seem to possess that same <u>mood</u> of inner safety and protection. They do not possess a peoples' intelligence, and yet certainly they live their lives as if they understood anatomy in all of its aspects—they seem so completely allied with the conditions of the flesh. There seems to be no other word for such a state except for the old descriptions of "a state of grace."

Here Protestant theology is also contradictory. On the one hand it declared that man is a good creature, a child of God, while on the other hand it declared that man is touched by original sin, and his powers forever impaired.

(Long pause at 5:27.) On any account, it certainly appears that a man falls in or out of grace at least from the standpoint of physical existence. Yet I know from my own afterdeath experiences that all life is continually protected, and that this protection is indeed one of the characteristics of the state of grace. I was aware of that feeling as I painted. On occasion I felt as if the ideas for the paintings themselves came from elsewhere; knocked at my door, so to speak, and then greeted <u>me</u> with welcome—as if I were the honored quest.

(Long pause.) I connect a state of grace with the early dawn *(pause)*, and I felt as if each day contained its own power, a power that flowed through my paintings, and even solved problems for me ahead of time, so that as soon as a given problem was pointed out to me I knew that it had already been solved.

In the same way, when I began a painting I knew that it was already finished, that it would complete itself through me, while on other occasions I felt that my brush could even paint without me—it seemed that knowledgeable.

It may very well be that the majority of artists have the same feelings. I tried to suggest this state of grace when I painted children in particular. I only knew it had a gigantic energy that was used constantly on our behalf.

(Long pause at 5:35, in an intent delivery.) What a strange new art could be developed if man could teach himself *(long pause)* to follow the designs of his own heart, forming a life that was a work of art in itself. *(Long pause.)* It is even possible, I used to think, that nature needed us as badly as we needed nature.

Protestantism was not easy on the animals. It was taken for granted that the creatures of the earth possessed no souls. When I *(pause)* worked on a painting of an animal, however, I always felt the animal's state of grace.

I did not proclaim my ideas to the world, as I have said, but I am convinced indeed that no decent artist ever would have invented Protestantism, for he would be aware of its <u>mean approach</u> *(pause)* overall, for life itself, and its creatures. *(Long pause.)* Man was supposedly banished to earth life, suffering the consequences of original sin—a concept believed in also by the Roman church. Hence, man was seen to need redemption—but no artist, looking at man or nature, could escape feeling life's great vitality, and certainly every painting is a celebration of life, regardless of its subject matter.

(5:44 PM. "I have to have a sip of something," Jane said. I gave her some ginger ale. She had a cigarette. Her delivery had been steady and intent. I yawned. There was a patient hollering down the hall: "Oh God, God, God, God...." I heard the supper trays in the hall also. To get some fresh air I shut off the air conditioner and opened the windows.

(Supper didn't come until 6:30, though. By then I'd read Jane the prayer and checked the TV for the evening. Forty minutes later I'd finished feeding her. I went shopping at the <u>Acme</u> on the south side. I didn't get home until 8:30, and finished eating supper at 9:45 PM.)

DELETED SESSION
AUGUST 21, 1983 4:45 PM SUNDAY

(No session was held yesterday, Saturday. The day was hot—over 90 degrees— and sunny. Jane lay nude on her back, and the air conditioner was on high. As soon as I arrived I noticed the swelling in her lower left abdomen. I'd noticed it yesterday also—but today I thought it was more prominent. It covered a rather large area under her pubic hair, and I could see that the inside of her left leg was also showing enlargement. The area, Jane said, was a little tender to the touch, but otherwise not bothersome. But now Jane's groin looked uneven. The area was discolored, as though if left alone long enough a boil might develop.

(Fred hadn't noticed anything day before yesterday, although I had, without paying any attention to it, nor had staff personnel. Today, when Jan returned with the aspirin to go with Jane's lunch I pointed the swelling out to her. It turned out Jan had noticed it this morning when Jane was taken to hydro—yet she hadn't done any-thing about it. Now she said Jane had a hernia—right away leaping to a most unwelcome, and possibly erroneous, conclusion. Jane didn't seem all that disturbed, though, saying the swelling was related to the movement of muscles in her upper left leg. She'd referred to this muscular activity several times lately. I asked Jan to have the area checked. She said she'd put it on the chart. Fred isn't in the hospital today.

(At 3:25 Jan cleaned Jane after a BM. Jan had called Fred, who is to see Jane tomorrow. And again Jan repeated that she thought Jane had a hernia. "I've seen them develop that way."

(Late in the afternoon Jane did get some work done. She read the last couple of pages for August 15, and the first two for August 17. Then she began to read her daily allotment of 10 pages of galleys for Seven. I ended up taking a nap in the easy chair. Supper came at 6:35. I left at 7:20, after checking the TV programs for the night. I forgot to read Jane the prayer, and she didn't remind me to do so—if she remembered. And Jane speculated that the swelling might be caused by her catheter. "Maybe it isn't in right?..."

(Today, Sunday, was hot and bright. I got there at 1:15, carrying the book on Rembrandt that I'd found at the screen door last night when I got home, plus my reg-ular bag of goodies; a heavy, awkward load. Jane lay nude on her left side, facing the

window. I turned her back on her back. Right away she told me that the head nurse had told her this morning that she had an <u>abscess</u> in her groin—not a hernia. "They" usually treated such a development with antibiotics or by making a small incision for drainage, the nurse had said. Fred hasn't been in yet. I thought Jane looked somewhat relieved.

(Now I told her that out of curiosity I'd asked my own pendulum this morning if she'd had a hernia. The question had been on my mind, so I decided to attempt to resolve it on my own. I seldom use the pendulum for such questions. In fact, I haven't used it for a number of weeks for anything. My pendulum had told me that Jane didn't have a hernia. It had also said that the swelling was related to muscular movement in the leg. At least the first portion of my answer had been correct, I thought. I didn't have any idea as to how the abscess could be related to muscular motion in the leg, though, although I didn't rule it out. It may be a question that we'll never resolve. I haven't gone back to the pendulum since. It would take time and effort to pursue the second portion of my answer, and I doubt if I'll do so. At the same time I'd like to know. My pendulum answer had made me feel better, though.

(During the course of the afternoon Jan, who was taking care of Jane again today, said one thing that made me uneasy—that there was a note on Jane's chart that she <u>wasn't</u> to get weighed. By Fred. We're not sure if this means he's acceded to Jane's request to forget about weight. I do believe Jane is losing weight. [Jan hasn't mentioned her misdiagnosis of Jane's abscess as a hernia.]

(Fred never did show up while I was at 330 today. People took Jane's vitals as usual. She had a BM. I'd told Jane I had to leave earlier than usual so I could mow some grass. She was uncomfortable lying on her right side, where I'd turned her, so I put her back on her back at 4:20. She had a cigarette. She'd already read some galleys for Seven *earlier. Now she felt like some dictation.)*

One thing that strikes me most strangely is the development of your electric light. I should think this must have revolutionized the art of painting—for it obviously is as easy for you to paint during the night as during the day.

This certainly provides additional time that we did not have, *(long pause)*, but the entire idea of having streets and houses so lit up after dark is amazing and delightful to me. In my time few people went abroad after darkness, for the lights that we had were of such poor quality. *(Pause.)* We did have some lamplighters, yet the entire period of the nighttime was somehow mysterious and untrustworthy.

I am not even sure, however, how closely your artificial light copies normal daylight—or if your light has an artificiality *(long pause)* that casts unnatural light effects. I understand you do have various kinds of light, and wonder about their yellowing capacity. Still, your social lives certainly must be entirely different than ours *(long pause)*, so the day is stretched into the night. I find it, again, most amazing.

I wonder also about the shadows cast by such light—whether they seem artificial or real. If I understand properly, many paintings are shown in art galleries, all utilizing the same kind of artificial light, though I understand that there would be variations here, of course.

(Long pause at 4:55.) Artificial light must also be highly advantageous to people in winter climes, where the days are very short. It makes me wonder how I would have used such light had I possessed it, and what changes its use might bring about particularly in the choice of color. *(Long pause.)* I always thought that candles lent an air of mystery to light itself, and it is quite difficult for me to understand that artists do not paint by candlelight now.

(4:49. "That's all for the minute," Jane said. I explained to her some of my ideas about the pros and cons of artificial light. She'd heard all of this before, of course—how it was especially tricky to paint flesh tones under warm artificial light, and so forth. I added that I used to wonder whether I could learn to paint at night by diligent practice. The odd thing now is that with the Rembrandt material in mind, I now find myself wondering if I could learn to paint by <u>candlelight</u>—a reversal of the usual procedure these days. Unheard of, actually, I said. I'm intrigued to try it, though.

(I'd told Jane earlier that I wanted to leave before her supper tray arrived, so as she had a cigarette now I began putting away my paraphernalia. "I don't know," she said. "I feel a little more Rembrandt, but you want to leave...." I said that that was okay, that I could stay to get the material. I regarded that as a creative endeavor that would replace whatever I might do at the house over the same amount of time.

(5:10.) Generally speaking, in my time the night had a poor reputation. It was believed by many to harbor all kinds of demons and evil spirits. *(Long pause.)* These same beliefs were spread throughout Europe, and in a strange manner at various times even nature itself was considered suspect.

Everything that was natural would decay, and only the soul, it was thought, would endure, and then only under very special circumstances.

(Long pause.) Forests in particular were considered to hide all kinds of demons and their cohorts, and few people ever traveled abroad at night without the strongest feelings of dismay. In larger cities those reactions were not as strong, but they still existed.

(Long pause at 5:15.) Night seemed to have a mysterious, unhealthy cast that was dispelled with the coming of dawn. *(Long pause.)* Even the shadiest tree that brought relief from the heat in the daytime was regarded with entirely dif-

ferent feelings as the coming of night approached. *(Long pause.)* I imagine that any dramatic painting almost always contained that same <u>battle</u> as the artist attempts to show the great comforting aspects of nature, while struggling against the darker concepts that speak of nature's inevitable decay.

We knew that the body decayed, of course—yet what was it that escaped? It must be the soul— and yet even then we had beliefs that marred the soul's capacity for truth or goodness. All of these feelings, in one way or another, were reflected in our paintings. And each new painting was like another world, to be created and examined. The idea was that nothing could exist in a painting, truly, unless it first existed somewhere else. I was never sure what this something else meant, but I certainly do know that white was considered the color of the soul and of goodness in general, while the darks in the painting represented the opposite.

In a fashion many of our paintings were dramas in which, only half-knowingly, we worked out the problems of good and evil.

(5:23. "Just a minute," Jane said. Then with exasperation: "That damn catheter just leaked." She meant only a few drops, however—but she was not referring to an isolated incident. It's been a little while now since Jane's catheter was changed, so that's something at least. Her urine is still not clear, however.

("Give me a sip of something and I'll go right back." She had a cigarette. I decided to leave at 5:30 "I can get a little more," she said.)

(5:33.) Some things have not changed very drastically between your time and mine.

Many of the symbols that your civilization uses would be quite familiar to people in my era. I refer specifically to the symbols of good and evil—and even though you do utilize artificial light to illuminate the night's darkness, still in your dreams and other art forms darkness is recognized as a sign of evil, in opposition to the qualities of light.

You end up with a kind of shorthand—villains have dark hair, while heroes or heroines are blond. If I understand correctly, your movies and television dramas use the same kind of symbolism, so that the screen has only to show a thunderstorm and lightning, and this is a signal itself of the appearance of the villain or his facsimile.

(Long pause.) I do not know if such symbolism is natural within man's own psyche, or whether it is the result of religious superstition dating backward into the earliest of centuries. Very often the same kind of symbolism applies to the seasons. Winter landscapes often represent the darkness of the soul, and skyscapes of a full moon surrounded by dark billowing clouds also represent feelings of man's ancient terror. Since my own afterdeath experiences have shown

me no inkling of true evil or darkness, then thus far I could only wonder at their prevalence both in life and in art.

(5:42.) My own present existence seems fully experienced, dramatic and full of challenges — and all this, again, without any experience with evil or darkness. More and more I wonder where and when man first came upon ideas of evil, and what purpose such ideas have held. It seems to me they have no purpose, and yet I know there is a reason for everything. And so I know that man must have invented the idea of evil for a purpose that is not yet available to me.

I can also honestly state that while I met many scoundrels in life, I never met anyone who was evil on purpose, and somehow even the worst of men try to justify their acts. I do not believe that the symbolism of good and evil belongs in a painting, either. Certainly there are other ways of achieving a dramatic effect. Yet the reason for the invention of evil thus far escapes me.

It is so prevalent, however, that it seems that man would not let it go without a struggle—so again I wonder at its origin.

(Long pause at 5:50 PM. "My throat's dry," Jane said, so I gave her some ginger ale. "I was getting that he was really honestly curious," she said, "about the good-and-evil thing...."

(She could have gotten more, she added, but I was really tired. I hated to miss out on any material, I told her, but.... I read her the prayer, and then turned her on her left side, waiting for supper. I left at 6:20.)

DELETED SESSION
AUGUST 29, 1983 2:55 PM MONDAY

(The last session was held eight days ago, on August 21. I'll summarize each day's events as briefly as possible.

(August 22. Fred and Ken Wrigley had been in to see her this morning. Fred had wanted Dr. Sonsire to look at the abscess, but he's out of town. At 1:15 Dr. Marshall came in. He wants to give Jane a "slight" anesthetic early tomorrow morning, by intravenous injection. "Just enough so you're comfortable. Then I'll give you a local in the groin area." This would allow him to drain the abscess in her left groin. He only had to touch the swelling and look at it briefly to know what it was. I told him Jane was frightened by the thought of anesthetic. "Don't worry, Jane, you won't be out at all—just comfortable so I can make a little slit there and drain that thing."

(Dr. Marshall, who was still wearing his greens from the operating room, said the abscess was definitely an infection. He didn't know whether it was related to the bladder when I asked him. "I don't know, because of her skin."

*("You mean it could go right through the skin from an external source?" I
asked. "That's very possible," he said. "Don't worry, Jane, you won't be unconscious."*
*(Not until he'd left did we wonder whether the procedure would be carried out
in 331. Jane cried a little, and I wiped away her tears. I thought the idea of infection penetrating the skin a bit far out. Through the afternoon aides put a hot pack—
a wiener-shaped hot water bag wrapped in a towel—on the abscess. At 7:00 LuAnn
came in while Jane was eating supper. She brought aspirin and a form for me to sign,
a release. Jane would be going to an OR—an operating room —between 10 and 11
AM for the procedure. Jane was again upset, but continued eating. Lu Ann brought
in another form for me to check—one containing routine questions about Jane's medical history. I knew all the answers. It was several pages long, but easy going. I took
the form out to the nurses' station, and Sharon got me an extra copy for my files.*
*(LuAnn had told us the anesthesiologist—a Dr. John—would be in to inter-
view Jane. He showed up after supper, and as I was getting ready to leave. Dr. John
was a black from a foreign country [I think], and a little hard to understand. He
agreed with the procedure Dr. Marshall had outlined for us. He said Jane cannot eat
after midnight. He will have nothing to do with giving Jane the local—only the IV
relaxant, something like Valium. The surgical procedure would take less than an
hour tomorrow morning. After that Jane can resume eating and taking medications.
Jane received the interview better than I thought she would, although she doesn't like
any of it; nor was she drawn to Dr. John.*
*(I wrote to Tam Mossman, Jane's editor at Prentice Hall, that this material
shows Jane's life while doing Rembrandt, and while she's also proofreding the galleys
for her Oversoul Seven novel.*
*(Jane read five pages from August 18 and 10 pages of the galleys for Seven,
while all this was going on. I worked on mail and tried to reassure her as much as I
could. "By this time tomorrow the whole thing will be over." When I left at 8:09 the
street lights were on. It was the first time I'd noticed them on at that hour. I was
reminded that before too long they would be lit every night when I left the hospital,
at whatever hour.*
*(August 23, Tuesday. Debbie Harris visited Jane last night, and my wife called
me after her visitor had left. "What are you thinking about?" I joked. "Guess," Jane
said. I tried to cheer her up.*
*(I called the nurses' station at 10:30 this morning, and asked the nurse who
answered—Barbara, whom neither Jane nor I can place—to say hello to Jane for me
and to wish her well. Barbara said that the schedule now was for Jane to go to the
OR by noon. I'd half expected a delay. Yet—when I got to 330 shortly after 1:00, I
discovered the procedure had been done. Jane was back, and Jean Reome was with
her; she had just finished shaving a portion of Jane's pubic hair, where the incision*

had been made—_after_ the procedure had been carried out. Jane looked okay. There was a tube in her left forearm, and she was on Lactated Ringer's with 5% Dextrose–Viaflex. Patty had inserted the tube in a big hurry before Jane went to the _emergency room_ for the procedure—not the OR as scheduled.

(I had almost as much trouble getting a straight story as to what had happened as Jane had telling it to me. There had been numerous foul-ups [although that may be too strong a word]. Jane went to the ER by 10:30, right after my call, instead of the OR at noon. She wasn't given any intravenous anesthetic as Dr. John had described it—only a Valium pill in the ER. And that hadn't been ground up, Jane said. Dr. Marshall had given her a local as the only anesthetic, and the injection had hurt, Jane said. Dr. John did not put in an appearance at all. The heparin lock was necessary, Jane was told, in case they wanted to add an IV anesthetic to the procedure. It's also in place if Fred decides to add an antibiotic. Blood tests were taken in the ER, but we have no word on any results.

(The above notes describe only part of the confusion of this morning, though. Jane was taken to hydro this morning after all, after having been told last night that she wouldn't go. Her dressings were left off after hydro, as usual. Then word was sent up that Jane was to go back downstairs to the ER, so Patty had to hurry to insert the heparin lock, and others put the dressings back on. Then Dr. Marshall himself came up to 331 to get her—he'd been waiting for his patient in the ER, and she hadn't showed up. Jane was quickly put on a stretcher and hustled downstairs. Jean Reome went with her and was a great comfort—and I thanked her.

(Jane said Dr. Marshall "did a lot of squeezing and pushing" on the abscess, and Jean added that he got "a couple of cups of stuff out of it." The procedure didn't hurt, Jane said, but she felt the pressure. Packing tape had been inserted into the incision so it wouldn't heal before all the infection was drained out. The tape is perhaps two feet long.

(I told Jane that her belly now looked "equalized." She's been informed that she doesn't go to hydro tomorrow morning. All in all, things had worked out well. Jane was quite sleepy. The glucose feeding is adjusted so that a bare drop at a time goes into Jane's system. I made a quick sketch of the apparatus. I watch each drop form in the joint where the tube from Jane's arm joins the underside of the bag. Ever so slowly each drop forms at the end of the tube leading from the bag, to finally fall the inch or so distance into the tube leading to Jane's arm—but each of those drops has to clear two more connections on that journey.

(Jane slept most of the afternoon and up until supper time—the aftereffects of the Valium, several people told us. She slept also in relief that it was over. When she woke up at times I would tell her things—for instance, that I'd filled out the forms for her absentee ballots and mailed them today, after making copies for our files. She *is now permanently registered, and will receive ballots as long as we don't move.*

(I should note that yesterday I'd written to Tam about his helping me get Seth's Dreams finished—an idea I've had for some time. I have no idea at the moment as to whether Tam is free enough to help with such a project, which would be lengthy indeed, but I felt I wanted to ask. It's one way to solve a challenge. Jane was quite in favor of the idea, which helps, so we'll see what may develop. The point I'd made to Tam yesterday, and also explained to Jane, was that keeping up with her current work precluded my having enough time to get Dreams out. I enjoyed the Rembrandt, of course, but besides that it's very important she does new creative work and that I help her get it out each day. Handling a backlog of work then becomes almost impossible. "I don't care if you do Rembrandt for a year," I'd told her. "The important thing is that you're able to do <u>something</u>, and that's a good sign."

(Today, August 23, people continued to place hot packs on the little incision. The bandage comes off tomorrow, Lu Ann said. She added that the glucose is "sugar water and electrolytes to replace body fluids." Jane slept a lot while I worked on mail. Her temperature was up a bit, to 100 degrees, but she felt well. And now she admitted that the abscess had hurt her quite a bit—only she hadn't told anybody. "It figures," I said. She didn't want any supper except cereal and milk, and bread, butter, and jelly. I left at 8:00 after checking the TV programs for the night. We didn't go over the prayer. No galleys today.

(August 24, Wednesday. Jane did okay today. She still felt long periods of drowsiness—the aftereffects of the Valium, people said, because of her small size physically. We've received no results of any of the blood tests, either connected with the Synthroid group or the abscess. There has been drainage from the incision, although she doesn't wear a large bandage there. "I was determined I wasn't going to call you," she said. "I'm dependent enough on you as it is." She referred to the fact that she was really glad I'd called yesterday morning before the surgical procedure.

(She read no galleys for Seven today. And wonder of wonders—the supper tray came at 4:55. Cathy said it was sent up early for Jane because she's been getting the supper so late. The irony of the situation is that Jane isn't even hungry, since she didn't finish lunch until about 2:15. I read her the prayer before leaving at 7:10. Jane said she'd try to call.

(August 25, Thursday. Fred Kardon came in at 1:15, and went to get a nurse, Jean Reome. They rolled Jane back and forth while he checked the hole in her right hip. Then Fred put on sterile gloves and took the packing out of Jane's abscess incision—a couple of feet of it, it looked like. Jean squeezed out some drainage—from the upper leg, where it had been swollen. Fred said he'd stop if it hurt Jane as he explored the incision with tweezers. Then he put in fresh packing tape, which took a while because of the way he had to work it inside the wound. This hurt Jane some-

what.

(*Then Fred told Jane he wants her to go to x-ray after she leaves hydro. There a rubber tube will be inserted into the incision and filled with dye. Another tube will be put in the hole in her right hip. Then x-rays will be taken to see where the dye migrates within the body. The cause of the infection must be internal, Fred said, since Dr. Marshall couldn't find any opening in the skin. Where did the abscess come from? "I don't know," Fred said. "I don't know if this is the tip of an iceberg, or if it's nothing. But I'd like to find out. Okay?"*

(*Jane agreed very reluctantly indeed. I could tell she was upset again. There were tears after Fred left. "But what could it be?" she asked Jean. Fred had done his best to make the situation clear to Jane, but I could see that she was unconvinced. I didn't envy Fred his position.*

(*At 1:55, just after the lunch tray had come, the head nurse brought in a release for me to sign. "Some x-ray procedures require a release," she said. "Is this a surgical procedure?" Jane asked. "No." I asked the nurse, whose name I didn't know, if I could have a copy of the form, since it contained a description of the x-ray procedure. I wanted it for my own files. She said we were entitled to a copy, but that other forms would have to be filled out. She was reserved, I could see. We settled for a copy of the procedure, which she'd write out and send to me via one of the staff. At 2:30 Patty brought in the slip of paper: Sinogram (R) ischiol and (L) groin wounds. Jane was still upset—When Patty brought the paper her face screwed up again. Tears were close. Perhaps it's my wife's general situation, I thought, the years of it, but any threat raised by even x-ray strikes deeply—the fears are aroused once more. Yet she shook her head no when I asked her if anything was wrong. Of course there is.*

(*I had to leave by 3:10 to get to the dentist myself by 3:30. No sessions or galleys were read before I left. Jane was on her back, having a cigarette. She still doesn't really agree that the x-ray procedure has any value. "I suppose I'm worried that they'll scratch around enough, and find something, and want me to have an operation," she said. And that, I said, was it. "And you wouldn't be worried, is that it?" she asked. "No, I'd be worried to some extent," I said, "especially since I'd be wondering where that infection came from in the first place."*

(*I turned Jane on her left side at 3:02, left for the dentist at 3:10, and got back to 330 at 4:25. Paul O'Neill had to do filling work on three teeth, plus cleaning them. He also told me he could come to the hospital to take impressions for new dentures for Jane, "when her weight stabilizes. Just let me know." I was surprised that he could work in the hospital.*

(*4:35. Peg Gallagher visited. She had with her a transcript she'd made of her phone conversation with the "healer and clairvoyant" from Washington state. The guy is right on some things, has others backward. Jane and I asked Peg—when the guy calls again, as we're sure he will—to tell him thanks, to send energy if he cares to, but that we don't want him hopping on a plane to come here; it's not necessary. He's right, though, about Jane setting up defenses and blocking her own energy. We thanked Peg for the trouble she's gone to. I do not really believe she understands our own attitudes here. I tried during her visit to explain our ideas about healers—that we think there's something to it all, but that usually the process is much too simplified and trite. After all, I said, if healing worked so well, Jane ought to be able to leave her bed and walk out of the hospital, for surely enough people around the country have contacted us to say that they're really focusing on helping her psychically. Obviously, to my mind, the healing comes from within the stricken person, and until permission is given for it to take place, or acquiescence or understanding is achieved in sufficient amount, there will be blockages and delays.*

(I explained to Jane that a more basic question is why she developed the abscess to begin with, instead of the advocated medical treatments afterward. Jane replied that she believes she "gathered together a lot of poisons in my body, and I got rid of them through the abscess." This to me is a perfectly logical explanation. Peggy agreed. At first the two of us said that this thinking meant that the x-ray examination tomorrow should show that the body is okay internally. A little thought revealed that that statement may not be true—Jane created a situation that required medical assistance; unless the abscess was simply allowed to grow until it burst [as I'd thought it might do eventually]. So now she may require more help medically in dealing with the aftereffects of the abscess. But I liked her intuitive response as to the reason the abscess developed to begin with. She regrets giving permission for the x-ray procedures tomorrow, and said she wouldn't have if left alone. Peg left. And, I thought, Jane may have had her basic right to do her own thing compromised once again by peer pressure. I'd signed the release form almost automatically. The head nurse and I had talked it over with her—but neither of us has seriously considered Jane's rights in the matter. The nurse had __expected__ permission to be given, I realized later. I wondered about her reaction if that permission had been withheld. And the doctors'.

(Jane read some galleys. Supper came after 7:00. I left at about 8:15, after checking the TV programs for the evening. We said no prayer. "Thanks for staying, Bob," Jane said. "I love you." It had been a difficult day for both of us. She didn't call later.

(August 26, Friday. I got there at 1:08, on a day that was very hot and bright. 330 was brilliant with light. Jane lay nude on her back, smoking. She'd just returned from having the sinogram done. I was surprised. I'd called Jean Reome at 10:30, and she'd told me "they" didn't do that kind of work in the mornings. Yet it turned out that Jane was taken to x-ray at 11:00 AM—but she had to be brought all the way back upstairs because nobody had put a name tag on her wrist for x-ray before tak-

ing her down there.

(A Dr. Neilson in the x-ray department had done the work. "Nice enough," Jane said, but he hadn't known anything about her case because her chart was late getting down to him. "My knee kept hitting the x-ray machine," Jane said. "They took a lot of pictures."

(First, though: Linda, a night-duty RN, had tried to irrigate Jane's catheter at 5:00 AM, but couldn't because it was plugged. She had to change it by herself because no help was available, and tried and tried again before she managed to do the job. Jane had an early BM. She also had a good breakfast before hydro, then more to eat after she came back to 330. But this involved another foul-up—for contradictory messages had been relayed to the nurses' station at A-3, involving hydro and x-ray: First the catheter was to be shut off during her visit to x-ray, and then it wasn't, so that she'd have a full bladder. I do not know whether it was shut off in x-ray or was-n't; sometimes from my position as an outside observer it's practically impossible to get a straight, single-line story of an event; too many people are involved that I don't see, and so forth. In any case, Jane had been scheduled to go to x-ray at 8:30, but could-n't because she was still in hydro at 8:30, so she was brought back upstairs.

(When she did finally get into x-ray, Jane said, dye was injected into the abscess incision and the right hip with a small catheter, and "it wasn't too bad." A nurse kept trying to get Jane to straighten out her legs more, but she couldn't do it. Jane really yelled when they tried to pull out from under her a sheet, without lifting her. She was in x-ray for l fi hours, "either taking pictures or maneuvering me to get them." The doctor looked at some of the x-rays as they were developed [I guess], but didn't say anything to Jane.

(Now, Jane said, all she wants is for Fred to tell her that the pictures didn't reveal anything untoward, and that all is okay. She hadn't heard anything by lunch at 1:40. All in all, she disliked the experience, yet came through it all right. Jean Reome stopped in briefly. She said there was much less drainage in the abscess inci-sion than there had been yesterday. It had been "unpacked" in 330 before Jane went to hydro, and Jean thought there was no packing in it now. There's but a small ban-dage over the incision site. Jane enjoyed her lunch. Debbie Harris and Elsbeth had visited last night. "There's no doubt about it," my wife said. "My appetite is a lot bet-ter than it used to be." And she's right.

(I told Jane I wanted to leave by 5:30 tonight, so I had time to go food shop-ping. I took her name tag off her left wrist to keep in our files, as well as a length of the packing tape from a jar sitting on the desk. After lunch Jane read Rembrandt ses-sions for August 18, 19, and 21—the last one being given five days ago. Then she did some galleys on Seven.

(At 3:50 I called Fred's office to see if we could get word on the results of the *x-ray procedure. Fred wasn't there, but his nurse said his wife was, and that she'd ask Marsha to check and call us. Dawn came in and asked me to stay to feed Jane because the staff is so short-handed. I agreed. I read Jane the two notes I'd written this morning. [These concerned the interactions between Jane and me, with speculations that some of these had helped set her symptoms into motion; the other note dealt with my insight that illness can form a bridge between "life" and "death" in ways we don't suspect.] Jane agreed with both of them, saying the personal one "hit home" to her, all of it, as I read it. After we'd talked them over both of us took naps while waiting for the supper tray. Jane reported that she'd had a very vivid and beneficial dream related to what I'd written. I'd given her a beautifully handcrafted desk made out of carved gorgeous wood. The symbolism is obvious. Jane was physically okay in her dream, walking and so forth. She also said that she'd bestowed upon me some of the characteristics of the Six-Million-Dollar Man [the TV character].*

(Supper came at 6:35. We hadn't heard from either of the Kardons. I read Jane the prayer at 7:43, and was getting ready to leave when Sarah, an RN, came in to tell us that Fred was on the phone at the nurses' station. I waited in 330, the phone in my lap. The phone rang. Fred said he'd gotten his information secondhand from Marsha—he hasn't seen the x-rays himself or talked to Dr. Neilson. Jane said things to me that I couldn't decipher as I talked with Fred. And Fred began to tell me things I didn't want to hear. I had a strange feeling of unreality as he gave me his information—the results of the x-ray procedure: There is, he said, a "deep connection" into Jane's intestine from the site of the abscess in her left groin area. They aren't sure whether the connection is with the large or the small intestine—if the former, it could be into the colon. The solution, Fred said, is to keep food out of the intestine until the opening has time to heal. "If it doesn't heal, it can mean something drastic," Fred said, "like an operation, and she can't stand anything like that."

(Fred wants to have Jane agree to subclavian feeding, where a tiny opening is made surgically into a vein beneath a collar bone and a feeding tube inserted so that large amounts of protein can be feed directly into the bloodstream "to build her up, put some weight on her." At the same time he talked, I picked up contradictions, for Fred also said—I think—that such openings don't heal by themselves. Part of what he said concerned building up Jane's strength for any future moves that may be necessary, like an operation, I believe.

("I know your wife is very strong-willed," he said, "and no one has the right to force anything on her. She'd be on the tube a long time...." He promised to go along with whatever decision Jane made, but he wanted me to explain what I could to her tonight. He said he'd see her tomorrow morning.

(When I explained the situation to Jane, she took it well. She'd already known the gist of the conversation, since my responses to Fred's material made that obvious.

I even hinted at the prospect of an operation if she didn't try the feeding program— but we'll see. She'd eaten well today. I didn't know what to think. I hadn't been quick enough to think to ask Fred if he thought the opening into the intestine was a fistu- la—but more, was it possibly the same opening she'd had months ago, when she'd been admitted to the hospital last April 20? I reminded Jane that she'd been put on a feeding tube then—the nose tube, though, not the subclavian, which she's never had.

(August 27, Saturday. Fred called me just before I ate lunch. He repeated much of what he'd said yesterday afternoon, though now he said he doesn't think the opening into her intestine— large or small—will heal itself. In addition, he wants to have Jane given an enema with a dye in it, as an aid in helping to pinpoint the location of the opening. More x-rays. I'd had at least the impression after talking to Jane yesterday that she might possibly agree to the subclavian feeding, but now Fred told me he didn't think she would. If she does agree, he said, I'm to tell one of the nurses. A surgeon has to insert the tube beneath the collarbone. Fred asked me if we knew of a surgeon who could do the work, or preferred a certain individual. I said no on both accounts.

("What I want to do and what I do are probably two different things," Jane said as we talked after lunch was over at 2:20. She said Fred had told her this morn- ing that the feeding would take months. This was a surprise to me, or else I hadn't grasped what he'd said on the telephone yesterday afternoon. It seems like an impos- sible procedure. Jane was very concerned about shutting down many of the body's normal functions for so long a period. She'd have no BM's, for example—though obviously, Fred had told her, she wouldn't feel hungry. She wouldn't get any solid food at all. We didn't know—and were half-afraid to ask—what other long-term effects such a prolonged situation might have upon a body, and Jane specifically thinks it's much better to use the body than to not use it. "If you follow that line of reasoning back far enough," I said, "then you can say that that's why we're here not using the body."

("All right." she said, "so I'm trying to use what I've learned...."

(3:17. "And I don't want anything sprung on me, like tests," she said as she read more galleys for Seven. She talked about not liking the idea of the enema. "I'm not going to do anything tomorrow. I don't have to go to hydro, either. I want the whole day off...."

(I had a sharp headache that came and went. I felt it was related to the situ- ation with my wife, and to the fact that tomorrow I planned to start putting Dreams into shape so that either Tam or I could start working on it. I've discussed with Jane, if briefly, my idea of asking Tam to help us out getting the book ready for publica- tion; she's agreed. Jane had a BM late in the afternoon, and Jean Reome came in to

clean her up. We hadn't known Jean was here today, but she'd had to come in to do charts. The staff is very short-handed: "It's been a rough two weeks." A lot of people are out on disability and maternity leave. The supper tray came at 6:35. I left at 7:20, after reading Jane the prayer.

(August 28, Sunday. Last night when I got home I found mail to the effect that there will be no Democratic primary election on September 13, but that Jane will be eligible to vote in the general election in November. She's now permanently registered for absentee ballots as long as we don't move. I also found the flap copy for Seven, *sent to us by Bill O'Hearn from production at Prentice-Hall. I'm to call him tomorrow morning about whether we have to return the galleys for* Seven, *since Jane hasn't made any changes in them. I want her to finish reading them this weekend.*

(3:31. Jane told me she's decided not to go the subclavian route. Nor does she want the enema-dye process. She is going to trust her body to heal itself, instead. We had a long talk, but I didn't try to pressure her into changing her mind. Basically she's right, I agreed. She'll be telling Fred the next time she sees him. She doesn't want to turn off bodily functions for months—though obviously, she said if she took a sudden turn for the worse she'd reconsider her decision. I said that the only thing that was going to get us out of our present lifestyle was a change in beliefs, and she replied that her decision was a step in that direction. She didn't seem to feel any better after our talk, which was emotional at times, but I thought that was natural enough, everything considered. I said I didn't know if she'd made the right decision, but that I hoped she had, and that I'd be glad to go along with her on it. She wants to concentrate upon the prayer and self- suggestion. Those are very good approaches.

(Jane was hoping she'd be relaxed enough today to do some Rembrandt, but at the moment that seems a ways off. She read the flap copy for Seven, *and had me change one word. As the afternoon passed I discerned that she wasn't too happy with certain other portions of the copy, so we worked those problems out. This came about after I remarked that here she was going to okay something she really didn't like, and that that reaction to life situations was one of the reasons she was in her present dilemma. So she made the changes, and they worked out very well. She finished the* Seven *galleys, also.*

(Late in the afternoon Jane asked me to bring in some of the recent Rembrandt sessions, so she can read them to "prime the pump" for new material. Steve Blumenthal called about visiting this evening, and we decided to forgo that. I read the prayer after supper, and left at 7:40 PM.

(I should add to the material above, for Sunday, that Jane said, "They took a whole lot of blood out of my lower left leg this morning, before breakfast. I don't know why they didn't use my arm." And she hasn't seen Fred yet, to give him her decision not to have subclavian feeding.

(August 29, Monday. I got to 330 at 1:10 PM, after mailing the Seven *galleys, plus the flap copy, to Bill O'Hearn. Doing this involved two calls with him. The day was hot and sunny. Jane lay nude on her left side, and had done so since 11:00 AM. I turned her back on her back and gave her a cigarette. She'd eaten well before going to hydro, but wanted more after returning. Patty didn't get in to do this until after 10:30—too late. Jane said that last night she discovered that now she's getting the second daily dose of Synthroid with the antidepressant late at night. In other words, if she misses one she misses the other.*

(After lunch she reread the Rembrandt sessions for August 21 and August 19, in that order. She finished at 2:35. And doing this did "prime the pump," for 20 minutes later she began dictation.

(2:55.) Wherever I have traveled there has always been light—and so it seems to me that existence itself must emerge from just that origin.

This makes me wonder even more about the light effects within a painting. *(Pause.)* It now appears clear that each figure should be painted as if it were indeed filled with its own luminosity, so that the light seems to tremble within the form itself, struggling to burst forth with its own true brilliance.

(Jane doesn't know it—I don't think—but the above paragraph very accurately reflects what has often been said about Rembrandt's late work—that his figures seem to contain within themselves their own light source, so that they attain an extraordinary internal luminosity.

(Pause.) The shadows of course would indicate mystery—but not the mystery of evil—but the struggle for fulfillment. Evil cannot be explained simply as the absence of good *(pause)*, but it does exist only because of man's greater expectation. Perhaps in the light of man's great inner knowledge of himself, any lesser performance is experienced as evil by contrast. This would go a long way in explaining the great contrast that seems to exist between good and evil.

As a child grows into an adult, perhaps we grow into our own more knowledgeable selves, so that looking back we see clearly that what we experienced as evil was instead a step along the way—lower only in light of the further height we hoped to achieve.

In a painting the artist tries to express himself, but the painting-to-be yearns to come into fulfillment also, so sometimes there is a kind of pull and tug between the artist and his own painting. He may feel that the painting wants to go one way while he wants to go another. The dilemma could be resolved if he but understood that his way and the painting's way were two versions—

(3:05. Georgia looked in. "Who's that?" Jane asked, breaking off her delivery. "Who's that?" Georgia repeated, then left.)

—of a larger path that led to his fulfillment and the painting's fulfillment also. Then the feeling of strain would be understood as simply a surge of motion in the process of resolving itself.

That phrase explains my own present situation to some extent, for I feel myself moving in still newer directions while trying to hold on to old familiar ways as well.

(Long pause at 3:09. "That's it for the minute," Jane said. "I think there'll be more. I'll have a sip of coffee. I'm glad I got some, anyway." Her delivery had been rather quiet, with pauses. I lit a cigarette for her. She said she'd asked Steve and Tracy for a copy of her translation of the Sumari singing she'd come through with during their recent visit. "Some of those English versions were delightful," she said, "and they might lead me into more—know what I mean?"

("Yes."

(3:13. "In fact, I guess I will get more," she said as she smoked. I was getting chilly, so I turned off the air conditioner. "How can you get chilly with all those clothes on?" Jane asked with a grin.

("I'm only wearing a shirt and undershirt," I said. Almost always I get chilly after sitting in 330 with the air conditioner on for a couple of hours. "Let me know when you're ready."

("I'm ready."

(3:19.) I look back at my own paintings, but when I do so I see those that I painted in physical terms, and those that were executed mentally—and to me both kinds of paintings are equally real, for they are part of the greater creative life that still remains to some extent hidden and mysterious only because I have yet to grow into my full <u>understanding</u>.

(Long pause at 3:21.) An artist's creative life as it is usually understood represents only the smallest portion of the inner life from which it constantly emerges. Sometimes, for example, it takes an artist years before he consciously understands how he produced certain delightful effects in a painting done years before. The conscious life is always trying to catch up with the greater intuitive and creative existence that is the heritage of each individual.

(Pause at 3:24.) In some strange manner, however, even while my existence seems elsewhere, a portion of myself remains with my paintings, and to some extent, again, the paintings themselves search for the greater fulfillment that I was not able to give them in the past. Thus, the Rembrandt that I was lives dearly in my own consciousness—and still that same Rembrandt has grown into what I am.

My paintings represent my signature *(long pause)*, the artistic track that I left behind me—yet it is true to say that those tracks or that signature emerged from the future as surely as from the past. And if I painted my paintings backward you would not be able to tell the difference *(pause)*, because time is simply one of the mediums we use in creating our existences.

(Beginning at 3:30, Jane took such a long pause that I began to wonder if she'd fallen asleep. Then slowly:)

We are all part of people who have loved us, and they are a part of us in the same fashion. *(Pause.)* Often we merge our thoughts with theirs, or they share in our own awareness without ever being conscious of the alliance.

(3:33. "Just a minute....")

So in a fashion, while I painted for myself, and for the love of painting, and for a livelihood, I also created my work on behalf of all those people who loved me, and whose love I returned. I was expressing not only my own view of life, but that view as it was also refined and reflected in the minds and hearts of family and friends. I expressed life in a certain fashion for them. I painted what they might have painted if they could. At the same time I was engaged upon my own particular unique journey, that still continues, compelled by a familiar yearning that has always been with me.

The universe itself <u>fulfills</u> itself by expressing itself through me—

(3:38. "Hi, Jane." It was Cathy, come to take Jane's temperature and write down her intake of liquids for breakfast and lunch. A minute later another RN named Sharon came to take Jane's blood pressure.

("Gee," Jane said as soon as they'd left, "I was right in the middle of that— really lost in it—"

("I could tell."

("I've had it before," Jane said as we talked, "but I've got that feeling that he's winding it up. I had the feeling before, though, didn't I?"

("Sure—and you've gotten some great stuff since then," I laughed. I said I'd begun to wonder if such material came to Jane, or was available, in segments; that when the conclusion of a segment arrived, she could choose to end the work, or to delve into the next segment to see where that one led. Jane said it was a good thought.

(I told her it was time for her to be turned on her side. She asked me to read her the last part of the session. Then she took up where she'd left off at the interruption.

(3:54.)—and every other individual expresses portions of myself for me *(long pause)*, so that each action we perform is performed for ourselves in our own unique fashion, and yet also speaks for millions and millions of other identities, to which we are in one way or another connected.

At some hypothesized other end of the universe, it is true to say that I am now taking down the notes that you are writing, and that you are speaking the words that are being spoken now, and that your wife, with her own unique abilities, forms the bridge upon which we can meet and salute each other.

(*Pause.*) We can thus in recognition figuratively smile and go our own ways, or we can follow the bridge through upper arches with further connections—

(*3:59. LuAnn came in to give Jane eye drops. Jane groaned after the nurse had left. "I was way down in it again when she came in—I was really feeling those arches. What was it, what was I saying?" I read it to her, and she tried again.*)

(*4:01.*) —the further connections of knowing and understanding.

("*I guess that what I felt was that there was something strange there just before LuAnn came in," Jane said. "I was really getting real strange feelings, like you said in your note just before...."*)

(*And, I wondered, had something unique been interrupted—broken, even—by the entrance of another personality at just that particular moment? What a pity, just to get eye drops!*

("*I'll have a cigarette, then turn over," Jane said, "and see if I can get something on my side."*)

(*4:05. "Mighty unfortunate that happened just when it did," I said.*)

("*Yes—I was getting some kind of an image."*)

(*4:15. I turned Jane on her right side, facing me. However, we couldn't get her comfortable. Her right shoulder bothered her especially, I could see that I should have turned her much earlier. "I'm not going to be able to do anything this way, I can tell you that," Jane said, as she struggled to get more at ease. I finished a card to a fan that I'd started then checked the TV programs for tonight.*)

(*Still, by 4:45 Jane was dozing as she lay on her right side and I worked on mail. Finally she slept. At 5:18 I decided to take a nap myself. Both of us slept soundly until 6:10, when I got up and shut off the air conditioner and opened the windows. Supper came in five minutes. I read Jane the prayer at 7:25, and left 330 at 7:30. Jane didn't manage to call later in the evening.*)

DELETED SESSION
AUGUST 30, 1983 3:44 PM TUESDAY

(*Jane called this Part 2.*)

(*I reached 330 at 1:20, after stopping at the printer's to pick up the copy of the Essays for Dreams. I plan to send them to Tam tomorrow. The copies turned out well, and I showed them to Jane. Already I feel a sense of relief that someone is, or soon will be, working on Seth's Dreams, so that we can get it into eventual production at Prentice-Hall.*

(Jane lay nude on her left side when I got there, so I turned her back on her back. The day was hot but cloudy. It was going to rain. I've noticed it before—One has a rather spectacular view of the sky from the hospital's parking lot in back of the emergency room. There aren't any trees so close by that they interrupt the view, and the hills circle around far enough away and low enough on the horizon so that one gets an open feeling. The ambience at the hill house is quite different, of course.

(It did begin to rain at 2:15, after lunch. I turned off the air conditioner and opened the two windows so we could hear the weather for a change. I showed Jane the last page of the essays, containing her Sumari Healing Song. Then she read the letter from Bill Kautz, concerning Bill's intent to have Seth Speaks *published in Japanese. Then I read her the session for yesterday, which I hadn't typed yet. Jane is quite intrigued by that session, for in it Rembrandt appears to be closing out his material—or extending it into new and unsuspected realms. We had many interruptions yesterday after 3:30, just when Jane was getting into the heart of that material. Most unfortunate, we agreed, for new things were evidently trying to manifest themselves in that session.*

(I also read her my own quick notes for the session, in an effort to recast the whole affair for her. Jane had come through with some vivid visual material on her own during the interruptions, and I plan to recount all of it as soon as possible. At the same time she was quite discouraged by the interruptions, although today she said, "Well, I guess what you read means that the changes aren't really gone or dead...." She was quite intent on trying to recapture the feeling of yesterday's material; she said she kept trying to get more Rembrandt.

(3:43. "Oh, I've got a bunch of stuff running around in my head," she said. "I don't know whether I can pull it all together or what.... Oh heck, I'll see what I can do—"

I am an old man, bearded and bleary eyed, I dream of stone quarries, and of rock piled high *(long pause)*—but so sweetly carved that no blemish shows.

(Long pause.) No cruel or jagged cut mars the smooth surfaces of stone, but all appears one, as if by the earth grown: a marble man *(long pause)* from the ribs of the earth, formed complete and joyous, invincible as a god. A perfect man beyond death or any imperfection, blown into being by this magical stone—a true son of rock loins, safe from decay or the harm of agonized thoughts such as men have. A son of rock, yet more alive than any man. So behold, though I am an old man, bearded and bleary eyed, still I father a son more vital than a youth, and when my own limbs lie silent as stone, that son will live on.

(There were already interruptions around us: In a room close by a woman began calling loudly for a nurse, over and over, as Jane gave her material. There was

the clatter of equipment in the hall. Jane's own delivery was interrupted by many long pauses, only a few of which are indicated here. Her voice had a different, almost harsh quality at times, as though taking on a version or characteristic of the material she was giving. Neither one of us was sure of what was going on, for that matter. Who was speaking?

(3:55.) The season is spring, and the Vatican shines like a celestial city, and the pope proclaims. Yet for all his station the pope cannot command my statue to kneel, to kiss his royal robes.

(More noise.) Earthly children fall into the arms of decay, molding, their curls, once so fancy, fade—but my son stands beyond bodily ruin or harm, to be commanded by no man. His thoughts are protected from all prying eyes (long pause), and he surveys the universe itself without blinking, my son of stone whose life is within. His dreams are protected—

(4:00. Now we had more interruptions. Peggy Gallagher visited, bringing with her the typed version of a long conversation she'd had with a "healer" from Washington State. Peggy had put a lot of work into this, and we thanked her. The guy was both right and wrong, I told Peg, without trying to go into a lot of detail. I did tell Peg that I couldn't help wonder why this fellow kept trying to contact Jane, who wasn't turned on by his efforts, when there must be many within his own locale who could benefit directly. I've grown a bit cynical, I'm afraid. In a nice way I tried to explain to Peggy that this person was attracted to Jane because she was well-known, and that whether he admitted it or not, that played a large part in his efforts at "healing." A number of other healers have written us—often motivated, I believe, by similar interests. Not that we wouldn't take any healing any of these people could send our way, I told Peg: We'd be glad to accept it. Yet Jane still lies in her bed. Naturally her own attitude—and mine—play a part here. I told Jane later that after the essays in Dreams are read we'd probably be bombarded with more "healings."

(4:42. Jane was very eager to hear what she'd delivered so far. I'd just started to read the material to her when Lorrie and Dawn came in to turn my wife on her left side. Her vitals had been taken while Peggy was here: temperature 98 degrees, blood pressure excellent, pulse the same. Jane's liquid intake including lunch was also good: 995 cc's.

(By now Jane was mad at all the interruptions. She was also upset because earlier I'd mentioned I'd like to leave early, comparatively, so I could go shopping. "Here we're losing all that time and you're leaving early," she said. I sat beside her, my back to the windows. "Say what you can, Hon, that's all...." I said. Already I had my suspicions as to what was going on in the session, although neither of us had said anything about that yet. "And it's all poetry," she said.

(When Jane did resume dictation her pace was somewhat faster. She picked up *on the last sentence she'd given after I'd read her all of the material:)*

—and safe as jeweled fruit, forever escaping earthen rot. I am an old man, bearded and bleary eyed, and I dream of stone quarries, as if from these I could breed perfect men: a race of angels *(long pause)* that were natives to the heavens and earth alike. In my own dreams my thoughts possess me, rolling like marbles of mixed colors that swirl—but each one is clear as the sky so that a thousand heavens turn and flash through my mind.

(5:00.) Oh, to be father of such a new breed *(long pause)*, marble-pure, clear-eyed but with thoughts as fluid as a flowing stream, sweet and cool to the touch, a step—no, sweet and cool to the touch, a <u>statue</u> breed free of disease *(pause)*, more pure than our father made us, with thoughts never confused.

Aegean hills reach steeply toward the blue heavens, and far beneath the sea *(long pause)* is so ancient that it hides man's own history, and his memories fall afloat in the dark waters below, whose depths are unknown—but I would raise a new breed of men. Carved fresh from the marble heart of earth, with loins that would rise miles above the sea.

I am an old man, bearded and bleary eyed, and some would say near-demented, yet a new sanity stares within my mind like a white gliding moon, and new marble dreams awaken me to a white, white dawn.

The fleshpots of Rome are full. Rome wears a courtesan's gown. The world resounds with infidels' swords *(pause)*, but I would form a breed apart. Pure as a youth before desire, whose needs are met without praying for bread, and whose marble eyes roam over the universe itself.

(Long pause at 5:12.) I have cut away all blemish from my son of stone. Let David sing victorious, for no man can command one of his fingers to move half an inch, or bend his will against his own.

(5:14. "My throat's dry," Jane said. I gave her a sip of ginger ale. She was quite comfortable lying on her side.)

No wonder the God of the Israelites forbade the creation of graven images—for even he was jealous of the perfection of stone, carved, curved, complete within itself, to heaven and hell unknown.

(5:17.) No soiled blood swirls through my son's veins, which are forever cleansed, unclogged and free as the hidden springs that rush through rock, past the white, white moonlight that sparkles like stone. My son's stone eyes see celestial hills. He is forever ageless. Though born from my mind's loins.

(5:21. "Boy, I'll have part of a cigarette," Jane said after a long pause. "I can't wait to see that—it sure feels powerful to me. I don't know if it comes across like that, but —"

("Sure it does," I said. "Even the subject matter—stone—makes it feel that

way."

(Jane grinned. "I think I know who it is.... Do you?")

("Sure," I said. "I thought of it right away—that is, I had an idea...." Neither of us mentioned a name in this little game, though. The name I had in mind was Michelangelo. Partly this was because Rembrandt had mentioned him. But Michelangelo had carved David. I had in mind a photograph of the statue of David, without being clear on details. Nor had I seen the photo for a long time. I remembered a stunning work of art well over life-size.

("I've got to go to the john," I said.)

("Before you go just write this down.")

(5:24.) So, frolic with eternity's playmates. My ageless youth *(pause)*, dancing invisibly though your marble legs move without any man seeing their motion *(long pause)*, so swift that no eye can follow even the smallest slight shift. Yet you dance eternally to your own rhythm, turning swifter than leaves do in the autumn wind.

(5:28. "Okay," Jane said. I put out Jane's cigarette. I read her the material from 4:42 when I came back from the john. "What do you think of that?")

("Weird," she said, obviously pleased. I told her the material was pretty damn good when she asked what I thought of it. She lay quietly for a little while. "I guess I've got a little more.")

(5:44.) I am an old man, bearded and bleary eyed. My life spills out of me drop by drop. Into what bucket does my life pour?

(Long pause.) Will it be saved and reused, cleansed and born again into another braver form? Even so, my son needs no transfusion, for the life that I have given him lives as much now as before.

This dream man builds celestial cities greater far than Rome. He gives no sacrifice and demands none, for he is complete having no demands of others. Yet his own dreams build even newer heavens than our fathers ever knew, and his stone-eyed sanity shines like white moonlight on the monuments *(long pause)* and carved gravestones *(long pause)* of men born by flesh and blood, fated to follow the fate of broken bones. How clear-eyed my son sees. How blind they are who would not recognize my David's life of stone.

(5:53. "Can I have another sip of ginger ale?" Jane asked.)

(I gave it to her. "You know who carved the statue of David, don't you?" I asked.)

("Yes. Michelangelo. But I don't know anything about him.")

("I don't either, though I've got a book on him—one of those Time-Life *jobs, like on Rembrandt.... I didn't even know what Michelangelo's statue of David celebrated. The triumph of David over Goliath? I told Jane I thought I remembered*

something about an over-life-sized magnificent statue of a nude warrior carrying a sword and shield—although I was almost certainly wrong about such details.

(I broke off typing this material to search the house for the book on Michelangelo—and discovered that I couldn't find it. I know I had it, possibly given to us by a friend some time ago. I now think that in turn I gave the volume away myself, possibly to George Rhoads....

(5:55.) Adorn my son's curls with flowers and laurel leaves and my son will still live when these remnants of summer are gone. (Very long pause.) Unmarked by a woman, no mars ever have touched his mind. Never possessed by summer's fever, his cool thoughts roam where the blighted cannot go.

Dear son of my mind's loins, let your silent lips speak. How beautiful their sound, how melodious the voice that only sounds (long pause) through choirs of silent stone.

(6:00. "That's one of the wildest things I've ever done," Jane said. I tried to describe to her the little I thought I remembered of photographs of David. Jane had "such a sense of power when I do it that I became concerned that I get the right words and the right rhythm...." She was pleased when I told her the statue of David was larger than life, for she'd had a feeling that the piece was like that. She'd also had an image of a head with curly hair in profile, like Zeus. I remember being most impressed by the David. It's truly a work of genius. Jane doesn't know what it looks like.

(6:05.) I died tomorrow, yesterday or today—what does it matter? Only that I am free of calamity and the restless chatter of unresolved thoughts.

So David strikes out for me, leading an army (long pause) of angels whose wings, stone-carved, move light as feathers. (Long pause.) And David now guides me higher, past stone-edged clouds, whereupon my soul now needs to speak to another whose name is nameless—and yet it resounds through all my stone-deaf loins.

Who speaks through David's unmoving lips, and whose name do my own lips try to speak? What sound is it that echoes through my stone-still mind?

(6:12. "Oh, that's it," Jane exclaimed. We heard the sound of the supper trays in the hall. I turned her back on her back as we waited for supper. She didn't know why she'd come through with the Michelangelo material. She'd felt somewhat nervous when yesterday's session had been interrupted so often, for she'd felt she was on the verge of trying something different. But to switch in mid-session from one historical character—Rembrandt—to another—Michelangelo—was quite an event, and certainly not one expected by us. Certainly both of us are open to things we'd have rejected in earlier years. There are many questions.)

DELETED SESSION
SEPTEMBER 2, 1983 3:00 PM FRIDAY

(I got there at 1:08, after stopping to mail the Preface and the first few sessions of Dreams *to Tam. I'd made an early morning trip to the printer's to have the material copied. The day had turned sunny and warm. Jane lay nude on her back. Jean Reome, an RN, was with her, reading* If We Live Again. *Both women asked me to bring in a copy of* Emir *so Jean could borrow it. "I promise to bring it back...." I helped Jean move my wife up on the bed.*

(Jane had had time to eat a full breakfast before going to hydro. Debbie Harris had visited her last night. Elsbeth had called me this morning. I'd finished the session for August 30. Lunch came at 1:20. Jane's appetite has been excellent lately, and she ate well now also. I worked on these notes and checked mail while she ate. She finished at 2:25. Five minutes later Peggy, an RN, came in to empty her Foley. Then Jane read the last three pages of the session for August 30. She was quite eager to get to dictation, and mentioned it several times as she had lunch. She also told me that the last session constituted Part Two of the Rembrandt work—and that that part may already be over. We speculated about what would come next. Would it be— obviously —Part Three?

(As was the case in Part Two, a name wasn't given to us today either. This time, however, both of us arrived at the name in question quite easily. Jane's delivery today was easier and faster by a good deal than it had been for Part Two.)

What does it matter my name *(pause)*, for I saw the future from my own time. Even my art was but a means to spy out the secrets of truth. *(Long pause.)* Restless and wild, I could not stay inside my own mind, but ever wandered into the realms of future time. I was haunted by the future's ghost. I saw men swim far beneath the sea in ships that made me catch my breath. They were so miraculous and secure.

(Now there began outside our window [three floors down on the street] a racket set up by some sort of machinery that sounded like it was being used to drill or gouge away concrete. Jane kept going, though it was a little difficult to hear her at times.)

My vision kept sliding where it didn't belong *(pause)*, and I saw wars and catastrophes and follies that only waited for the calendar's change—and what I saw I captured in feverish sketches and notes. I drew the plans for the future, and no matter how I tried I kept sliding into days that hadn't yet come, and their brilliance nearly dazed me till I returned hastily to my own rooms, but they could not hold me. The present and the future kept melting together, and I slipped dizzily from one to the other. The voices of the future called me to follow while my body held back. Through the months and the weeks nothing contented me, for I saw my own world as if it were already passed and finished, and like the dead covered with stone.

It was difficult to complete anything, for I was constantly being called from one reality to another, until the future seemed more real than the past, and the present disappeared in the tension between.

(Long pause at 3:11.) I learned to be content enough with small victories (long pause), stealing from the future what knowledge I could—but not fastened in time as all my companions, but adrift between the centuries, marking battles and celebrations whose banners would not show in the world that I knew.

I was like a time machine, though unfocused, caught between worlds that shimmered aglow. No one believed me, so that my world seemed sad and hollow, yet I sang with triumph *(long pause)*, flying with the wind of tomorrow.

(3:16. "Okay, that would be the end of the section," Jane said.

("Uh—Part Two or Three?"

("I don't know. I lost track, but it's probably Part Three."

("You know who that was speaking, don't you?"

("Sure, da Vinci."

("Right." According to the dictionary Leonardo da Vinci lived from 1452-1519. 67 years old, in other words. Italian painter, sculptor, architect, engineer and scientist.

(And soon Jane was back delivering more material.

(3:17.) You can begin to read the universe at any point—and I am Rembrandt now, half-dozing in a comfortable chair, listening to the pigeons that coo outside the window—

(3:20. The TV gal came in to collect for next week. After she left I read to Jane what she'd given so far today. Rembrandt has mentioned both Michelangelo and da Vinci in his text. Jane wanted to give more material before the late-afternoon round of visits from staff people began. Her pace picked up a bit as she resumed dictation at the point of interruption.)

—only barely remembering the thoughts I just had, and I would if I could—and I can—apologize to da Vinci, since I thought him a dandy, and never considered the strange problems he had. I treasure, now more than ever, the contentment I took with my own time, with domestic issues, the price of trinkets—even the problems that kept me concentrated, I suppose, in the elaborate, labyrinthian ways of my own world. My old snuffboxes even seem more dear to me now than ever, and I would have had no heart for the kind of exploration da Vinci knew. I was concerned, as you know, with the nature of eternity, yet surely I was blessed to enjoy the candles' warmth, and to take joy in the taste of fine food and the drinking of good wine. Perhaps I had the best of both worlds—and they all served to give me a <u>stability</u> that allows me to travel now in ways I never could have before. But as you reached my mind, my world view if you prefer, so it would naturally lead to *(pause)* the world view of others, for all of our paths cross again and again.

(Long pause at 3:34. "Have to wait a minute," Jane said.)

(3:35.) You used artists as a focus, and started walking on a path that had several destinations at once, so that a <u>cluster</u> of world views fell like a cluster of flowers into your hand. You enjoy their aroma.

(Very long pause at 3:37.) I suppose I keep my old world intact within my mind, returning to it, knowing it is always there, alive as ever. Though I have left it, its reality remains unbroken, and I learn from it even now—as I learn from you as your understanding of your world seeps into my knowledge.

(Long pause at 3:39. "That's it for the minute," Jane said. "I guess the carnival outside has stopped for a few minutes.")

(Jane wasn't referring to the commotion in the street—which had finally tailed off—but to loud talking and other noses in the hall. "I got up and shut the door," I said.

("I know. Read me that back. Halfway through today's dictation I started to feel which way it was going to go....")

(3:45. "I have a good feeling about that now," Jane said after I'd finished. She repeated herself, with enthusiasm. "Now I see where it's going to go—like you went up in a rocketship and wondered if you'd ever return. But you made it okay.")

(3:48. I lit a cigarette for her. An aide looked in—someone we don't know—saw that Jane was smoking, and said she'd return a bit later to get her blood pressure. "I'll do all my other patients first," she said.

(I turned Jane on her left side before the interruptions started. The sun had evidently become clouded over, for the curtains were dull now. "It's funny about creative work," Jane said as she tried to get comfortable. "You know you have a destination, but you don't know if you get there or not until you've done it.")

(I should add that before today's session I'd told her that I hadn't been able to find the Time-Life book I remembered having on Michelangelo. I'd searched the house. I wasn't too surprised—for as I looked about I remembered giving that book to George Rhoads some time ago, along with a number of other art books I thought I no longer needed.

(The book on Michelangelo had also been given to us, I knew, but I don't recall the circumstances. I'm sure I hadn't ordered it. Although I've always greatly admired Michelangelo's work, it hadn't turned me on the way some other artists do—

Rembrandt, say. Yet his sculpture had an effect upon my memory, particularly that of David, and the Pieta. Too bad, I said to Jane. Now I'll have to dig up a photo of David some other way.)

DELETED SESSION
SEPTEMBER 3, 1983 4:16 PM SATURDAY

(For the first time in a long while I didn't have to make any stops on my way to the hospital. This morning I finished numbering the pages of Dreams, *preparatory to having them copied to send to Tam next week. [I'd called the printers this morning, but they're closed—and, I suppose, they may not be open Monday, the Labor Day holiday. I also called MacGreevey's, or tried to, about the copy paper they are supposed to order for me; they're closed also.]*

(The day was sunny and nice. Jane lay on her left side, and I put her on her back at once. Lunch came soon, and Jane ate well. She'd also had a good breakfast before going to hydro—bacon and eggs—and could have eaten more after returning to 330, but there wasn't anyone available to feed her. I do think she's losing weight, however.

(I told Jane I thought the manuscript for Dreams *was long enough that it could be published in two volumes, like "Unknown" Reality. After talking it over we decided that we wouldn't say anything about this possibility to Tam, Prentice-Hall, or anyone else—unless they mentioned it. Jane was all for getting it out in one book, and so was I. "I'll worry about two volumes if they suggest it," she said.*

(There followed after lunch our usual routine. I held up the session for September 2 so that she could read it more easily. Jane also wanted to be turned early so that she could get some more dictation before the flurry of visits by RN's and aides began—checking her vitals, and so forth. In addition, her catheter was leaking; when I turned her I found it was wet and needed changing. I finally pressed the call button for help, and the wet chuck was changed. An hour after I'd turned her, the nurse, Sharon, tried to irrigate the catheter, but without much success; it seemed to be plugged. I worked on mail while my wife's vital were checked one by one. Temperature, 98 degrees. 580 cc's liquid for breakfast and lunch: low. Sharon, after another attempt to clear the catheter, finally told Jane it may have to be changed later tonight; she's going to keep a watch. Jane was unhappy.

(Dawn set out to see if we could get the supper tray at an earlier hour. Yesterday the other Sharon [Poley] and Lorrie had tried the same thing; the tray will be sent to rehab, and rerouted to us around the corner.

(4:03. I put Jane back on her back—and it appeared that her catheter was

draining much better. Jane had a cigarette. "I'd like to get more dictation, but I'm
afraid to get it because it might mean the end," she said. She'd mentioned a likely
ending to the Rembrandt material earlier this afternoon, also, just as she has on other
recent days.

(Finally, as I worked on mail, she said, "I might get a little more.")

("Going to take a chance, huh?" I asked. "Wait 'till I get my pad.... Okay.")

Indeed, life and death are only conditions *(pause)* in the larger sphere of existence.

Our identities are eternally valid, whether we are alive in earthly terms or not. We leave our traces in all spheres of existence, and consciousness is always victorious, regardless of its circumstances. It is never quenched or quelled.

For a while these messages seemed to be discontinuous. They are in their fashion ever ongoing. Each of us is connected to the other, and all are couched secure and safe *(pause)*, heading for destinations that are ever new.

In a manner of speaking, I continue to produce my paintings, and new versions of them. *(Long pause.)* Now and then I rest from images, but only to learn greater combinations. *(Pause.)* I study the ingredients of inner imagery, and am beginning to feel my way toward an art that is truly multidimensional.

I bid you then, good sir, a fine good day, as if I were my old self in my studio, and you had come to visit. I must leave your company for my other pursuits—and indeed, you must leave mine for the same reason.

Enjoy the dear clarity of physical reality and the seasons which so enrich the senses, for those are memories that will go with you always as you paint the greater picture of existence and discover your own hearth in that greater clime.

(Long pause at 4:25. "I don't know, " Jane finally said. "I think that's it."

("Hmm. That was very well done, Hon."

("I felt that was going to happen."

("It bothers me, too. I feel sad."

("Doesn't it? It leaves you with a gap—what am I going to do now? I was really fond of him." Jane laughed a little. "It started on your birthday—"

(Sharon came in to check Jane's catheter, and was pleased to see that it appeared to be draining okay now.

("Yeah, I was fond of it too," I said.

(Jane laughed again. "I guess I was waiting to see if he could be teased to stay around longer, you know? But I guess not."

(4:30. "Gee," I said, "it'll really be strange, not to have that to look forward to each day.... Well, that means you're supposed to move ahead to something new. I was thinking of that earlier today."

(And how creative a performance Jane's Rembrandt material was, I thought,

for those other portions of her personality not only knew how to come through with the material in the first place, but when to end it. And the ending was certainly a painful experience from our ordinary conscious standpoints.

(Jane said she was thinking of The World View of Jane Roberts—*to my surprise. I'd mentioned the idea some time ago. She also wondered if she could do a Seth book; she was worried about the volume of the voice. I replied that when we were alone, doing book dictation, the voice wasn't a problem. Jane even wondered if she could get into a Seth trance. I said that that was no problem either, since she was doing related work now, talking about such pursuits, and so forth.*

(Jane said, "I might even be mad at him because I got sick." This was an important clue to her thinking. Its resolution might be of great benefit. I said that my only question was how she'd cope with the interruptions while she was in a Seth trance. I thought that it would be little or no problem that she'd adapt to that situation as easily as she had when delivering the Rembrandt material.

("I don't see why Seth just doesn't put me in a good trance and do The Way Toward Health *and heal me at the same time," Jane said. "This is the time when I used to call Tam up and tell him I'd finished a book," she added sadly.*

(We'd planned to turn her over after her cigarette so she wouldn't be so long on her back all the way through supper. The room was quiet and cool. Goodbye, Rembrandt.

(But I did know there was endless creativity "out there" as well as "in here," waiting. "What's next?" I asked. "I suppose that's what you should be thinking about, no matter how you feel. And me too."

(Jane agreed. I'd hardly finished turning her on her right side, facing me, when the supper tray came. Unbelievable, I said to Dawn as she walked in with it. While I fed Jane I thought of the latest massive gorgeous art book of Rembrandt's paintings that I'd ordered last month, and brought in to show Jane. It still sat in the closet, wrapped in brown paper. Jane hasn't even seen it. I thought that now I might have time to show it to her.

(And yes, as I typed this session the next day tears came to my eyes when I reached Rembrandt's farewell. This material has an emotional pull or attraction for me—and for Jane, I'm sure—that none of her other works had. It strikes home in a number of ways. Both of us always feel that certain nostalgia when a Seth book comes to an end—but those feelings are always ameliorated by the knowledge that there'll "always" be another Seth book. The Cézanne *and the* James *books are fine, and each one is unique. In some way, however, the uniqueness of the Rembrandt work embodies depths of feeling or emotion unique to it alone.*

(The last two paragraphs of Rembrandt are especially good, I think. The last paragraph, in which he reminds me to enjoy "the dear clarity of physical reality and

the seasons" etc., is very evocative, for it reminds me of what I try to do each night as I lay in bed with the windows open so I can hear the katydids and treetoads....

(And I think that Rembrandt's obvious attachment and affection for physical life serves as a powerful connective between his reality and ours, obviously making it easier for us to identify with him. It also reminds me of questions I had earlier in these sessions, when I wondered at the feelings of those who had "died," and left loved ones behind. There seems to be an equal exchange, then, and the fact of transition doesn't erase strong emotional connections. [The intellect would be involved also, of course.]

(I still remember especially two observations made by Rembrandt—to the effect that "I felt my way through life," and "the woes I experienced in physical life I now see were quite unimportant in a larger context." Neither of these quotations are literal by any means, but they express strong attractions for me.)

DELETED SESSION
SEPTEMBER 7, 1983 3:45 PM WEDNESDAY

(Got there at 1:10 PM on a very hot and sunny day—over 90 degrees. I stopped to pick up a combo pack for our home copier at MacGreevey's, and went to the printer's to pick up a batch of sessions that I'd had copied to send to Tam for Dreams. Earlier this morning I'd delivered those sessions to the printer, and also mailed Tam the previous day's batch.

(Jane was asleep on her left side, with the air conditioner on high and the TV set going. She'd had a good breakfast before going to hydro, but hadn't been able to get any bread and jelly after coming back—everyone was too busy. Several of the staff said they didn't feel well this morning. There's a "bug" going around the hospital. Evidently Jane had had her own reaction to this yesterday with her own chills and hot flashes. She got her antidepressant early last night and it had "knocked me out." And she'd slept well through the night, she said.

(I'd brought in Tam's letter of Sept. 2 for her to read—hardly anything in it about Dreams— and before leaving this noon had hurriedly picked up what I thought were the pages for the last Rembrandt session I had to type—for August 29— but when I presented them to her I discovered I'd picked up only one-half a page plus its carbons, omitting several previous pages, so she had nothing to read on that score.

(I told her that when I'd turned the corner on to Holley Road after leaving the hospital last night I'd immediately noticed that our lawn had been mowed front, side, and back. I burst out laughing. When I pulled in to the driveway Margaret Bumbalo came over and said she'd seen "little green men" cutting the grass that after-

noon. *Of course Joe and John had done it, and I was very grateful. Not only that, Margaret asked me over for supper—baked chicken, delicious squash, salad, etc. During the meal I asked Joe if he'd like to buy our air conditioner, and he said yes. I'd been joking. I'd give it to them for all their kindnesses if they can use it. It's sat unused in the cellar since 1976. Joe and John said they'd be over to get it, probably tomorrow. When I got home I hunted up the literature for it, which I still had on file.*

(This morning I'd also written to Bill Kautz and Eleanor Friede, re the Japanese Seth Speaks *proposal, and* Emir. *When I went to file my letter with Bill's previous letter, I couldn't find that missive, or the carbon of my reply. This was most vexing. I've run into the same occasion before, though not often. A letter is missing, and I start hunting for it. The more time I spend doing this the more determined I become to find the missing item. This time, though, I didn't find Bill's first letter, and used over half an hour in the search. I finally had to break off my hunt to finish Eleanor's letter. And now I'm left wondering where on earth I filed Bill's letter, and why. I know my action made sense to me at the time.*

(During supper last night Margaret had said Jane's chills and fever, though brief, could mean a low-grade infection. This had been on my mind. When I learned today that staff members weren't feeling well—a few were quite ill—I felt relieved. And Jane seems to be okay. I finished the job of cutting her fingernails, which I'd stopped yesterday when she began to shiver. What she wanted to do today, she said, was "to do dictation on a poem or something." I started on the mail while waiting to see if anything came through for her.

(At 3:40, I finally turned her on her right side, facing me as I sat in my chair. She was so uncomfortable lying on her right shoulder that I thought dictation would- n't happen. However, within five minutes Jane began a poem. We had three inter- ruptions while Jane was giving it, though they aren't noted below. It was getting to be time for the routine "vitals" to be taken—blood pressure, temperature—which was down to 97.4 from 100 the day before—and pulse. After she'd finished the poem we went over it line by line to make sure I typed it the way she wanted it. We have no title yet:)

> *Messengers run up and down*
> *the stony steps*
> *of my inner world.*
> *Men loiter in doorways*
> *and women call out*
> *from second-story windowsills.*
> *Children play*

in the streets and alleyways.
The dawn rises, the twilight falls, a faithful replica
of the exterior world.
But the inner geography came first.
The inner hills and mountains form

the fabric I hang
my experience on,
and these twin worlds
mirror each
the larger dimensions
of my soul.

(Jane finished the poem at 4:10. She was really uncomfortable on her right shoulder. Still, at 4:28 she began another poem—but this one was cut off by another interruption, and she didn't go back to it:

Once I thought that love
could cure all ills

(At 4:40 I put Jane on her right side, until I turned her back on her back to eat supper at 5:30. She didn't eat well. I left at 6:56, after reading her the prayer. She didn't call me later.)

DELETED SESSION
SEPTEMBER 8, 1983 4:00 PM THURSDAY

(Jane delivered this little poem as she lay on her back in bed in 330. It took her only 11 minutes, including several long pauses. The air conditioner was off for the moment, the curtains drawn, and the room was quiet. After she'd finished, we went over the poem to make sure I had the lineage and punctuation indicated the way she wanted them to be. She gave no title.)

When I was very young
I thought that the world
and my world were one.
I could wiggle a finger or a toe,
or nudge a grain of sand on a distant shore.

At night I could travel
as far as I wanted,
though my body lay quiet
beneath the bed covers.
There were velvet soft paths that I traveled alone
'till hungry for breakfast
I'd return home.
I traveled more miles
than as if I'd taken a plane
but there were no charges made or
taxes paid.

(4:11 PM.)

THE SETH AUDIO COLLECTION

RARE RECORDINGS OF SETH SPEAKING through Jane Roberts are now available on audiocassette and CD. These Seth sessions were recorded by Jane's student, Rick Stack, during Jane's classes in Elmira, New York, in the 1970's. The majority of these selections have never been published in any form. Volume I, described below, is a collection of some of the best of Seth's comments gleaned from over 120 Seth Sessions. Additional selections from The Seth Audio Collection are also available. For information ask for our free catalogue.

Volume I of The Seth Audio Collection consists of six (1-hour) cassettes plus a 34-page booklet of Seth transcripts. Topics covered in Volume I include:

- Creating your own reality – How to free yourself from limiting beliefs and create the life you want.
- Dreams and out-of-body experiences.
- Reincarnation and Simultaneous Time.
- Connecting with your inner self.
- Spontaneity–Letting yourself go with the flow of your being.
- Creating abundance in every area of your life.
- Parallel (probable) universes and exploring other dimensions of reality.
- Spiritual healing, how to handle emotions, overcoming depression and much more.

FOR A FREE CATALOGUE of Seth related products including a detailed description of The Seth Audio Collection, please send your request to the address below.

ORDER INFORMATION:
If you would like to order a copy of The Seth Audio Collection Volume I, please send your name and address, with a check or money order payable to New Awareness Network, Inc. for $60 (Tapes), or $70 (CD's) plus shipping charges. United States residents in New York State must add sales tax.

Shipping charges: U.S.—$7.00, Canada—$8, Europe—$20, Australia, Asia & South Pacific—$22, South America—$18
Rates are UPS for U.S. & Airmail for International—Allow 2 weeks for delivery
Alternate Shipping—Surface—$9.00 to anywhere in the world—Allow 5-8 weeks

Mail to: **NEW AWARENESS NETWORK INC.**
P.O. BOX 192,
Manhasset, New York 11030
(516) 869-9108 between 9:00-5:00 p.m. Monday-Friday EST
Visit us on the Internet—www.sethcenter.com

Books by Jane Roberts from Amber-Allen Publishing

Seth Speaks: The Eternal Validity of the Soul. This essential guide to conscious living clearly and powerfully articulates the furthest reaches of human potential, and the concept that each of us creates our own reality.

The Nature of Personal Reality: Specific, Practical Techniques for Solving Everyday Problems and Enriching the Life You Know.. In this perennial bestseller, Seth challenges our assumptions about the nature of reality and stresses the individual's capacity for conscious action.

The Individual and the Nature of Mass Events. Seth explores the connection between personal beliefs and world events, how our realities merge and combine "to form mass reactions such as the overthrow of governments, the birth of a new religion, wars, epidemics, earthquakes, and new periods of art, architecture, and technology."

The Magical Approach: Seth Speaks About the Art of Creative Living. Seth reveals the true, magical nature of our deepest levels of being, and explains how to live our lives spontaneously, creatively, and according to our own natural rhythms.

The Oversoul Seven Trilogy (The Education of Oversoul Seven, The Further Education of Oversoul Seven, Oversoul Seven and the Museum of Time). Inspired by Jane's own experiences with the Seth Material, the adventures of Oversoul Seven are an intriguing fantasy, a mind-altering exploration of our inner being, and a vibrant celebration of life.

The Nature of the Psyche. Seth reveals a startling new concept of self, answering questions about the inner reality that exists apart from time, the origins and powers of dreams, human sexuality, and how we choose our physical death.

The "Unknown" Reality, Volumes One and Two. Seth reveals the multidimensional nature of the human soul, the dazzling labyrinths of unseen probabilities involved in any decision, and how probable realities combine to create the waking life we know.

Dreams, "Evolution," and Value Fulfillment, Volumes One and Two. Seth discusses the material world as an ongoing self-creation—the product of a conscious, self-aware and thoroughly animate universe, where virtually every possibility not only exists, but is constantly encouraged to achieve its highest potential.

The Way Toward Health. Woven through the poignant story of Jane Roberts' final days are Seth's teachings about self-healing and the mind's effect upon physical health.

Available in bookstores everywhere.

CPSIA information can be obtained
at www.ICGtesting.com
Printed in the USA
FFOW03n1047131017
40848FF